# ALCOHOL, TOBACCO, AND ILLICIT DRUGS

ISSN 1938-8896

# ALCOHOL, TOBACCO, AND ILLICIT DRUGS

Stephen Meyer

**INFORMATION PLUS® REFERENCE SERIES**
Formerly Published by Information Plus, Wylie, Texas

GALE
CENGAGE Learning·

Detroit • New York • San Francisco • New Haven, Conn • Waterville, Maine • London

GALE
CENGAGE Learning®

Alcohol, Tobacco, and Illicit Drugs

Stephen Meyer

Kepos Media, Inc.: Steven Long and Janice Jorgensen, Series Editors

Project Editors: Elizabeth Manar, Kathleen J. Edgar, Kimberley McGrath

Rights Acquisition and Management: Margaret Chamberlain-Gaston

Composition: Evi Abou-El-Seoud, Mary Beth Trimper

Manufacturing: Rita Wimberley

For product information and technology assistance, contact us at
**Gale Customer Support, 1-800-877-4253.**
For permission to use material from this text or product,
submit all requests online at **www.cengage.com/permissions.**
Further permissions questions can be e-mailed to
**permissionrequest@cengage.com**

Cover photograph: © Konstantin Yolshin/Shutterstock.com.

Gale
27500 Drake Rd.
Farmington Hills, MI 48331-3535

ISBN-13: 978-0-7876-5103-9 (set)          ISBN-10: 0-7876-5103-6 (set)
ISBN-13: 978-1-56995-786-8               ISBN-10: 1-56995-786-X

ISSN 1938-8896

This title is also available as an e-book.
ISBN-13: 978-1-56995-838-4 (set)
ISBN-10: 1-56995-838-6 (set)
Contact your Gale sales representative for ordering information.

Printed in the United States of America
1 2 3 4 5          17 16 15 14 13

# TABLE OF CONTENTS

# PREFACE

*Alcohol, Tobacco, and Illicit Drugs* is part of the *Information Plus Reference Series*. The purpose of each volume of the series is to present the latest facts on a topic of pressing concern in modern American life. These topics include the most controversial and studied social issues of the 21st century: abortion, capital punishment, care of senior citizens, crime, the environment, health care, immigration, minorities, national security, social welfare, water, women, youth, and many more. Even though this series is written especially for high school and undergraduate students, it is an excellent resource for anyone in need of factual information on current affairs.

By presenting the facts, it is the intention of Gale, Cengage Learning to provide its readers with everything they need to reach an informed opinion on current issues. To that end, there is a particular emphasis in this series on the presentation of scientific studies, surveys, and statistics. These data are generally presented in the form of tables, charts, and other graphics placed within the text of each book. Every graphic is directly referred to and carefully explained in the text. The source of each graphic is presented within the graphic itself. The data used in these graphics are drawn from the most reputable and reliable sources, such as from the various branches of the U.S. government and from private organizations and associations. Every effort has been made to secure the most recent information available. Readers should bear in mind that many major studies take years to conduct and that additional years often pass before the data from these studies are made available to the public. Therefore, in many cases the most recent information available in 2013 is dated from 2010 or 2011. Older statistics are sometimes presented as well if they are landmark studies or of particular interest and no more-recent information exists.

Although statistics are a major focus of the *Information Plus Reference Series*, they are by no means its only content. Each book also presents the widely held positions and important ideas that shape how the book's subject is discussed in the United States. These positions are explained in detail and, where possible, in the words of their proponents. Some of the other material to be found in these books includes historical background, descriptions of major events related to the subject, relevant laws and court cases, and examples of how these issues play out in American life. Some books also feature primary documents or have pro and con debate sections that provide the words and opinions of prominent Americans on both sides of a controversial topic. All material is presented in an evenhanded and unbiased manner; readers will never be encouraged to accept one view of an issue over another.

## HOW TO USE THIS BOOK

Both legal and illicit drugs—substances that can affect a person's mood or physiology—are used by people from all segments of American society. Legal drugs include prescription medications as well as popular and widely available substances such as alcohol, tobacco, and caffeine. Illegal drugs are those with no currently accepted medical use in the United States, such as heroin, lysergic acid diethylamide, ecstasy, and inhalants. This book provides an overview of legal and illicit drugs, including their health impact, addictive nature, and potential for abuse. Also discussed are the political and economic ramifications of such substances; their use among youth; possible treatments; drug trafficking; and antidrug efforts and campaigns.

*Alcohol, Tobacco, and Illicit Drugs* consists of nine chapters and three appendixes. Each chapter is devoted to a particular aspect of alcohol, tobacco, and illicit drugs in the United States. For a summary of the information that is covered in each chapter, please see the synopses that are provided in the Table of Contents. Chapters generally begin with an overview of the basic facts and background information on the chapter's topic, then proceed to examine subtopics of particular interest. For example, Chapter 4: Illicit Drugs, begins with an overview of illicit drug use in the United States, assessing the relationship between drug usage and factors such as age, race, and gender. The chapter proceeds to investigate the frequency with which specific types of illicit drugs are used, providing statistics on drug-related deaths as well as detailed usage statistics for marijuana, psychotherapeutics (including synthetic stimulants such as methamphetamine), cocaine, hallucinogens, and inhalants. Usage of other dangerous drugs, notably heroin and anabolic steroids, is also discussed, as is the use of illicit drugs during pregnancy. The chapter then offers an analysis of drug arrest, conviction, and sentencing statistics, before concluding with a broad examination of the relationship between illicit drug use and crime. Readers can find their way through a chapter by looking for the section and subsection headings, which are clearly set off from the text. They can also refer to the book's extensive Index if they already know what they are looking for.

## Statistical Information

The tables and figures featured throughout *Alcohol, Tobacco, and Illicit Drugs* will be of particular use to readers in learning about this issue. These tables and figures represent an extensive collection of the most recent and valuable statistics on alcohol, tobacco, illicit drugs, and related issues—for example, graphics cover the amount of alcoholic beverages consumed per capita by American citizens over the past several decades; alcohol's involvement in fatal automobile crashes; the diseases associated with tobacco use; the number of youth who use illicit drugs; and the prevalence rates of hallucinogen use among students. Gale, Cengage Learning believes that making this information available to readers is the most important way to fulfill the goal of this book: to help readers understand the issues and controversies surrounding alcohol, tobacco, and illicit drugs in the United States and to reach their own conclusions.

Each table or figure has a unique identifier appearing above it for ease of identification and reference. Titles for the tables and figures explain their purpose. At the end of each table or figure, the original source of the data is provided.

To help readers understand these often complicated statistics, all tables and figures are explained in the text. References in the text direct readers to the relevant statistics. Furthermore, the contents of all tables and figures are fully indexed. Please see the opening section of the Index at the back of this volume for a description of how to find tables and figures within it.

## Appendixes

Besides the main body text and images, *Alcohol, Tobacco, and Illicit Drugs* has three appendixes. The first is the Important Names and Addresses directory. Here, readers will find contact information for a number of government and private organizations that can provide further information on alcohol, tobacco, and/or illicit drugs. The second appendix is the Resources section, which can also assist readers in conducting their own research. In this section the author and editors of *Alcohol, Tobacco, and Illicit Drugs* describe some of the sources that were most useful during the compilation of this book. The final appendix is the Index. It has been greatly expanded from previous editions and should make it even easier to find specific topics in this book.

## ADVISORY BOARD CONTRIBUTIONS

The staff of Information Plus would like to extend its heartfelt appreciation to the Information Plus Advisory Board. This dedicated group of media professionals provides feedback on the series on an ongoing basis. Their comments allow the editorial staff who work on the project to make the series better and more user-friendly. The staff's top priority is to produce the highest-quality and most useful books possible, and the Information Plus Advisory Board's contributions to this process are invaluable.

The members of the Information Plus Advisory Board are:

- Kathleen R. Bonn, Librarian, Newbury Park High School, Newbury Park, California

- Madelyn Garner, Librarian, San Jacinto College, North Campus, Houston, Texas

- Anne Oxenrider, Media Specialist, Dundee High School, Dundee, Michigan

- Charles R. Rodgers, Director of Libraries, Pasco-Hernando Community College, Dade City, Florida

- James N. Zitzelsberger, Library Media Department Chairman, Oshkosh West High School, Oshkosh, Wisconsin

## COMMENTS AND SUGGESTIONS

The editors of the *Information Plus Reference Series* welcome your feedback on *Alcohol, Tobacco, and Illicit Drugs*. Please direct all correspondence to:

Editors
*Information Plus Reference Series*
27500 Drake Rd.
Farmington Hills, MI 48331-3535

CHAPTER 1

# DRUGS: A DEFINITION

Drugs are nonfood chemicals that alter the way a person thinks, feels, functions, or behaves. This includes everything from prescription medications, to illegal chemicals such as heroin, to popular and widely available substances such as alcohol, tobacco, and caffeine. A wide variety of laws, regulations, and government agencies exist to control the possession, sale, and use of drugs. Different drugs are held to different standards based on their perceived dangers and usefulness, a fact that sometimes leads to disagreement and controversy.

Illegal drugs are those with no currently accepted medical use in the United States, such as heroin, lysergic acid diethylamide (LSD), and marijuana. It is illegal to buy, sell, possess, and use these drugs except for research purposes. They are supplied only to registered, qualified researchers. (Some states and local jurisdictions have decriminalized certain uses of specific amounts of marijuana, but federal laws supersede these state and local marijuana decriminalization laws. For a more detailed discussion on the legalization of marijuana, see Chapter 9.)

By contrast, legal drugs are drugs whose sale, possession, and use as intended are not forbidden by law. Their use may be restricted, however. For example, the U.S. Drug Enforcement Administration (DEA) controls the use of legal psychoactive (mood- or mind-altering) drugs that have the potential for abuse. These drugs, which include narcotics, depressants, and stimulants, are available only with a prescription and are called controlled substances. The term *illicit drugs* is used by the Substance Abuse and Mental Health Services Administration to describe both controlled substances that are used in violation of the law and drugs that are completely illegal.

The goal of the DEA is to ensure that controlled substances are readily available for medical use or research purposes while preventing their illegal sale and abuse. The agency works toward accomplishing this goal by requiring people and businesses that manufacture, distribute, prescribe, and dispense controlled substances to register with the DEA. Registrants must abide by a series of requirements that relate to drug security, records accountability, and adherence to standards. The DEA also enforces the controlled substances laws and regulations of the United States by investigating and prosecuting those who violate these laws.

The U.S. Food and Drug Administration (FDA) also plays a role in drug control. This agency regulates the manufacture and marketing of prescription and nonprescription drugs. It also requires that the active ingredients in a product be safe and effective before allowing the drug to be sold.

Alcohol and tobacco are monitored and specially taxed by the Alcohol and Tobacco Tax and Trade Bureau (TTB). The TTB was formed in January 2003 as a provision of the Homeland Security Act of 2002, which split the Bureau of Alcohol, Tobacco, and Firearms (ATF) into two new agencies. One of these agencies, the TTB, took over the taxation duties for alcohol, tobacco, and firearms and remained a part of the U.S. Department of the Treasury. The TTB also ensures that alcohol and tobacco products are legally labeled, advertised, and marketed; regulates the qualification and operations of distilleries, wineries, and breweries; tests alcoholic beverages to ensure that their regulated ingredients are within legal limits; and screens applicants who wish to manufacture, import, or export tobacco products.

The other agency split from the former ATF is the reformed ATF: the Bureau of Alcohol, Tobacco, Firearms, and Explosives. The ATF has become a principal law enforcement agency within the U.S. Department of Justice, enforcing federal criminal laws and regulating the firearms and explosives industries. It also investigates illegal trafficking of alcohol and tobacco products.

In June 2009 Congress and President Barack Obama (1961–) enacted legislation that gave the FDA authority to oversee the sale and advertising of tobacco. The legislation granted the FDA various liberties, including regulating the levels of nicotine and other ingredients in cigarettes, banning tobacco manufacturers from selling candy-flavored or menthol cigarettes, requiring larger warning signs on tobacco packaging, and preventing the sale of so-called mild or light cigarettes.

## FIVE CATEGORIES OF SUBSTANCES

Drugs may be classified into five categories:

- Depressants, including alcohol and tranquilizers—these substances slow down the activity of the nervous system. They produce sedative (calming) and hypnotic (trancelike) effects as well as drowsiness. If taken in large doses, depressants can cause intoxication (drunkenness).

- Hallucinogens, including marijuana, phencyclidine, and LSD—hallucinogens produce abnormal and unreal sensations such as seeing distorted and vividly colored images. Hallucinogens can also produce frightening psychological responses such as anxiety, depression, and the feeling of losing control of one's mind.

- Narcotics, including heroin and opium, from which morphine and codeine are derived—narcotics are drugs that alter the perception of pain and induce sleep and euphoria (an intense feeling of well-being; a "high").

- Stimulants, including caffeine, nicotine, cocaine, amphetamine, and methamphetamine—these substances speed up the processing rate of the central nervous system. They can reduce fatigue, elevate mood, increase energy, and help people stay awake. In large doses stimulants can cause irritability, anxiety, sleeplessness, and even psychotic behavior. Caffeine is the most commonly used stimulant in the world.

- Other compounds, including anabolic steroids and inhalants—anabolic steroids are a group of synthetic substances that are chemically related to testosterone and are promoted for their muscle-building properties. Inhalants are solvents and aerosol products that produce vapors that have psychoactive effects. These substances dull pain and can produce euphoria.

Table 1.1 provides an overview of alcohol, nicotine, and other selected psychoactive substances. It includes the DEA schedule for each drug listed. Developed as part of the Controlled Substances Act (CSA) of 1970, the DEA drug schedules are categories into which controlled substances are placed depending on their characteristics such as medical use, potential for abuse, safety, and danger of dependence. Table 1.2 provides a list of commonly abused prescription drugs, along with their DEA schedules. The types of drugs categorized in each of the five schedules, with examples, are shown in Table 1.3.

## DRUGS DISCUSSED IN THIS BOOK

This book focuses on substances that are widely used throughout the world: alcohol, tobacco, and illicit drugs. Not only are alcohol and tobacco legal, relatively affordable, and more or less socially acceptable (depending on time, place, and circumstance) but also they are important economic commodities. Industries exist to produce, distribute, and sell these products, creating jobs and income and contributing to economic well-being. Thus, whenever discussions of possible government regulation of alcohol and tobacco arise, the topic brings with it significant economic and political issues.

Illicit drugs are those that are unlawful to possess or distribute under the CSA. Some controlled substances can be taken under the supervision of health care professionals who are licensed by the DEA. The CSA provides penalties for the unlawful manufacture, distribution, and dispensing of controlled substances, based on the schedule of the drug or substance. Nonetheless, illicit drugs have fostered huge illicit drug marketing and drug trafficking (buying and selling) networks. (See Chapter 8.) Tobacco, beer, wine, and spirits are exempt from the CSA and the DEA drug schedules.

Figure 1.1, Figure 1.2, and Figure 1.3 show trends in cigarette, illicit drug, and alcohol use from 1900 to the first decade of the 21st century. They also provide an overview of the ebb and flow of the use and abuse of these substances in the United States. This chapter will take a historical look at the use and abuse of each substance, and the chapters that follow will present more up-to-date information.

## WHAT ARE ABUSE AND ADDICTION?

Many drugs, both legal and illicit, have the potential for abuse and addiction. Research and treatment experts identify three general levels of interaction with drugs: use, abuse, and dependence (or addiction). In general, abuse involves a compulsive use of a substance and impaired social or occupational functioning. Dependence (addiction) includes these traits, plus evidence of physical tolerance (a need to take increasingly higher doses to achieve the same effect) or withdrawal symptoms when use of the drug is stopped.

The progression from use to dependence is complex, as are the abused substances themselves. Researchers find no standard boundaries between using a substance, abusing a substance, and being addicted to a substance.

# TABLE 1.1

## Commonly abused drugs

| Substances: category and name | Examples of commercial and street names | DEA schedule[a]/how administered[b] | Acute effects/health risks |
|---|---|---|---|
| **Tobacco** | | | |
| Nicotine | Found in cigarettes, cigars, bidis, and smokeless tobacco (snuff, spit tobacco, chew) | Not scheduled/smoked, snorted, chewed | Increased blood pressure and heart rate/chronic lung disease; cardiovascular disease; stroke; cancers of the mouth, pharynx, larynx, esophagus, stomach, pancreas, cervix, kidney, bladder, and acute myeloid leukemia; adverse pregnancy outcomes; addiction |
| **Alcohol** | | | |
| Alcohol (ethyl alcohol) | Found in liquor, beer, and wine | Not scheduled/swallowed | In low doses, euphoria, mild stimulation, relaxation, lowered inhibitions; in higher doses, drowsiness, slurred speech, nausea, emotional volatility, loss of coordination, visual distortions, impaired memory, sexual dysfunction, loss of consciousness/increased risk of injuries, violence, fetal damage (in pregnant women): depression; neurologic deficits; hypertension; liver and heart disease; addiction; fatal overdose |
| **Cannabinoids** | | | |
| Marijuana | Blunt, dope, ganja, grass, herb, joint, bud, Mary Jane, pot, reefer, green, trees, smoke, sinsemilla, skunk, weed | I/smoked, swallowed | Euphoria; relaxation; slowed reaction time; distorted sensory perception; impaired balance and coordination; increased heart rate and appetite; impaired learning, memory; anxiety; panic attacks; psychosis/cough; frequent respiratory infections; possible mental health decline; addiction |
| Hashish | Boom, gangster, hash, hash oil, hemp | I/smoked, swallowed | |
| **Opioids** | | | |
| Heroin | Diacetylmorphine: smack, horse, brown sugar, dope, H, junk, skag, skunk, white horse, China white; cheese (with OTC cold medicine and antihistamine) | I/injected, smoked, snorted | Euphoria; drowsiness; impaired coordination; dizziness; confusion; nausea; sedation; feeling of heaviness in the body; slowed or arrested breathing/constipation; endocarditis; hepatitis; HIV; addiction; fatal overdose |
| Opium | Laudanum, paregoric: big O, black stuff, block, gum, hop | II, III, V/swallowed, smoked | |
| **Stimulants** | | | |
| Cocaine | Cocaine hydrochloride: blow, bump, C, candy, Charlie, coke, crack, flake, rock, snow, toot | II/snorted, smoked, injected | Increased heart rate, blood pressure, body temperature, metabolism; feelings of exhilaration; increased energy, mental alertness; tremors; reduced appetite; irritability; anxiety; panic; paranoia; violent behavior; psychosis/weight loss; insomnia; cardiac or cardiovascular complications; stroke; seizures; addiction |
| Amphetamine | Biphetamine, Dexedrine: bennies, black beauties, crosses, hearts, LA turnaround, speed, truck drivers, uppers | II/swallowed, snorted, smoked, injected | Also, for cocaine—nasal damage from snorting |
| Methamphetamine | Desoxyn: meth, ice, crank, chalk, crystal, fire, glass, go fast, speed | II/swallowed, snorted, smoked, injected | Also, for methamphetamine—severe dental problems |
| **Club drugs** | | | |
| MDMA (methylenedioxymethamphetamine) | Ecstasy, Adam, clarity, Eve, lover's speed, peace, uppers | I/swallowed, snorted, injected | MDMA—mild hallucinogenic effects; increased tactile sensitivity, empathic feelings; lowered inhibition; anxiety; chills; sweating; teeth clenching; muscle cramping/sleep disturbances; depression; impaired memory; hyperthermia; addiction |
| Flunitrazepam[c] | Rohypnol: forget-me pill, Mexican Valium, R2, roach, Roche, roofies, roofinol, rope, rophies | IV/swallowed, snorted | Flunitrazepam—sedation; muscle relaxation; confusion; memory loss; dizziness; impaired coordination/addiction |
| GHB[c] | Gamma-hydroxybutyrate: G, Georgia home boy, grievous bodily harm, liquid ecstasy, soap, scoop, goop, liquid X | I/swallowed | GHB—drowsiness; nausea; headache; disorientation; loss of coordination; memory loss/unconsciousness; seizures; coma |
| **Dissociative drugs** | | | |
| Ketamine | Ketalar SV: cat Valium, K, Special K, vitamin K | III/injected, snorted, smoked | Feelings of being separate from one's body and environment; impaired motor function/anxiety; tremors; numbness; memory loss; nausea |
| PCP and analogs | Phencyclidine: angel dust, boat, hog, love boat, peace pill | I, II/swallowed, smoked, injected | Also, for ketamine—analgesia; impaired memory; delirium; respiratory depression and arrest; death |
| Salvia divinorum | Salvia, Shepherdess's Herb, Maria Pastora, magic mint, Sally-D | Not scheduled/chewed, swallowed, smoked | Also, for PCP and analogs—analgesia; psychosis; aggression; violence; slurred speech; loss of coordination; hallucinations |
| Dextromethorphan (DXM) | Found in some cough and cold medications: Robotripping, Robo, Triple C | Not scheduled/swallowed | Also, for DXM—euphoria; slurred speech; confusion; dizziness; distorted visual perceptions |

**TABLE 1.1**

**Commonly abused drugs** [CONTINUED]

| Substances: category and name | Examples of commercial and street names | DEA schedule[a]/how administered[b] | Acute effects/health risks |
|---|---|---|---|
| **Hallucinogens** | | | |
| LSD | Lysergic acid diethylamide: acid, blotter, cubes, microdot, yellow sunshine, blue heaven | I/swallowed, absorbed through mouth tissues | Altered states of perception and feeling; hallucinations; nausea |
| Mescaline | Buttons, cactus, mesc, peyote | I/swallowed, smoked | Also, for LSD and mescaline—increased body temperature, heart rate, blood pressure; loss of appetite; sweating; sleeplessness; numbness; dizziness; weakness; tremors; impulsive behavior; rapid shifts in emotion |
| Psilocybin | Magic mushrooms, purple passion, shrooms, little smoke | I/swallowed | Also, for LSD—flashbacks, Hallucinogen Persisting Perception Disorder |
| | | | Also, for psilocybin—nervousness; paranoia; panic |
| **Other compounds** | | | |
| Anabolic steroids | Anadrol, Oxandrin, Durabolin, Depo-Testosterone, Equipoise: roids, juice, gym candy, pumpers | III/injected, swallowed, applied to skin | Steroids—no intoxication effects/hypertension; blood clotting and cholesterol changes; liver cysts; hostility and aggression; acne; in adolescents—premature stoppage of growth; in males—prostate cancer, reduced sperm production, shrunken testicles, breast enlargement; in females—menstrual irregularities, development of beard and other masculine characteristics |
| Inhalants | Solvents (paint thinners, gasoline, glues): gases (butane, propane, aerosol propellants, nitrous oxide); nitrites (isoamyl, isobutyl, cyclohexyl): laughing gas, poppers, snappers, whippets | Not scheduled/inhaled through nose or mouth | Inhalants (varies by chemical)—stimulation; loss of inhibition; headache; nausea or vomiting; slurred speech; loss of motor coordination; wheezing/cramps; muscle weakness; depression; memory impairment; damage to cardiovascular and nervous systems; unconsciousness; sudden death |

[a]Schedule I and II drugs have a high potential for abuse. They require greater storage security and have a quota on manufacturing, among other restrictions. Schedule I drugs are available for research only and have no approved medical use; Schedule II drugs are available only by prescription (unrefillable) and require a form for ordering. Schedule III and IV drugs are available by prescription, may have five refills in 6 months, and may be ordered orally. Some Schedule V drugs are available over the counter.

[b]Some of the health risks are directly related to the route of drug administration. For example, injection drug use can increase the risk of infection through needle contamination with staphylococci, HIV, hepatitis, and other organisms.

[c]Associated with sexual assaults.

SOURCE: Adapted from "Commonly Abused Drugs," National Institute on Drug Abuse, National Institutes of Health, March 2011, http://www.drugabuse.gov/sites/default/files/cadchart_2.pdf (accessed February 11, 2013)

# TABLE 1.2

## Commonly abused prescription drugs

| Substances: category and name | Examples of commercial and street names | DEA schedule[a]/how administered | Intoxication effects/health risks |
|---|---|---|---|
| **Depressants** | | | |
| Barbiturates | Amytal, Nembutal, Seconal, Phenobarbital: barbs, reds, red birds, phennies, tooies, yellows, yellow jackets | II, III, IV/injected, swallowed | Sedation/drowsiness, reduced anxiety, feelings of well-being, lowered inhibitions, slurred speech, poor concentration, confusion, dizziness, impaired coordination and memory/slowed pulse, lowered blood pressure, slowed breathing, tolerance, withdrawal, addiction; increased risk of respiratory distress and death when combined with alcohol |
| Benzodiazepines | Ativan, Halcion, Librium, Valium, Xanax, Klonopin: candy, downers, sleeping pills, tranks | IV/swallowed | For barbiturates—euphoria, unusual excitement, fever, irritability/life-threatening withdrawal in chronic users |
| Sleep medications | Ambien (zolpidem), Sonata (zaleplon), Lunesta (eszopiclone) | IV/swallowed | |
| **Opioids and morphine derivatives[b]** | | | |
| Codeine | Empirin with Codeine, Fiorinal with Codeine, Robitussin A-C, Tylenol with Codeine: Captain Cody, Cody, schoolboy; (with glutethimide: doors & fours, loads, pancakes and syrup) | II, III, IV/injected, swallowed | Pain relief, euphoria, drowsiness, sedation, weakness, dizziness, nausea, impaired coordination, confusion, dry mouth, itching, sweating, clammy skin, constipation/slowed or arrested breathing, lowered pulse and blood pressure, tolerance, addiction, unconsciousness, coma, death; risk of death increased when combined with alcohol or other CNS depressants |
| Morphine | Roxanol, Duramorph: M, Miss Emma, monkey, white stuff | II, III/injected, swallowed, smoked | For fentanyl—80–100 times more potent analgesic than morphine |
| Methadone | Methadose, Dolophine: fizzies, amidone (with MDMA: chocolate chip cookies) | II/swallowed, injected | For oxycodone—muscle relaxation/twice as potent analgesic as morphine; high abuse potential |
| Fentanyl and analogs | Actiq, Duragesic, Sublimaze: Apache, China girl, dance fever, friend, goodfella, jackpot, murder 8, TNT, Tango and Cash | II/injected, smoked, snorted | For codeine—less analgesia, sedation, and respiratory depression than morphine |
| Other opioid pain relievers: Oxycodone HCL Hydrocodone Bitartrate Hydromorphone Oxymorphone Meperidine Propoxyphene | Tylox, Oxycontin, Percodan, Percocet: Oxy, O.C., oxycotton, oxycet, hillbilly heroin, percs Vicodin, Lortab, Lorcet: vike, Watson-387 Dilaudid: juice, smack, D, footballs, dillies Opana, Numorphan, Numorphone: biscuits, blue heaven, blues, Mrs. O, octagons, stop signs, O Bomb Demerol, meperidine hydrochloride: demmies, pain killer Darvon, Darvocet | II, III, IV/chewed, swallowed, snorted, injected, suppositories | For methadone—used to treat opioid addiction and pain; significant overdose risk when used improperly |
| **Stimulants** | | | |
| Amphetamines | Biphetamine, Dexedrine, Adderall: bennies, black beauties, crosses, hearts, LA turn around, speed, truck drivers, uppers | II/injected, swallowed, smoked, snorted | Feelings of exhilaration, increased energy, mental alertness/increased heart rate, blood pressure, and metabolism, reduced appetite, weight loss, nervousness, insomnia, seizures, heart attack, stroke |
| Methylphenidate | Concerta, Ritalin: JIF, MPH, R-ball, Skippy, the smart drug, vitamin R | II/injected, swallowed, snorted | For amphetamines—rapid breathing, tremor, loss of coordination, irritability, anxiousness, restlessness/delirium, panic, paranoia, hallucinations, impulsive behavior, aggressiveness, tolerance, addiction For methylphenidate—increase or decrease in blood pressure, digestive problems, loss of appetite, weight loss |
| **Other compounds** | | | |
| Dextromethorphan (DXM) | Found in some cough and cold medications: Robotripping, Robo, Triple C | Not scheduled/swallowed | Euphoria, slurred speech/increased heart rate and blood pressure, dizziness, nausea, vomiting, confusion, paranoia, distorted visual perceptions, impaired motor function |

[a]Schedule I and II drugs have a high potential for abuse. They require greater storage security and have a quota on manufacturing, among other restrictions. Schedule I drugs are available for research only and have no approved medical use. Schedule II drugs are available only by prescription and require a new prescription for each refill. Schedule III and IV drugs are available by prescription, may have five refills in 6 months, and may be ordered orally. Most Schedule V drugs are available over the counter.

[b]Taking drugs by injection can increase the risk of infection through needle contamination with staphylococci, HIV, hepatitis, and other organisms. Injection is a more common practice for opioids, but risks apply to any medication taken by injection.

SOURCE: Adapted from "Commonly Abused Prescription Drugs Chart," National Institutes of Health, National Institute on Drug Abuse, October 2011, http://www.drugabuse.gov/sites/default/files/rx_drugs_placemat_508c_10052011.pdf (accessed February 11, 2013)

**TABLE 1.3**

### Drug schedules established by the Controlled Substance Act (CSA), 1970

**Schedule I**

• The drug or other substance has a high potential for abuse.
• The drug or other substance has no currently accepted medical use in treatment in the United States.
• There is a lack of accepted safety for use of the drug or other substance under medical supervision.
• Examples of Schedule I substances include heroin, gamma hydroxybutyric acid (GHB), lysergic acid diethylamide (LSD), marijuana, and methaqualone.

**Schedule II**

• The drug or other substance has a high potential for abuse.
• The drug or other substance has a currently accepted medical use in treatment in the United States or a currently accepted medical use with severe restrictions.
• Abuse of the drug or other substance may lead to severe psychological or physical dependence.
• Examples of Schedule II substances include morphine, phencyclidine (PCP), cocaine, methadone, hydrocodone, fentanyl, and methamphetamine.

**Schedule III**

• The drug or other substance has less potential for abuse than the drugs or other substances in Schedules I and II.
• The drug or other substance has a currently accepted medical use in treatment in the United States.
• Abuse of the drug or other substance may lead to moderate or low physical dependence or high psychological dependence.
• Anabolic steroids, codeine and hydrocodone products with aspirin or Tylenol®, and some barbiturates are examples of Schedule III substances.

**Schedule IV**

• The drug or other substance has a low potential for abuse relative to the drugs or other substances in Schedule III.
• The drug or other substance has a currently accepted medical use in treatment in the United States.
• Abuse of the drug or other substance may lead to limited physical dependence or psychological dependence relative to the drugs or other substances in Schedule III.
• Examples of drugs included in Schedule IV are alprazolam, clonazepam, and diazepam.

**Schedule V**

• The drug or other substance has a low potential for abuse relative to the drugs or other substances in Schedule IV.
• The drug or other substance has a currently accepted medical use in treatment in the United States.
• Abuse of the drug or other substances may lead to limited physical dependence or psychological dependence relative to the drugs or other substances in Schedule IV.
• Cough medicines with codeine are examples of Schedule V drugs.

SOURCE: Adapted from *Drugs of Abuse, 2011 Edition*, U.S. Department of Justice, Drug Enforcement Administration, 2011, http://www.justice.gov/dea/docs/drugs_of_abuse_2011.pdf (accessed February 11, 2013)

**FIGURE 1.1**

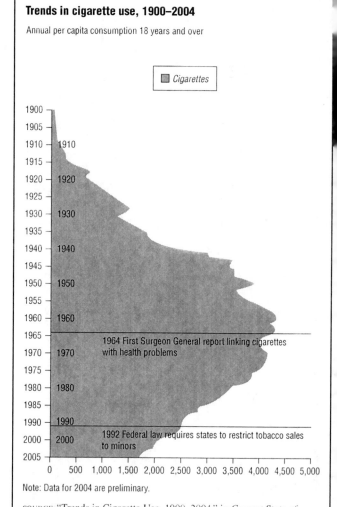

### Trends in cigarette use, 1900–2004

Annual per capita consumption 18 years and over

Note: Data for 2004 are preliminary.

SOURCE: "Trends in Cigarette Use, 1900–2004," in *Current State of Drug Policy: Successes and Challenges*, Executive Office of the President of the United States, Office of National Drug Control Policy, March 2008, http://www.ncjrs.gov/ondcppubs/publications/pdf/successes_challenges.pdf (accessed February 11, 2013). Data from Miller, R. U.S. cigarette consumption 1900 to date. In Harr W. ed. Tobacco Yearbook. Bowling Green KY. Cockrel Corporation 1981.

---

They believe these lines vary widely from substance to substance and from individual to individual.

In addition, scientists have been working to understand why some people who use addictive substances become addicted and why others do not or can more easily break the addiction. The results of many studies of identical and fraternal (nonidentical) twins and families with histories of substance abuse and addiction indicate that there is a genetic component to addiction. For example, in "Are There Genetic Influences on Addiction: Evidence from Family, Adoption, and Twin Studies" (*Addiction*, vol. 103, no. 7, July 2008), Arpana Agrawal and Michael T. Lynskey of the Washington University School of Medicine in St. Louis, Missouri, review studies that examined the genetic basis for addiction. The

researchers determine that inheritance accounts for a wide range of influence on addiction—from 30% to 70%. Other factors, such as gender, age, social influences, and cultural characteristics, interact with one's genetics, resulting in an individual's susceptibility to addictive behavior.

### Physiological, Psychological, and Sociocultural Factors

Some researchers maintain that the principal causes of substance use are external social influences, such as peer pressure, whereas the principal causes of substance abuse and/or dependence are psychological and physiological needs and pressures, including inherited tendencies. Additionally, psychoactive drug use at an early age may be a risk factor (a characteristic that increases likelihood) for subsequent dependence.

FIGURE 1.2

## Trends in illicit drug use, 1900–2005

Percent marijuana and cocaine users among those ages 18–25

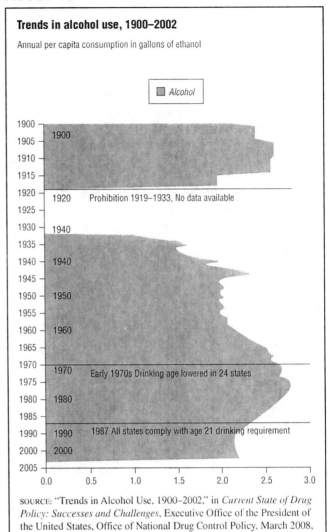

1900–1971 No data available for cocaine and marijuana usage

1973 President Nixon declares war on drugs

1985 "Just say no" campaign started

1996 Marijuana approved for medical use in California and Arizona

Note: Data for cocaine past year unavailable for 1971–1972.

SOURCE: "Trends in Illicit Drug Use, 1900–2005," in *Current State of Drug Policy: Successes and Challenges*, Executive Office of the President, Office of National Drug Control Policy, March 2008, http://www.ncjrs.gov/ondcppubs/publications/pdf/successes_challenges.pdf (accessed February 11, 2013)

FIGURE 1.3

## Trends in alcohol use, 1900–2002

Annual per capita consumption in gallons of ethanol

Prohibition 1919–1933, No data available

Early 1970s Drinking age lowered in 24 states

1987 All states comply with age 21 drinking requirement

SOURCE: "Trends in Alcohol Use, 1900–2002," in *Current State of Drug Policy: Successes and Challenges*, Executive Office of the President of the United States, Office of National Drug Control Policy, March 2008, http://www.ncjrs.gov/ondcppubs/publications/pdf/successes_challenges.pdf (accessed February 11, 2013)

Physically, mood-altering substances affect brain processes. Most drugs that are abused stimulate the reward or pleasure center of the brain by causing the release of dopamine, which is a neurotransmitter—a chemical in the brain that relays messages from one nerve cell to another.

Psychologically, a person may become dependent on a substance because it relieves pain, offers escape from real or perceived problems, or makes the user feel more relaxed or confident in certain social settings. A successful first use of a substance may reduce the user's fear of the drug and thus lead to continued use and even dependence.

Socially, substance use may be widespread in some groups or environments. The desire to belong to a special group is a strong human characteristic, and those who use one or more substances may become part of a subculture that encourages and promotes use. An individual may be influenced by one of these groups to start using a substance, or he or she may be drawn to such a group after starting use somewhere else. In addition, a person—especially a young person—may not have access to alternative rewarding or pleasurable groups or activities that do not include substance use.

Researchers have identified complex relationships between physiological, psychological, and cultural factors that influence drinking and drinking patterns. Constraints (inhibitory factors) and motivations influence drinking patterns. In turn, drinking patterns influence the relationship between routine activities that are related to drinking and acute (immediate) consequences of drinking.

### Definitions of Abuse and Dependence

Two texts provide the most commonly used medical definitions of substance abuse and dependence. The *Diagnostic and Statistical Manual of Mental Disorders*

(*DSM*) is published by the American Psychiatric Association. The *International Classification of Diseases* (*ICD*) is published by the World Health Organization (WHO). Even though the definitions of dependence in these two manuals are almost identical, the definitions of abuse are not.

**THE *DSM* DEFINITION OF ABUSE.** The text revision of the fourth edition of the *DSM, Diagnostic and Statistical Manual of Mental Disorders-IV Text Revision* (*DSM-IV-TR*), was published in 2000 and was the most recent revision available as of April 2013. (The publication of the *DSM-V* is scheduled for May 2013.) The *DSM-IV-TR* defines abuse as an abnormal pattern of recurring use that leads to "significant impairment or distress," marked by one or more of the following during a 12-month period:

- Failure to fulfill major obligations at home, school, or work (e.g., repeated absences, poor performance, or neglect)

- Use in hazardous or potentially hazardous situations, such as driving a car or operating a machine while impaired

- Legal problems, such as arrest for disorderly conduct while under the influence of the substance

- Continued use in spite of social or interpersonal problems caused by the use of the substance, such as fights or family arguments

**THE *ICD* DEFINITION OF HARMFUL USE.** The 10th and most recent revision (as of April 2013) of the *ICD* (*ICD-10*), which was endorsed by the 43rd World Health Assembly in May 1990 and has been used by WHO member states since 1994, uses the term *harmful use* rather than *abuse*. (The publication of the *ICD-11* in its final form is expected in 2015.) It defines harmful use as "a pattern of psychoactive substance use that is causing damage to health," either physical or mental.

Because the *ICD-10* manual is targeted toward international use, its definition must be broader than the *DSM-IV-TR* definition, which is intended for use in the United States. Cultural customs of substance use vary widely, sometimes even within the same country.

**DEFINITIONS OF DEPENDENCE.** In general, the *DSM-IV-TR* and the *ICD-10* manuals agree that dependence is present if three or more of the following occur during a 12-month period:

- Increasing need for more of the substance to achieve the same effect (occurs as the user builds up a tolerance to the substance), or a reduction in effect when using the same amount as used previously

- Withdrawal symptoms if use of the substance is stopped or reduced

- Progressive neglect of other pleasures and duties

- A strong desire to take the substance or a persistent but unsuccessful desire to control or reduce the use of the substance

- Continued use in spite of physical or mental health problems caused by the substance

- Use of the substance in larger amounts or over longer periods of time than originally intended, or difficulties in controlling the amount of the substance used or when trying to stop using it

- Considerable time spent in obtaining the substance, using it, or recovering from its effects

### Progression from Use to Dependence

The rate at which individuals progress from drug use to drug abuse to drug dependence (or addiction) depends on many of the aforementioned factors. In general, each level is more dangerous, more invasive in the user's life, and more likely to cause social interventions, such as family pressure to enter treatment programs or prison sentences for drug offenses, than the previous level.

Figure 1.4 is a diagram of the progression from drug use to addiction. Notice that the intensification of use leads to abuse and that abuse leads to dependence. The right side of the diagram shows social interventions that are appropriate at various stages of drug use, abuse, and dependence. The dotted lines on the left side of the diagram show that relapse after recovery may lead to renewed drug use, abuse, or dependence.

## THE HISTORY OF ALCOHOL USE

Ethyl alcohol (ethanol), the active ingredient in beer, wine, and other liquors, is the oldest known psychoactive drug. It is also the only type of alcohol that is used as a beverage. Other alcohols, such as methanol and isopropyl alcohol, when ingested even in small amounts can produce severe negative health effects and often death.

The basic characteristics of alcoholic beverages have remained unchanged from early times. Beer and wine are created through the natural chemical process called fermentation. Fermentation can produce beverages with an alcohol content of up to 14%. More potent drinks, such as rum or vodka (known as spirits or liquors), can be produced through distillation. This is a process that involves using heat to separate and concentrate the alcohol found in fermented beverages and can result in drinks that have an alcoholic content of 40% or more.

### Early Uses and Abuses of Alcohol

Beer and wine have been used since ancient times in religious rituals, celebrations of councils, coronations, war, peacemaking, festivals, and the rites of birth, initiation, marriage, and death. In ancient times, just as in the 21st century, the use of beer and wine sometimes led to

FIGURE 1.4

**Drug use, abuse, and dependence**

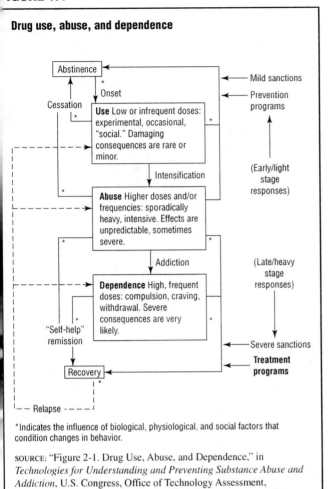

*Indicates the influence of biological, physiological, and social factors that condition changes in behavior.

SOURCE: "Figure 2-1. Drug Use, Abuse, and Dependence," in *Technologies for Understanding and Preventing Substance Abuse and Addiction*, U.S. Congress, Office of Technology Assessment, September 1994, www.fas.org/ota/reports/9435.pdf (accessed February 11, 2013). Data from the National Academy of Sciences, Institute of Medicine.

drunkenness. One of the earliest works on temperance (controlling one's drinking or not drinking at all) was written in Egypt nearly 3,000 years ago. These writings can be thought of as similar to present-day pamphlets that espouse moderation in alcohol consumption. Similar recommendations have been found in early Greek, Roman, Indian, Japanese, and Chinese writings, as well as in the Bible.

**Drinking in Colonial America**

In colonial America people drank much more alcohol than they do in the 21st century, with estimates ranging from three to seven times more alcohol per person per year. Liquor was used to ease the pain and discomfort of many illnesses and injuries such as the common cold, fever, broken bones, toothaches, frostbite, and the like. Parents often gave liquor to children to relieve their minor aches and pains or to help them sleep. Until 1842, when modern surgical anesthesia began with the use of ether, only heavy doses of alcohol were consistently effective to ease pain during operations.

As early as 1619 drunkenness was illegal in the Virginia Colony. It was punished in various ways: whipping, placement in the stocks, fines, and even wearing a red D (for "Drunkard"). By the 18th century all classes of people were getting drunk with greater frequency, even though it was well known that alcohol affected the senses and motor skills and that drunkenness led to increased crime, violence, accidents, and death.

**Temperance**

In 1784 Benjamin Rush (1746–1813), a physician and signer of the Declaration of Independence, published the booklet *An Inquiry into the Effects of Ardent Spirits on the Mind and Body*. The pamphlet became popular among the growing number of people who were concerned about the excessive drinking of many Americans. Such concern gave rise to the temperance movement.

The temperance movement in the United States spanned the 19th and early 20th centuries. Initially, the goal of the movement was to promote moderation in the consumption of alcohol. By the 1850s large numbers of people were completely giving up alcohol, and by the 1870s the goal of the temperance movement was to promote abstinence from alcohol. Reformers were concerned about the effects of alcohol on the family, the labor force, and the nation, all of which needed sober participants if they were to remain healthy and productive. Temperance supporters also saw alcoholism as a problem of personal immorality.

**Prohibition**

Temperance organizations lobbied for the prohibition of alcohol in the United States during the early years of the 20th century. One of the leading temperance organizations was the Anti-Saloon League, which created print materials to convince the public that alcohol should be banned. Figure 1.5 is one of the league's flyers, which showed that families who drank alcohol had a higher rate of child death than families who abstained from alcohol. However, the Anti-Saloon League's research did not take into account other factors that might affect the rate of child death among families, such as poverty. In addition, the league used sensationalist images in its print materials, such as children with gravestones above their heads, to sway public opinion.

In 1919 reform efforts led to the passage of the 18th Amendment of the U.S. Constitution, which prohibited the "manufacture, sale, or transportation of intoxicating liquors" and their importation and exportation. The Volstead Act of 1919, which passed over President Woodrow Wilson's (1856–1924) veto, was the Prohibition law that enforced the 18th Amendment.

Outlawing alcohol did not stop most people from drinking; instead, alcohol was manufactured and sold illegally by gangsters, who organized themselves efficiently and gained considerable political influence from the

**FIGURE 1.5**

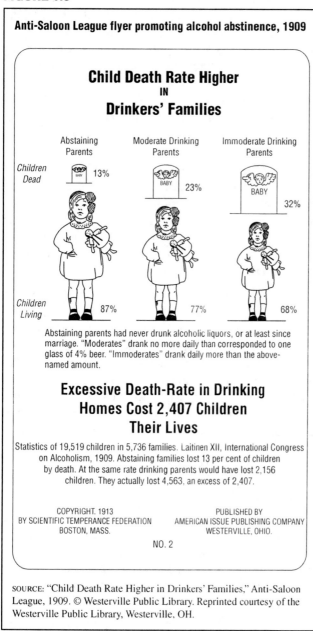

**Anti-Saloon League flyer promoting alcohol abstinence, 1909**

## Child Death Rate Higher
### IN
## Drinkers' Families

Abstaining Parents

Moderate Drinking Parents

Immoderate Drinking Parents

Children Dead — 13% — 23% — 32%

Children Living — 87% — 77% — 68%

Abstaining parents had never drunk alcoholic liquors, or at least since marriage. "Moderates" drank no more daily than corresponded to one glass of 4% beer. "Immoderates" drank daily more than the above-named amount.

## Excessive Death-Rate in Drinking Homes Cost 2,407 Children Their Lives

Statistics of 19,519 children in 5,736 families. Laitinen XII, International Congress on Alcoholism, 1909. Abstaining families lost 13 per cent of children by death. At the same rate drinking parents would have lost 2,156 children. They actually lost 4,563, an excess of 2,407.

COPYRIGHT. 1913
BY SCIENTIFIC TEMPERANCE FEDERATION
BOSTON, MASS.

PUBLISHED BY
AMERICAN ISSUE PUBLISHING COMPANY
WESTERVILLE, OHIO.

NO. 2

SOURCE: "Child Death Rate Higher in Drinkers' Families," Anti-Saloon League, 1909. © Westerville Public Library. Reprinted courtesy of the Westerville Public Library, Westerville, OH.

money they earned. In addition, many individuals illegally brewed alcoholic beverages at home or smuggled alcohol from Canada and Mexico. Ultimately, the 18th Amendment was repealed in 1933 with the passage of the 21st Amendment.

### Understanding the Dangers of Alcohol

As the decades passed, recognition of the dangers of alcohol increased. In 1956 the American Medical Association endorsed classifying and treating alcoholism as a disease. In 1970 Congress created the National Institute on Alcohol Abuse and Alcoholism, which established a public commitment to alcohol-related research. During the 1970s, however, many states lowered their drinking age to 18 when the legal voting age was lowered to this age.

Traffic fatalities rose after these laws took effect, and many such accidents involved people between the ages of 18 and 21 years who had been drinking and driving. Organizations such as Mothers against Drunk Driving and Students against Drunk Driving sought to educate the public about the great harm drunk drivers had done to others. As a result, and because of pressure from the federal government, by 1988 all states raised their minimum drinking age to 21. The National Highway Traffic Safety Administration of the U.S. Department of Transportation estimates in *Traffic Safety Facts, 2010 Data: Young Drivers* (May 2012, http://www-nrd.nhtsa.dot.gov/Pubs/811622.pdf) that laws making 21 the minimum drinking age saved an estimated 28,230 lives between 1975 and 2010. By 1989 warning labels noting the deleterious effects of alcohol on health were required on all retail containers of alcoholic beverages. Nonetheless, the misuse and abuse of alcohol remain major health and social problems in the 21st century.

## THE HISTORY OF TOBACCO USE

Tobacco is a commercially grown plant that contains nicotine, an addictive drug. Tobacco is native to North America, where since ancient times it has played an important part in Native American social and religious customs. Additionally, Native Americans believed that tobacco had medicinal properties, so it was used to treat pain, epilepsy, colds, and headaches.

### From Pipes to Cigarettes

As European explorers and settlers came to North America during the 15th and 16th centuries, Native Americans introduced them to tobacco. Its use soon spread among the settlers, and then throughout Europe and Asia, although some rulers and nations opposed it and sought to outlaw it. At that point tobacco was smoked in pipes, chewed, or taken as snuff. Snuff is finely powdered tobacco that can be chewed, rubbed on the gums, or inhaled through the nose.

Cigar smoking was introduced to the United States in about 1762. Cigars are tobacco leaves that are rolled and prepared for smoking. The U.S. consumption of cigars exceeded 4 billion in 1898, according to various tobacco-related websites. However, cigarettes (cut tobacco rolled in a paper tube) would soon become the choice of most smokers, thanks to the 1881 invention of a cigarette-making machine that allowed them to be mass-produced and sold cheaply.

### Early Antismoking Efforts in the United States

The first antismoking movement in the United States was organized during the 1830s (just as the temperance movement was growing in the country). Reformers characterized tobacco as an unhealthy and even fatal habit. Tobacco use was linked to increased alcohol use and lack of cleanliness. Antismoking reformers also suggested that obacco exhausted the soil, wasted money, and promoted aziness, promiscuity, and profanity. Their efforts to limit r outlaw smoking were met with only small, temporary uccesses until well into the 20th century.

## A Boom in Smoking in the United States

The Centers for Disease Control and Prevention reports n *Surveillance for Selected Tobacco-Use Behaviors— United States, 1900–1994* (*Morbidity and Mortality Weekly Report*, vol. 43, no. SS03, November 18, 1994) that cigarette usage increased dramatically during the early 1900s, with the total consumption increasing from 2.5 billion cigarettes in 1901 to 13.2 billion cigarettes in 1912. In 1913 the R. J. Reynolds Company introduced Camel cigarettes, an event that is often called the birth of the modern cigarette. During World War I (1914–1918) cigarettes were shipped to U.S. troops fighting overseas (this also occurred during World War II [1939–1945]). They were included in soldiers' rations and were dispensed by groups such as the American Red Cross and the Young Men's Christian Association. Women began openly smoking in larger numbers as well, which was something that tobacco companies noticed; in 1919 the first advertisement featuring a woman smoking cigarettes appeared.

Cigarette smoking was very common and an accepted part of society, but doubts about its safety were growing. On July 12, 1957, following a joint report by the National Cancer Institute, the National Heart Institute, the American Cancer Society, and the American Heart Association, the U.S. surgeon general Leroy E. Burney (1906–1998), a smoker himself, delivered the official statement "Lung Cancer and Excessive Cigarette Smoking" (http://www .traumaf.org/Lung%20Cancer%20and%20Excessive%20 Cigarette%20Smoking.pdf), in which he declared that "the weight of the evidence is increasingly pointing in one direction: that excessive smoking is one of the causative factors in lung cancer." Nevertheless, cigarette ads of the 1950s touted cigarette smoking as pleasurable, sexy, relaxing, flavorful, and fun. (See Figure 1.6.)

## Health Risks Lead to Diminished Smoking

In 1964 the U.S. surgeon general Luther L. Terry (1911–1985) released *Smoking and Health: Report of the Advisory Committee to the Surgeon General of the Public Health Service* (http://profiles.nlm.nih.gov/NN/B/ B/M/Q/_/nnbbmq.pdf). This landmark document was the first widely publicized official recognition that cigarette smoking is a cause of lung cancer and laryngeal cancer in men, a probable cause of lung cancer in women, and the most important cause of chronic bronchitis.

Increased attention was paid to the potential health risks of smoking throughout the rest of the 1960s and 1970s. The first health warnings appeared on cigarette packages in 1966. In 1970 the WHO took a public stand

**FIGURE 1.6**

A cigarette advertisement from the 1950s. (© *Apic/Getty Images.*)

against smoking. On January 2, 1971, the Public Health Cigarette Smoking Act of 1969 went into effect, removing cigarette advertising from radio and television in the United States. A growing number of individuals, cities, and states filed lawsuits against U.S. tobacco companies. Some individuals claimed they had been deceived about the potential harm of smoking. A few states filed lawsuits to recoup money spent on smokers' Medicaid bills. In 1998, 46 states, five territories, and the District of Columbia signed the Master Settlement Agreement (http://ag.ca.gov/tobacco/msa.php) with the major tobacco companies to settle all state lawsuits for $206 billion. Excluded from the settlement were Florida, Minnesota, Mississippi, and Texas, which had already concluded previous settlements with the tobacco industry. Chapter 7 includes more information on the Master Settlement Agreement and its long-term effects.

As awareness of the hazards of smoking increased, researchers began reporting the dangers of secondhand smoke (also known as environmental tobacco smoke or passive smoke). State and federal regulators responded to these studies by imposing strict new laws that regulated smoking, particularly in public places. In 1995 California became the first state to pass a law that prohibited smoking in restaurants and bars; the statute went into effect in

1998. Delaware passed a similar restriction in 2002, and by 2012 more than half of U.S. states had implemented public smoking bans. According to Ryan Jaslow, in "Anti-smoking Laws Prevent Heart Attacks, Research Suggests" (CBSNews.com, October 30, 2012), Mayo Clinic researchers reported in 2012 that the number of heart attacks caused by exposure to secondhand smoke dropped 33% due to public smoking bans. Chapter 3 provides a more detailed overview of antismoking legislation in the United States, as well as a more thorough analysis of shifting public attitudes toward smoking since the late 20th century.

## THE EARLY HISTORY OF NARCOTIC, STIMULANT, AND HALLUCINOGEN USE

Humans have experimented with narcotic and hallucinogenic plants since before recorded history, discovering their properties as they tested plants for edibility or were attracted by the odors of some leaves when the leaves were burned. Ancient cultures used narcotic plants to relieve pain or to heighten pleasure and hallucinogenic plants to induce trancelike states during religious ceremonies. Natural substances, used directly or in refined extracts, have also served simply to increase or dull alertness, to invigorate the body, or to change the mood.

### Narcotic Use through the 19th Century

As mentioned earlier, narcotics, including heroin and opium, are drugs that alter the perception of pain and induce sleep and euphoria. Opium is a dried powdered extract that is derived from the opium poppy plant *Papaver somniferum*. Morphine and heroin are made from opium, and all three of these addicting narcotics are called opiates.

Opium itself has been used as a pain reliever in Europe and Asia for thousands of years. In 1805 Friedrich Sertürner (1793–1841), a German pharmacist, discovered how to isolate the highly potent morphine from opium. In 1832 the French chemist Pierre-Jean Robiquet (1780–1840) isolated codeine from opium, which is milder than morphine. It came to be used in cough remedies. The development of the hypodermic needle during the early 1850s made it easier to use morphine. It became a common medicine for treating severe pain, such as battlefield injuries. During the U.S. Civil War (1861–1865) so many soldiers became addicted to morphine that the addiction was later called soldier's disease.

The most potent narcotic that is derived from opium is heroin, which was first synthesized in 1874 by C. R. Alder Wright (1844–1894) at St. Mary's Hospital in London, England. In 1898 the Bayer Company of Elberfeld, Germany, began marketing the drug as a cough remedy and painkiller under the brand-name Heroin; the word was derived from the German word for "heroic,"

which was intended to convey the drug's power and potency. The drug was an instant success and was soon exported.

### Stimulant Use through the 19th Century

The use of stimulants dates back to about 3000 BC with South American societies. Even then, the people of this region knew that cocaine, which is extracted from the leaves of the coca tree *Erythroxylon coca*, was capable of producing euphoria, hyperactivity, and hallucinations. This small coca tree is native to tropical mountain regions in Peru and Bolivia.

After the Spanish conquest of the Incas during the early 1500s and the ensuing Spanish immigration into South America, coca was grown on plantations and used as wages to pay workers. The drug seemed to negate the effects of exhaustion and malnutrition, especially at high altitudes. Many South Americans still chew coca leaves to alleviate the effects of high altitudes.

The spread of the use of coca is attributed to Paolo Mantegazza (1831–1910), an Italian physician who came to value the restorative powers of coca while living in Lima, Peru, during the 1850s. He praised the drug, which led to interest in coca in the United States and Europe. In 1863 the French chemist Angelo Mariani (1838–1914) extracted cocaine from coca leaves and used it as the main ingredient in his coca wine, called Vin Mariani. Shortly thereafter, cough syrups and tonics holding drops of cocaine in solution became popular. Eventually, extracts from coca leaves not only appeared in wine but also in chewing gum, tea, and throat lozenges.

The temperance movement in the United States from 1800 to 1890 helped fuel the public's fondness for nonalcoholic products containing coca. During the mid-1880s Atlanta, Georgia, became one of the first major U.S. cities to forbid the sale of alcohol. It was there that the American inventor John Pemberton (1831–1888) first marketed Coca-Cola, a syrup that then contained extracts of both coca and the kola nut, as a "temperance drink."

### Hallucinogen Use through the 19th Century

Naturally occurring hallucinogens, which are derived from plants, have been used by various cultures for magical, religious, recreational, and health-related purposes for thousands of years. For more than 2,000 years Native American societies often used hallucinogens, such as the psilocybin mushroom (*Psilocybe mexicana*) of Mexico and the peyote cactus (*Lophophora williamsii*) of the U.S. Southwest, in religious ceremonies. Even though scientists were slow to discover the medicinal possibilities of hallucinogens, by 1919 they had isolated mescaline from the peyote cactus and recognized its resemblance to the adrenal hormone epinephrine (adrenaline).

Cannabis, also a hallucinogen, is the term generally applied to the Himalayan hemp plant *Cannabis sativa* from which marijuana, bhang, and ganja (hashish) are derived. Bhang is equivalent to the U.S.-style marijuana, consisting of the leaves, fruits, and stems of the plant. Ganja, which is prepared by crushing the flowering tips of cannabis and collecting a resinous paste, is more potent than marijuana and bhang.

Cannabis dates back more than 5,000 years to Central Asia and China; from there it spread to India and the Near East. Cannabis was highly regarded as a medicinal plant used in folk medicines. It was long valued as an analgesic (painkiller), topical anesthetic, antispasmodic, antidepressant, appetite stimulant, antiasthmatic, and antibiotic.

## NARCOTIC, STIMULANT, AND HALLUCINOGEN USE AT THE END OF THE 19TH CENTURY AND BEYOND

In late 19th-century America it was possible to buy, in a store or by mail order, many medicines (or alleged medicines) that contained morphine, cocaine, and even heroin. Until 1903 the soft drink Coca-Cola contained cocaine. The cocaine was removed and more caffeine (which was already present in the drink from the kola nut) was added. Pharmacies sold cocaine in pure form, as well as many drugs made from opium, such as morphine and heroin.

Beginning in 1898 heroin became widely available when the Bayer Company marketed it as a powerful cough suppressant. According to the Office of Technology Assessment, in *Technologies for Understanding and Preventing Substance Abuse and Addiction* (September 1994, http://www.princeton.edu/~ota/disk1/1994/9435/9435.PDF), physician prescriptions of these drugs increased from 1% of all prescriptions in 1874 to between 20% and 25% in 1902. These drugs were readily available and widely used, with little concern for negative health consequences.

Soon, however, cocaine, heroin, and other drugs were taken off the market for a number of reasons. A growing awareness of the dangers of drug use and food contamination led to the passage of laws such as the Pure Food and Drug Act of 1906. Among other things, the act required the removal of false claims from patent medicines. Medical labels also had to state the amount of any narcotic ingredient the medicine contained and whether that medicine was habit-forming. A growing temperance movement, the development of safe painkillers (such as aspirin), and more alternative medical treatments contributed to the passage of laws that limited drug use, although these laws did not completely outlaw the drugs.

Besides health-related worries, drug use had come to be associated with "undesirables" by the mid- to late 1800s. When drug users were thought to live only in the slums, drug use was considered solely a criminal problem; but when it was finally recognized in middle-class neighborhoods, it came to be seen as a mental health problem. By the start of the 20th century the use of narcotics was considered an international problem. In 1909 the International Opium Commission met to discuss worldwide drug use. This meeting led to the signing of a treaty two years later in the Netherlands requiring all signatories to pass laws that limited the use of narcotics for medicinal purposes. After nearly three years of debate, Congress passed the Harrison Narcotic Act of 1914, which called for the strict control of opium and coca (although coca is a stimulant and not a narcotic).

### Regulating Narcotics, Stimulants, and Hallucinogens

During the 1920s the federal government regulated drugs through the U.S. Department of the Treasury. In 1930 President Herbert Hoover (1874–1964) created the Federal Bureau of Narcotics and selected Harry J. Anslinger (1892–1975) to head it. Believing that all drug users were deviant criminals, Anslinger vigorously enforced the law for the next 32 years. Marijuana, for example, was presented as a "killer weed" that threatened the very fabric of American society.

Marijuana is thought to have been introduced to the United States by Mexican immigrants. Thus, according to the Office of Technology Assessment, in *Technologies for Understanding and Preventing Substance Abuse and Addiction*, it was widely believed that anti-Mexican attitudes, as well as Anslinger's considerable influence, prompted the passage of the Marijuana Tax Act of 1937. The act made the use or sale of marijuana without a tax stamp a federal offense. Because by this time the sale of marijuana was illegal in most states, buying a federal tax stamp would alert the authorities in a particular state to who was selling drugs. Naturally, no marijuana dealer wanted to buy a stamp and expose his or her identity to the authorities.

From the 1940s to the 1960s the FDA, based on the authority granted by the Food, Drug, and Cosmetic Act of 1938, began policing the sale of certain drugs. The act required the FDA to stipulate if specific drugs, such as amphetamines (stimulants) and barbiturates (depressants), were safe for self-medication.

After studying most amphetamines and barbiturates, the agency concluded that it simply could not declare them safe for self-medication. (See Table 1.1 for listings of stimulants and depressants.) Therefore, it ruled that these drugs could only be used under medical supervision—that is, with a physician's prescription. For all pharmaceutical products other than narcotics, this marked the beginning of the distinction between prescription and over-the-counter (without a prescription) drugs.

For 25 years undercover FDA inspectors identified pharmacists who sold amphetamines and barbiturates without a prescription and doctors who wrote illegal prescriptions. During the 1950s, with the growing sale of amphetamines, barbiturates, and, eventually, LSD and other hallucinogens at cafés, truck stops, flophouses, and weight-reduction salons and by street-corner pushers, FDA authorities went after these other illegal dealers. In 1968 the drug-enforcement responsibilities of the FDA were transferred to the Department of Justice.

## War on Drugs

From the mid-1960s to the late 1970s the demographic profile of drug users changed. Previously, drug use had generally been associated with minorities, lower classes, or young "hippies" and "beatniks." During this period drug use among middle- and upper-class whites became widespread and more generally accepted. Many of them began using cocaine, an expensive drug, which they considered to be nonaddictive and a status symbol. In addition, drugs had become much more prevalent in the military because they were cheap and plentiful in Vietnam.

Whereas some circles viewed drug use with wider acceptance, other public sectors came to see drugs as a threat to their communities—much as, 40 years earlier, alcohol had acquired a negative image, leading to Prohibition. Drugs not only symbolized poverty but also were associated with protest movements against the Vietnam War (1954–1975) and the so-called Establishment. Many parents began to perceive the widespread availability of drugs as a threat to their children. By the end of the 1960s such views began to acquire a political expression.

When Richard M. Nixon (1913–1994) ran for president in 1968, he included a strong antidrug plank in his law-and-order platform, calling for a War on Drugs. After he was elected president, Nixon created the President's National Commission on Marihuana and Drug Abuse, which published its findings in *Marihuana: A Signal of Misunderstanding* (March 1972, http://www.druglibrary .org/Schaffer/Library/studies/nc/ncmenu.htm). Nixon ignored the commission's findings, which called for the legalization of marijuana. Since that time the U.S. government has been waging the War on Drugs. In 1973 Congress authorized the formation of the DEA to reduce the supply of drugs. The following year the National Institute on Drug Abuse (NIDA) was created to lead the effort to reduce the demand for drugs and to direct research, federal prevention, and treatment services.

Under the Nixon, Ford, and Carter administrations federal spending tended to emphasize the treatment of drug abusers. Meanwhile, a growing number of parents, fearing that their children were being exposed to drugs, began pressuring elected officials and government agencies to do more about the growing use of drugs. In response, the NIDA began widely publicizing the dangers of marijuana and other drugs once thought not to be particularly harmful.

President Ronald Reagan (1911–2004) favored a strict approach to drug use, popularized the phrase "War on Drugs," and increased enforcement efforts. In *Technologies for Understanding and Preventing Substance Abuse and Addiction*, the Office of Technology Assessment states that the budget to fight drugs rose from $1.5 billion in fiscal year (FY) 1981 to $4.2 billion in FY 1989. By the end of the Reagan administration two-thirds of all drug control funding went for law enforcement and one-third went for treatment and prevention. First Lady Nancy Reagan (1921–) vigorously campaigned against drug use, urging children to "just say no!" The Crime Control Act of 1984 dramatically increased the penalties for drug use and drug trafficking.

INTRODUCTION OF CRACK COCAINE. Cocaine use increased dramatically during the 1960s and 1970s, but the drug's high cost restricted its use to the more affluent. During the early 1980s cocaine dealers discovered a way to prepare cocaine so that it could be smoked in small and inexpensive but powerful and highly addictive amounts. The creation of this so-called crack cocaine meant that poor people could now afford to use the drug and led to the creation of a new market. In addition, the acquired immunodeficiency syndrome (AIDS) epidemic caused some injection drug users to switch to smoking crack to avoid exposure to the human immunodeficiency virus (HIV), which can be contracted by sharing needles with an infected user.

Battles for control of the distribution and sale of the drug led to a violent black market. The easy availability of firearms and the huge amounts of money to be made selling crack and other drugs transformed many areas of the nation—but particularly the inner cities—into dangerous places.

The widespread fear of crack cocaine led to increasingly harsh laws and penalties. Authorities warned that crack was highly addictive and spreading rapidly, and they predicted a subsequent generation of "crack babies"—that is, babies born addicted to crack because their mothers were using it during pregnancy.

HEROIN GETS CHEAPER AND PURER. The dangers associated with crack cocaine caused changes in the use of heroin during the 1980s. Many reported deaths from heroin overdosing had lessened the drug's attraction. In addition, heroin had to be injected by syringe, and concerns regarding HIV infection contributed to the dangers of using the drug. During the 1990s an oversupply of heroin, innovations that produced a smokable variety of the drug, and the appearance of purer forms of the drug estored its attractiveness to the relatively small number of people who were addicted to so-called hard drugs. It was no longer necessary to take the drug intravenously—it could be sniffed like cocaine—although many users continued to use needles.

## The War Continues: The Office of National Drug Control Policy

The Anti-drug Abuse Act of 1988 created the Office of National Drug Control Policy (ONDCP), to be headed by a director—popularly referred to as the drug czar—who would coordinate the nation's drug policy. The Office of Technology Assessment reports in *Technologies for Understanding and Preventing Substance Abuse and Addiction* that spending for drug control rose from $4.2 billion in FY 1989 under President Reagan to $12.7 billion in FY 1993 under President George H. W. Bush (1924–). As was the case during the Reagan administration, the monetary split was roughly two-thirds for law enforcement and one-third for treatment and prevention. By 1990 every state that had once decriminalized the use of marijuana had repealed those laws.

The Office of Technology Assessment indicates that when President Bill Clinton (1946–) took office in 1993, he cut the ONDCP staff from 146 to 25, while at the same time raising the director of the ONDCP to cabinet status. Clinton called for 100,000 more police officers on the streets and advocated drug treatment on demand. According to the ONDCP, in *The National Drug Control Strategy, FY 2004 Budget Summary* (February 2003, http://www.ncjrs.gov/pdffiles1/ondcp/198157.pdf), drug control funding totaled $8.2 billion in FY 1998, with the split 52% for law enforcement and 48% for treatment and prevention. (It is important to note that during the mid-1990s changes were made in the list of expenditures included in this tally and that in 2003 the national drug control budget was restructured, thus making it difficult to analyze historical drug control spending trends before and after 1995. The FY 2004 budget summary provides a recalculation of historical tables from FYs 1995 to 2004.)

When he took office in 2001, President George W. Bush (1946–) promised to continue national efforts to eradicate illicit drugs in the United States and abroad. In May 2001 he appointed John P. Walters (1952?–) as the new drug czar. Together, they pledged to continue to reduce illicit drug use in the United States. Their proposed goals included increased spending on treatment, intensified work with foreign nations, and an adamant opposition to the legalization of any currently illicit drugs. The Bush administration also wove its antidrug message into its arguments for invading Afghanistan. Even though Bush's case was built primarily on the notion that Afghanistan's Taliban leaders were harboring the terrorist Osama bin Laden (1957?–2011), Bush regularly referred to Afghanistan's role as the world's biggest producer of opium poppies.

By 2008, however, some foreign policy experts viewed the Bush administration's opium poppy eradication program as both an economic and political disaster. In "Still Wrong in Afghanistan" (WashingtonPost.com, January 23, 2008), the veteran diplomat Richard Holbrooke (1944–2010) described the policy as arguably "the single most ineffective program in the history of American foreign policy." Citing the program's annual cost at roughly $1 billion, Holbrooke suggested that the policy actually helped strengthen "the Taliban and al-Qaeda, as well as criminal elements within Afghanistan," largely by driving "farmers with no other source of livelihood into the arms of the Taliban."

In June 2009 President Obama announced a major change in the United States' drug strategy for Afghanistan, in which resources were shifted from the eradication of poppy fields to the prohibition of supplies needed to grow opium and to more vigorous efforts to curtail drug smuggling operations. At the same time, the new policy aimed to help Afghan farmers with the cultivation of alternative crops. Nevertheless, these new efforts to curb the production of opium in Afghanistan also proved ineffective. Heidi Vogt reports in "Afghanistan Opium Poppy Cultivation Problem Grows in 2012" (Huffington Post.com, November 20, 2012) that opium poppy cultivation in Afghanistan increased 18% between 2011 and 2012.

### Questioning the War on Drugs

By 2007 there was considerable controversy surrounding the necessity and effectiveness of the War on Drugs. Decades of effort had led to large numbers of people serving prison sentences for manufacturing, selling, or using drugs. Yet, the illicit drug trade continued to thrive. Many critics argued that a different approach was necessary and questioned whether illicit drugs were an enemy worth waging war against, especially such a costly war during a time of rapidly rising federal budget deficits.

The American public also appeared to view the War on Drugs as a low priority. In *Economy Runaway Winner as Most Important Problem* (November 21, 2008, http://www.gallup.com/poll/112093/Economy-Runaway-Winner-Most-Important-Problem.aspx), Jeffrey M. Jones of the Gallup Organization notes that in 2008, 58% of adult Americans rated the economy as the top problem in the United States; drugs were not listed among the top-13 most important problems. Other problems seen as having a higher priority than drugs were the war in Iraq, unemployment, dissatisfaction with government leaders, national security, education, and terrorism.

During the fall of 2008 two reports were published that also documented inadequacies with the War on Drugs. In October 2008 the U.S. Government Accountability Office (GAO) released *Plan Colombia: Drug Reduction Goals Were Not Fully Met, but Security Has Improved; U.S. Agencies Need More Detailed Plans for Reducing Assistance* (http://www.gao.gov/assets/290/282 511.pdf). The GAO examined progress made toward the Colombian government's strategy "Plan Colombia," the goals of which included reducing the production of illicit drugs by half between 2000 and 2006 (with a focus on cocaine) and improving security in areas of Colombia that were held by illegal armed groups. The United States supported this plan and provided nearly $6 billion for its implementation. The GAO found that security had been increased and that opium poppy cultivation and heroin production had decreased by about half. However, coca cultivation and cocaine production had increased.

In November 2008 the Partnership for the Americas Commission of the Brookings Institution released *Rethinking U.S.-Latin American Relations: A Hemispheric Partnership for a Turbulent World* (http://www.brookings.edu/~/media/research/files/reports/2008/11/24%20latin%20america%20partnership/1124_latin_america_partnership.pdf). The report noted that "current U.S. counternarcotics policies are failing by most objective measures" and that "the only long-run solution to the problem of illegal narcotics is to reduce the demand for drugs in the major consuming countries, including the United States." The report also suggested that the United States should work to reduce the flow of guns to Mexico, which would help curb the flow of drugs to the United States; expand drug prevention programs in schools, especially those that emphasize drugs' disfiguring attributes to young people; and promote drug courts, which merge treatment with incarceration.

In the months that followed President Obama's inauguration, the new administration began showing signs of rethinking existing drug policy in the United States. Gil Kerlikowske (1949–), who was named the director of the ONDCP, called for an end to the War on Drugs and favored treatment over prison time for drug offenders. Certain federal drug policies began to change. For example, in 2009 Congress repealed the decades-old ban on federal funding for needle exchange programs.

Nonetheless, the Obama administration firmly opposed the legalization of marijuana.

In 2009 the Transform Drug Policy Foundation, a United Kingdom–based organization that promotes drug regulation and control, released *After the War on Drugs: Blueprint for Regulation* (http://www.tdpf.org.uk/Transform_Drugs_Blueprint.pdf). The foundation recognized the failure of the War on Drugs and the increasing recognition of this failure around the world. It suggested that many countries have not changed their drug policies because of a deep concern about what might happen if drugs are legalized. To diminish this fear of the unknown, the foundation proposed models of legal drug regulation and control, along with rationales for each model, to control drug production, supply, and use.

Charles Shaw suggests in "European Blueprint Signals Way for America to End the War on Drugs" (Guardian.co.uk, November 15, 2010) that the United States is addicted to the War on Drugs. He notes that no real drop in the use of or demand for drugs has occurred as a result of the war, yet the United States continues spending billions of dollars on this failed policy—culminating in a total of $1 trillion spent over 40 years. Shaw discusses the Transform Drug Policy Foundation's *Blueprint for Regulation* as well as *Drug Policy Guide* (March 2010, http://idpc.net/sites/default/files/library/IDPC%20Drug%20Policy%20Guide_Version%201.pdf) by the International Drug Policy Consortium, a worldwide group of nongovernmental organizations. The consortium notes that the approach of trying to eradicate the supply of illegal drugs has been ineffective. It proposes that countries should focus on reducing the harmful consequences of drug use on individuals rather than on fighting drug use. Shaw agrees and suggests that "the primary drivers of this issue are economic: money and jobs." He calculates that the U.S. criminal justice system employs more workers than Wal-Mart and McDonald's combined. He also explains, "And just like military spending, any attempts to cut criminal justice or prison budgets is considered political suicide."

Thus, in early 2013 continuing the War on Drugs was an increasingly controversial approach in the United States and around the world, but resistance to change and the lack of a clear approach that could effectively curb the use of drugs remained a problem.

## CHAPTER 2

# ALCOHOL

Contrary to popular belief, ethanol (the alcohol in alcoholic beverages) is not a stimulant, but a depressant. Even though many of those who drink alcoholic beverages feel relaxation, pleasure, and stimulation, these feelings are caused by the depressant effects of alcohol on the brain.

## WHAT CONSTITUTES A DRINK?

In the United States a standard drink contains about 0.5 ounces (14.8 mL) of pure alcohol. The following beverages contain nearly equal amounts of alcohol and are approximately standard drink equivalents:

- One shot (1.5 ounces, or 44.4 mL) of spirits (80-proof whiskey, vodka, gin, and so on)

- One 2.5-ounce (73.9-mL) glass of a cordial, liqueur, or aperitif

- One 5-ounce (147.9-mL) glass of table wine

- One 3- to 4-ounce (88.7- to 118.3-mL) glass of fortified wine, such as sherry or port

- One 12-ounce (354.9-mL) bottle or can of beer

- One 8- to 9-ounce (236.6- to 266.2-mL) bottle or can of malt liquor

## ALCOHOL CONSUMPTION IN THE UNITED STATES

After caffeine, alcohol is the most commonly used drug in the United States. Although researchers frequently count how many people are drinking and how often, the statistics do not necessarily reflect the true picture of alcohol consumption in the United States. People tend to underreport their drinking. Furthermore, survey interviewees are typically people living in households; therefore, the results of survey research may not include the homeless, a portion of the U.S. population that is traditionally at risk for alcoholism (alcohol dependence).

## Alcohol: A Lucrative Business

As Table 2.1 shows, yearly expenditures on alcoholic beverages have increased steadily since 1935. In 1980 annual total expenditures on alcoholic beverages topped $45.4 billion; by 2011 this figure nearly quadrupled, to $162.9 billion. Overall, in 2011 consumers spent $86.5 billion on packaged alcoholic beverages, or beverages to be consumed at home, compared with $76.3 billion spent on alcoholic beverages consumed away from home. Restaurants and bars represented the largest share of alcoholic beverage sales in 2011, accounting for nearly $58 billion (36%). By comparison, liquor stores accounted for $42.5 billion (26%) of alcoholic beverage sales.

## Individual Consumption of Alcohol

The data for alcohol consumption mentioned in the previous section are per capita figures, which are determined by taking the total consumption of alcohol per year and dividing by the total resident population, including children. This figure is useful for showing how consumption changes from year to year because it takes into account changes in the size of the resident population. Nonetheless, babies and small children generally do not consume alcohol, so it is also useful to look at consumption figures that are based on U.S. residents aged 12 years and older.

Table 2.2 shows the percentage of respondents aged 12 years and older who reported consuming alcohol in the past month in 2010 and 2011 when questioned for the annual National Survey on Drug Use and Health, which is conducted by the Substance Abuse and Mental Health Services Administration. In 2011, 51.8% of this total population had consumed alcohol in the month before the survey, a figure that was identical to the percentage of the total population that had consumed alcohol within the previous month in 2010. A higher percentage of males had consumed alcoholic beverages in the past

**TABLE 2.1**

## Total alcoholic beverages expenditures, 1935–2011

| | Packaged alcoholic beverages at home | | | | Alcoholic drinks away from home | | | | All alcoholic beverages |
|---|---|---|---|---|---|---|---|---|---|
| Year | Liquor stores | Food stores | All other | Total[a] | Eating and drinking places[b] | Hotels and motels[b] | All other | Total[a] | Total[a] |
| | | | | | Million dollars | | | | |
| 1935 | 305 | 65 | 199 | 569 | 964 | 81 | 20 | 1,065 | 1,634 |
| 1936 | 435 | 95 | 220 | 750 | 1,195 | 97 | 24 | 1,316 | 2,066 |
| 1937 | 504 | 113 | 235 | 852 | 1,299 | 109 | 28 | 1,436 | 2,288 |
| 1938 | 479 | 111 | 227 | 817 | 1,246 | 98 | 26 | 1,370 | 2,187 |
| 1939 | 517 | 122 | 237 | 876 | 1,365 | 103 | 28 | 1,496 | 2,372 |
| 1940 | 602 | 131 | 244 | 977 | 1,459 | 113 | 30 | 1,602 | 2,579 |
| 1941 | 758 | 151 | 271 | 1,180 | 1,753 | 124 | 37 | 1,914 | 3,094 |
| 1942 | 1,081 | 194 | 311 | 1,586 | 2,176 | 145 | 47 | 2,368 | 3,954 |
| 1943 | 1,395 | 225 | 361 | 1,981 | 2,744 | 194 | 60 | 2,998 | 4,979 |
| 1944 | 1,734 | 252 | 393 | 2,379 | 3,144 | 219 | 69 | 3,432 | 5,811 |
| 1945 | 2,070 | 272 | 422 | 2,764 | 3,609 | 236 | 79 | 3,924 | 6,688 |
| 1946 | 2,443 | 368 | 472 | 3,283 | 3,984 | 272 | 91 | 4,347 | 7,630 |
| 1947 | 2,540 | 341 | 481 | 3,362 | 4,178 | 274 | 96 | 4,548 | 7,910 |
| 1948 | 2,487 | 475 | 484 | 3,446 | 4,172 | 272 | 100 | 4,544 | 7,990 |
| 1949 | 2,359 | 550 | 479 | 3,388 | 4,029 | 258 | 110 | 4,397 | 7,785 |
| 1950 | 2,399 | 569 | 487 | 3,455 | 4,028 | 259 | 126 | 4,413 | 7,868 |
| 1951 | 2,646 | 617 | 526 | 3,789 | 4,341 | 272 | 152 | 4,765 | 8,554 |
| 1952 | 2,786 | 668 | 545 | 3,999 | 4,442 | 281 | 176 | 4,899 | 8,898 |
| 1953 | 2,830 | 698 | 552 | 4,080 | 4,482 | 282 | 196 | 4,960 | 9,040 |
| 1954 | 2,942 | 685 | 562 | 4,189 | 4,454 | 274 | 218 | 4,946 | 9,135 |
| 1955 | 3,060 | 717 | 584 | 4,361 | 4,552 | 290 | 226 | 5,068 | 9,429 |
| 1956 | 3,408 | 756 | 616 | 4,780 | 4,753 | 309 | 238 | 5,300 | 10,080 |
| 1957 | 3,642 | 806 | 645 | 5,093 | 4,861 | 325 | 252 | 5,438 | 10,531 |
| 1958 | 3,841 | 868 | 656 | 5,365 | 4,910 | 330 | 261 | 5,501 | 10,866 |
| 1959 | 4,056 | 919 | 678 | 5,653 | 5,014 | 356 | 289 | 5,659 | 11,312 |
| 1960 | 4,137 | 966 | 690 | 5,793 | 5,039 | 378 | 317 | 5,734 | 11,527 |
| 1961 | 4,120 | 979 | 695 | 5,794 | 4,975 | 395 | 337 | 5,707 | 11,501 |
| 1962 | 4,494 | 1,071 | 714 | 6,279 | 5,172 | 427 | 365 | 5,964 | 12,243 |
| 1963 | 4,665 | 1,169 | 725 | 6,559 | 5,306 | 458 | 385 | 6,149 | 12,708 |
| 1964 | 4,958 | 1,272 | 761 | 6,991 | 5,465 | 493 | 408 | 6,366 | 13,357 |
| 1965 | 5,247 | 1,382 | 809 | 7,438 | 5,681 | 541 | 440 | 6,662 | 14,100 |
| 1966 | 5,676 | 1,535 | 864 | 8,075 | 5,981 | 593 | 487 | 7,061 | 15,136 |
| 1967 | 6,005 | 1,539 | 904 | 8,448 | 6,222 | 623 | 551 | 7,396 | 15,844 |
| 1968 | 6,576 | 1,708 | 955 | 9,234 | 6,642 | 667 | 587 | 7,896 | 17,130 |
| 1969 | 7,034 | 1,834 | 987 | 9,855 | 6,878 | 691 | 624 | 8,193 | 18,048 |
| 1970 | 7,671 | 2,110 | 1,064 | 10,845 | 7,652 | 760 | 657 | 9,069 | 19,914 |
| 1971 | 8,506 | 2,297 | 1,102 | 11,905 | 8,026 | 849 | 678 | 9,553 | 21,458 |
| 1972 | 8,810 | 2,702 | 1,113 | 12,625 | 7,911 | 961 | 704 | 9,576 | 22,201 |
| 1973 | 9,236 | 3,105 | 1,254 | 13,595 | 8,747 | 1,069 | 757 | 10,573 | 24,168 |
| 1974 | 9,948 | 3,600 | 1,355 | 14,903 | 9,371 | 1,167 | 778 | 11,316 | 26,219 |
| 1975 | 10,681 | 4,080 | 1,519 | 16,280 | 10,324 | 1,315 | 887 | 12,526 | 28,806 |
| 1976 | 11,170 | 4,209 | 1,717 | 17,096 | 11,088 | 1,555 | 947 | 13,590 | 30,686 |
| 1977 | 11,686 | 4,603 | 1,946 | 18,235 | 11,981 | 1,713 | 1,266 | 14,960 | 33,195 |
| 1978 | 12,179 | 5,211 | 2,222 | 19,612 | 13,342 | 2,023 | 1,303 | 16,668 | 36,280 |
| 1979 | 13,528 | 5,903 | 2,480 | 21,911 | 15,152 | 2,306 | 1,435 | 18,893 | 40,804 |
| 1980 | 14,977 | 6,995 | 2,816 | 24,788 | 16,722 | 2,450 | 1,484 | 20,656 | 45,444 |
| 1981 | 15,648 | 7,629 | 3,141 | 26,418 | 17,976 | 2,751 | 1,528 | 22,255 | 48,673 |
| 1982 | 15,984 | 8,147 | 3,378 | 27,509 | 18,371 | 2,849 | 1,488 | 22,708 | 50,217 |
| 1983 | 16,818 | 8,999 | 3,878 | 29,695 | 19,038 | 3,051 | 1,620 | 23,709 | 53,404 |
| 1984 | 15,997 | 10,132 | 4,158 | 30,287 | 19,863 | 3,220 | 1,691 | 24,774 | 55,061 |
| 1985 | 17,058 | 10,361 | 4,152 | 31,571 | 20,659 | 3,371 | 1,816 | 25,846 | 57,417 |
| 1986 | 17,350 | 10,755 | 5,031 | 33,136 | 22,291 | 3,406 | 1,935 | 27,632 | 60,768 |
| 1987 | 17,283 | 9,164 | 4,156 | 30,603 | 23,232 | 3,281 | 3,524 | 30,036 | 60,639 |
| 1988 | 17,007 | 9,436 | 4,406 | 30,848 | 24,227 | 3,419 | 3,863 | 31,510 | 62,357 |
| 1989 | 17,292 | 10,073 | 4,917 | 32,282 | 24,748 | 3,397 | 4,201 | 32,346 | 64,627 |
| 1990 | 18,597 | 10,844 | 5,435 | 34,875 | 26,528 | 3,376 | 4,634 | 34,539 | 69,414 |
| 1991 | 19,123 | 10,770 | 5,810 | 35,703 | 27,200 | 3,249 | 4,838 | 35,286 | 70,989 |
| 1992 | 18,418 | 10,700 | 6,647 | 35,754 | 27,727 | 3,318 | 5,233 | 36,278 | 72,042 |
| 1993 | 18,370 | 11,146 | 6,801 | 36,318 | 28,393 | 3,305 | 5,253 | 36,951 | 73,270 |
| 1994 | 18,846 | 11,735 | 6,940 | 37,520 | 29,227 | 3,416 | 5,303 | 37,946 | 75,467 |
| 1995 | 18,850 | 12,280 | 7,135 | 38,264 | 30,194 | 3,423 | 5,205 | 38,822 | 77,086 |
| 1996 | 19,922 | 12,953 | 7,467 | 40,343 | 31,379 | 3,427 | 5,191 | 39,996 | 80,339 |
| 1997 | 20,864 | 12,798 | 6,759 | 40,421 | 33,427 | 3,734 | 5,721 | 42,882 | 83,303 |
| 1998 | 21,859 | 14,139 | 6,934 | 42,931 | 35,688 | 5,524 | 6,093 | 47,306 | 90,237 |
| 1999 | 22,725 | 15,159 | 7,439 | 45,322 | 38,090 | 7,505 | 6,882 | 52,478 | 97,800 |
| 2000 | 24,350 | 15,847 | 8,022 | 48,218 | 41,533 | 6,842 | 10,556 | 58,931 | 107,149 |
| 2001 | 25,168 | 16,888 | 8,214 | 50,270 | 44,130 | 5,293 | 15,241 | 64,664 | 114,934 |
| 2002 | 27,951 | 17,356 | 10,119 | 55,426 | 47,173 | 4,625 | 7,461 | 59,259 | 114,685 |

**otal alcoholic beverages expenditures, 1935–2011** [CONTINUED]

| | Packaged alcoholic beverages at home | | | | Alcoholic drinks away from home | | | | All alcoholic beverages |
|---|---|---|---|---|---|---|---|---|---|
| ear | Liquor stores | Food stores | All other | Total[a] | Eating and drinking places[b] | Hotels and motels[b] | All other | Total[a] | Total[a] |
| | | | | | Million dollars | | | | |
| ?003 | 28,623 | 17,520 | 11,032 | 57,175 | 44,077 | 4,679 | 8,023 | 56,779 | 113,954 |
| ?004 | 30,613 | 18,056 | 11,853 | 60,523 | 49,943 | 4,914 | 9,084 | 63,941 | 124,464 |
| ?005 | 32,103 | 18,603 | 12,739 | 63,446 | 51,248 | 5,065 | 9,301 | 65,614 | 129,059 |
| ?006 | 34,600 | 18,968 | 13,421 | 66,988 | 53,570 | 5,133 | 10,975 | 69,677 | 136,666 |
| ?007 | 36,791 | 19,545 | 13,333 | 69,670 | 54,130 | 5,090 | 10,274 | 69,493 | 139,163 |
| ?008 | 38,137 | 20,340 | 20,357 | 78,834 | 54,733 | 5,189 | 9,896 | 69,818 | 148,652 |
| ?009 | 38,732 | 20,289 | 18,711 | 77,731 | 53,698 | 5,024 | 10,539 | 69,261 | 146,992 |
| ?010 | 39,936 | 20,738 | 20,099 | 80,774 | 54,768 | 5,081 | 12,120 | 71,969 | 152,743 |
| ?011 | 42,499 | 21,918 | 22,108 | 86,525 | 57,986 | 5,138 | 13,215 | 76,339 | 162,864 |

ªComputed from unrounded data.
ᵇIncludes tips.

SOURCE: "Table 4. Alcoholic Beverages: Total Expenditures," in "Food Expenditures," U.S. Department of Agriculture, Economic Research Service, October 1, 2012, http://www.ers.usda.gov/datafiles/Food_Expenditures/Food_Expenditures/table4.xls (accessed February 11, 2013)

**TABLE 2.2**

**Percentage of past-month alcohol use, binge alcohol use, and heavy alcohol use among drinkers aged 12 and older, by demographic characteristics, 2010 and 2011**

| Demographic characteristic | Alcohol use (2010) | Alcohol use (2011) | Binge alcohol use (2010) | Binge alcohol use (2011) | Heavy alcohol use (2010) | Heavy alcohol use (2011) |
|---|---|---|---|---|---|---|
| **Total** | **51.8** | **51.8** | **23.1** | **22.6** | **6.7**[a] | **6.2** |
| **Age** | | | | | | |
| 12–17 | 13.6 | 13.3 | 7.9 | 7.4 | 1.7 | 1.5 |
| 18–25 | 61.4 | 60.7 | 40.5 | 39.8 | 13.5[b] | 12.1 |
| 26 or older | 54.9 | 55.1 | 21.9 | 21.6 | 6.1 | 5.7 |
| **Gender** | | | | | | |
| Male | 57.3 | 56.8 | 30.9 | 30.0 | 10.1 | 9.4 |
| Female | 46.6 | 47.1 | 15.7 | 15.8 | 3.4 | 3.2 |
| **Hispanic origin and race** | | | | | | |
| Not Hispanic or Latino | 53.5 | 53.5 | 22.7 | 22.5 | 6.9[a] | 6.4 |
| White | 56.7 | 56.8 | 24.0 | 23.9 | 7.7[a] | 7.1 |
| Black or African American | 42.8 | 42.1 | 19.7 | 19.4 | 4.5 | 4.0 |
| American Indian or Alaska Native | 36.6 | 44.7 | 24.8 | 24.3 | 6.9 | 11.6 |
| Native Hawaiian or other Pacific Islander | * | * | * | * | * | 10.5 |
| Asian | 38.3 | 40.0 | 12.3 | 11.6 | 2.4 | 1.6 |
| Two or more races | 45.4 | 46.9 | 21.6 | 18.6 | 5.8 | 5.1 |
| Hispanic or Latino | 41.8 | 42.5 | 25.2 | 23.4 | 5.1 | 5.0 |

*Low precision; no estimate reported.
Notes: Some 2010 estimates may differ from previously published estimates due to updates.
Binge alcohol use is defined as drinking five or more drinks on the same occasion (i.e., at the same time or within a couple of hours of each other) on at least 1 day in the past 30 days.
Heavy alcohol use is defined as drinking five or more drinks on the same occasion on each of 5 or more days in the past 30 days; all heavy alcohol users are also binge alcohol users.
ªDifference between estimate and 2011 estimate is statistically significant at the 0.05 level.
ᵇDifference between estimate and 2011 estimate is statistically significant at the 0.01 level.

SOURCE: "Table 2.42B. Alcohol Use, Binge Alcohol Use, and Heavy Alcohol Use in the Past Month among Persons Aged 12 or Older, by Demographic Characteristics: Percentages, 2010 and 2011," in Results from the 2011 National Survey on Drug Use and Health: Detailed Tables, U.S. Department of Health and Human Services, Substance Abuse and Mental Health Services Administration, September 2012, http://www.samhsa.gov/data/NSDUH/2011SummNatFind DetTables/NSDUH-DetTabsPDFWHTML2011/2k11DetailedTabs/Web/PDFW/NSDUH-DetTabsCover2011.pdf (accessed February 11, 2013)

month than did females in both years. Table 2.2 also shows that alcohol consumption varies by race. A higher percentage of whites had used alcohol within the month before the survey than had African-Americans or Hispanics.

### Prevalence of Problem Drinking

Table 2.2 also shows the percentages of Americans aged 12 years and older who engaged in binge drinking or heavy alcohol use in the month before the survey.

Binge drinking means a person had five or more drinks on the same occasion, that is, within a few hours of each other. Heavy alcohol use means a person had five or more drinks on the same occasion on each of five or more days in the past 30 days. All heavy alcohol users are binge drinkers, but not all binge drinkers are heavy alcohol users.

In both 2010 and 2011 people aged 18 to 25 years were more likely than people in other age groups to be binge drinkers and heavy alcohol users. Much higher percentages of males binge drank and used alcohol heavily than females in the month before each of these surveys. Native Americans and Alaskan Natives (24.3%) were the most likely to have engaged in binge drinking in 2011, followed by whites (23.9%) and Hispanics (23.4%). Native Americans and Alaskan Natives (11.6%) were also more likely than all other groups to have engaged in heavy alcohol use in 2011, followed by Native Hawaiians and other Pacific Islanders (10.5%). By comparison, only 1.6% of Asian-Americans were heavy drinkers in 2011.

## DEFINING ALCOHOLISM

Most people consider an alcoholic to be someone who drinks too much alcohol and cannot control his or her drinking. Alcoholism, however, does not merely refer to heavy drinking or getting drunk a certain number of times. The diagnosis of alcoholism applies only to those who show specific symptoms of addiction, which the Institute of Medicine defines in *Dispelling the Myths about Addiction: Strategies to Increase Understanding and Strengthen Research* (1997) as a brain disease "manifested by a complex set of behaviors that are the result of genetic, biological, psychological, and environmental interactions."

In "The Definition of Alcoholism" (*Journal of the American Medical Association*, vol. 268, no. 8, August 26, 1992), Robert M. Morse and Daniel K. Flavin define alcoholism as "a primary, chronic disease with genetic, psychosocial, and environmental factors influencing its development and manifestations. The disease is often progressive and fatal. It is characterized by impaired control over drinking, preoccupation with the drug alcohol, use of alcohol despite adverse consequences, and distortions in thinking, most notably denial. Each of these symptoms may be continuous or periodic."

"Primary" refers to alcoholism as a disease independent from any other psychological disease (e.g., schizophrenia), rather than as a symptom of some other underlying disease. "Adverse consequences" for an alcoholic can include physical illness (such as liver disease or withdrawal symptoms), psychological problems, interpersonal difficulties (such as marital problems or domestic violence), and problems at work. "Denial" includes a number of psychological maneuvers by the drinker to avoid the fact that alcohol is the cause of his or her problems. Family and friends may reinforce an alcoholic's denial by covering up his or her drinking (e.g., calling an employer to say the alcoholic has the flu rather than a hangover). Such behavior is also known as enabling. In other words, family and friends make excuses for the drinker and enable him or her to continue drinking as opposed to having to face the repercussions of his or her alcohol abuse. Denial is a major obstacle in recovery from alcoholism.

In "Alcoholism" (August 9, 2012, http://www.mayoclinic.com/health/alcoholism/DS00340), the Mayo Clinic provides a very simple and straightforward definition of alcoholism: "Alcoholism is a chronic and often progressive disease that includes problems controlling your drinking, being preoccupied with alcohol, continuing to use alcohol even when it causes problems, having to drink more to get the same effect (physical dependence), or having withdrawal symptoms when you rapidly decrease or stop drinking. If you have alcoholism, you can't consistently predict how much you'll drink, how long you'll drink, or what consequences will occur from your drinking."

## ALCOHOLISM AND ALCOHOL ABUSE

The American Psychiatric Association (APA), which publishes the *Diagnostic and Statistical Manual of Mental Disorders* (*DSM*), first defined alcoholism in 1952. The *DSM-III*, the third edition of the APA's publication, renamed alcoholism as alcohol dependence and introduced the term *alcohol abuse*. According to the *DSM-III*'s definition of alcohol abuse, the condition involves a compulsive use of alcohol and impaired social or occupational functioning, whereas alcohol dependence includes physical tolerance and withdrawal symptoms when the drug is stopped. *DSM-IV-TR* refines these definitions further, but the basic definitions remain the same.

Maia Szalavitz reports in "Mental Health Manual Changes May Turn Binge Drinkers into Mild Alcoholics" (Time.com, January 24, 2013) that the fifth edition of the *DSM*, due to be published in May 2013, will introduce a major change to traditional classifications of alcohol use by combining alcohol abuse and alcohol dependence into a single condition called alcohol use disorder.

The World Health Organization publishes the *International Classification of Diseases* (*ICD*), which is designed to standardize health data collection throughout the world. The 10th edition (*ICD-10*) generally defines abuse and tolerance similarly to the *DSM-IV-TR*.

Alcoholism includes the following four symptoms: craving, loss of control, physical dependence, and tolerance. These symptoms are described in Table 2.3 and are

**TABLE 2.3**

**Four symptoms of alcoholism**

Alcoholism, also known as "alcohol dependence," is a disease that includes four symptoms:

- Craving: A strong need, or compulsion, to drink.
- Loss of control: The inability to limit one's drinking on any given occasion.
- Physical dependence: Withdrawal symptoms, such as nausea, sweating, shakiness, and anxiety, occur when alcohol use is stopped after a period of heavy drinking.
- Tolerance: The need to drink greater amounts of alcohol in order to "get high."

SOURCE: Adapted from "What Is Alcoholism?" in *FAQs for the General Public*, U.S. Department of Health and Human Services, National Institutes of Health, National Institute on Alcohol Abuse and Alcoholism, December 19, 2011, http://www.google.com/url?sa=t&rct=j&q=&esrc= s&source=web&cd=2&cad=rja&ved=0CDwQFjAB&url=http%3A%2F% 2Ffileserver.net-texts.com%2Fasset.aspx%3Fdl%3Dyes%26id%3D10749 &ei=QIUZUbq0Namu0AGvkoHoCQ&usg=AFQjCNGff8WIdyVGX8ffSRS swIHBtoyTfg&sig2=kPwWQTWCGdC_F_G8gt259Q (accessed February 11, 2013)

**TABLE 2.4**

**Four symptoms of alcohol abuse**

Alcohol abuse is defined as intentional overuse in cases of celebration, anxiety, despair, self-medication, or ignorance, resulting in one or more of the following occurring within a 12-month period:

- Failure to fulfill major role obligations at work, school, or home
- Recurrent drinking in physically hazardous situations
- Recurrent alcohol-related legal problems
- Continued alcohol use despite having persistent or recurrent social and/or interpersonal problems caused or exacerbated by the effects of alcohol.

SOURCE: Adapted from "Module 5. Diagnosis and Assessment of Alcohol Use Disorders," U.S. Department of Health and Human Services, National Institutes of Health, National Institute on Alcohol Abuse and Alcoholism, March 2005, http://pubs.niaaa.nih.gov/publications/Social/Module5 Diagnosis&Assessment/Module5.html (accessed February 11, 2013)

a result of changes in the functioning of the brain and underlying changes in gene expression as its cells adapt to the chronic heavy use and abuse of alcohol.

Those who are alcohol dependent—as well as those who are not—may manifest the symptoms of alcohol abuse. The primary symptoms of alcohol abuse are listed in Table 2.4. Other characteristics of alcohol abuse include the need to drink before facing certain situations, frequent drinking sprees, a steady increase in intake, solitary drinking, early morning drinking, and the occurrence of blackouts. For heavy drinkers, blackouts are not episodes of passing out, but are periods drinkers cannot remember later, even though they appeared to be functioning at the time.

### Prevalence of Alcohol Dependence, Alcohol Abuse, Binge Drinking, and Heavy Drinking

The National Institute on Alcohol Abuse and Alcoholism (NIAAA) notes in *Five Year Strategic Plan FY09–14* (2008, http://pubs.niaaa.nih.gov/publications/StrategicPlan/ StrategicPlan.doc) that 18 million Americans (8.5% of the

population aged 18 years and older) have alcohol use disorders (AUD; alcohol abuse and alcohol dependence).

Figure 2.1 shows the percentages of people who engaged in alcohol use, binge drinking, and heavy alcohol use in 2011 by age group. The graph shows that people aged 21 to 25 years are more likely to engage in binge drinking use than those in younger or older age groups. The rate of binge drinking use in this age group was slightly over 45% in 2011. The graph also shows that as people grow older, the proportion of people who use alcohol without manifesting binge drinking increases.

Table 2.2 compares the rates of binge drinking and heavy alcohol use for males and females across all age groups. In 2010 and 2011 the rate of binge drinking in males was nearly double that of females. The percentage of males who binge drank was 30.9% in 2010, before dropping slightly to 30% in 2011; by comparison, the percentage of females who binge drank was 15.7% in 2010 and 15.8% in 2011. Heavy alcohol use was much more prevalent in males than in females. Roughly 10% of males were heavy alcohol users in 2010 and 2011, whereas fewer than 3.5% of females were.

## ALCOHOL ABUSE AND ALCOHOLISM IN VARIOUS RACIAL AND ETHNIC GROUPS

The patterns of alcohol consumption vary across racial and ethnic groups. (See Table 2.2.) Low alcoholism rates occur in certain groups and individuals because of their customs or religion. Groups and individuals with multicultural backgrounds generally have fewer cultural or religious constraints regarding alcohol use and tend to have higher alcoholism rates. For example, alcohol is forbidden in Islam, so it is rare to find Muslims who engage in alcohol use. However, whites are a diverse population, both religiously and culturally. This group had the highest rate of alcohol use of all the groups listed in Table 2.2.

Certain populations may be at a higher or lower risk for binge or heavy alcohol use because of the way their bodies metabolize (chemically process) alcohol. For example, many Asian-Americans have an inherited deficiency of aldehyde dehydrogenase, a chemical that breaks down ethyl alcohol in the body. Without it, toxic substances build up after drinking alcohol and rapidly lead to flushing, dizziness, and nausea. Therefore, many Asian-Americans experience warning signals very early on and are less likely to continue drinking. Conversely, research results suggest that Native Americans or Alaskan Natives may lack these warning signals. They are less sensitive to the intoxicating effects of alcohol and are more likely to develop alcoholism. Table 2.2 shows that the prevalence of binge alcohol use and heavy alcohol use is low for Asian-Americans and high for Native Americans or Alaskan Natives.

FIGURE 2.1

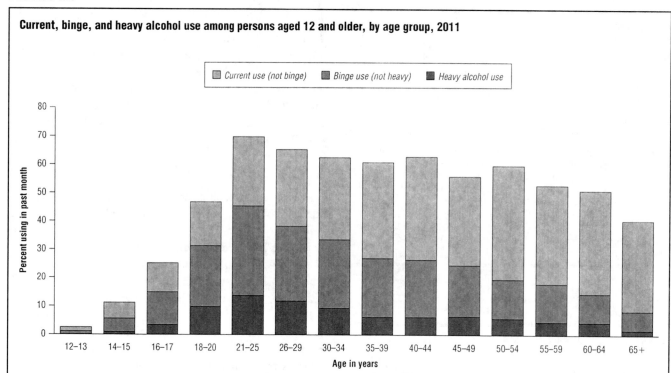

**Current, binge, and heavy alcohol use among persons aged 12 and older, by age group, 2011**

SOURCE: "Figure 3.1. Current, Binge, and Heavy Alcohol Use among Persons Aged 12 or Older, by Age, 2011," in *Results from the 2011 National Survey on Drug Use and Health: Summary of National Findings,* U.S. Department of Health and Human Services, Substance Abuse and Mental Health Services Administration, September 2012, http://www.samhsa.gov/data/NSDUH/2k11Results/NSDUHresults2011.pdf (accessed February 11, 2013)

## RISK FACTORS OF ALCOHOL USE DISORDERS

The development of AUD is the result of a complex mix of biological, psychological, and social factors including genetics, alcohol reactivity (sensitivity), and psychosocial factors. Genetics and alcohol reactivity are biological factors. The rest are psychosocial factors. Table 2.5 lists the factors that are involved in the development of AUD, which are discussed in the following sections.

### Biological Factors

**GENETICS.** A variety of studies investigating family history, adopted versus biological children living in the same families, and twins separated and living in different families all indicate that genetics play a substantial role in some forms of AUD. For example, R. Dayne Mayfield, R. Adron Harris, and Marc A. Schuckit indicate in "Genetic Factors Influencing Alcohol Dependence" (*British Journal of Pharmacology,* vol. 154, no. 2, May 2008) that relatives of alcoholics have four times the risk of developing alcohol dependence than do nonrelatives of alcoholics and that the identical twins of those dependent on alcohol have a higher risk of developing alcohol dependence than do fraternal twins or nontwin siblings. Most likely, many genes influence a range of characteristics that affect risk. Marc A. Schuckit of the University of California, San Diego, states in "An Overview of

**TABLE 2.5**

**Factors involved in the development of alcohol use disorders**

**Biological**
Genetics
Alcohol reactivity

**Psychosocial**
Social sanctions
Gender roles
Coping styles
Drinking motives and expectations
Depression
Sensation-seeking
Stress
Impulsivity
Interpersonal relationships
History of sexual assault or child abuse

SOURCE: Created by Sandra Alters for Gale, 2010

Genetic Influences in Alcoholism" (*Journal of Substance Abuse Treatment,* vol. 36, no. 1, January 2009) that "genes explain about 50% of the vulnerabilities leading to heavy drinking and associated problems." In "Assessing the Genetic Risk for Alcohol Use Disorders" (*Alcohol Research: Current Reviews,* vol. 34, no. 3, 2012), Tatiana Foroud and Tamara J. Phillips discuss the link between alcoholism and the human genome, asserting that alcoholism is determined by complex interactions between genes, rather than by individual genes themselves. Albert J. Arias and R. Andrew Sewell report in

"Pharmacogenetically Driven Treatments for Alcoholism: Are We There Yet?" (*CNS Drugs*, vol. 26, no. 6, June 1, 2012) that continued study of the genetic underpinnings of alcohol abuse has enabled scientists to experiment with increasingly sophisticated drug-based treatments for the disease.

**ALCOHOL REACTIVITY.** Alcohol reactivity refers to the sense of intoxication one has when drinking alcohol. Without early signals of intoxication, an individual may tend to drink more before feeling drunk and thus may develop a high physiological tolerance for alcohol. An individual with low alcohol reactivity to moderate doses of alcohol may be more likely to become an alcoholic over time than an individual with greater reactivity. Typically, the sons of alcoholics report a lower sense of intoxication and show fewer signs of intoxication when given moderate amounts of alcohol, compared with the sons of nonalcoholics, showing a likely genetic link to alcoholism as Schuckit describes.

## Psychosocial Factors

**SOCIAL SANCTIONS, GENDER ROLES, BIOLOGICAL DIFFERENCES, AND CULTURAL FACTORS.** Social sanctions are a mechanism of social control for enforcing a society's standards. Social sanctions may be one factor explaining why men drink more alcohol than women. Besides social sanctions against women drinking as heavily as men, American culture appears to identify alcohol consumption as more of a part of the male gender role than of the female gender role. However, gender differences in alcohol consumption are seen not only in the United States but also around the world.

Richard W. Wilsnack et al. explain in "Gender and Alcohol Consumption: Patterns from the Multinational GENACIS Project" (*Addiction*, vol. 104, no. 9, September 2009) that:

> gender differences in alcohol consumption remain universal [among countries], although the sizes of gender differences vary. More drinking and heavy drinking occur among men, more long-term abstention occurs among women, and no cultural differences or historical changes have entirely erased these differences. As there are relatively few universals in human social behavior, these findings suggest that biological differences play some role in how men and women drink. However, because the gender differences vary in magnitude across cultures and across different drinking patterns, it is also very likely that gender differences in drinking behavior are modified by cultural and not just biological factors.

**DRINKING MOTIVES, EXPECTATIONS, AND DEPRESSION/ DISTRESS.** People consume alcohol for various reasons: as part of a meal, to celebrate certain occasions, and to reduce anxiety in social situations. People also consume alcohol to cope with distress or depression or to escape from negative feelings. Those who have positive expectations for their drinking, such as the belief that alcohol will reduce distress, tend to drink more than those who have negative expectations, such as the belief that alcohol will interfere with the ability to cope with distress. In general, Shelly F. Greenfield et al. indicate in "Substance Abuse in Women" (*Psychiatric Clinics of North America*, vol. 33, no. 2, June 2010) that men have more positive expectations concerning alcohol consumption than women. In addition, women are more likely than men to drink alcohol in response to distress and negative emotions. The researchers note, however, that even though these generalizations can be made, the relationships among depression, general distress, and alcohol consumption are quite complex.

**IMPULSIVITY, SENSATION-SEEKING, BEHAVIORAL UNDERCONTROL, AND ANTISOCIALITY.** In "Sex Difference in Alcoholism: Who Is at a Greater Risk for Development of Alcoholic Complication?" (*Life Sciences*, vol. 87, nos. 5–6, July 31, 2010), Asli F. Ceylan-Isik, Shawna M. McBride, and Jun Ren of the University of Wyoming, Laramie, indicate that impulsivity, sensation-seeking, and behavioral undercontrol (not controlling one's behavior well) are consistently associated with alcohol use and problems in men rather than in women. The researchers suggest this may occur because "women perceive greater social and health sanctions for drinking while alcohol and alcoholism may counter desirable feminine traits."

Antisociality is a personality disorder that includes a chronic disregard for the rights of others and an absence of remorse for the harmful effects of these behaviors on others. People with this disorder are usually involved in aggressive and illegal activities. They are often impulsive and reckless and are more likely to become alcohol dependent. Males are more likely than females to demonstrate antisociality.

**ALCOHOL USE AND INTERPERSONAL RELATIONSHIPS, RAISING CHILDREN, CHILD ABUSE, AND SEXUAL ASSAULT.** Married couples often have strongly similar levels of drinking. It is unclear whether men and women with problem drinking patterns seek out partners with similar drinking patterns or whether either is influenced by the other to drink during the marriage. However, marital discord is often present when spouses' drinking patterns differ significantly.

Being a victim of sexual assault and/or child abuse is a risk factor for AUD. Women who have been sexually assaulted, whether during childhood or as an adult, are at an increased risk for problem drinking and alcohol abuse. According to Karen A. Kalmakis of the University of Massachusetts, Amherst, in "Cycle of Sexual Assault and Women's Alcohol Misuse" (*Journal of the American Academy of Nurse Practitioners*, vol. 22, no. 12, December 2010), over half of the individuals who enter substance abuse treatment programs report a history of physical or sexual abuse. She notes that these individuals are primarily women and that they mostly abuse alcohol. Kalmakis explains that women who experienced sexual abuse and then misuse alcohol are more likely to experience subsequent sexual assault as an adult than are women who do not misuse alcohol. She concludes, "The psychological impact of women's childhood sexual abuse, combined with their alcohol misuse, makes them vulnerable to further victimization, creating a cycle of alcohol misuse and victimization."

Daniel F. Becker and Carlos M. Grilo, in investigating the psychosocial factors of drug and alcohol abuse in adolescents, note that women are not the only victims of this abuse/misuse cycle. The researchers suggest in "Prediction of Drug and Alcohol Abuse in Hospitalized Adolescents: Comparisons by Gender and Substance Type" (*Behaviour Research and Therapy*, vol. 44, no. 10, October 2006) that a history of child abuse is a risk factor for drug and alcohol abuse in both males and females. Researchers have also studied the ways that alcohol abuse adversely affects the ability of parents to raise their children effectively. For example, in "Explicating the Social Mechanisms Linking Alcohol Use Behaviors and Ecology to Child Maltreatment" (*Journal of Sociology and Social Welfare*, vol. 39, no. 4, December 2012), Bridget Freisthler and Megan R. Holmes of the University of California, Los Angeles, analyze the link between alcoholism and child abuse. The researchers focus on the ways in which certain social situations (such as weddings or other special occasions) are tied to alcohol consumption and in turn how these situations can lead to inadequate supervision, disruptive and unsafe household environments, and other circumstances that put children at risk of abuse or neglect. Freisthler and Holmes conclude that increasing understanding of the "specific social mechanisms" by which alcohol consumption leads to child maltreatment can help lead to improved intervention techniques and practices.

## EFFECTS OF PARENTAL ALCOHOLISM ON CHILDREN

Living with someone who has an alcohol problem affects every member of the family. Children often suffer many problems as a result. In the fact sheet "Children of Addicted Parents: Important Facts" (2013, http://www.nacoa.net/pdfs/addicted.pdf), the National Association for Children of Alcoholics (NACoA) estimates that there are over 28 million children of alcoholics in the United States, including 11 million under the age of 18 years.

As mentioned earlier, relatives of alcoholics have four times the risk of alcoholism than do nonrelatives. Jodi M. Gilman, James M. Bjork, and Daniel W.

Hommer of the NIAAA note in "Parental Alcohol Use and Brain Volumes in Early and Late-Onset Alcoholics" (*Biological Psychiatry*, vol. 62, no. 6, September 15, 2007) that many factors contribute to this increased risk. Some of these contributing factors are a genetic predisposition to alcoholism as well as a poor diet, unstable parental relationships, and alcohol exposure in the womb. Their research adds another factor, however: the effect of a family history of heavy drinking on brain volume. Gilman, Bjork, and Hommer find that alcoholic patients who had a family history of heavy drinking had significantly smaller brain volumes than did alcoholic patients with no family history of heavy drinking. The researchers conclude that "parental alcohol use may increase risk for alcoholism in offspring in part by a genetic and/or environmental effect that may be related to reduced brain growth."

The NACoA also notes that children of alcoholics are more likely to suffer from attention-deficit/hyperactivity disorder, behavioral problems, and anxiety disorders. They tend to score lower on tests that measure cognitive and verbal skills. Furthermore, children of alcoholics are more likely to be truant, repeat grades, drop out of school, or be referred to a school counselor or psychologist.

## UNDERAGE DRINKING, ADVERTISING, AND THE LAW

One issue of particular concern to health experts, regulators, and parents is the prevalence of underage drinking. The Johns Hopkins Bloomberg School of Public Health reports in "Alcohol Advertising and Youth" (April 2007, http://www.camy.org/factsheets/sheets/Alcohol_Advertising_and_Youth.html) that many factors help shape the underage drinking culture in the United States, including parental behavior, peer pressure, and the pervasiveness of alcohol in popular culture. It also indicates that alcohol advertising plays a key role in encouraging teenagers to drink. Indeed, according to the Bloomberg School, advertisements for alcoholic beverages often appeal to the adolescent desire for "immediate gratification, thrills and/or social status." A number of studies show that this type of advertising can be very effective. For example, in "Does Alcohol Advertising Promote Adolescent Drinking? Results from a Longitudinal Assessment" (*Addiction*, vol. 100, no. 2, February 2005), Phyllis L. Ellickson et al. identify a link between high school drinking and exposure to in-store beer marketing and alcohol advertisements in magazines. Likewise, researchers at the Center on Alcohol Marketing and Youth, which is part of the Johns Hopkins Bloomberg School of Public Health, note in *State Laws to Reduce the Impact of Alcohol Marketing on Youth: Current Status and Model Policies* (May 1, 2012, http://www.camy.org/action/Legal_Resources/State%20Ad%20Laws/CAMY_State_Alcohol_Ads_Report_2012.pdf) that the alcohol industry spends $4 billion on marketing each year. To counter the influence of alcohol lvertising on underage drinking habits, the report recommends a number of legislative changes at the state level, including a prohibition on linking alcohol to athletic achievement, on portraying images of intoxication, and on directly targeting minors with marketing efforts.

## SHORT-TERM EFFECTS OF ALCOHOL ON THE BODY

When most people think about how alcohol affects them, they think of a temporary light-headedness or a hangover the next morning. Many are also aware of the serious damage that continuous, excessive alcohol use can do to the liver. Alcohol, however, affects many organs of the body and has been linked to cancer, mental and/or physical retardation in newborns, heart disease, and other health problems.

Low to moderate doses of alcohol produce a slight, brief increase in heartbeat and blood pressure. Large doses can reduce the pumping power of the heart and produce irregular heartbeats. In addition, blood vessels within muscles constrict, but those at the surface expand, causing rapid heat loss from the skin and a flushing or reddening. Thus, large doses of alcohol decrease body temperature and, additionally, may cause numbness of the skin, legs, and arms, creating a false feeling of warmth. Figure 2.2 illustrates and describes in more detail the path that alcohol takes through the body after it is consumed.

Alcohol affects the endocrine system (a group of glands that produce hormones) in several ways. One effect is increased urination. Urination increases not only because of fluid intake but also because alcohol stops the release of vasopressin (an antidiuretic hormone) from the pituitary gland. This hormone controls how much water the kidneys reabsorb from the urine as it is being produced and how much water the kidneys excrete. Therefore, heavy alcohol intake can result in both dehydration and an imbalance in electrolytes, which are chemicals dissolved in body fluids that conduct electrical currents. Both of these conditions are serious health hazards.

Alcohol is sometimes believed to be an aphrodisiac (sexual stimulant). Whereas low to moderate amounts of alcohol can reduce fear and decrease sexual inhibitions, larger doses tend to impair sexual performance. Alcoholics sometimes report difficulties in their sex life.

**FIGURE 2.2**

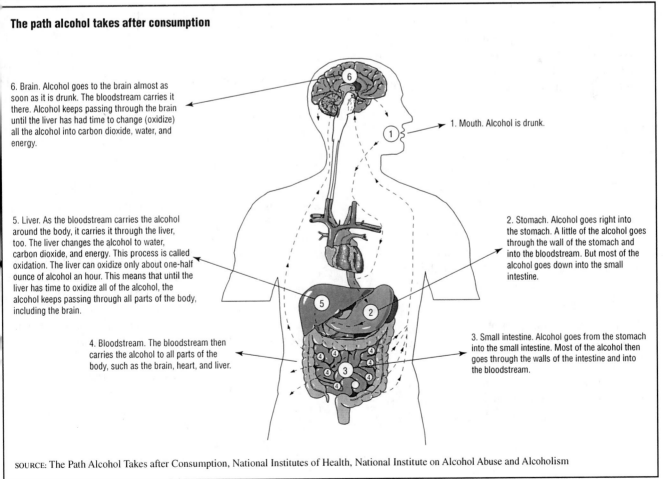

The path alcohol takes after consumption

6. Brain. Alcohol goes to the brain almost as soon as it is drunk. The bloodstream carries it there. Alcohol keeps passing through the brain until the liver has had time to change (oxidize) all the alcohol into carbon dioxide, water, and energy.

1. Mouth. Alcohol is drunk.

5. Liver. As the bloodstream carries the alcohol around the body, it carries it through the liver, too. The liver changes the alcohol to water, carbon dioxide, and energy. This process is called oxidation. The liver can oxidize only about one-half ounce of alcohol an hour. This means that until the liver has time to oxidize all of the alcohol, the alcohol keeps passing through all parts of the body, including the brain.

2. Stomach. Alcohol goes right into the stomach. A little of the alcohol goes through the wall of the stomach and into the bloodstream. But most of the alcohol goes down into the small intestine.

4. Bloodstream. The bloodstream then carries the alcohol to all parts of the body, such as the brain, heart, and liver.

3. Small intestine. Alcohol goes from the stomach into the small intestine. Most of the alcohol then goes through the walls of the intestine and into the bloodstream.

SOURCE: The Path Alcohol Takes after Consumption, National Institutes of Health, National Institute on Alcohol Abuse and Alcoholism

## Intoxication

The speed of alcohol absorption affects the rate at which one becomes intoxicated. Intoxication occurs when alcohol is absorbed into the blood faster than the liver can oxidize it (or break it down into water, carbon dioxide, and energy). In a 160-pound (72.6-kg) man, alcohol is metabolized at a rate of about one drink every two hours. The absorption of alcohol is influenced by several factors:

- Body weight—heavier people are less affected than lighter people by the same amount of alcohol because there is more blood and water in their system to dilute the alcohol intake. In addition, the greater the body muscle weight, the lower the blood alcohol concentration (BAC) for a given amount of alcohol.

- Speed of drinking—the faster alcohol is drunk, the faster the BAC level rises.

- Presence of food in the stomach—eating while drinking slows down the absorption of alcohol by increasing the amount of time it takes the alcohol to get from the stomach to the small intestine.

- Drinking history and body chemistry—the longer a person has been drinking, the greater his or her tolerance (in other words, the more alcohol it takes him or her to get drunk). An individual's physiological functioning or "body chemistry" may also affect his or her reactions to alcohol. Women are more easily affected by alcohol regardless of weight because women metabolize alcohol differently than men. Women are known to have less body water than men of the same body weight, so equivalent amounts of alcohol result in higher concentrations of alcohol in the blood of women than men.

As a person's BAC rises, there are somewhat predictable responses in behavior.

- At a BAC of about 0.05 grams (g) of alcohol per 1 deciliter (dL) of blood, thought processes, judgment, and restraint are more lax. The person may feel more at ease socially. Also, reaction time to visual or auditory stimuli slows down as the BAC rises. (It should be noted that a measurement of g/dL—a mass/volume measure—is approximately equal to a volume/volume—or a percentage—measurement when calculating BAC and that the two are often used interchangeably; so a BAC of 0.05 g/dL can also mean a BAC of 0.05%.)

- At 0.10 g/dL, voluntary motor actions become noticeably clumsy. (It is illegal to drive with a BAC of 0.08 g/dL or higher.)

- At 0.20 g/dL, the entire motor area of the brain becomes significantly depressed. The person staggers, may want to lie down, may be easily angered, or may shout or weep.

- At 0.30 g/dL, the person generally acts confused or may be in a stupor.

- At 0.40 g/dL, the person usually falls into a coma.

- At 0.50 g/dL or more, the medulla is severely depressed, and death generally occurs within several hours, usually from respiratory failure. The medulla is the portion of the brainstem that regulates many involuntary processes, such as breathing.

Without immediate medical attention, a person whose BAC reaches 0.50 g/dL will almost certainly die. Death may even occur at a BAC of 0.40 g/dL if the alcohol is consumed quickly and in a large amount, causing the BAC to rise rapidly.

## Sobering Up

Time is the only way to rid the body of alcohol. The more slowly a person drinks, the more time the body has to process the alcohol, so less alcohol accumulates in the bloodstream. In addition, having food in the stomach slows the absorption of alcohol there. Drinking slowly while eating and alternating nonalcoholic beverages with alcoholic beverages helps keep the BAC at lower levels than drinking more quickly on an empty stomach.

According to Brown University, in "Alcohol & Your Body" (2013, http://brown.edu/Student_Services/Health_Services/Health_Education/alcohol,_tobacco,_&_other_drugs/alcohol/alcohol_&_your_body.php), five drinks consumed in quick succession by a 175-pound (79.4-kg) man will produce a BAC of 0.125 g/dL. In a 150-pound (68-kg) man this intake will produce a higher BAC of 0.145 g/dL. In a 125-pound (56.7-kg) woman it will produce an even higher BAC of 0.202 g/dL. It will take six hours for the BAC level of the 125-pound woman to drop to 0.112, which is still high above the legal driving limit of 0.08 g/dL.

## Hangovers

Hangovers cause a great deal of misery as well as absenteeism and loss of productivity at school or work. A person with a hangover experiences two or more physical symptoms after drinking and fully metabolizing alcohol. The major symptoms of a hangover are listed in Table 2.6, but the causes of these symptoms are not well known. Gemma Prat, Ana Adan, and Miguel Sánchez-Turet of the University of Barcelona review explanations of hangovers in "Alcohol Hangover: A Critical Review of Explanatory Factors" (*Human Psychopharmacology: Clinical and Experimental*, vol. 24, no. 4, June 2009). The primary hypotheses as to the causes of hangovers are that they are a physiological response to withdrawal from alcohol, impurities produced during fermentation that are present in alcoholic beverages, or by-products that are produced by the body during the metabolism of alcohol. Fluctuations in body hormones and dehydration intensify hangover symptoms.

**mptoms of a hangover**

dy aches
arrhea
zziness/lightheadedness
y mouth/thirst
tigue
adache
itability
ck of alertness/difficulty concentrating
usea

SURCE: Created by Sandra Alters for Gale, 2010

There is no scientific evidence to support popular angover cures, such as black coffee, raw egg, chili epper, steak sauce, "alkalizers," and vitamins. To treat hangover, health care practitioners usually prescribe ed rest as well as eating food and drinking nonalcoholic uids.

## LONG-TERM EFFECTS OF ALCOHOL ON THE BODY

The results of scientific research help health care ractitioners and the general public understand both the ositive and negative health consequences of drinking lcohol. Thomas F. Babor and Katherine Robaina iden-ify in "Public Health, Academic Medicine, and the lcohol Industry's Corporate Social Responsibility ctivities" (*American Journal of Public Health*, vol. 03. no. 2, February 2013) a link between alcohol con-umption and a range of health problems and diseases, ncluding breast cancer, cirrhosis of the liver, heart dis-ase, and tuberculosis. Citing statistics from the World Health Organization, the researchers state that alcohol onsumption causes 3.8% of all deaths worldwide. In "Alcohol-Attributable Cancer Deaths and Years of Potential Life Lost in the United States" (*American ournal of Public Health*, vol. 103, no. 4, April 2013), David E. Nelson et al. report that alcohol consumption esulted in 19,500 cancer deaths in 2009, greater than the number of deaths due to ovarian cancer or melanoma and oughly two-thirds the number of deaths due to prostate ancer that year.

Not all the effects of alcohol consumption are harmful o health, however. In "Alcohol on Trial: The Evidence" *Southern Medical Journal*, vol. 98, no. 1, January 2005), Ronald C. Hamdy and Melissa McManama Aukerman list evels of alcohol consumption and the relative risk for total mortality (death) for a variety of diseases and conditions. Their data show that men aged 40 to 85 years who drank up to, and possibly slightly over, two drinks per day had a ower total mortality risk than those who did not drink. That is, this level of drinking was good for the men's overall health and life expectancy. According to David

M. Goldberg and George E. Soleas of the University of Toronto, in "Wine and Health: A Paradigm for Alcohol and Antioxidants" (*Journal of Medical Biochemistry*, vol. 30, no. 2, June 2011), the ethanol found in alcoholic beverages has been found to reduce clotting of the arteries, while also diminishing the risk of type 2 diabetes, which is a major cause of arteriosclerotic vascular disease.

Benjamin Taylor et al. compare in "Alcohol and Hypertension: Gender Differences in Dose-Response Relationships Determined through Systematic Review and Meta-Analysis" (*Addiction*, vol. 104, no 12, December 2009) alcohol consumption versus relative risk of hypertension (chronic high blood pressure) in women versus men. Alcohol consumption of between two and four drinks per week, with only one drink per day on any occasion, lowered the risk of hypertension in women. Once that level of alcohol consumption was reached, however, the risk of hypertension in women rose as their alcohol consumption rose. With men, low levels of alcohol consumption were not protective against hypertension as in women. Furthermore, the more men drank, the higher their risk of hypertension.

In "Effects of Beer, Wine, and Liquor Intakes on Bone Mineral Density in Older Men and Women" (*American Journal of Clinical Nutrition*, February 25, 2009), Katherine L. Tucker et al. of Tufts University indicate that bone density can also benefit from alcohol consumption. In reporting on Tucker et al.'s study, Anne Harding explains in "Moderate Drinking May Help Bone Density" (Reuters, March 20, 2009) that "people who enjoy a glass or two of wine or beer every day could be helping to keep their bones strong." However, Harding cautions that "drinking more—and choosing hard liquor instead of wine or beer—may actually weaken bones."

The studies mentioned in this section provide only a small sample of the wide variety and large number of studies that have been conducted on the long-term effects of alcohol consumption on health. With so many studies and so many health-related factors to take into account, how does a person know how much alcohol is beneficial and how much is too much? The World Cancer Research Fund and the American Institute for Cancer Research state in *Food, Nutrition, Physical Activity, and the Prevention of Cancer: A Global Perspective* (2007, http://eprints.ucl.ac.uk/4841/1/4841.pdf): "If alcoholic drinks are consumed, limit consumption to no more than two drinks a day for men and one drink a day for women." Their justification for this statement is as follows: "The evidence on cancer justifies a recommendation not to drink alcoholic drinks. Other evidence shows that modest amounts of alcoholic drinks are likely to reduce the risk of coronary heart disease."

In "Alcoholic Beverages and Cardiovascular Disease" (March 31, 2011, http://www.heart.org/HEARTORG/Get

tingHealthy/NutritionCenter/Alcoholic-Beverages-and-Cardiovascular-Disease_UCM_305864_Article.jsp), the American Heart Association states: "If you drink alcohol, do so in moderation. This means an average of one to two drinks per day for men and one drink per day for women.... Drinking more alcohol increases such dangers as alcoholism, high blood pressure, obesity, stroke, breast cancer, suicide and accidents. Also, it's not possible to predict which people will develop problems with alcoholism. Consumption of alcohol can have beneficial or harmful effects, depending on the amount consumed, age and other characteristics of the person consuming the alcohol."

## EFFECTS OF ALCOHOL ON SEX AND REPRODUCTION

Alcohol consumption can affect sexual response and reproduction in profound ways. Many alcoholics suffer from erectile dysfunction (impotence) and/or reduced sexual drive. Valentina Boddi et al. suggest in "Priapus Is Happier with Venus Than with Bacchus" (*Journal of Sexual Medicine*, vol. 7, no. 8, August 2010) that male alcohol consumption of four or more drinks per day was associated with a greater risk of erectile dysfunction as shown by a reduction in penile blood flow. The researchers also note that this level of alcohol consumption "was associated with low perceived partner's sexual desire, worse couple relationship, and smoking abuse." Many alcoholics suffer from depression, which may further impair their sexual function. In addition, Jerrold S. Greenberg, Clint E. Bruess, and Sarah C. Conklin report in *Exploring the Dimensions of Human Sexuality* (2011) that alcohol use is associated with poor sperm quality in men.

In premenopausal women chronic heavy drinking can contribute to a variety of reproductive disorders. According to Greenberg, Bruess, and Conklin, these disorders include the cessation of menstruation, irregular menstrual cycles, failure to ovulate, early menopause, increased risk of spontaneous miscarriages, and lower rates of conception. Some of these disorders can be caused directly by the interference of alcohol with the hormonal regulation of the reproductive system. They may also be caused indirectly through other disorders that are associated with alcohol abuse, such as liver disease, pancreatic disease, malnutrition, or fetal abnormalities.

### Fetal Alcohol Spectrum Disorders

Alcohol consumption during pregnancy can result in severe harm to the fetus (unborn child). The development of such defects can begin early in pregnancy when the mother-to-be may not even know she is pregnant, and such defects are likely to be exacerbated by binge drinking. For example, Lisa A. DeRoo et al. reveal in "First-Trimester Maternal Alcohol Consumption and the Risk of Infant Oral Clefts in Norway: A Population-Based Case-Control Study" (*American Journal of Epidemiology*, vol. 168, no. 6, September 15, 2008) that women who binge drank during their first trimester of pregnancy were twice as likely as nondrinkers to give birth to an infant having a cleft lip, cleft palate, or both. Other alcohol-related birth defects include malformations and abnormal development of the heart, bones, and kidneys.

It should be noted that drinking during pregnancy can cause more than physical alcohol-related birth defects. Exposure to alcohol in the womb can cause a variety of conditions that are collectively called fetal alcohol spectrum disorders (FASD). Alcohol-related birth defects make up only one aspect of FASD. Children with FASDs can exhibit not only physical birth defects but also a complex pattern of behavioral and cognitive dysfunctions, which are listed in Table 2.7. Together, FASDs include effects that are physical, cognitive, and behavioral; cannot be cured; and last throughout the life of the affected individual.

Fetal alcohol syndrome (FAS) is the most severe FASD. An individual with FAS has characteristic facial anomalies, growth deficiency, and central nervous system abnormalities. Children with these facial anomalies and the central nervous system abnormalities of FAS but who have normal growth patterns are said to have partial FAS. Children exposed to alcohol before birth who do not have the facial characteristics typical of FAS, but who have severe central nervous system dysfunction have the FASD called alcohol-related neurodevelopmental disorder (ARND).

In "Fetal Alcohol Spectrum Disorders (FASDs): Data and Statistics" (August 16, 2012, http://www.cdc.gov/ncbddd/fasd/data.html), the Centers for Disease Control and Prevention (CDC) notes that FAS rates range from 0.2 to 1.5 per 1,000 live births in results of CDC studies, and from 0.5 to 2 per 1,000 live births in results from other studies. In addition, the CDC reports that other prenatal alcohol-related conditions that are less severe than FAS, such as ARND and alcohol-related birth defects (ARBD), occur approximately three times as often as FAS. ARND and ARBD were formerly and collectively known as fetal alcohol effects. In

**TABLE 2.7**

**Characteristics typical of fetal alcohol spectrum disorders (FASD)**

Characteristic facial features (fetal alcohol syndrome only)
Delayed motor development
Difficulties in learning and in abstract thinking
Disregard for authority
Disruptive and impulsive behavior
Growth deficiency
Hyperactivity
Low birth weight
Low IQ
Poor social skills
Short attention span
Slow reaction time

SOURCE: Created by Sandra Alters for Gale, 2010

he 21st century all prenatal alcohol-related conditions are collectively known as FASD.

In February 2005 the U.S. surgeon general Richard Carmona (1949–) issued an advisory on alcohol use during pregnancy. Key points of the advisory are listed in Table 2.8. As noted in the advisory, there is no known safe level of alcohol consumption during pregnancy. The CDC emphasizes, along with the surgeon general, that FAS and other prenatal alcohol-related disorders are 100% preventable if a woman does not drink alcohol while she is pregnant or if she is of reproductive age and is not using birth control. Even so, data show that some women who might become pregnant, or who are pregnant, consume alcohol and put themselves at risk for having a child with FASD.

Table 2.9 shows that 9.4% of pregnant women consumed alcohol in the past month in 2010–11 when questioned for the annual National Survey on Drug Use and Health. This figure was down from 9.9% in 2008–09. In 2008–09 approximately one-fifth (20.4%) of pregnant women drank during their first trimester of pregnancy, a time when all the organ systems of the fetus are developing; in 2010–11 this percentage dropped to 18.4%. In contrast, the percentage of pregnant women who drank

## TABLE 2.8

### Key points in the U.S. Surgeon General's advisory on alcohol use during pregnancy, 2005

**Based on the current, best science available we now know the following:**

- Alcohol consumed during pregnancy increases the risk of alcohol related birth defects, including growth deficiencies, facial abnormalities, central nervous system impairment, behavioral disorders, and impaired intellectual development.
- No amount of alcohol consumption can be considered safe during pregnancy.
- Alcohol can damage a fetus at any stage of pregnancy. Damage can occur in the earliest weeks of pregnancy, even before a woman knows that she is pregnant.
- The cognitive deficits and behavioral problems resulting from prenatal alcohol exposure are lifelong.
- Alcohol-related birth defects are completely preventable.

**For these reasons:**

1. A pregnant woman should not drink alcohol during pregnancy.
2. A pregnant woman who has already consumed alcohol during her pregnancy should stop in order to minimize further risk.
3. A woman who is considering becoming pregnant should abstain from alcohol.
4. Recognizing that nearly half of all births in the United States are unplanned, women of childbearing age should consult their physician and take steps to reduce the possibility of prenatal alcohol exposure.
5. Health professionals should inquire routinely about alcohol consumption by women of childbearing age, inform them of the risks of alcohol consumption during pregnancy, and advise them not to drink alcoholic beverages during pregnancy.

SOURCE: Adapted from "Surgeon General's Advisory on Alcohol Use in Pregnancy," in *News Release: U.S. Surgeon General Releases Advisory on Alcohol Use in Pregnancy*, U.S. Department of Health and Human Services, February 21, 2005, http://www.surgeongeneral.gov/pressreleases/sg02222005.html (accessed February 11, 2013)

## TABLE 2.9

### Percentage of past-month alcohol use among females aged 15–44, by pregnancy status, 2008–09 and 2010–11

| | Total[a] | | Pregnancy status | | | |
| | | | Pregnant | | Not pregnant | |
| Demographic/pregnancy characteristic | 2008–2009 | 2010–2011 | 2008–2009 | 2010–2011 | 2008–2009 | 2010–2011 |
|---|---|---|---|---|---|---|
| Total | 52.6 | 53.4 | 9.9 | 9.4 | 54.4 | 55.1 |
| **Age** | | | | | | |
| 15–17 | 22.9 | 21.4 | 16.7 | 8.8 | 22.9 | 21.6 |
| 18–25 | 57.8 | 57.5 | 9.8 | 8.2 | 60.7 | 60.1 |
| 26–44 | 55.2 | 56.7 | 9.6 | 10.2 | 57.1 | 58.5 |
| **Hispanic origin and race** | | | | | | |
| Not Hispanic or Latino | 55.2 | 55.9 | 9.8 | 10.6 | 57.1 | 57.6 |
| White | 59.3 | 60.2 | 9.2 | 11.0 | 61.5 | 62.0 |
| Black or African American | 46.1 | 45.6 | 16.5 | 8.4 | 47.2 | 47.1 |
| American Indian or Alaska Native | 48.2 | 44.2 | * | * | 50.0 | 45.6 |
| Native Hawaiian or other Pacific Islander | * | * | * | * | * | * |
| Asian | 33.6 | 40.0 | * | * | 35.0 | 41.1 |
| Two or more races | 51.8 | 55.6 | * | * | 54.1 | 57.5 |
| Hispanic or Latino | 40.3 | 42.4 | 10.6 | 4.8 | 41.8 | 44.0 |
| **Trimester[b]** | | | | | | |
| First | N/A | N/A | 20.4 | 18.4 | N/A | N/A |
| Second | N/A | N/A | 6.2 | 7.9 | N/A | N/A |
| Third | N/A | N/A | 3.5 | 3.0 | N/A | N/A |

*Low precision; no estimate reported.
N/A: Not applicable.
Note: Some 2008–2009 estimates may differ from previously published estimates due to updates.
[a]Estimates in the total column are for all females aged 15 to 44, including those with unknown pregnancy status.
[b]Pregnant females aged 15 to 44 not reporting trimester were excluded.

SOURCE: "Table 6.76B. Alcohol Use in the Past Month among Females Aged 15 and 44, by Pregnancy and Demographic Characteristics: Percentages, Annual Averages Based on 2008–2009 and 2010–2011," in *Results from the 2011 National Survey on Drug Use and Health: Detailed Tables*, U.S. Department of Health and Human Services, Substance Abuse and Mental Health Services Administration, September 2012, http://www.samhsa.gov/data/NSDUH/2011SummNatFindDetTables/NSDUH-DetTabsPDFWHTML2011/2k11DetailedTabs/Web/PDFW/NSDUH-DetTabsSect6peTabs71to78-2011.pdf (accessed February 11, 2013)

during their second trimester rose, from 6.2% in 2008–09 to 7.9% in 2010–11.

## ALCOHOL'S INTERACTION WITH OTHER DRUGS

Because alcohol is easily available and such an accepted part of American social life, people often forget that it is a drug. When someone takes a medication while drinking alcohol, he or she is taking two drugs. Alcohol consumed with other drugs—for example, an illegal drug such as cocaine, an over-the-counter (without a prescription) drug such as cough medicine, or a prescription drug such as an antibiotic—may make the combination harmful or even deadly or may counteract the effectiveness of a prescribed medication.

To promote the desired chemical or physical effects, a medication must be absorbed into the body and must reach its site of action. Alcohol may prevent an appropriate amount of the medication from reaching its site of action. In other cases alcohol can alter the drug's effects once it reaches the site. Alcohol interacts negatively with more than 150 medications. Table 2.10 shows some possible interactions when combining alcohol and other types of drugs.

The U.S. Food and Drug Administration recommends that anyone who regularly has three alcoholic drinks per day should check with a physician before taking aspirin, acetaminophen, or any other over-the-counter painkiller. Combining alcohol with aspirin, ibuprofen, or related pain relievers may promote stomach bleeding. Combining alcohol with acetaminophen may promote liver damage.

## ALCOHOL-RELATED DEATHS

Kenneth D. Kochanek et al. of the CDC report in "Deaths: Final Data for 2009" (*National Vital Statistics Reports*, vol. 60, no. 3, December 29, 2011) that 24,518 people in the United States died from alcohol-induced causes in 2009. This category includes deaths from dependent use of alcohol, nondependent use of alcohol, and accidental alcohol poisoning. It excludes accidents, homicides, and other causes indirectly related to alcohol use, as well as deaths because of FAS. In 2009, 15,183 people died from alcoholic liver disease.

## MOTOR VEHICLE AND PEDESTRIAN ACCIDENTS

In *Traffic Safety Facts 2010: A Compilation of Motor Vehicle Crash Data from the Fatality Analysis Reporting System and the General Estimates System* (2012, http://www-nrd.nhtsa.dot.gov/Pubs/811659.pdf), the National Highway Traffic Safety Administration (NHTSA) of the U.S. Department of Transportation defines a fatal traffic crash as alcohol related if either the driver or an involved pedestrian has a BAC of 0.01 g/dL or greater. If either the driver or an involved pedestrian has a BAC of 0.08 g/dL

or greater, the individual is considered to be intoxicated and the crash is classified as alcohol impaired. However, neither definition means that alcohol is necessarily the cause of the accident.

The NHTSA reports that 32,885 people were killed in traffic accidents in 2010, with 11,948 of them in alcohol-related crashes. (See Table 2.11.) These alcohol-related traffic deaths represented 36% of all car crash fatalities in 2010. The percentage of alcohol-related traffic fatalities has declined somewhat steadily from a high of 55% in 1982, and leveled out from about the mid-1990s to 2010. The peak number of fatalities occurred in 1990, when 44,599 traffic accident deaths, including both alcohol-related accidents (46%) and nonalcohol-related accidents (53%), were recorded.

A number of important factors have contributed to the decline of drunk driving fatalities. Mothers against Drunk Driving was founded in 1980. This organization's most significant achievement was lobbying to get the legal drinking age raised to 21 in all states, which occurred in 1988. There were also successful campaigns such as "Friends Don't Let Friends Drive Drunk." The use of seat belts has also helped reduce deaths in motor vehicle accidents.

By August 2005 all 50 states, the District of Columbia, and Puerto Rico had lowered the BAC limit for drunk driving from 0.1 g/dL to 0.08 g/dL. According to the Insurance Institute for Highway Safety, in "DUI/DWI Laws" (http://www.iihs.org/laws/dui.aspx), as of April 2013, 41 states and the District of Columbia also had administrative license revocation laws, which require prompt, mandatory suspension of driver's licenses when drivers fail or refuse to take the BAC test. This immediate suspension, before conviction and independent of criminal procedures, is invoked immediately after arrest.

In both 2001 and 2010 drivers aged 21 to 44 years were the most likely to be involved in fatal crashes in which the driver had a BAC of 0.08 g/dL or higher, and their percentages have predominantly risen. (See Table 2.12.) The percentage of drivers within the 21- to 24-year-old age group increased from 33% in 2001 to 34% in 2010, while the percentage of drivers in the 25- to 34-year-old age group increased from 28% to 30%; the percentage of drivers in the 35- to 44-year-old age group remained the same at 25%. Those in the 45- to 54-year-old age group accounted for 19% of fatal crashes in which the driver had a BAC of 0.08 g/dL or higher in 2001; this percentage increased to 21% in 2010.

In 2010 the percentage of male drivers (24%) involved in fatal crashes who had a BAC of 0.08 g/dL or greater was nine percentage points higher than female drivers (15%) involved in fatal crashes. (See Table 2.12.) When compared with 2001, the percentage of drunk male and female drivers in fatal accidents in 2010 remained the same for males, at 24%, and increased by two

TABLE 2.10

**Interactions between alcohol and various medications**

| Drug class (conditions or which they are used) | Generic name | Brand name | Availability | Type of interaction |
|---|---|---|---|---|
| Analgesics (pain relief) | Aspirin<br>Acetaminophen | various<br>e.g., Tylenol | Rx and OTC | • Aspirin increases gastric emptying, leading to faster alcohol absorption in the small intestine; may also inhibit gastric ADH.<br>• Alcohol enhances acetaminophen metabolism into a toxic product, potentially causing liver damage. |
| Antibiotics (microbial infections) | Erythromycin<br>Isoniazid | various<br>Nydrazid, Rifamate, Rifater | Rx | • Erythromycin may increase gastric emptying, leading to faster alcohol absorption in the small intestine.<br>• Alcohol increases the risk of isoniazid-related liver disease. |
| Anticonvulsants (seizure disorders) | Phenytoin | Dilantin | Rx | • Chronic alcohol consumption induces phenytoin breakdown. |
| Antihistamines (allergies, colds) | Diphenhydramine<br>Chlorpheniramine<br>Clemastine<br>Hydroxyzine<br>Promethazine<br>Cyproheptadine | e.g., Benadryl<br>various<br><br>Atarax, Vistaril<br>Phenergan<br>Periactin | Rx and OTC | • Alcohol enhances the effects of these agents on the central nervous system (CNS), such as drowsiness, sedation, and decreased motor skills.<br>• The interactions are more pronounced in elderly people.<br>• No documented interactions exist with nonsedating antihistamines (i.e., certrizine, hismanal, loratidine). |
| Anticoagulants (prevention of blood clots) | Warfarin | Coumadin | Rx | • Acute alcohol intake may increase anticoagulation by decreasing warfarin metabolism; chronic alcohol ingestion decreases anticoagulation by increasing warfarin metabolism. |
| Antidiabetic agents (blood sugar regulation) | Chlorpropamide<br>Glipizide<br>Glyburide<br><br>Tolbutamide<br>Metformin | Diabinese<br>Glucotrol<br>DiaBeta, Glynase, Micronase<br>Orinase<br>Glucophage | Rx | • Alcohol consumption by diabetic patients taking these medications increases the risk of lower-than-normal blood sugar levels (i.e., hypoglycemia).<br>• Chlorpropamide, glyburide, and tolbutamide can cause disulfiram-like interactions after alcohol ingestion.<br>• Metformin may cause increased levels of lactic acid in the blood after alcohol consumption. |
| Barbiturates (anesthesia, pain relief) | Phenobarbital | various | Rx | • Chronic alcohol intake increases barbiturate metabolism by cytochrome P450.<br>• Alcohol enhances the sedative and hypnotic effects on the CNS. |
| Benzodiazepines (sedative agents) | Alprazolam<br>Chlordiazepoxide<br>Clonazepam<br>Clorazepate<br>Diazepam<br>Lorazepam<br>Midazolam<br>Oxazepam<br>Temazepam<br>Triazolam | Xanax<br>Librium<br>Klonopin<br>Tranxene<br>Valium<br>Ativan<br>Versed<br>Serax<br>Restoril<br>Halcion | Rx | • Alcohol enhances the effects of these agents on the CNS, such as drowsiness, sedation, and decreased motor skills. |
| Histamine $H_2$ receptor antagonists (ulcers, heart burn) | Cimetidine<br>Nizatidine<br>Ranitidine | Tagamet<br>Axid<br>Zantac | Rx and OTC | • The agents inhibit ADH in the stomach, thereby reducing alcohol first-pass metabolism (see figure 1), as well as increase gastric emptying. As a result, BALs are higher than expected for a given alcohol dose; this effect increases over time. |
| Immune modulators (rheumatoid arthritis) | Methotrexate | Rheumatrex | Rx | • Immune modulators (i.e., medications that affect immune cell function) are associated with a risk of liver damage, which is increased in combination with alcohol. |
| Muscle relaxants | Carisoprodol<br>Cyclobenzaprine | Soma<br>Flexeril | Rx | • Alcohol consumption enhances impairment of physical abilities (e.g., driving) and increases sedation.<br>• Carisoprodol produces an opiate-like high when taken with alcohol; it is metabolized to meprobamate and sometimes abused as a street drug. |

percentage points for females, from 13% to 15%; thus the gap between the two groups narrowed over the course of the decade.

Alcohol was related to a higher percentage of fatal crashes by motorcycles (28%) in 2010 than for crashes involving automobiles and light trucks (23% and 22%,

**TABLE 2.10**

**Interactions between alcohol and various medications** [CONTINUED]

| Drug class (conditions for which they are used) | Generic name | Brand name | Availability | Type of interaction |
|---|---|---|---|---|
| NSAIDs (pain relief and inflammation) | Ibuprofen Flurbiprofen Fenoprofen Ketoprofen Naproxen Diclofenac | e.g., Motrin various Nalfon Orudis Naprosyn Voltaren | Rx and OTC | • Alcohol consumption increases the associated risk of gastrointestinal bleeding. |
| Opioids (pain relief) | Codeine Hydromorphone Fentanyl Morphine Meperidine Propoxyphene | various Dilaudid generic various e.g., Demerol Darvon, Wygesic | Rx | • Alcohol enhances the effects of these agents on the CNS, such as drowsiness, sedation, and decreased motor skills. |
| Sedatives and hypnotics | Chloral hydrate Meprobamate | Noctec Equanil, Miltown | Rx | • Alcohol inhibits the metabolism of these agents and produces a depressant effect on the CNS that includes sleepiness, disorientation, incoherence, and confusion. |
| Tricyclic antidepressants (depression) | Amitriptyline Clomipramine Desipramine Doxepin Imipramine Nortriptyline Trimipramine | Elavil, Endep Anafranil Norpramin Adapin, Sinequan Tofranil Aventyl, Pamelor Surmontil | Rx | • Alcohol consumption increases the risk of sedation and a sudden drop in blood pressure when a person stands up (i.e., orthostatic hypotension). |
| Herbal medications (sleep aids) | Chamomile Echinacea Valerian | various preparations | OTC | • Alcohol may accentuate the drowsiness that is associated with these herbal preparations. |

ADH = alcohol dehydrogenase. BAL = blood alcohol level. NSAIDs = nonsteroidal anti-inflammatory drugs. OTC = over the counter. Rx = prescription.

SOURCE: Ron Weathermon and David W. Crabb, "Table 3. Interactions between Alcohol and Various Classes of Medication," in "Alcohol and Medication Interactions," *Alcohol, Research & Health*, vol. 23, no. 1, 1999, http://pubs.niaaa.nih.gov/publications/arh23-1/40-54.pdf (accessed February 11, 2013)

**TABLE 2.11**

**Fatalities in motor accidents, by blood alcohol concentration (BAC) at time of crash, 1982 and 1985–2010**

| Year | BAC = 0.00 Number | BAC = 0.00 Percent | BAC = 0.01 – 0.07 Number | BAC = 0.01 – 0.07 Percent | Alcohol-impaired driving fatalities (BAC = 0.08+) Number | Alcohol-impaired driving fatalities (BAC = 0.08+) Percent | BAC = 0.01+ Number | BAC = 0.01+ Percent | Total fatalities* Number | Total fatalities* Percent |
|---|---|---|---|---|---|---|---|---|---|---|
| 1982 | 19,771 | 45 | 2,912 | 7 | 21,113 | 48 | 24,025 | 55 | 43,945 | 100 |
| 1985 | 22,589 | 52 | 2,974 | 7 | 18,125 | 41 | 21,098 | 48 | 43,825 | 100 |
| 1990 | 23,823 | 53 | 2,901 | 7 | 17,705 | 40 | 20,607 | 46 | 44,599 | 100 |
| 1991 | 23,025 | 55 | 2,480 | 6 | 15,827 | 38 | 18,307 | 44 | 41,508 | 100 |
| 1992 | 22,726 | 58 | 2,352 | 6 | 14,049 | 36 | 16,401 | 42 | 39,250 | 100 |
| 1993 | 23,979 | 60 | 2,300 | 6 | 13,739 | 34 | 16,039 | 40 | 40,150 | 100 |
| 1994 | 24,948 | 61 | 2,236 | 5 | 13,390 | 33 | 15,626 | 38 | 40,716 | 100 |
| 1995 | 25,768 | 62 | 2,416 | 6 | 13,478 | 32 | 15,893 | 38 | 41,817 | 100 |
| 1996 | 26,052 | 62 | 2,415 | 6 | 13,451 | 32 | 15,866 | 38 | 42,065 | 100 |
| 1997 | 26,902 | 64 | 2,216 | 5 | 12,757 | 30 | 14,973 | 36 | 42,013 | 100 |
| 1998 | 26,477 | 64 | 2,353 | 6 | 12,546 | 30 | 14,899 | 36 | 41,501 | 100 |
| 1999 | 26,798 | 64 | 2,235 | 5 | 12,555 | 30 | 14,790 | 35 | 41,717 | 100 |
| 2000 | 26,082 | 62 | 2,422 | 6 | 13,324 | 32 | 15,746 | 38 | 41,945 | 100 |
| 2001 | 26,334 | 62 | 2,441 | 6 | 13,290 | 31 | 15,731 | 37 | 42,196 | 100 |
| 2002 | 27,080 | 63 | 2,321 | 5 | 13,472 | 31 | 15,793 | 37 | 43,005 | 100 |
| 2003 | 27,328 | 64 | 2,327 | 5 | 13,096 | 31 | 15,423 | 36 | 42,884 | 100 |
| 2004 | 27,413 | 64 | 2,212 | 5 | 13,099 | 31 | 15,311 | 36 | 42,836 | 100 |
| 2005 | 27,423 | 63 | 2,404 | 6 | 13,582 | 31 | 15,985 | 37 | 43,510 | 100 |
| 2006 | 26,633 | 62 | 2,479 | 6 | 13,491 | 32 | 15,970 | 37 | 42,708 | 100 |
| 2007 | 25,611 | 62 | 2,494 | 6 | 13,041 | 32 | 15,534 | 38 | 41,259 | 100 |
| 2008 | 23,499 | 63 | 2,115 | 6 | 11,711 | 31 | 13,826 | 37 | 37,423 | 100 |
| 2009 | 21,051 | 62 | 1,972 | 6 | 10,759 | 32 | 12,731 | 38 | 33,883 | 100 |
| 2010 | 20,838 | 63 | 1,720 | 5 | 10,228 | 31 | 11,948 | 36 | 32,885 | 100 |

*Totals include fatalities in crashes in which there was no driver present.
Note: National Highway Traffic Safety Administration (NHTSA) estimates alcohol involvement when alcohol test results are unknown.

SOURCE: "Table 13. Persons Killed, by Highest Blood Alcohol Concentration (BAC) at Time of Crash, 1982–2010," in *Traffic Safety Facts 2010: A Compilation of Motor Vehicle Crash Data from the Fatality Analysis Reporting System and the General Estimates System*, U.S. Department of Transportation, National Highway Traffic Safety Administration, National Center for Statistics and Analysis, 2012, http://www-nrd.nhtsa.dot.gov/Pubs/811659.pdf (accessed February 11, 2013)

espectively). (See Table 2.12.) Fatal crashes involving large trucks were very unlikely to be alcohol related (2%).

In 2001 over half of all pedestrians aged 25 to 44 years who were killed in a traffic accident had a BAC of 0.08 g/dL or greater. (See Table 2.13.) In 2010 the percent-ages within the age subgroups of this group dropped below 50%. In contrast, among pedestrians aged 21 to 24 and 45 to 54 years who were killed in a traffic accident and who had a BAC of 0.08 g/dL or greater, the percentage rose during this span, from 45% and 43%, respectively, in 2001 to 48% and 46%, respectively, in 2010.

## TABLE 2.12

Drivers with a blood alcohol concentration (BAC) of 0.08 or higher involved in motor vehicle crashes, by age, gender, and vehicle type, 2001 and 2010

| | Total drivers | | | | | | |
|---|---|---|---|---|---|---|---|
| | 2001 | | | 2010 | | | Change in percentage with BAC = 0.08+ 2001–2010 |
| | Total number of drivers | BAC = 0.08+ | | Total number of drivers | BAC = 0.08+ | | |
| Drivers involved in fatal crashes | | Number | Percent of total | | Number | Percent of total | |
| Total | 57,586 | 12,233 | 21% | 44,440 | 9,694 | 22% | +1 |
| Drivers by age group (years) | | | | | | | |
| 16–20 | 7,992 | 1,420 | 18% | 4,487 | 827 | 18% | 0 |
| 21–24 | 6,037 | 1,979 | 33% | 4,585 | 1,545 | 34% | +1 |
| 25–34 | 11,584 | 3,213 | 28% | 8,540 | 2,566 | 30% | +2 |
| 35–44 | 11,261 | 2,839 | 25% | 7,313 | 1,845 | 25% | 0 |
| 45–54 | 8,346 | 1,601 | 19% | 7,490 | 1,592 | 21% | +2 |
| 55–64 | 4,714 | 543 | 12% | 5,554 | 769 | 14% | +2 |
| 65–74 | 3,156 | 224 | 7% | 2,894 | 230 | 8% | +1 |
| 75+ | 3,290 | 132 | 4% | 2,666 | 130 | 5% | +1 |
| Drivers by gender | | | | | | | |
| Male | 41,901 | 10,120 | 24% | 31,965 | 7,721 | 24% | 0 |
| Female | 14,919 | 1,903 | 13% | 11,811 | 1,810 | 15% | +2 |
| Drivers by vehicle type | | | | | | | |
| Passenger cars | 27,444 | 6,235 | 23% | 17,623 | 4,082 | 23% | 0 |
| Light trucks | 20,704 | 4,706 | 23% | 17,322 | 3,895 | 22% | −1 |
| Large trucks | 4,779 | 56 | 1% | 3,446 | 61 | 2% | +1 |
| Motorcycles | 3,261 | 951 | 29% | 4,629 | 1,285 | 28% | −1 |

Numbers shown for groups of drivers do not add to the total number of drivers due to unknown/not reported or other data not included.

SOURCE: "Table 3. Drivers with a BAC of .08 or Higher Involved in Fatal Crashes, by Age, Gender, and Vehicle Type, 2001 and 2010," in *Traffic Safety Facts 2010 Data: Alcohol-Impaired Driving*, U.S. Department of Transportation, National Highway Traffic Safety Administration, National Center for Statistics and Analysis, April 2012, http://www-nrd.nhtsa.dot.gov/Pubs/811606.pdf (accessed February 11, 2013)

## TABLE 2.13

Pedestrians killed in motor vehicle crashes, by age group and percentage blood alcohol concentration (BAC), 2001 and 2010

| Age (years) | 2001 | | | | | 2010 | | | | |
|---|---|---|---|---|---|---|---|---|---|---|
| | Number of fatalities | % with BAC = 0.00 | % with BAC = 0.01 − 0.07 | % with BAC = 0.08+ | % with BAC = 0.01+ | Number of fatalities | % with BAC = 0.00 | % with BAC = 0.01 − 0.07 | % with BAC = 0.08+ | % with BAC = 0.01+ |
| 16–20 | 294 | 67 | 4 | 29 | 33 | 282 | 73 | 4 | 23 | 27 |
| 21–24 | 275 | 47 | 8 | 45 | 53 | 277 | 46 | 7 | 48 | 54 |
| 25–34 | 564 | 44 | 5 | 51 | 56 | 599 | 44 | 7 | 49 | 56 |
| 35–44 | 912 | 42 | 6 | 52 | 58 | 573 | 49 | 5 | 46 | 51 |
| 45–54 | 800 | 51 | 6 | 43 | 49 | 798 | 49 | 5 | 46 | 51 |
| 55–64 | 465 | 64 | 5 | 31 | 36 | 615 | 63 | 4 | 33 | 37 |
| 65–74 | 402 | 83 | 4 | 14 | 17 | 361 | 82 | 3 | 14 | 18 |
| 75–84 | 479 | 91 | 3 | 6 | 9 | 326 | 93 | 2 | 5 | 7 |
| 85+ | 177 | 92 | 3 | 5 | 8 | 139 | 95 | 2 | 3 | 5 |
| Total* | 4,368 | 59 | 5 | 36 | 41 | 3,970 | 60 | 5 | 35 | 40 |

*Excludes pedestrians under 16 years old and pedestrians of unknown age.

SOURCE: "Table 6. Alcohol Involvement for Pedestrians Killed in Fatal Crashes by Age, 2001 and 2010," in *Traffic Safety Facts 2010 Data: Pedestrians*, U.S. Department of Transportation, National Highway Traffic Safety Administration, National Center for Statistics and Analysis, August 2012, http://www-nrd.nhtsa.dot.gov/Pubs/811625.pdf (accessed February 11, 2013)

**TABLE 2.14**

**Arrests for alcohol-related offenses and driving under the influence, 1970–2011**

[In thousands]

| | Alcohol-related offenses* | Driving under the influence |
|---|---|---|
| 1970 | 2,849 | 424 |
| 1971 | 2,914 | 490 |
| 1972 | 2,835 | 604 |
| 1973 | 2,539 | 654 |
| 1974 | 2,297 | 617 |
| 1975 | 3,044 | 909 |
| 1976 | 2,790 | 838 |
| 1977 | 3,303 | 1,104 |
| 1978 | 3,406 | 1,205 |
| 1979 | 3,455 | 1,232 |
| 1980 | 3,535 | 1,304 |
| 1981 | 3,745 | 1,422 |
| 1982 | 3,640 | 1,405 |
| 1983 | 3,729 | 1,613 |
| 1984 | 3,153 | 1,347 |
| 1985 | 3,418 | 1,503 |
| 1986 | 3,325 | 1,459 |
| 1987 | 3,248 | 1,410 |
| 1988 | 2,995 | 1,294 |
| 1989 | 3,180 | 1,333 |
| 1990 | 3,270 | 1,391 |
| 1991 | 3,000 | 1,289 |
| 1992 | 3,061 | 1,320 |
| 1993 | 2,886 | 1,229 |
| 1994 | 2,698 | 1,080 |
| 1995 | 2,578 | 1,033 |
| 1996 | 2,677 | 1,014 |
| 1997 | 2,510 | 986 |
| 1998 | 2,451 | 969 |
| 1999 | 2,238 | 931 |
| 2000 | 2,218 | 916 |
| 2001 | 2,224 | 947 |
| 2002 | 2,401 | 1,020 |
| 2003 | 2,301 | 1,006 |
| 2004 | 2,373 | 1,014 |
| 2005 | 2,374 | 997 |
| 2006 | 2,463 | 1,039 |
| 2007 | 2,552 | 1,056 |
| 2008 | 2,620 | 1,110 |
| 2009 | 2,576 | 1,112 |
| 2010 | 2,439 | 1,088 |
| 2011 | 2,201 | 930 |

Note: These data were compiled by the Federal Bureau of Investigation through the Uniform Crime Reporting (UCR) Program. On a monthly basis, law enforcement agencies report the number of offenses that become known to them in the following crime categories: murder and nonnegligent manslaughter, forcible rape, robbery, aggravated assault, burglary, larceny-theft, motor vehicle theft, and arson. Arrest statistics are compiled as part of this monthly data collection effort. Participating law enforcement agencies are instructed to count one arrest each time a person is taken into custody, notified, or cited for criminal infractions other than traffic violations. Annual arrest figures do not measure the number of individuals taken into custody because one person may be arrested several times during the year for the same type of offense or for different offenses. A juvenile is counted as a person arrested when he/she commits an act that would be a criminal offense if committed by an adult.
The number of agencies reporting and the populations represented vary from year to year. Due to National Incident-Based Reporting System conversion efforts beginning in 1991 as well as other reporting problems, complete arrest data were not available for a small number of jurisdictions for certain years.
This table presents data from all law enforcement agencies submitting complete reports for 12 months.
*Alcohol-related offenses include driving under the influence, liquor law violations, drunkenness, disorderly conduct, and vagrancy.

SOURCE: "Table 4.27.2011. Arrests for Alcohol-Related Offenses and Driving under the Influence, 1970–2011," in *Sourcebook of Criminal Justice Statistics Online*, U.S. Department of Justice, Bureau of Justice Statistics, University at Albany School of Criminal Justice, Hindelang Criminal Justice Research Center, 2013, http://www.albany.edu/sourcebook/tost_4.html (accessed February 11, 2013)

## ALCOHOL-RELATED OFFENSES

Table 2.14 shows arrest trends for alcohol-related offenses and driving under the influence between 1970 and 2011. Arrests were the highest for alcohol-related offenses from 1975 to 1992, with 1981 being the peak year. Arrests for driving under the influence were the highest from 1977 to 1996, with 1983 being the peak year. In 2011 there were 2.2 million alcohol-related arrests; 930,000 of those arrests were for driving under the influence.

Doris J. James of the Bureau of Justice Statistics (BJS) mentions in *Profile of Jail Inmates, 2002* (July 2004, http://bjs.ojp.usdoj.gov/content/pub/pdf/pji02.pdf) that in 2002, 33.4% of convicted jail inmates reported that they had been under the influence of alcohol alone (not in combination with any other drug) when they committed their offenses. This figure had decreased since 1996. A higher percentage of jail inmates used alcohol when committing a violent offense than did those committing other types of crimes, such as property or drug offenses. As of April 2013, these data were the most recent from the BJS.

## CHAPTER 3

# TOBACCO

During the mid-20th century smoking in the United States was often associated with adventure, relaxation, and romance; movie stars oozed glamour on-screen while smoking, and movie tough guys were never more masculine than when lighting up. Songs such as "Smoke Gets in Your Eyes" topped the list of most popular songs. Smoking became a rite of passage for young males and a sign of increasing independence for young females.

Since the 1990s, however, there has been an increase in opposition to tobacco use. Health authorities warn of the dangers of smoking and chewing tobacco, and nonsmokers object to secondhand smoke—because of both the smell and the health dangers of breathing smoke from other people's cigarettes. In the 21st century a smoker is more likely to ask for permission before lighting up, and the answer is often "no." Because of health concerns, smoking has been banned on airplanes, in hospitals, and in many workplaces, restaurants, and bars. In 2012, 80% of respondents to a Gallup Organization poll believed that cigarette smoking was very harmful to adults who smoke, down from a high of 84% in 2006. (See Figure 3.1.)

This increased awareness of the dangers of cigarettes has coincided with a steady decline in the percentage of Americans who smoke. Lydia Saad of the Gallup Organization reports in *One in Five U.S. Adults Smoke, Tied for All-Time Low* (August 22, 2012, http://www.gallup.com/poll/156833/one-five-adults-smoke-tied-time-low.aspx) that in 2001–05 a quarter (25%) of American adults smoked cigarettes; by 2011–12 this proportion had dropped to just over one-fifth (21%) of the population. (See Table 3.1.) Among age demographics, the largest percentage drop occurred among adults aged 18 to 29 years. In 2001–05 more than one-third (34%) of 18- to 29-year-olds smoked cigarettes; by 2011–12 this figure had dropped to 25%, a decline of nine percentage points. Still, as Table 3.1 shows, in 2012 adults between the ages of 18 and 29 were the most likely to smoke cigarettes among all demographic age groups.

## PHYSICAL PROPERTIES OF NICOTINE

Tobacco is a plant native to the Western Hemisphere. It contains nicotine, a drug that is classified as a stimulant, although it has some depressive effects as well. Nicotine is a poisonous alkaloid that is the major psychoactive (mood-altering) ingredient in tobacco. Alkaloids are carbon- and nitrogen-containing compounds that are found in some families of plants. They have both poisonous and medicinal properties.

Nicotine's effects on the body are complex. The drug affects the brain and central nervous system as well as the hypothalamus and pituitary glands of the endocrine (hormone) system. Nicotine easily crosses the blood-brain barrier—a series of capillaries and cells that control the flow of substances from the blood to the brain. It accumulates in the brain faster than caffeine or heroin but slower than Valium, a sedative medicine that is used to treat anxiety. In the brain nicotine imitates the actions of the hormone epinephrine (adrenaline) and the neurotransmitter acetylcholine, both of which heighten awareness. Nicotine also triggers the release of dopamine, which enhances feelings of pleasure, and endorphins, which have a calming effect.

As noted earlier, nicotine acts as both a stimulant and a depressant. By stimulating certain nerve cells in the spinal cord, nicotine relaxes the nerves and slows some reactions, such as the knee-jerk reflex. Small amounts of nicotine stimulate some nerve cells, but these cells are depressed by large amounts of nicotine. In addition, nicotine stimulates the brain cortex (the outer layer of the brain) and affects the functions of the heart and lungs.

## TRENDS IN TOBACCO USE
### Cigarettes

CONSUMPTION DATA. According to the Centers for Disease Control and Prevention (CDC), in "The National Tobacco Control Program" (*Chronic Disease Notes and*

## FIGURE 3.1

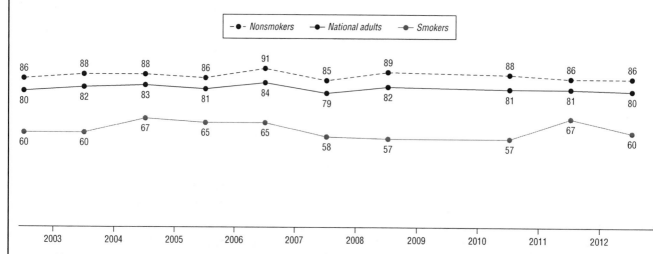

**Public opinion on the harmfulness of smoking, 2003–12**

IN GENERAL, HOW HARMFUL DO YOU FEEL SMOKING IS TO ADULTS WHO SMOKE?

% very harmful

- ● - Nonsmokers      — ● — National adults      — ● — Smokers

## TABLE 3.1

**Percentage of adults who smoke, by age group, 2001–05, 2006–10, and 2011–12**

| | 2001–2005 | 2006–2010 | 2011–2012 | Change, 2011–2012 vs. 2001–2005 |
|---|---|---|---|---|
| | % | % | % | pct. pts. |
| National adults | 25 | 22 | 21 | −4 |
| 18 to 29 years | 34 | 28 | 25 | −9 |
| 30 to 49 years | 28 | 25 | 23 | −5 |
| 50 to 64 years | 24 | 23 | 22 | −2 |
| 65 and older | 11 | 11 | 12 | +1 |

*Reports*, vol. 14, no. 3, Fall 2001), the consumption of cigarettes, the most widely used tobacco product, has decreased over the past generation among adults. After increasing rather consistently for 60 years, the per capita (per person) consumption of cigarettes peaked during the 1960s at well over 4,000 cigarettes per year. The steady decline in smoking came shortly after 1964, when the Advisory Committee to the Surgeon General concluded in *Smoking and Health: Report of the Advisory Committee to the Surgeon General of the Public Health Service* (1964, http://profiles.nlm.nih.gov/NN/B/B/M/Q/_/nnbbmq.pdf) that cigarette smoking is a cause of lung and laryngeal cancer in men, a probable cause of lung cancer in women, and the most important cause of chronic bronchitis in both genders.

By 2006 the annual per capita consumption of cigarettes for those aged 18 years and older was 1,691. These data are taken from *Tobacco Outlook* (September 26, 2006, http://usda.mannlib.cornell.edu/usda/ers/TBS//2000s/2006/TBS-09-26-2006.pdf) by Tom Capehart of the Economic Research Service (ERS). This was the final report provided by the ERS on this topic because the ERS discontinued this publication along with another tobacco-related publication, the *Tobacco Briefing Room*, after a tobacco buyout was formalized by the U.S. Department of Agriculture (USDA) in February 2005. The tobacco buyout is a part of the Fair and Equitable Tobacco Reform Act of 2004 and is formally known as the Tobacco Transition Payment Program. (See Chapter 7.) Several USDA agencies discontinued their tobacco programs after the buyout. As of April 2013, none of the programs had been reinstituted nor were any governmental agencies collecting these data.

Each year the Substance Abuse and Mental Health Services Administration surveys U.S. households on drug use for the National Survey on Drug Use and Health (NSDUH). According to the NSDUH, in *Results from the 2011 National Survey on Drug Use and Health: Detailed Tables* (September 2012, http://www.samhsa.gov/), 62.8% of the U.S. population in 2011 had smoked cigarettes at some point during their lifetime and 22.1% were current smokers (meaning they had smoked within the month before the survey). (See Table 3.2.)

In 2011 men (24.3%) were more likely than women (19.9%) to be current smokers. (See Table 3.2.) Additionally, whites (23.5%) were more likely to be current smokers than African-Americans (21.5%), Hispanics (18.5%), or Asian-Americans (11.7%). Those aged 18 to 25 years had the highest rate of current smoking, at 33.5%, compared with 7.8% for those aged 12 to 17 years and 21.9% for those aged 26 years and older. As Figure 3.2 shows, in 2011 smoking rates were relatively low among minors

## TABLE 3.2

### Percentage of lifetime, past-year, and past-month cigarette users, by age group, gender, and ethnicity, 2010 and 2011

| Demographic characteristic | Lifetime (2010) | Lifetime (2011) | Past year (2010) | Past year (2011) | Past month (2010) | Past month (2011) |
|---|---|---|---|---|---|---|
| Total | 64.2[b] | 62.8 | 27.0[a] | 26.1 | 23.0[a] | 22.1 |
| **Age** | | | | | | |
| 12–17 | 20.5[a] | 19.1 | 14.2[a] | 13.2 | 8.4 | 7.8 |
| 18–25 | 62.3 | 61.0 | 43.2 | 42.3 | 34.3 | 33.5 |
| 26 or older | 70.0[a] | 68.6 | 25.8 | 24.9 | 22.8 | 21.9 |
| **Gender** | | | | | | |
| Male | 69.2[a] | 67.9 | 30.0 | 28.8 | 25.4 | 24.3 |
| Female | 59.6[a] | 58.0 | 24.3 | 23.5 | 20.7 | 19.9 |
| **Hispanic origin and race** | | | | | | |
| Not Hispanic or Latino | 66.2[a] | 65.1 | 27.3 | 26.6 | 23.5 | 22.7 |
| White | 70.2 | 69.4 | 28.3 | 27.4 | 24.4 | 23.5 |
| Black or African American | 53.8[a] | 50.9 | 25.7 | 25.2 | 22.6 | 21.5 |
| American Indian or Alaska Native | 63.4 | 69.7 | 35.7 | 43.1 | 31.1 | 36.5 |
| Native Hawaiian or other Pacific Islander | * | * | * | 21.0 | * | 18.4 |
| Asian | 39.7 | 40.2 | 14.4 | 14.4 | 10.9 | 11.7 |
| Two or more races | 68.0 | 67.7 | 33.5 | 34.5 | 27.6 | 29.4 |
| Hispanic or Latino | 52.9[a] | 50.2 | 25.4[a] | 23.2 | 20.0 | 18.5 |

*Low precision; no estimate reported.
Note: Some 2010 estimates may differ from previously published estimates due to updates.
[a]Difference between estimate and 2011 estimate is statistically significant at the 0.05 level.
[b]Difference between estimate and 2011 estimate is statistically significant at the 0.01 level.

SOURCE: "Table 2.22B. Cigarette Use in Lifetime, Past Year, and Past Month among Persons Aged 12 or Older, by Demographic Characteristics: Percentages, 2010 and 2011," in *Results from the 2011 National Survey on Drug Use and Health: Detailed Tables*, U.S. Department of Health and Human Services, Substance Abuse and Mental Health Services Administration, September 2012, http://www.samhsa.gov/data/NSDUH/2011SummNatFindDetTables/NSDUH-DetTabsPDFWHTML2011/2k11DetailedTabs/Web/PDFW/NSDUH-DetTabsSect2peTabs22to26-2011.pdf (accessed February 12, 2013)

## FIGURE 3.2

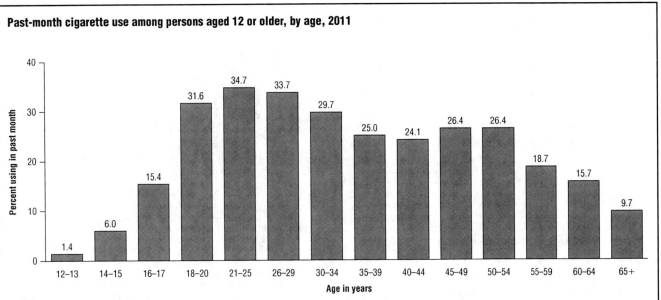

Past-month cigarette use among persons aged 12 or older, by age, 2011

SOURCE: "Figure 4.3. Past Month Cigarette Use among Persons Aged 12 or Older, by Age, 2011," in *Results from the 2011 National Survey on Drug Use and Health: Summary of National Findings*, U.S. Department of Health and Human Services, Substance Abuse and Mental Health Services Administration, September 2012, http://www.samhsa.gov/data/NSDUH/2k11Results/NSDUHresults2011.pdf (accessed February 12, 2013)

FIGURE 3.3

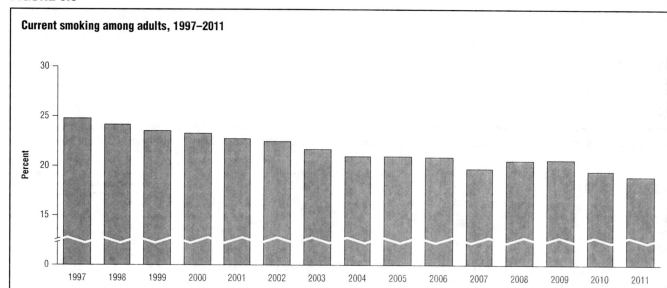

**Current smoking among adults, 1997–2011**

Notes: Data are based on household interviews of a sample of the civilian noninstitutionalized population. Current smokers were defined as those who had smoked more than 100 cigarettes in their lifetime and now smoke every day or some days. The analyses excluded persons with unknown smoking status (about 2% of respondents each year).

SOURCE: P. M. Barnes et al., "Figure 8.1. Prevalence of Current Smoking among Adults Aged 18 Years and over: United States, 1997–2011," in *Early Release of Selected Estimates Based on Data from the 2011 National Health Interview Survey*, U.S. Department of Health and Human Services, Centers for Disease Control and Prevention, National Center for Health Statistics, June 2012, http://www.cdc.gov/nchs/data/nhis/earlyrelease/earlyrelease201206 .pdf (accessed February 12, 2013)

aged 12 to 13 years (1.4%); however, these rates increased significantly among those aged 14 to 15 years (6%) and 16 to 17 years (15.4%). Overall, rates of current cigarette smoking declined from 23% in 2010 to 22.1% in 2011. (See Table 3.2.)

The National Health Interview Survey (NHIS), which is conducted annually by the National Center for Health Statistics, reports findings similar to those of the NSDUH. In *Early Release of Selected Estimates Based on Data from the 2011 National Health Interview Survey* (June 19, 2012, http://www.cdc.gov/nchs/data/ nhis/earlyrelease/earlyrelease201206.pdf), the NHIS indicates that 18.9% of adults in the United States were current smokers in 2011, down from 24.7% in 1997. (See Figure 3.3.) Like the NSDUH, the NHIS finds that men are more likely than women to smoke. Of adult men, 21.5% were current smokers in 2011. Of adult women, 16.5% were current smokers. (See Figure 3.4.) Women (64.6%) were more likely than men (53.7%) to have never smoked.

Using different age groups than the NSDUH, the NHIS survey finds that younger people smoked at a slightly lower rate than older people in 2011. Figure 3.5 shows that those aged 45 to 64 years were slightly more likely to smoke than those aged 18 to 44 years. In contrast, the rate of smoking in the 65-and-older age group was dramatically lower than in either of the two younger groups. Men in all age categories were

FIGURE 3.4

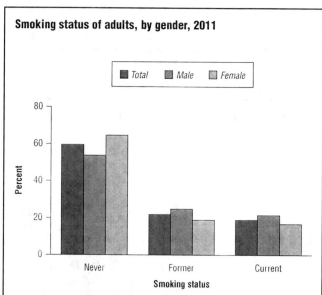

**Smoking status of adults, by gender, 2011**

Notes: Data are based on household interviews of a sample of the civilian noninstitutionalized population. Current smokers were defined as those who had smoked more than 100 cigarettes in their lifetime and now smoke every day or some days. The analyses excluded 0.3% of persons with unknown smoking status.

SOURCE: P. M. Barnes et al., "Figure 8.2. Percent Distribution of Smoking Status among Adults Aged 18 and over, by Sex: United States, 2011," in *Early Release of Selected Estimates Based on Data from the 2011 National Health Interview Survey*, U.S. Department of Health and Human Services, Centers for Disease Control and Prevention, National Center for Health Statistics, June 2012, http://www.cdc.gov/nchs/data/ nhis/earlyrelease/earlyrelease201206.pdf (accessed February 12, 2013)

**Current adult smokers, by age group and gender, 2011**

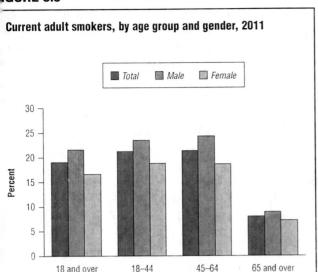

Notes: Data are based on household interviews of a sample of the civilian noninstitutionalized population. Current smokers were defined as those who had smoked more than 100 cigarettes in their lifetime and now smoke every day or some days. The analyses excluded 0.3% of persons with unknown smoking status.

SOURCE: P. M. Barnes et al., "Figure 8.3. Prevalence of Current Smoking among Adults Aged 18 and over, by Age Group and Sex: United States, 2011," in *Early Release of Selected Estimates Based on Data from the 2011 National Health Interview Survey*, U.S. Department of Health and Human Services, Centers for Disease Control and Prevention, National Center for Health Statistics, June 2012, http://www.cdc.gov/nchs/data/nhis/earlyrelease/earlyrelease201206.pdf (accessed February 12, 2013)

**FIGURE 3.6**

**Current adult smokers, by ethnicity, 2011**

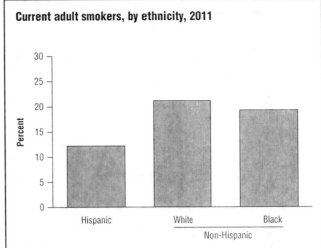

Notes: Data are based on household interviews of a sample of the civilian noninstitutionalized population. Current smokers were defined as those who had smoked more than 100 cigarettes in their lifetime and now smoke every day or some days. The analyses excluded 0.3% of persons with unknown smoking status. Estimates are age-sex-adjusted using the projected 2000 U.S. population as the standard population and using five age groups: 18–24, 25–34, 35–44, 45–64, and 65 and over.

SOURCE: P. M. Barnes et al., "Figure 8.4. Age-Sex-Adjusted Prevalence of Current Smoking among Adults Aged 18 and over, by Race/Ethnicity: United States, 2011," in *Early Release of Selected Estimates Based on Data from the 2011 National Health Interview Survey*, U.S. Department of Health and Human Services, Centers for Disease Control and Prevention, National Center for Health Statistics, June 2012, http://www.cdc.gov/nchs/data/nhis/earlyrelease/earlyrelease 201206.pdf (accessed February 12, 2013)

more likely than women in the same age group to smoke.

Furthermore, the NHIS finds that the prevalence of current smoking among various races and ethnicities was highest for non-Hispanic whites (21.1%) in 2011. (See Figure 3.6.) Non-Hispanic African-Americans (19.2%) were less likely to smoke than non-Hispanic whites, whereas Hispanics (12.1%) were the least likely to smoke among the three groups.

In 2011 the Gallup Organization looked at smoking by state to determine which states had the highest and which states had lowest percentage of smokers. The results are shown in Table 3.3. The states with the highest percentage of smokers were clustered in the central and southeastern portion of the United States. The state with the highest percentage of smokers was Kentucky, where 29% of residents smoked. In six additional states—Arkansas, Louisiana, Mississippi, Missouri, Ohio, and Oklahoma—more than a quarter (26%) of residents smoked in 2011. The states with the lowest percentage of smokers were scattered around the United States. The state with the lowest percentage of smokers was Utah (11%), followed by California (15%), Hawaii (16%), Massachusetts (17%), Minnesota (17%), New Hampshire (17%), and North Dakota (17%).

## Cigars, Pipes, and Other Forms of Tobacco

The NSDUH reports in *Results from the 2011 National Survey on Drug Use and Health: Summary of National Findings* (September 2012, http://www.samhsa.gov/data/NSDUH/2k11Results/NSDUHresults2011.pdf) that 3.2% of those aged 12 years and older were current users of smokeless tobacco (chewing tobacco and/or snuff) and 5% were current users of cigars in 2011. Only 0.8% smoked pipes. These percentages remained relatively constant between 2002 and 2011. However, the overall use of tobacco products has declined modestly since 2002, from 30.4% of people aged 12 years and older using tobacco products in that year to 26.5% in 2011. The current use of cigarettes by people aged 12 years and older has declined as well, from 26% in 2002 to 22.1% in 2011. Among minors aged 12 to 17 years, tobacco use declined by one-third during the same period, from 15.2% in 2002 to 10% in 2011. (See Figure 3.7.)

## ADDICTIVE NATURE OF NICOTINE

Is tobacco addictive? In *The Health Consequences of Smoking—Nicotine Addiction: A Report of the Surgeon General* (1988, http://profiles.nlm.nih.gov/NN/B/B/Z/D/_/nnbbzd.pdf), researchers first examined this question. They determined that the pharmacological (chemical and physical) effects and behavioral processes that contribute

**TABLE 3.3**

**States with highest and lowest percentages of smokers, 2011**

| Percentage who smoke is 25% or more | % smoke |
|---|---|
| Kentucky | 29 |
| Missouri | 26 |
| Oklahoma | 26 |
| Louisiana | 26 |
| Mississippi | 26 |
| Arkansas | 26 |
| Ohio | 26 |
| Tennessee | 25 |
| Alabama | 25 |
| West Virginia | 25 |
| Indiana | 25 |

| Percentage who smoke is lower than 20% | % smoke |
|---|---|
| Utah | 11 |
| California | 15 |
| Hawaii | 16 |
| North Dakota | 17 |
| Massachusetts | 17 |
| Minnesota | 17 |
| New Hampshire | 17 |
| Idaho | 18 |
| New Jersey | 18 |
| Oregon | 18 |
| Vermont | 18 |
| Connecticut | 18 |
| Washington | 19 |
| Maryland | 19 |
| Kansas | 19 |
| District of Columbia | 19 |
| Virginia | 19 |
| New York | 19 |

SOURCE: Elizabeth Mendes, "States with the Highest Percentage of Smokers, States with the Lowest Percentage of Smokers," in *Smoking Rates Remain Highest in Kentucky, Lowest in Utah*, The Gallup Organization, November 17, 2011, http://www.gallup.com/poll/150779/smoking-rates-remain-highest-kentucky-lowest-utah.aspx (accessed February 12, 2013). Copyright © 2011 Gallup, Inc. All rights reserved. The content is used with permission; however, Gallup retains all rights of republication.

to tobacco addiction are similar to those that contribut in the addiction to drugs such as heroin and cocaine Many researchers consider nicotine to be as potentiall addictive as cocaine and heroin and note that it can creat dependence quickly in some users. After more than 2: years since the surgeon general's report—with study afte study confirming the addictive nature of nicotine while also zeroing in on characteristics that increase the like lihood for addiction, such as genetics, ethnicity, and eve tobacco additives such as menthol—the National Institut on Drug Abuse states conclusively in "Tobacco Addic tion (Nicotine)" (July 2012, http://www.drugabuse.gov drugs-abuse/tobacco-addiction-nicotine) that nicotine i not only "highly addictive" but also "one of the mos heavily used addictive drugs" in the United States According to Alyssa Brown of the Gallup Organization in *In U.S., Smokers Light Up Less Than Ever* (Septembe 13, 2012, http://www.gallup.com/poll/157466/smokers light-less-ever.aspx), in 2012 more than two-third: (68%) of all smokers considered themselves addicted t cigarettes. (See Figure 3.8.)

Cigarette smoking results in the rapid distribution o nicotine throughout the body, reaching the brain withi 10 seconds of inhalation. However, the intense effects o nicotine disappear in a few minutes, causing smokers to continue smoking frequently throughout the day to main tain its pleasurable effects and to prevent withdrawal Tolerance develops after repeated exposure to nicotine and higher doses are required to produce the same initial stimulation. Because nicotine is metabolized (chemically processed) fairly quickly, disappearing from the body in a

**FIGURE 3.7**

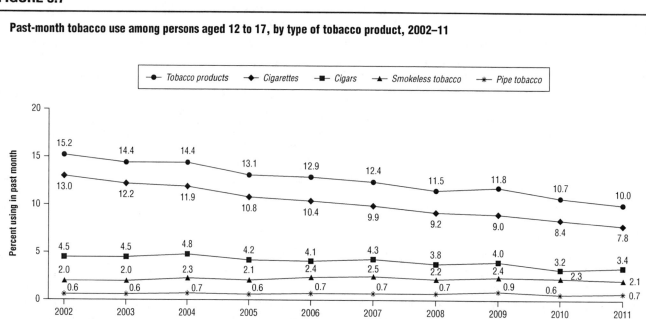

Past-month tobacco use among persons aged 12 to 17, by type of tobacco product, 2002–11

SOURCE: "Figure 4.2. Past Month Tobacco Use among Youths Aged 12 to 17: 2002–2011," in *Results from the 2011 National Survey on Drug Use and Health: Summary of National Findings*, U.S. Department of Health and Human Services, Substance Abuse and Mental Health Services Administration, September 2012, http://www.samhsa.gov/data/NSDUH/2k11Results/NSDUHresults2011.pdf (accessed February 12, 2013)

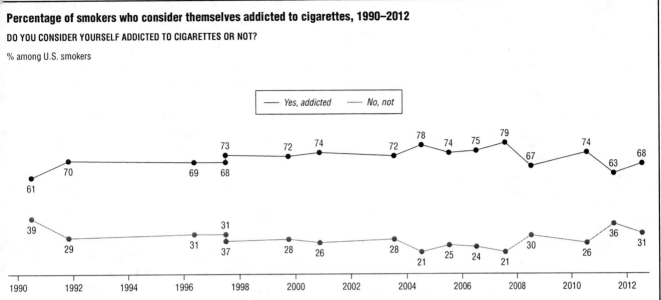

**Percentage of smokers who consider themselves addicted to cigarettes, 1990–2012**

DO YOU CONSIDER YOURSELF ADDICTED TO CIGARETTES OR NOT?

% among U.S. smokers

— Yes, addicted    — No, not

SOURCE: Alyssa Brown, "Do You Consider Yourself Addicted to Cigarettes or Not?" in *In U.S., Smokers Light up Less Than Ever*, The Gallup Organization, September 13, 2012, http://www.gallup.com/poll/157466/smokers-light-less-ever.aspx (accessed February 16, 2013). Copyright © 2012 Gallup, Inc. All rights reserved. The content is used with permission; however, Gallup retains all rights of republication.

ew hours, some tolerance is lost overnight. Smokers ˈften report that the first cigarette of the day is the most ˌatisfying. The more cigarettes smoked during the day, ˌhe more tolerance develops, and the less effect subseˌquent cigarettes have.

### ˈs There a Genetic Basis for Nicotine Addiction?

Smoking is influenced by both environment and ˌgenetics, as are all addictions. (See Chapter 1.) The ˈesults of many scientific studies, such as M. K. Ho and Rachel F. Tyndale's "Overview of the Pharmacogenomˌics of Cigarette Smoking" (*Pharmacogenomics Journal*, ˌvol. 7, no. 2, April 2007), show that between 11% and ˈ78% of the initiation of smoking and between 28% and ˈ84% of the maintenance of dependent smoking behavior ˈare genetically influenced. In addition, 28% to 84% of the ˈnumber of cigarettes an individual smokes is genetically ˈinfluenced as is 31% to 75% of nicotine dependence. The ˈranges in these data are due to the variations in the results ˈof numerous studies. Ho and Tyndale conclude that ˈ"taken together, these studies suggest a substantial ˈgenetic contribution to most aspects of smoking."

### Nicotine May Not Be the Only Substance in Cigarettes Linked to Addiction

Research results suggest that nicotine may not be the ˈonly ingredient in tobacco involved with addiction. Varˈious compounds called monoamine oxidase (MAO) inhibitors are found in high concentrations in cigarette ˈsmoke. MAO is an enzyme that is responsible for breakˈing down the brain chemical dopamine. The decrease in MAO results in higher dopamine levels and may be another reason that smokers continue to smoke—to sustain the high dopamine levels that result in pleasurable effects and the desire for repeated cigarette use.

One issue that complicates any efforts by a longtime smoker to quit is nicotine withdrawal, which is often referred to as craving. This urge for nicotine is not well understood by researchers. Withdrawal may begin within a few hours after the last cigarette. According to the National Institute on Drug Abuse, high levels of craving may persist six months or longer. Besides craving, withdrawal can include irritability, attention deficits, interruption of thought processes, sleep disturbances, and increased appetite.

Some researchers also point out the behavioral aspects that are involved in smoking. The purchasing, handling, and lighting of cigarettes may be just as pleasing psychologically to the user as the chemical properties of the tobacco itself.

## HEALTH CONSEQUENCES OF TOBACCO USE
### Respiratory System Effects

Cigarette smoke contains almost 4,000 different chemical compounds, many of which are toxic, mutagenic (capable of increasing the frequency of mutation, or change, in the genetic material), and carcinogenic (cancer causing). At least 43 carcinogens have been identified in tobacco smoke. Besides nicotine, the most damaging substances are tar and carbon monoxide (CO). Smoke also contains hydrogen cyanide and other chemicals that can damage the respiratory system. These substances and nicotine are absorbed into the body through the linings of the mouth, nose, throat, and lungs. About 10 seconds later they are delivered by the bloodstream to the brain.

Tar, which adds to the flavor of cigarettes, is released by the burning of tobacco. As it is inhaled, it enters the alveoli (air cells) of the lungs. There, the tar hampers the action of cilia (small, hairlike extensions of cells that clean foreign substances from the lungs), allowing the substances in cigarette smoke to accumulate.

CO affects the blood's ability to distribute oxygen throughout the body. CO is chemically similar to carbon dioxide ($CO_2$), which bonds with the hemoglobin in blood so that the $CO_2$ can be carried to the lungs for elimination. Hemoglobin has two primary functions: to carry oxygen to all parts of the body and to remove excess $CO_2$ from the body's tissues. CO bonds to hemoglobin more tightly than $CO_2$ and leaves the body more slowly, which allows CO to build up in the hemoglobin, in turn reducing the amount of oxygen the blood can carry. The lack of adequate oxygen is damaging to most of the body's organs, including the heart and brain.

## Diseases and Conditions Linked to Tobacco Use

The results of medical research show an association between smoking and cancer, as well as heart and circulatory disease, fetal growth retardation, and low birth weight babies. The 1983 *Health Consequences of Smoking—Cardiovascular Disease: Report of the Surgeon General* (http://profiles.nlm.nih.gov/NN/B/B/T/D/_/nnbbtd.pdf) linked cigarette smoking to cerebrovascular disease (strokes) and associated it with cancer of the uterine cervix. Two 1992 studies showed that people who smoke double their risk of forming cataracts, the leading cause of blindness. Several other studies linked smoking to unsuccessful pregnancies, increased infant mortality, and peptic ulcer disease. In 2004 the U.S. surgeon general Richard Carmona (1949–) released *The Health Consequences of Smoking: A Report of the Surgeon General* (http://www.cdc.gov/tobacco/data_statistics/sgr/2004/complete_report/index.htm), which revealed for the first time that cigarette smoking causes diseases in nearly every organ of the body. In December 2010 the U.S. surgeon general Regina Benjamin (1956–) released *How Tobacco Smoke Causes Disease: The Biology and Behavioral Basis for Smoking-Attributable Disease: A Report of the Surgeon General* (http://www.surgeongeneral.gov/library/reports/tobaccosmoke/full_report.pdf). This report pictorially shows the long list of health consequences and diseases that are caused by smoking. (See Figure 3.9.)

The National Cancer Institute notes in "Cigar Smoking and Cancer" (October 27, 2010, http://www.cancer.gov/cancertopics/factsheet/Tobacco/cigars) that cigar smoking is associated with cancers of the lip, tongue, mouth, throat, larynx (voice box), lungs, esophagus (food

tube), and possibly the pancreas. Those who smoke cigar daily and inhale the smoke have an increased risk for developing heart and lung disease.

Smokeless tobacco, which includes chewing tobacco and snuff, also creates health hazards for its users. The National Cancer Institute explains that smokeless tobacco is associated with cancers of the lip, gum, mouth, esophagus, and pancreas. It can also cause heart disease, gum disease, and precancerous white patches in the mouth. It is not a safer alternative to smoking. In addition, smokeless tobacco use can lead to nicotine addiction and may, therefore, lead to smoking.

## Premature Aging

Smoking cigarettes contributes to premature aging in a variety of ways. The results of research conducted over nearly four decades, such as Akimichi Morita et al.'s "Molecular Basis of Tobacco Smoke-Induced Premature Skin Aging" (*Journal of Investigative Dermatology Symposium Proceedings*, vol. 14, no. 1, August 2009), show that smoking enhances facial aging and skin wrinkling. The researchers also note that cigarette smoking results in "smoker's face," which consists of a gray pallor and deep wrinkles. Cigarette smoking is also associated with the development of gray hair, cataracts, diabetes, weak bones, and atherosclerosis (a hardening of the walls of the arteries caused by the buildup of fatty deposits on the inner walls of the arteries that interferes with blood flow).

Why do these changes occur? Lowell Dale of the Mayo Clinic explains in "Is It True That Smoking Causes Wrinkles?" (October 21, 2011, http://www.mayoclinic.com/health/smoking/AN00644) that nicotine tightens blood vessels, which decreases blood flow to the body's organs, depriving them of the proper amount of oxygen and nutrients that they need for good health. The skin, which is the body's largest organ, also receives less oxygen and nutrients than it needs, especially vitamin A. This vitamin is critical to regenerating new skin cells, which are essential to healthy, youthful-looking skin. In addition, the lack of proper skin nutrition damages structural proteins within the skin, resulting in skin sagging and wrinkling. Dale states a startling fact: "Smoking can speed up the normal aging process of your skin, contributing to wrinkles. These skin changes may occur after only 10 years of smoking."

In "Cigarette Smoke Induces Cellular Senescence via Werner's Syndrome Protein Down-Regulation" (*American Journal of Respiratory and Critical Care Medicine*, vol. 179, no. 4, February 15, 2009), Toru Nyunoya et al. report that cigarette smokers have the same cell defect as individuals with the genetic premature aging disease Werner's syndrome. Research results show that both cigarette smokers and individuals with Werner's syndrome do not produce enough of a protein

FIGURE 3.9

**Health consequences linked to smoking and exposure to secondhand smoke**

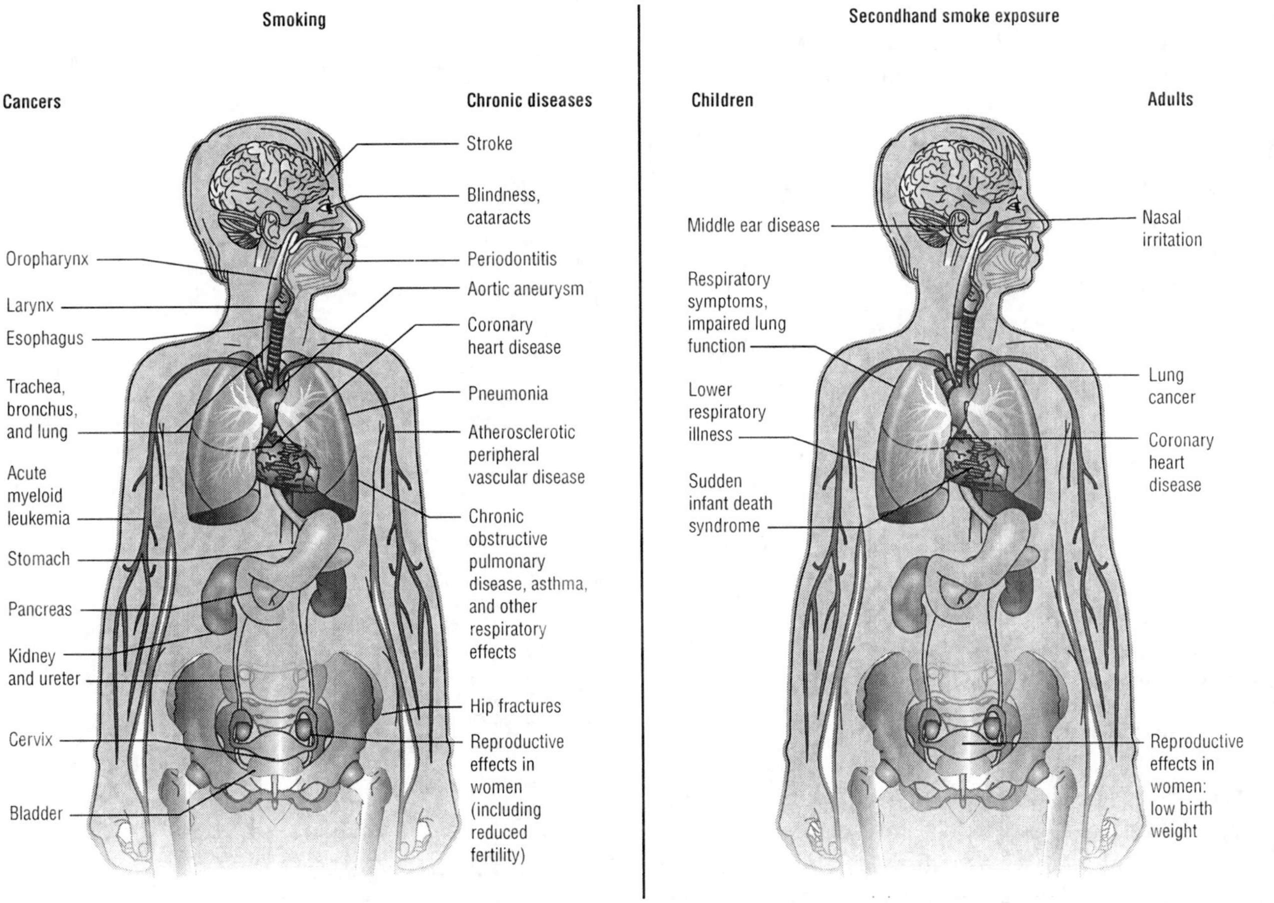

SOURCE: "Figure 1.1. The Health Consequences Causally Linked to Smoking and Exposure to Secondhand Smoke," in *How Tobacco Smoke Causes Disease: The Biology and Behavioral Basis for Smoking-Attributable Disease: A Report of the Surgeon General*, U.S. Department of Health and Human Services, Office on Smoking and Health, December 9, 2010, http://www.surgeongeneral.gov/library/reports/tobaccosmoke/full_report.pdf (accessed February 12, 2013)

alled WRN, which protects and repairs genetic material in the body. In addition, an extract of cigarette smoke is found to reduce WRN production in cultured lung cells in the laboratory. Not enough of WRN leads to premature aging. This information may help researchers develop a treatment for premature aging in smokers.

Although smoking is damaging to the body, research shows that the body begins to rebound shortly after a smoker quits smoking. For example, in "Quit Smoking Improves Gastroesophageal Reflux Symptoms and Quality of Life" (*Health*, vol. 3, no. 11, November 2011), Kou Nakajima et al. report that even though cigarettes have been linked to gastroesophageal reflux disease, quitting smoking can lead to dramatic improvements in a patient's condition, in many cases even eliminating the need for a medical procedure to remedy the disorder. According to Toshiji Ishiwata et al., in "Improvement in Skin Color Achieved by Smoking Cessation" (*International Journal*

*of Cosmetic Science*, vol. 35, no. 2, April 2013), studies show that skin discoloration associated with smoking can begin to show signs of reversal as early as four to 12 weeks after a smoker quits.

**Interactions with Other Drugs**

Smoking can have adverse effects when combined with over-the-counter (without a prescription) and prescription medications that a smoker may be taking. In many cases smoking reduces the effectiveness of medications, such as pain relievers (acetaminophen), antidepressants, tranquilizers, sedatives, ulcer medications, and insulin. With estrogen and oral contraceptives, smoking may increase the risk of heart and blood vessel disease and can cause strokes and blood clots.

Robert G. Smith notes in "An Appraisal of Potential Drug Interactions in Cigarette Smokers and Alcohol Drinkers" (*Journal of the American Podiatric Medical*

*Association*, vol. 99, no. 1, January–February 2009) that many drug interactions with smoking have been identified, and therefore smokers should be screened by their physicians for potential harmful drug interactions. In addition, individuals may need to take higher doses of some medications while they are current smokers and may need to reduce dosages when they quit.

## SMOKING AND PUBLIC HEALTH

A study during the 1920s found that men who smoked two or more packs of cigarettes per day were 22 times more likely than nonsmokers to die of lung cancer. At the time, these results surprised researchers and medical authorities alike. Roughly 40 years later the U.S. government first officially recognized the negative health consequences of smoking. In 1964 the Advisory Committee to the Surgeon General released *Smoking and Health*, which was a ground-breaking survey of studies on tobacco use. In the report the U.S. surgeon general Luther L. Terry (1911–1985) stated that cigarette smoking increased overall mortality in men and caused lung and laryngeal cancer, as well as chronic bronchitis. Terry concluded, "Cigarette smoking is a health hazard of sufficient importance in the United States to warrant appropriate remedial action," but what action should be taken was left unspecified at that time.

Later surgeons general issued additional reports on the health effects of smoking and the dangers to nonsmokers of secondhand smoke. Besides general health concerns, the reports addressed specific health consequences and populations. Table 3.4 shows a listing of reports of the surgeons general and the years in which they were published. The later reports concluded that smoking increases the morbidity (proportion of diseased people in a particular population) and mortality (proportion of deaths in a particular population) of both men and women.

In 1965 Congress passed the Federal Cigarette Labeling and Advertising Act, which required the following health warning on all cigarette packages: "Caution: Cigarette smoking may be hazardous to your health." The Public Health Cigarette Smoking Act of 1969 strengthened the warning to read: "Warning: The Surgeon General has determined that cigarette smoking is dangerous to your health." Still later acts resulted in four different health warnings to be used in rotation.

In June 2009 President Barack Obama (1961–) signed the Family Smoking Prevention and Tobacco Control Act. The act gave the U.S. Food and Drug Administration (FDA) regulatory authority over tobacco products and required that cigarette packages and advertisements have larger and more visible graphic health warnings. The FDA reveals in "FDA Unveils New Cigarette Health Warnings" (June 21, 2011, http://www.fda.gov/downloads/ForConsumers/ConsumerUpdates/UCM259865.pdf) that two of the proposed warnings were "Smoking can kill you," with an accompanying photo of

**TABLE 3.4**

**Surgeon General's reports on smoking and health, 1964–2012**

| | |
|---|---|
| 1964 | Smoking and Health: Report of the Advisory Committee to the Surgeon General of the Public Health Service |
| 1967 | The Health Consequences of Smoking: A Public Health Service Review |
| 1968 | The Health Consequences of Smoking: 1968 Supplement to the 1967 Public Health Service Review |
| 1969 | The Health Consequences of Smoking: 1969 Supplement to the 1967 Public Health Service Review |
| 1971 | The Health Consequences of Smoking |
| 1972 | The Health Consequences of Smoking |
| 1973 | The Health Consequences of Smoking |
| 1974 | The Health Consequences of Smoking |
| 1975 | The Health Consequences of Smoking |
| 1976 | The Health Consequences of Smoking: A Reference Edition |
| 1979 | The Health Consequences of Smoking, 1977–1978 |
| 1979 | Smoking and Health |
| 1980 | The Health Consequences of Smoking for Women |
| 1981 | The Health Consequences of Smoking: The Changing Cigarette |
| 1982 | The Health Consequences of Smoking: Cancer |
| 1983 | The Health Consequences of Smoking: Cardiovascular Disease |
| 1984 | The Health Consequences of Smoking: Chronic Obstructive Lung Disease |
| 1985 | The Health Consequences of Smoking: Cancer and Chronic Lung Disease in the Workplace |
| 1986 | The Health Consequences of Involuntary Smoking |
| 1988 | The Health Consequences of Smoking: Nicotine Addiction |
| 1989 | Reducing the Health Consequences of Smoking: 25 Years of Progress |
| 1990 | Smoking and Health: A National Status Report |
| 1990 | The Health Benefits of Smoking Cessation |
| 1992 | Smoking and Health in the Americas |
| 1994 | SGR 4 Kids: The Surgeon General's Report for Kids about Smoking |
| 1995 | Preventing Tobacco Use among Young People |
| 1998 | Tobacco Use among U.S. Racial/Ethnic Minority Groups |
| 2000 | Reduce Tobacco Use |
| 2001 | Women and Smoking |
| 2004 | The Health Consequences of Smoking |
| 2006 | The Health Consequences of Involuntary Exposure to Tobacco Smoke |
| 2007 | Children and Secondhand Smoke Exposure: Excerpts from the Health Consequences of Involuntary Exposure to Tobacco Smoke |
| 2008 | Treating Tobacco Use and Dependence: 2008 Update |
| 2010 | How Tobacco Smoke Causes Disease: The Biology and Behavioral Basis for Smoking-Attributable Disease |
| 2012 | Preventing Tobacco Use among Youth and Young Adults |

SOURCE: Created by Stephen Meyer for Gale, 2013

a dead person, and "Cigarettes cause cancer," with an accompanying photo of a smoker suffering from mouth cancer. Responding to the new regulations, the major tobacco companies filed a legal challenge, arguing that the rules violated basic protections of their right to free speech. In "FDA Changes Course on Graphic Warning Labels for Cigarettes" (CNN.com, March 20, 2013), Steve Almasy reports that in March 2012 a federal judge initially ruled in favor of the tobacco companies; in August of that year the U.S. Court of Appeals for the District of Columbia Circuit upheld the ruling by a 2–1 vote. Almasy notes that the FDA announced in March 2013 that it would not appeal the verdict to the U.S. Supreme Court, opting instead to "create new warning labels to comply with the 2009 law."

## DEATHS ATTRIBUTED TO TOBACCO USE

According to the 2012 surgeon general's report *Preventing Tobacco Use among Youth and Young Adults* (http://www.surgeongeneral.gov/library/reports/preventing-youth-tobacco-use/full-report.pdf), cigarette smoking is he leading cause of preventable death and disability in he United States and produces substantial health-related conomic costs to society. The report notes that smoking auses an estimated 443,000 deaths in the United States nnually. Nationwide, smoking kills more people each ear than alcohol, drug abuse, car crashes, murders, uicides, fires, and the acquired immunodeficiency syn-lrome (AIDS) combined.

In 2011 diseases linked to smoking accounted for our of the top-five causes of death in the United States. See Table 3.5.) The CDC explains in "Health Effects of :igarette Smoking" (January 10, 2012, http://www.cdc gov/tobacco/data_statistics/fact_sheets/health_effects/ ffects_cig_smoking/index.htm) that smoking can dou-le, and in some cases quadruple, a person's chance of uffering coronary heart disease, which remains the lead-ng cause of death in the United States. The CDC also eports that smoking increases the risk of developing ung cancer by 23 times in men and 13 times in women. n fact, smoking is responsible for roughly 90% of all ung cancer deaths in men and 80% of all lung cancer leaths in women.

In *Cancer Facts and Figures, 2012* (2012, http:// vww.cancer.org/acs/groups/content/@epidemiology urveilance/documents/document/acspc-031941.pdf), the American Cancer Society estimates that 160,340 Ameri-:ans died of lung and bronchus cancer in 2012. Even hough not all lung and bronchus cancer deaths are directly attributable to smoking, a large proportion of them are. Lung cancer is the leading cause of cancer mortality in ooth men and women in the United States. It has been the leading cause of cancer deaths among men since the early 1950s and, in 1987, it surpassed breast cancer to become the leading cause of cancer deaths in women.

## SECONDHAND SMOKE

Secondhand smoke, also known as environmental tobacco smoke or passive smoke, is a health hazard for nonsmokers who live or work with smokers. In the fact sheet "Secondhand Smoke and Cancer" (January 12, 2011, http://www.cancer.gov/cancertopics/factsheet/Tobacco/ ETS), the National Cancer Institute defines secondhand smoke as "the smoke given off by a burning tobacco product and the smoke exhaled by a smoker."

The article "Non-smoking Wives of Heavy Smokers Have a Higher Risk of Lung Cancer: A Study from Japan" (*British Medical Journal*, vol. 282, no. 6259, January 17, 1981) by Takeshi Hirayama of the National Cancer Centre Research Institute was the first scientific paper on the harm-ful effects of secondhand smoke. Hirayama studied 91,540 nonsmoking wives of smoking husbands and a similarly sized group of nonsmoking women who were married to nonsmokers. He discovered that nonsmoking wives of husbands who smoked faced a 40% to 90% elevated risk of lung cancer (depending on how frequently their husband smoked) compared with the wives of nonsmoking husbands.

Other studies followed. The U.S. Environmental Pro-tection Agency (EPA) concluded in *Respiratory Health Effects of Passive Smoking: Lung Cancer and Other Disorders* (December 1992, http://cfpub2.epa.gov/ncea/ cfm/recordisplay.cfm?deid=2835) that the "widespread exposure to environmental tobacco smoke (ETS) in the United States presents a serious and substantial public health impact." In "Environmental Tobacco Smoke and Lung Cancer in Nonsmoking Women: A Multicenter

**TABLE 3.5**

**Death rates for the five leading causes of death, 2010 and 2011, with percentage changes**

[Data are based on a continuous file of records received from the states. Rates are per 100,000 population; age-adjusted rates per 100,000 U.S. standard population based on the year 2000 standard. Figures for 2011 are based on weighted data rounded to the nearest individual, so categories may not add to totals.]

| Rank[a] | Cause of death, based on the International Classification of Diseases, tenth revision, 2008 edition, 2009. Codes in parentheses. | | Number | Death rate | Age-adjusted death rate | | |
|---|---|---|---|---|---|---|---|
| | | | | | 2011 | 2010 | Percent change |
| — | All causes | | 2,512,873 | 806.5 | 740.6 | 747.0 | −0.9 |
| 1 | Diseases of heart | (I00–I09,I1 1,I13,I20–I51) | 596,339 | 191.4 | 173.7 | 179.1 | −3.0 |
| 2 | Malignant neoplasms | (C00–C97) | 575,313 | 184.6 | 168.6 | 172.8 | −2.4 |
| 3 | Chronic lower respiratory diseases | (J40–J47) | 143,382 | 46.0 | 42.7 | 42.2 | 1.2 |
| 4 | Cerebrovascular diseases | (I60–I69) | 128,931 | 41.4 | 37.9 | 39.1 | −3.1 |
| 5 | Accidents (unintentional injuries) | (V01–X59, Y85–Y86)[b, c] | 122,777 | 39.4 | 38.0 | 38.0 | 0.0 |

—Category not applicable.
[a]Rank based on number of deaths.
[b]For unintentional injuries, suicides, preliminary and final data may differ significantly because of the truncated nature of the preliminary file.
[c]New *International Classification of Diseases* (ICD-10) subcategories were introduced for the existing X34 (victim of earthquakes).
Note: Data are subject to sampling and random variation.

SOURCE: Adapted from Donna L. Hoyert and Jiaquan Xu, "Table B. Deaths and Death Rates for 2011 and Age-Adjusted Death Rates and Percentage Changes in Age-Adjusted Rates from 2010 to 2011 for the 15 Leading Causes of Death in 2011: United States, Final 2010 and Preliminary 2011," in "Deaths: Preliminary Data 2011," *National Vital Statistics Reports*, vol. 61, no. 6, October 10, 2012, http://www.cdc.gov/nchs/data/nvsr/nvsr61/nvsr61_06.pdf (accessed February 12, 2013)

Study" (*Journal of the American Medical Association*, vol. 271, no. 22, June 8, 1994), a large case-control study on secondhand smoke, Elizabeth T. H. Fontham et al. found compelling links between passive smoke and lung cancer. In 2000 the Environmental Health Information Service's *Ninth Report on Carcinogens* classified secondhand smoke as a Group A (human) carcinogen. According to the EPA, there is no safe level of exposure to such Group A toxins.

In 2005 more evidence accumulated on the risks of secondhand smoking. Paolo Vineis et al. revealed in "Environmental Tobacco Smoke and Risk of Respiratory Cancer and Chronic Obstructive Pulmonary Disease in Former Smokers and Never Smokers in the EPIC Prospective Study" (*British Medical Journal*, vol. 330, no. 7486, February 5, 2005) that those who had been exposed to secondhand smoke during childhood for many hours each day had more than triple the risk of developing lung cancer compared with people who were not exposed. In addition, Sarah M. McGhee et al. showed in "Mortality Associated with Passive Smoking in Hong Kong" (*British Medical Journal*, vol. 330, no. 7486, February 5, 2005) that there is a correlation between an increased risk of dying from various causes (including lung cancer and other lung diseases, heart disease, and stroke) and the number of smokers in the home. The risk increased by 24% when one smoker lived in the home and by 74% with two smokers in the household.

In 2006 the 31st report of the surgeon general on smoking—*The Health Consequences of Involuntary Exposure to Tobacco Smoke* (http://www.surgeongeneral.gov/library/secondhandsmoke/report/fullreport.pdf)—was published. The report noted that:

> With regard to the involuntary exposure of nonsmokers to tobacco smoke, the scientific evidence now supports the following major conclusions:
>
> 1. Secondhand smoke causes premature death and disease in children and in adults who do not smoke.
>
> 2. Children exposed to secondhand smoke are at an increased risk for sudden infant death syndrome (SIDS), acute respiratory infections, ear problems, and more severe asthma. Smoking by parents causes respiratory symptoms and slows lung growth in their children.
>
> 3. Exposure of adults to secondhand smoke has immediate adverse effects on the cardiovascular system and causes coronary heart disease and lung cancer.
>
> 4. The scientific evidence indicates that there is no risk-free level of exposure to secondhand smoke.
>
> 5. Many millions of Americans, both children and adults, are still exposed to secondhand smoke in their homes and workplaces despite substantial progress in tobacco control.

> 6. Eliminating smoking in indoor spaces fully protects nonsmokers from exposure to secondhand smoke. Separating smokers from nonsmokers, cleaning the air, and ventilating buildings cannot eliminate exposures of nonsmokers to secondhand smoke.

In 2007 an excerpt of this report was published: *Children and Secondhand Smoke Exposure: Excerpts from the Health Consequences of Involuntary Exposure to Tobacco Smoke* (http://www.surgeongeneral.gov/library/smokeexposure/report/fullreport.pdf). The purpose of the publication was to highlight the serious consequences of secondhand smoke exposure on the health of children, to emphasize that they are more heavily exposed to secondhand smoke than are adults, and to urge that children be protected from this unnecessary threat to their health.

The 2012 surgeon general's report *Preventing Tobacco Use among Youth and Young Adults* emphasizes the dangers of secondhand smoke and notes that secondhand smoke exposure causes middle ear disease, impaired lung function, lower respiratory illness, and SIDS in children. In adults, secondhand smoke can cause lung cancer and coronary heart disease. Also, pregnant women who are exposed to secondhand smoke have an increased risk of giving birth to low birth weight babies.

Even though the percentage of those who perceive secondhand smoke to be very harmful has increased since 1994, this percentage has not increased in recent years. (See Figure 3.10.) In 2011, 56% of all people and 63% of nonsmokers said secondhand smoke is very harmful. Meanwhile, the percentage of smokers who believed that secondhand smoke is very harmful declined between 2008 and 2011, from 36% to 28%.

## THIRDHAND SMOKE

According to Jonathan P. Winickoff et al., in "Beliefs about the Health Effects of 'Thirdhand' Smoke and Home Smoking Bans" (*Pediatrics*, vol. 123, no. 1, January 2009), "thirdhand smoke is residual tobacco smoke contamination that remains after the cigarette is extinguished." The researchers find an association between parents believing that thirdhand smoke harms children and their banning smoking in the home.

Discussions and research results regarding thirdhand smoke have appeared in the medical literature only since 2009. Just a few studies on the existence and harmfulness of thirdhand smoke were available as of April 2013. For example, Marie-Hélène Becquemin et al. were the first to show that particles from cigarette smoke that fall onto furniture and other surfaces can become airborne long after a cigarette is extinguished. Once airborne, these potentially harmful particles can be inhaled and enter the lungs. The researchers published their findings in

**Public opinion on the harmfulness of secondhand smoke, 1995–2011**

IN GENERAL, HOW HARMFUL DO YOU FEEL SECONDHAND SMOKE IS TO ADULTS?

% very harmful

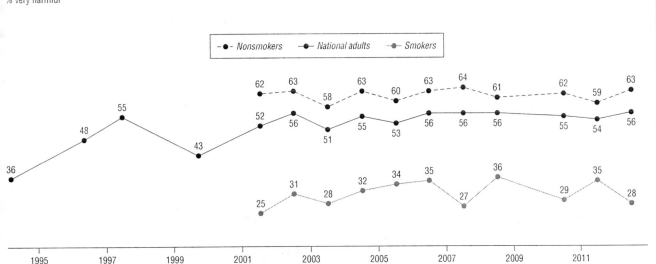

SOURCE: Alyssa Brown, "In General, How Harmful Do You Feel Secondhand Smoke Is to Adults?" in *Few U.S. Smokers Say Secondhand Smoke Is Very Harmful*, The Gallup Organization, September 28, 2012, http://www.gallup.com/poll/157793/few-smokers-say-secondhand-smoke-harmful.aspx (accessed February 12, 2013). Copyright © 2012 Gallup, Inc. All rights reserved. The content is used with permission; however, Gallup retains all rights of republication.

"Third-Hand Smoking: Indoor Measurements of Concentration and Sizes of Cigarette Smoke Particles after Resuspension" (*Tobacco Control*, vol. 19, no. 4, August 2010). In "Pediatrician Interventions and Thirdhand Smoke Beliefs of Parents" (*American Journal of Preventive Medicine*, vol. 43, no. 5, November 2012), Jeremy E. Drehmer et al. find that pediatrician warnings on the potential impact of thirdhand smoke on infants and children have exerted a noticeable impact on the smoking habits of parents.

## A MOVEMENT TO BAN SMOKING

Many efforts have been initiated over the years to control public smoking or to separate smokers and nonsmokers. In 1975 Minnesota became the first state in the nation to require the separation of smokers and nonsmokers following passage of the Clean Indoor Air Act. The purpose of the law was to protect public health, public comfort, and the environment by banning smoking in public places and at public meetings, except in designated smoking areas.

Other states soon followed. In 1977 Berkeley became the first community in California to limit smoking in restaurants and other public places. In 1990 San Luis Obispo, California, became the first city to ban smoking in all public buildings, bars, and restaurants. In 1994 smoking was restricted in many government buildings in California. That same year the fast-food giant McDonald's banned

smoking in all of its establishments. In 1995 New York City banned smoking in the dining areas of all restaurants with more than 35 seats. As of July 2003, all public and private workplaces in New York City became smoke-free, including bars and restaurants. Laws vary from state to state and from city to city, but by 2005 smoking was banned in most workplaces, hospitals, government buildings, museums, schools, theaters, and restaurants throughout the United States.

As shown in Figure 3.11, support for banning smoking in public places has risen steadily since 2001. In 2001 just over three-eighths (39%) of those surveyed by the Gallup Organization thought that smoking should be banned in all public places; by 2011 this figure had grown to 59%. In addition, in 2011 nearly one out of five (19%) Americans felt that smoking should be "totally illegal" throughout the United States.

## STOPPING SMOKING

In "Current Cigarette Smoking among Adults—United States, 2011" (*Morbidity and Mortality Weekly Report*, vol. 61, no. 44, November 9, 2012), the CDC estimates that there were 43.8 million current smokers in 2011. This number was high, but the CDC notes that "in recent years, several advances in tobacco control have occurred in the United States. These include implementation of the 2009 Family Smoking Prevention and Tobacco Control Act, which granted the Food and Drug

**FIGURE 3.11**

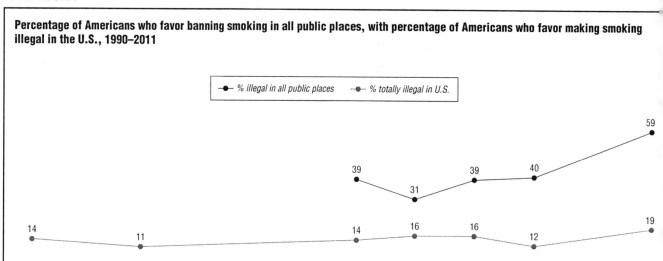

Percentage of Americans who favor banning smoking in all public places, with percentage of Americans who favor making smoking illegal in the U.S., 1990–2011

SOURCE: Frank Newport, "Support for Making Smoking Illegal in All Public Places, and Totally Illegal across Country," in *For First Time, Majority in U.S. Supports Public Smoking Ban*, The Gallup Organization, July 15, 2011, http://www.gallup.com/poll/148514/First-Time-Majority-Supports-Public-Smoking-Ban.aspx (accessed February 12, 2013). Copyright © 2011 Gallup, Inc. All rights reserved. The content is used with permission; however, Gallup retains all rights of republication.

Administration the authority to regulate the manufacture, distribution, and marketing of tobacco products. Although not affecting these 2011 findings, the federal mass media campaign conducted in early 2012, which included graphic personal stories on the adverse health impact of smoking, might contribute to future decreases in prevalence."

Many current cigarette smokers report they are trying to stop smoking—or would like to. In *In U.S., Smokers Light up Less than Ever*, the Gallup Organization asked smokers in July 2012 if they would like to give up smoking. Seventy-eight percent answered yes. This figure was down from 82% in 2004 but up from 63% in 1989.

**Global Efforts to Reduce Tobacco Use**

According to the World Health Organization (WHO), in *WHO Report on the Global Tobacco Epidemic, 2011: Warning about the Dangers of Tobacco* (2011, http://whqlibdoc.who.int/publications/2011/9789240687813_eng.pdf), tobacco use kills approximately 6 million people worldwide annually; 600,000 of these die because of exposure to secondhand smoke. Of the world's 1 billion smokers, half are expected to die from smoking-related diseases. According to the WHO, most deaths occur in low- and middle-income countries.

The WHO is working diligently to curb smoking around the world. In May 2003 member states of the WHO adopted the world's first international public health treaty for global cooperation in reducing the negative health consequences

of tobacco use. The WHO Framework Convention on Tobacco Control (2003, http://www.who.int/tobacco/framework/WHO_FCTC_english.pdf) was designed to reduce tobacco-related deaths and disease worldwide. In February 2005 the treaty came into force after 40 member countries had ratified it (become bound by it). Each of the other 128 countries that signed the treaty but did not ratify it was to work toward this goal in their country. The WHO notes in "Parties to the WHO Framework Convention on Tobacco Control" (December 7, 2012, http://www.who.int/fctc/signatories_parties/en/) that there were 168 signatories to the treaty as of December 2012. The United States signed the treaty in May 2004, indicating its general acceptance, but as of December 2012 it had not yet ratified the treaty. The treaty has many measures, which include requiring countries to impose restrictions on tobacco advertising, sponsorship, and promotion; creating new packaging and labeling of tobacco products; establishing clean indoor air controls; and promoting taxation as a way to cut consumption and fight smuggling.

In *WHO Report on the Global Tobacco Epidemic, 2008: The MPOWER Package* (2008, http://www.who.int/tobacco/mpower/mpower_report_full_2008.pdf), the WHO configures the primary measures of the treaty into the acronym MPOWER, which stands for:

- Monitor tobacco use and prevention policies
- Protect people from tobacco smoke
- Offer help to quit tobacco use
- Warn about the dangers of tobacco

- Enforce bans on tobacco advertising, promotion, and sponsorship
- Raise taxes on tobacco

The WHO indicates that young females are being targeted by tobacco companies, especially in developing countries and in many countries in which women traditionally do not smoke. The WHO suggests that tobacco companies are working to weaken this cultural taboo in their "advertising, promotion and sponsorship, including charitable donations to women's causes." It also notes that many poorer nations, in which tobacco controls are weak, rely on income from the tobacco business for revenue. The state-owned China National Tobacco Corporation is given as one example of this fiscal reliance.

The WHO notes in *WHO Report on the Global Tobacco Epidemic, 2011* that between 2008 and 2011, 30 nations worldwide implemented new policies aimed at curbing tobacco use; of these, more than half of the countries were classified as low or middle income. By 2011, 3.8 billion people, or 55% of the earth's population, were covered by at least one MPOWER measure.

## Benefits of Stopping

The 1990 *Health Benefits of Smoking Cessation: A Report of the Surgeon General* (http://profiles.nlm.nih.gov/NN/B/B/C/T/_/nnbbct.pdf) noted that quitting offers major and immediate health benefits for both sexes and for all ages. This first comprehensive report on the benefits of quitting showed that many of the ill effects of smoking can be reversed. The subsequent 2004 surgeon general's report *Health Consequences of Smoking* revealed that deaths attributable to smoking can be reduced dramatically if the prevalence of smoking is cut.

The 2010 surgeon general's report *How Tobacco Smoke Causes Disease* states that of smokers who try to quit at any one time, less than 5% are successful. According to the report, smokers who quit early in life (aged 25 to 34 years) reduce their risk of dying from all causes to the same level as lifetime nonsmokers. Those who quit slightly later in life (aged 35 to 44 years) reduce their risk of dying from all causes to nearly the same level as nonsmokers. Even those who quit after the age of 45 years reduce their risk of dying to a level in between that of nonsmokers and smokers. Nonetheless, for lung cancer alone, "there is a persistent elevated risk in former smokers compared with lifetime nonsmokers of the same age even after a long abstinence." The report adds, "Evidence indicates that lung cancer risk increases far more strongly with each additional year of smoking than it increases for a higher average number of cigarettes smoked per day."

## Quitting and Pregnancy

In *Results from the 2011 National Survey on Drug Use and Health: Summary of National Findings*, the NSDUH finds that in 2010–11, 17.6% of pregnant women smoked cigarettes in the month before the survey. (See Figure 3.12.) This percentage of smokers was lower than among women who were not pregnant (25.4%),

**FIGURE 3.12**

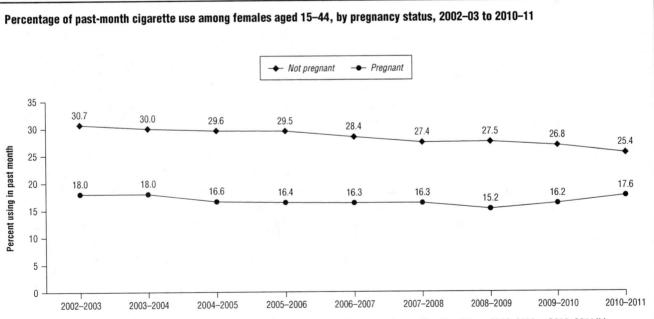

Percentage of past-month cigarette use among females aged 15–44, by pregnancy status, 2002–03 to 2010–11

SOURCE: "Figure 4.5. Past Month Cigarette Use among Women Aged 15 to 44, by Pregnancy Status: Combined Years 2002–2003 to 2010–2011," in *Results from the 2011 National Survey on Drug Use and Health: Summary of National Findings*, U.S. Department of Health and Human Services, Substance Abuse and Mental Health Services Administration, September 2012, http://www.samhsa.gov/data/NSDUH/2k11Results/NSDUHresults2011.pdf (accessed February 12, 2013)

although it represented an increase from the 15.2% of pregnant women who reported smoking in the past month in 2008–09.

Smoking during pregnancy can compromise the health of the developing fetus (unborn child). According to the 2010 surgeon general's report *How Tobacco Smoke Causes Disease*, evidence suggests the possibility of a causal relationship between maternal smoking and ectopic pregnancy, a situation in which the fertilized egg implants in the fallopian tube rather than in the uterus. This situation is quite serious and is life-threatening to the mother. Smoking by pregnant women is also linked to an increased risk of miscarriage, stillbirth, premature delivery, and SIDS and is a cause of low birth weight in infants. A woman who stops smoking before pregnancy or during her first trimester (three months) of pregnancy significantly reduces her chances of having a low birth weight baby. Additionally, it takes smokers longer to get pregnant than nonsmokers; some smokers are unable to become pregnant. In general, however, women who quit are as likely to get pregnant as those who have never smoked.

## Complaints about Quitting

A major side effect of smoking cessation is nicotine withdrawal. The short-term consequences of nicotine withdrawal may include anxiety, irritability, frustration, anger, difficulty concentrating, and restlessness. Possible long-term consequences are urges to smoke and increased appetite. Nicotine withdrawal symptoms peak in the first few days after quitting and subside during the following weeks. Improved self-esteem and an increased sense of control often accompany long-term abstinence.

One of the most common complaints among former smokers is that they gain weight when they stop smoking. Many reasons explain this weight gain, but two primary reasons are the metabolism changes associated with nicotine withdrawal and the change in food habits by many former smokers as a result of their attempts to manage withdrawal cravings. To combat weight gain, some former smokers start exercise programs.

## Ways to Stop Smoking

Nicotine replacement treatments can be effective for many smokers. Nicotine patches and gum are two types of nicotine replacement therapy (NRT). The nicotine in a patch is absorbed through the skin, and the nicotine in the gum is absorbed through the mouth and throat. NRT helps a smoker cope with nicotine withdrawal symptom that discourage many smokers from trying to stop. Nicotine patches and gum are available over the counter. Other NRT products are the nicotine nasal spray and the nicotine inhaler, which are available by prescription.

Another product marketed to combat the use of cigarettes—electronic cigarettes (e-cigarettes; plastic devices that are fashioned to look like cigarettes)—drew serious criticism from the FDA in 2010. E-cigarettes contain liquid nicotine. When the user inhales through the device, a battery heats up the nicotine into a vapor. In September 2010 the FDA sent warning letters to five e-cigarette distributors for violations of the federal Food, Drug, and Cosmetic Act. The violations included poor manufacturing practices and unsubstantiated claims that the devices can help smokers quit their addiction. In the press release "FDA Acts against 5 Electronic Cigarette Distributors" (September 9, 2010, http://www.fda.gov/NewsEvents/Newsroom/PressAnnouncements/ucm225224.htm), the FDA states that "a company cannot claim that its drug can treat or mitigate a disease, such as nicotine addiction, unless the drug's safety and effectiveness have been proven. Yet all five companies claim without FDA review of relevant evidence that the products help users quit smoking cigarettes."

The nonnicotine therapy bupropion (an antidepressant drug) is also available by prescription for the relief of nicotine withdrawal symptoms. In addition, behavioral treatments, such as smoking-cessation programs, are useful for some smokers who want to quit. Behavioral methods are designed to create an aversion to smoking, develop self-monitoring of smoking behavior, and establish alternative coping responses.

Besides smoking-cessation therapies, a number of organizations offer programs and support groups that are aimed at helping smokers quit. Notable among these are the Smoking Cessation Program at Cedars-Sinai Medical Center in Los Angeles, California, and the American Academy of Family Physicians "Ask and Act" Tobacco Cessation Program. Furthermore, the Employee Assistance Program sponsors a number of smoking-cessation services and programs throughout the country. The website Smokefree.gov, a joint venture of the National Cancer Institute, the National Institutes of Health, the U.S. Department of Health and Human Services, and USA.gov, provides online information and resources that are designed to help people quit smoking.

CHAPTER 4

# ILLICIT DRUGS

Illegal drugs are those with no currently accepted medical use in the United States, such as heroin, lysergic acid diethylamide (LSD), and marijuana. (Some states and local jurisdictions have decriminalized certain uses of specific amounts of marijuana, but federal laws supersede these state and local marijuana decriminalization laws. For a more detailed discussion on the legalization of marijuana, see Chapter 9.) Controlled substances are legal drugs whose sale, possession, and use are restricted because they are psychoactive (mood- or mind-altering) drugs that have the potential for abuse. These drugs are medications, such as certain narcotics, depressants, and stimulants, that physicians prescribe for various conditions. The term *illicit drugs* is used by the Substance Abuse and Mental Health Services Administration (SAMHSA) to mean both illegal drugs and controlled substances that are used illegally.

## WHO USES ILLICIT DRUGS?

The National Survey on Drug Use and Health (NSDUH) is an annual survey that is conducted by SAMHSA, and its 2011 survey results are published in *Results from the 2011 National Survey on Drug Use and Health: Summary of National Findings* (September 2012, http://www.samhsa.gov/data/NSDUH/2k11Results/NSDUHesults2011.pdf). The NSDUH reveals that an estimated 22.5 million Americans aged 12 years and older were current illicit drug users in 2011. By "current" SAMHSA means the people who were surveyed about their drug use and who had taken an illicit drug during the month before participating in the survey. (Current users are "past month" users.) This figure represented 8.7% of the U.S. population in 2011.

Table 4.1 presents a demographic profile of this population of drug users. In 2011, 21.4% of those aged 18 to 25 years and 10.1% of those aged 12 to 17 years were current illicit drug users. In contrast, only 6.3% of those aged 26 years and older were current illicit drug users.

Figure 4.1 shows a more detailed look at current illicit drug use by age. In 2011, 18- to 20-year-olds accounted for the highest percentage of illicit drug users. At 23.8% of their population, nearly one-quarter of young people aged 18 to 20 years were current illicit drug users in that year. The 21-to-25-year-old age group had the second-highest percentage of current illicit drug users (19.9%), followed by 16- and 17-year-olds (17.2%).

Regarding other demographics of illicit drug use, Table 4.1 shows that a higher proportion of males than females were current, past-year, or lifetime illicit drug users in both 2010 and 2011. (Past-year users took a specific drug during the 12 months before taking the SAMHSA survey and lifetime users took a specific drug at least once during their lifetime.) Individuals of two or more races had the highest percentage of current illicit drug users in their population in 2011 (13.5%). Native Americans or Alaskan Natives were next (13.4%), followed by Native Hawaiians or other Pacific Islanders (11%) and African-Americans (10%). Asian-Americans (3.8%) had the lowest percentage of current illicit drug users in their population.

Table 4.2 shows drug use statistics by military veteran status for 2002–04, 2005–07, and 2008–10. Among adults aged 18 years and older, veterans (5.6%) were less likely than nonveterans (8.7%) to use illicit drugs in 2008–10. In contrast, veterans were more likely to use alcohol (58.8%) than nonveterans (55.5%) during this same period.

## WHICH ILLICIT DRUGS ARE USED MOST FREQUENTLY?

Figure 4.2 shows the types of illicit drugs that were used in 2011 and how many people used those drugs in that year. More than four out of five (80.4%) current illicit drug users used marijuana—18.1 million people of the 22.5 million illicit drug users. According to the

**TABLE 4.1**

**Use of illicit drugs among persons aged 12 and older, by time of use and demographic characteristics, 2010–11**

| Demographic characteristic | Lifetime (2010) | Lifetime (2011) | Past year (2010) | Past year (2011) | Past month (2010) | Past month (2011) |
|---|---|---|---|---|---|---|
| **Total** | 47.3 | 47.0 | 15.3 | 14.9 | 8.9 | 8.7 |
| **Age** | | | | | | |
| 12–17 | 25.8 | 25.5 | 19.5 | 19.0 | 10.1 | 10.1 |
| 18–25 | 57.3 | 56.9 | 35.2 | 35.2 | 21.6 | 21.4 |
| 26 or older | 48.2 | 48.0 | 11.4 | 10.8 | 6.6 | 6.3 |
| **Gender** | | | | | | |
| Male | 52.4 | 51.4 | 18.3 | 17.7 | 11.2 | 11.1 |
| Female | 42.5 | 42.9 | 12.6 | 12.2 | 6.8 | 6.5 |
| **Hispanic origin and race** | | | | | | |
| Not Hispanic or Latino | 49.0 | 48.9 | 15.4 | 14.9 | 9.1 | 8.8 |
| White | 51.1 | 51.1 | 15.4 | 15.0 | 9.1 | 8.7 |
| Black or African American | 45.1 | 45.4 | 16.7 | 16.0 | 10.7 | 10.0 |
| American Indian or Alaska Native | 58.4 | 59.1 | 22.6 | 24.4 | 12.1 | 13.4 |
| Native Hawaiian or other Pacific Islander | * | * | 10.3 | * | 5.3 | 11.0 |
| Asian | 25.2 | 22.5 | 8.7 | 7.2 | 3.5 | 3.8 |
| Two or more races | 57.6 | 56.9 | 22.5 | 23.3 | 12.6 | 13.5 |
| Hispanic or Latino | 37.2 | 36.7 | 15.3 | 14.5 | 8.1 | 8.4 |

*Low precision; no estimate reported.

Note: Illicit drugs include marijuana/hashish, cocaine (including crack), heroin, hallucinogens, inhalants, or prescription-type psychotherapeutics used nonmedically, including data from original methamphetamine questions but not including new methamphetamine items added in 2005 and 2006.

SOURCE: "Table 1.19B. Illicit Drug Use in Lifetime, Past Year, and Past Month among Persons Aged 12 or Older, by Demographic Characteristics: Percentages, 2010 and 2011," in *Results from the 2011 National Survey on Drug Use and Health: Detailed Tables*, U.S. Department of Health and Human Services, Substance Abuse and Mental Health Services Administration, September 2012, http://www.samhsa.gov/data/NSDUH/2011SummNatFindDetTables/NSDUH-DetTabsPDFWHTML2011/2k11DetailedTabs/Web/PDFW/NSDUH-DetTabsSect1peTabs19to23-2011.pdf (accessed February 13, 2013)

**FIGURE 4.1**

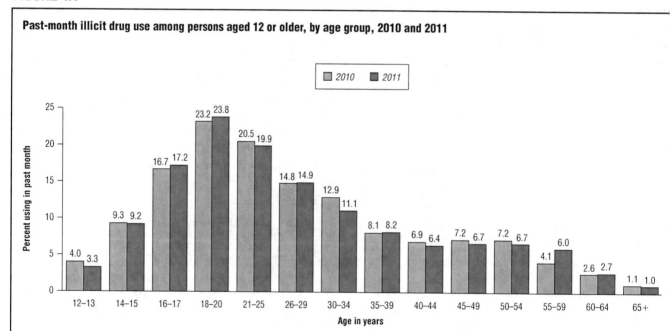

**Past-month illicit drug use among persons aged 12 or older, by age group, 2010 and 2011**

SOURCE: "Figure 2.5. Past Month Illicit Drug Use among Persons Aged 12 or Older, by Age: 2010 and 2011," in *Results from the 2011 National Survey on Drug Use and Health: Summary of National Findings*, U.S. Department of Health and Human Services, Substance Abuse and Mental Health Services Administration, September 2012, http://www.samhsa.gov/data/NSDUH/2k11Results/NSDUHresults2011.pdf (accessed February 13, 2013)

NSDUH, those who used only marijuana made up nearly two-thirds (64.3%) of the population of current illicit drug users in 2011.

Between 2002 and 2011, 5.8% to 7% of people aged 12 years and older had used marijuana in the month prior to being surveyed. (See Figure 4.3.) Psychotherapeutics

TABLE 4.2

**Drug use among military veterans, by drug type, 2002–10**

| | Number of users (thousands) | | | Percentage who used | | |
|---|---|---|---|---|---|---|
| | 2002–2004 | 2005–2007 | 2008–2010 | 2002–2004 | 2005–2007 | 2008–2010 |
| **Veteran** | | | | | | |
| Any illicit drug[a] | 1,222 | 1,259 | 1,336 | 4.6 | 5.0 | 5.6 |
| Marijuana | 931 | 940 | 1,053 | 3.5 | 3.7 | 4.4 |
| Cocaine | 202 | 164 | 130 | 0.8 | 0.6 | 0.5 |
| Heroin | 11 | 22 | 12 | 0.0 | 0.1 | 0.0 |
| Methamphetamine | 40 | 43 | 16 | 0.1 | 0.2 | 0.1 |
| Nonmedical use of any psychotherapeutic drug[b] | 322 | 407 | 366 | 1.2 | 1.6 | 1.5 |
| Cigarettes | 6,761 | 6,055 | 5,242 | 25.3 | 24.0 | 21.9 |
| Alcohol | 15,478 | 14,583 | 14,042 | 58.0 | 57.7 | 58.8 |
| **Non-veteran** | | | | | | |
| Any illicit drug[a] | 15,344 | 16,249 | 17,749 | 8.2 | 8.3 | 8.7 |
| Marijuana | 11,700 | 11,985 | 13,623 | 6.3 | 6.1 | 6.7 |
| Cocaine | 1,763 | 2,016 | 1,447 | 0.9 | 1.0 | 0.7 |
| Heroin | 125 | 176 | 192 | 0.1 | 0.1 | 0.1 |
| Methamphetamine | 598 | 534 | 343 | 0.3 | 0.3 | 0.2 |
| Nonmedical use of any psychotherapeutic drug[b] | 4,994 | 5,582 | 5,614 | 2.7 | 2.9 | 2.8 |
| Cigarettes | 50,626 | 52,042 | 51,495 | 27.2 | 26.7 | 25.3 |
| Alcohol | 100,010 | 107,285 | 112,714 | 53.8 | 55.0 | 55.5 |

[a]Any illicit drug includes marijuana/hashish, cocaine (including crack), heroin, hallucinogens, inhalants, or any prescription-type psychotherapeutic drugs used nonmedically.
[b]Nonmedical use of prescription-type psychotherapeutics includes the nonmedical use of pain relievers, tranquilizers, stimulants, or sedatives and does not include over-the-counter drugs.

SOURCE: "Table 34. Substance Use in the Past Month by Veteran Status, Aged 18 or Older, 2002–2004, 2005–2007, and 2008–2010," in *National Drug Control Strategy: Data Supplement 2012*, Executive Office of the President, Office of National Drug Policy, 2012, http://www.whitehouse.gov/sites/default/files/page/files/2012_data_supplement_final.pdf (accessed February 16, 2013)

**FIGURE 4.2**

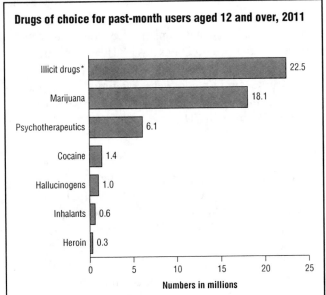

**Drugs of choice for past-month users aged 12 and over, 2011**

| | Numbers in millions |
|---|---|
| Illicit drugs* | 22.5 |
| Marijuana | 18.1 |
| Psychotherapeutics | 6.1 |
| Cocaine | 1.4 |
| Hallucinogens | 1.0 |
| Inhalants | 0.6 |
| Heroin | 0.3 |

*Illicit drugs include marijuana/hashish, cocaine (including crack), heroin, hallucinogens, inhalants, or prescription-type psychotherapeutics used nonmedically.

SOURCE: "Figure 2.1. Past Month Illicit Drug Use among Persons Aged 12 or Older: 2011," in *Results from the 2011 National Survey on Drug Use and Health: Summary of National Findings*, U.S. Department of Health and Human Services, Substance Abuse and Mental Health Services Administration, September 2012, http://www.samhsa.gov/data/NSDUH/2k11Results/NSDUHresults2011.pdf (accessed February 13, 2013)

was the next most used group of illicit drugs, ranging from 2.7% of the population in 2002 to 2.4% of the population in 2011. Psychotherapeutics are a group of drugs that include pain relievers, tranquilizers, stimulants (including methamphetamine), and sedatives. This group does not include over-the-counter (without a prescription) drugs. The next most used illicit drugs were cocaine and hallucinogens, ranging from 0.5% to 1% and from 0.4% to 0.5% of the population, respectively.

## DRUG-RELATED DEATHS

Sherry L. Murphy of the Centers for Disease Control and Prevention (CDC) reports in "Deaths: Final Data for 1998" (July 24, 2000, http://www.cdc.gov/nchs/data/nvsr/nvsr48/nvs48_11.pdf) that there were 16,926 drug-related deaths in 1998, or 6.3 deaths per 1,000 population. Kenneth D. Kochanek et al. of the CDC note in "Deaths: Final Data for 2009" (December 29, 2011, http://www.cdc.gov/nchs/data/nvsr/nvsr60/nvsr60_03.pdf) that by 2009 the number of drug-related deaths more than doubled to 39,147. The rate doubled as well, reaching 12.6 deaths per 1,000 population. In this annual CDC report, drug-related deaths include those due directly to the use of either legal or illegal drugs but exclude deaths due indirectly to drug use, such as unintentional injuries or homicides.

**FIGURE 4.3**

**Past-month use of selected illicit drugs among persons aged 12 or older, 2002–11**

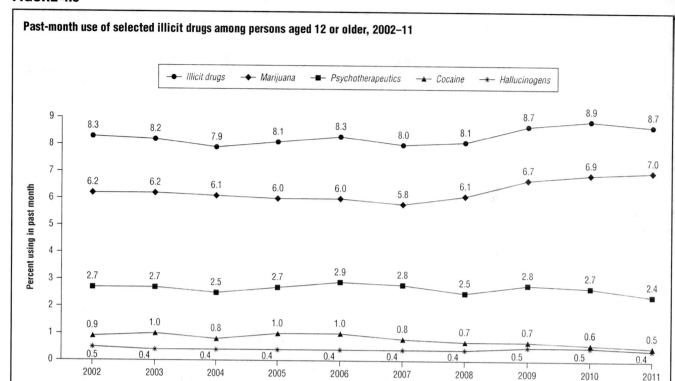

SOURCE: "Figure 2.2. Past Month Use of Selected Illicit Drugs among Persons Aged 12 or Older: 2002–2011," in *Results from the 2011 National Survey on Drug Use and Health: Summary of National Findings*, U.S. Department of Health and Human Services, Substance Abuse and Mental Health Services Administration, September 2012, http://www.samhsa.gov/data/NSDUH/2k11Results/NSDUHresults2011.pdf (accessed February 13, 2013)

## CANNABIS AND MARIJUANA

*Cannabis sativa*, the hemp plant from which marijuana is made, grows wild throughout most of the world's tropic and temperate regions, including Mexico, the Middle East, Africa, and India. For centuries its therapeutic potential has been explored, including uses as an analgesic (painkiller) and anticonvulsant. However, with the advent of new, synthetic drugs and the passage of the Marijuana Tax Act of 1937, interest in marijuana—even for medicinal purposes—faded. In 1970 the Controlled Substances Act (CSA) classified marijuana as a Schedule I drug because it has "no currently accepted medical use in treatment in the United States," though this classification is debated by those in favor of using it for medical and recreational purposes. (See Chapter 9.)

Besides regular marijuana, there are two alternate forms: ditchweed and sinsemilla. All three are tobacco-like substances that are produced by drying the leaves and flowery tops of cannabis plants. The Office of National Drug Control Policy (ONDCP) explains in *National Drug Control Strategy: Data Supplement 2012* (2012, http://www .whitehouse.gov/sites/default/files/page/files/2012_data_sup plement_final.pdf) that potency varies considerably among the three. The potency of the drug depends on how much of the chemical THC (delta-9-tetrahydrocan nabinol) is present. Ditchweed, or wild U.S. marijuana, is the least potent form of marijuana and generally has a

THC content of less than 0.5%. Sinsemilla is the most potent form of marijuana. The name is Spanish for "without seed" and refers to the unpollinated, and therefore seedless, female cannabis plant. Generally, marijuana cultivated in the United States has a THC content of about 2% to 3%, whereas the marijuana from other countries has a higher potency, in recent years ranging from about 6% to 7%. In contrast, the potency of sinsemilla is roughly between 12% to 13% THC.

### Effects of Marijuana

Marijuana is usually smoked in the form of loosely rolled cigarettes called joints, in hollowed-out commercial cigars called blunts, or in water pipes called bongs. Sometimes it is ingested. The effects are felt within minutes, usually peaking in 10 to 30 minutes and lingering for two to three hours. Low doses induce restlessness and an increasing sense of well-being, followed by a dreamy state of relaxation and, frequently, hunger. Changes in sensory perception—a more vivid sense of sight, smell, touch, taste, and hearing—may occur, with subtle alterations in thought formation and expression. However, the National Institute on Drug Abuse reports in *DrugFacts: Marijuana* (December 2012, http://www .drugabuse.gov/publications/drugfacts/marijuana) that along with the pleasant side effects of smoking marijuana come some not-so-pleasant effects, including short-term memory loss, possible abnormalities in heart rhythm and an increased risk of heart attack, and lung damage.

The immediate physical effects of marijuana include a faster heartbeat (by as much as 50%), bloodshot eyes, and a dry mouth and throat. It can alter one's sense of time and reduce concentration and coordination. Some users experience lightheadedness and giddiness, whereas others feel depressed and sad. Many users have also reported experiencing severe anxiety attacks.

Even though the immediate effects of marijuana usually disappear in about four to six hours, it takes about three days for 50% of the drug to be broken down and eliminated from the body. It takes three weeks to completely excrete the THC from one marijuana cigarette. If a user smokes two joints per week, it takes months for all traces of the THC to disappear from the body.

## Hashish and Hash Oil

Two other drugs besides marijuana come from the cannabis plant: hashish and hash oil. Hashish is made from the THC-rich, tar-like material that can be collected from the cannabis plant. This resin is dried and compressed into a variety of forms, including balls and cakes. Larger pieces are broken into smaller pieces and smoked. Most hashish

comes from the Middle East, North Africa, Pakistan, and Afghanistan. Demand in the United States is limited.

Despite its name, hash oil is not directly related to hashish. It is produced by extracting the cannabinoids from the cannabis plant with a solvent. The color and odor of hash oil depend on the solvent that is used. Hash oil ranges from amber to dark brown and has a potency of about 15% THC. In terms of effect, a drop or two of hash oil on a cigarette is equal to a single marijuana joint.

## Prevalence of Use of Marijuana

Figure 4.4 shows the lifetime, annual, and 30-day (current) use of marijuana among 18- to 50-year-olds in 2011. Current and annual use generally drops with age—younger people are more likely to have used marijuana during the past month or past year than older people. However, by the age of 50, 76% of Americans in 2011 had tried marijuana at some point during their lifetime.

In 2011, 23% of 18-year-olds were current users of marijuana. (See Figure 4.4.) Use rates dropped to 20% for 19- to 20-year-olds, before climbing slightly to 22% for 21- to 22-year-olds. By the age of 30, 11% were current users of marijuana, and by the age of 50 this figure dropped to 6%.

For each year between 2002 and 2011 an average of 2.2 million people over the age of 12 years tried marijuana

## FIGURE 4.4

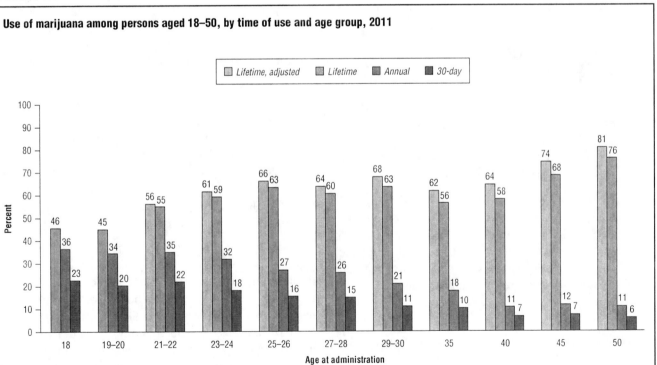

Use of marijuana among persons aged 18–50, by time of use and age group, 2011

Notes: Lifetime prevalence estimates were adjusted for inconsistency in self-reports of drug use over time.
Due to rounding some bars with the same number may have uneven height.

SOURCE: Lloyd D. Johnston et al., "Figure 4-3. Marijuana: Lifetime, Annual, and 30-Day Prevalence among Respondents of Modal Ages 18 through 50 by Age Group, 2011," in *Monitoring the Future National Survey Results on Drug Use, 1975–2011: Volume II, College Students and Adults Ages 19–50,* University of Michigan, Ann Arbor, Institute for Social Research, 2012, http://www.monitoringthefuture.org/pubs/monographs/mtf-vol2_2011.pdf (accessed February 13, 2013)

FIGURE 4.5

**New users of marijuana over age 12 and the mean age at first use among those aged 12–49, 2002–11**

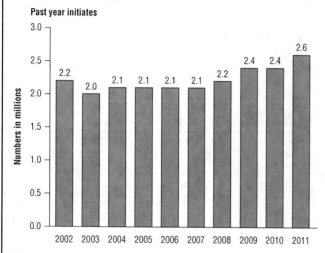

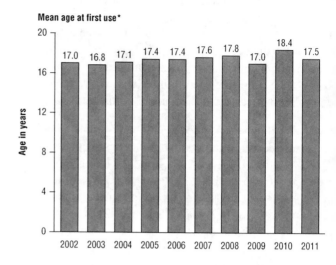

*Mean-age-at-first-use estimates are for recent initiates aged 12 to 49.

SOURCE: "Figure 5.4. Past Year Marijuana Initiates among Persons Aged 12 or Older and Mean Age at First Use of Marijuana among Past Year Marijuana Initiates Aged 12 to 49: 2002–2011," in *Results from the 2011 National Survey on Drug Use and Health: Summary of National Findings*, U.S. Department of Health and Human Services, Substance Abuse and Mental Health Services Administration, September 2012, http://www.samhsa.gov/data/NSDUH/2k11Results/NSDUHresults2011.pdf (accessed February 13, 2013)

for the first time. (See Figure 4.5.) The average age of those first-timers ranged from 16.8 years in 2003 to 18.4 years in 2010, indicating in general that the average age at which people tried marijuana for the first time is about 17.

## PSYCHOTHERAPEUTICS

Psychotherapeutics, a group of drugs that includes pain relievers, tranquilizers, stimulants (including methamphetamine), and sedatives, was the second-most used group of illicit drugs between 2002 and 2011. (See Figure 4.3.) During those years the use of psychotherapeutics among people aged 12 years and older ranged from 2.4% to 2.9% of this population.

Figure 4.3 shows that 2.4% of the population aged 12 years and older were current users of prescription-type psychotherapeutic drugs for nonmedical reasons in 2011. Use was down from 2.7% in 2010. According to the NSDUH, in 2011 pain relievers were the most used and sedatives were the least used psychotherapeutics.

### Pain Relievers

Table 4.3 shows the percentages of people aged 12 years and older who used prescription pain relievers for nonmedical reasons during their lifetime, during the past year, and during the past month in 2010 and 2011. Current users made up 1.7% of the population in 2011 and 2% in 2010. Approximately 4.3% of people had used painkillers for nonmedical reasons in 2011, and about 13.3% had tried them at least once during their lifetime.

Most current users of illicit pain relievers in 2010 and 2011 were young adults aged 18 to 25 years (4.4% in 2010 and 3.6% in 2011). (See Table 4.3.) Those aged 12 to 17 years were the next most likely to take these drugs (2.5% in 2010 and 2.3% in 2011). Only 1.5% of those aged 26 years and older were current illicit users of prescription pain relievers in 2010, a figure that dropped slightly to 1.4% in 2011.

The percentage of current users of illicit pain relievers among whites was approximately 2% of each population in 2010 and 2011. (See Table 4.3.) In 2011 Asian-Americans had a very low current rate of use at 0.6%. Native Americans or Alaskan Natives had a very high percentage of current users at 4% in 2010 and 4.6% in 2011. The 2011 percentage was more than two-and-a-half times the national average of 1.7% in that year.

NARCOTICS: OXYCODONE, HYDROCODONE, AND MORPHINE. Two prescription pain relievers that have been popular with users of illicit prescription drugs are oxycodone and hydrocodone, both of which are strong narcotic pain relievers. Narcotics are addictive drugs, such as morphine, codeine, and opium, and they reduce pain, alter mood and behavior, and usually induce sleep. Whereas morphine, codeine, and opium are natural narcotics extracted from the juice of the opium poppy, oxycodone and hydrocodone are semisynthetic narcotics; that is, they are made in the laboratory from codeine.

Oxycodone and hydrocodone are two of the most commonly prescribed narcotic painkillers in the United

**onmedical use of pain relievers among persons aged 12 and older, by time of use and demographic characteristics, 2010 and 2011**

Percentages]

| emographic characteristic | Lifetime (2010) | Lifetime (2011) | Past year (2010) | Past year (2011) | Past month (2010) | Past month (2011) |
|---|---|---|---|---|---|---|
| Total | 13.8 | 13.3 | 4.8 | 4.3 | 2.0 | 1.7 |
| **ge** | | | | | | |
| 2–17 | 9.2 | 8.6 | 6.3 | 5.9 | 2.5 | 2.3 |
| 8–25 | 23.9 | 22.2 | 11.1 | 9.8 | 4.4 | 3.6 |
| 6 or older | 12.6 | 12.4 | 3.6 | 3.2 | 1.5 | 1.4 |
| **ender** | | | | | | |
| Male | 15.8 | 15.5 | 5.6 | 4.8 | 2.3 | 2.0 |
| emale | 11.9 | 11.2 | 4.1 | 3.8 | 1.7 | 1.5 |
| **ispanic origin and race** | | | | | | |
| ot Hispanic or Latino | 14.2 | 13.7 | 4.8 | 4.3 | 2.0 | 1.8 |
| White | 15.3 | 14.9 | 5.1 | 4.6 | 2.1 | 1.9 |
| Black or African American | 10.6 | 10.8 | 3.6 | 3.5 | 1.6 | 1.4 |
| American Indian or Alaska Native | 19.4 | 15.2 | 8.9 | 8.1 | 4.0 | 4.6 |
| Native Hawaiian or other Pacific Islander | 6.4 | 11.3 | 3.4 | 2.8 | 2.4 | 1.2 |
| Asian | 6.3 | 5.0 | 3.2 | 1.7 | 0.7 | 0.6 |
| Two or more races | 17.3 | 15.2 | 7.0 | 5.2 | 2.4 | 2.5 |
| Hispanic or Latino | 11.3 | 10.8 | 4.9 | 4.3 | 2.0 | 1.6 |

ote: Some 2010 estimates may differ from previously published estimates due to updates.

OURCE: "Table 1.54B. Nonmedical Use of Pain Relievers in Lifetime, Past Year, and Past Month among Persons Aged 12 or Older, by Demographic Characteristics: Percentages, 2010 and 2011," in *Results from the 2011 National Survey on Drug Use and Health: Detailed Tables*, U.S. Department of Health and Human Services, Substance Abuse and Mental Health Services Administration, September 2012, http://www.samhsa.gov/data/NSDUH/2011SummNatFind DetTables/NSDUH-DetTabsPDFWHTML2011/2k11DetailedTabs/Web/PDFW/NSDUH-DetTabsSect1peTabs19to23-2011.pdf (accessed February 13, 2013)

States. Even though they are designed to have a less euphoric effect than morphine, they are still highly sought after by recreational users and addicts. Like morphine, these drugs have enough potential for abuse that they are classified as Schedule II substances.

Oxycodone is the active ingredient in many narcotic pain relievers, including those manufactured as time-release caplets or those containing other pain relievers such as aspirin and acetaminophen. Illicit users of oxycodone crush, chew, or dissolve and inject the drug so that they receive all the oxycodone at once, giving them a heroin-like high. Emergency departments report serious injuries and deaths from the abuse of oxycodone, often by teenagers and young adults. In *Monitoring the Future National Survey Results on Drug Use, 1975–2011, Volume I: Secondary School Students* (June 2012, http://www.monitoringthefuture.org/pubs/monographs/mtf-vol1_2011.pdf), Lloyd D. Johnston et al. of the University of Michigan report that 4.9% of high school seniors had tried oxycodone at least once during the past year.

Morphine is extracted from opium and is one of the most effective drugs known for pain relief. It is marketed in the form of oral solutions, sustained-release tablets, and injectable preparations. Morphine is used legally only in hospitals or hospice care, usually to control the severe pain that results from illnesses such as cancer. Tolerance and dependence develop rapidly in the morphine abuser. According to Johnston et al., the annual prevalence rate of morphine use for high school seniors in 2011 was 1.4%.

**Tranquilizers**

A tranquilizer is a calming medication that relieves tension and anxiety. Tranquilizers are central nervous system depressants and include a group of drugs called benzodiazepines. They are also known as sleeping pills, downers, or tranks. Benzodiazepines have a relatively slow onset but long duration of action. They also have a greater margin of safety than other depressants.

Johnston et al. note that most illicit tranquilizer use reported in recent years involved the drugs Valium and Xanax. In 2011, 1.6% of high school seniors had taken Valium during the previous year and 2.8% had taken Xanax. These figures represented a decline from 2010, when 1.9% of high school seniors had taken Valium within the past year and 3.7% had taken Xanax.

Prolonged use of excessive doses of tranquilizers may result in physical and psychological dependence. Because benzodiazepines are eliminated from the body slowly, withdrawal symptoms generally develop gradually, usually seven to 10 days after continued high doses are stopped. When these drugs are used illicitly, they are often taken with alcohol or marijuana to achieve a euphoric high.

ROHYPNOL: THE DATE RAPE DRUG. Rohypnol, another benzodiazepine, has become increasingly popular among young people. Manufactured as a short-term treatment for severe sleeping disorders, the drug is not marketed legally in the United States and must be smuggled in. It is widely known as a date rape drug because would-be rapists have been known to drop it secretly into a victim's drink to facilitate sexual assault. In a sufficiently large dose it can leave a victim physically incapacitated and cause amnesia that may prevent him or her from recalling an assault. Responding to pressure from the U.S. government, Roche, the Mexican producer of Rohypnol, began putting a blue dye in the pill so that it can be seen when dissolved in a drink. Johnston et al. indicate that in 2011, 1.3% of high school seniors used Rohypnol at least once during the previous year.

## Synthetic Stimulants

Stimulants (uppers) are drugs that produce a sense of euphoria or wakefulness. They are used to increase alertness, boost endurance and productivity, and suppress the appetite. Examples of stimulants are caffeine, nicotine, amphetamine, methamphetamine, and cocaine.

Potent stimulants, such as amphetamine and methamphetamine, make users feel stronger, more decisive, and self-possessed. Chronic users often develop a pattern of using uppers in the morning and depressants (downers), such as alcohol or sleeping pills, at night. Such manipulation interferes with normal body processes and can lead to mental and physical illness.

Large doses of stimulants can produce paranoia and auditory and visual hallucinations. Overdoses can also produce dizziness, tremors, agitation, hostility, panic, headaches, flushed skin, chest pain with palpitations, excessive sweating, vomiting, and abdominal cramps. When

withdrawing from stimulants, chronic high-dose user exhibit depression, apathy, fatigue, and disturbed sleep.

**AMPHETAMINE AND METHAMPHETAMINE.** Amphet amine has been used to treat sleeping disorders and dur ing World War II (1939–1945) it was used to keep soldiers awake. Abuse of amphetamine was noticed dur ing the 1960s. It was used by truck drivers to help them stay alert during long hauls, by athletes to help them train longer, and by many people to lose weight. An injectable form of amphetamine, methamphetamine, was abused by a subculture of people dubbed "speed freaks."

In 1965 the federal government realized that amphet amine products had tremendous potential for abuse, so it amended food and drug laws to place stricter controls on their distribution and use. All amphetamines are now Sched ule II drugs, in the same category as morphine and cocaine

Methamphetamine is a powerful stimulant that is relatively easy for drug traffickers to synthesize in homemade labs, so its illegal synthesis, distribution, and sale developed after new laws made amphetamine more difficult to get. Two products that come out of these clandestine labs are the injectable form of methamphetamine (meth) and the crystallized form (crystal meth or ice) that is smoked. Both forms are highly addictive and toxic. Chronic abuse results in a schizophrenic-like mental illness that is characterized by paranoia, picking at the skin, and hallucinations.

Figure 4.6 shows data on new users of methamphetamine during the past year between 2002 and 2011. In

**FIGURE 4.6**

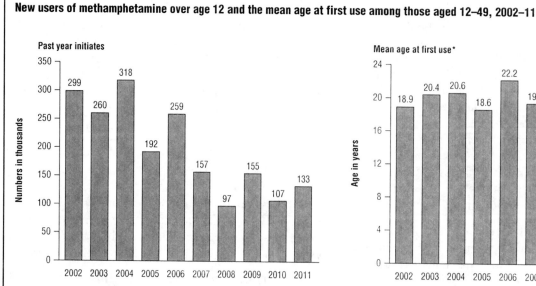

New users of methamphetamine over age 12 and the mean age at first use among those aged 12–49, 2002–11

*Mean-age-at-first-use estimates are for recent initiates aged 12 to 49.

SOURCE: "Figure 5.6. Past Year Methamphetamine Initiates among Persons Aged 12 or Older and Mean Age at First Use of Methamphetamine among Past Year Methamphetamine Initiates Aged 12 to 49: 2002–2011," in *Results from the 2011 National Survey on Drug Use and Health: Summary of National Findings*, U.S. Department of Health and Human Services, Substance Abuse and Mental Health Services Administration, September 2012, http://www .samhsa.gov/data/NSDUH/2k11Results/NSDUHresults2011.pdf (accessed February 13, 2013)

011, 133,000 people aged 12 years and older began sing methamphetamine. The number of methamphetnine initiates declined from 2002, but the downward end had a zigzag pattern. The 2011 figure was up from 07,000 methamphetamine initiates in 2010. However, igure 4.6 also shows that the mean (average) age at hich methamphetamine users first used the drug in 011 was 17.8 years, the youngest average since 2002 nd nearly 4.5 years younger than the highest mean age f 22.2 years in 2006. Johnston et al. note that in 2011 nnual methamphetamine use was approximately 1% for ll age subgroups within the 18- to 30-year-old span. (See igure 4.7.)

## edatives

Like tranquilizers, sedatives are calming, soothing rugs. They relieve tension and anxiety. Also, like tranquilzers, sedatives are central nervous system depressants, ut they include a group of drugs called barbiturates, vhich are generally stronger than tranquilizers. Barbituates have many street names, including barbs, yellows, nd reds.

Small therapeutic doses of sedatives calm nervous onditions; larger doses cause sleep within a short period. A feeling of excitement precedes the sedation. The prinary danger of sedatives is that too large a dose can ring a person through stages of sedation, sleep, and oma and ultimately cause death via respiratory failure

and cardiovascular complications. According to Johnston et al., the past-year use of sedatives by high school seniors gradually rose from 2.8% in 1992 to 7.2% in 2005, before slowly falling to 4.3% in 2011.

## COCAINE

After marijuana and psychotherapeutics, cocaine was the next most used illicit drug in 2011. (See Figure 4.3.) Cocaine, a powerful stimulant, is extracted from the leaves of the coca plant (*Erythroxylon coca*). The plant has been cultivated in the Andean highlands of South America since prehistoric times. In these regions of South America, coca leaves are frequently chewed for refreshment and relief from fatigue—in much the same way some North Americans chew tobacco.

Pure cocaine was first used during the 1880s as a local anesthetic in eye, nose, and throat surgeries. It was also used in dental procedures. Since then, other drugs, such as lidocaine and novocaine, have replaced it as an anesthetic.

Illicit cocaine is distributed as a white crystalline powder and is often contaminated (cut) with sugars or local anesthetics. The drug is commonly snorted. Less commonly, it is mixed with water and injected, which brings a more intense high because the drug reaches the brain more rapidly.

**IGURE 4.7**

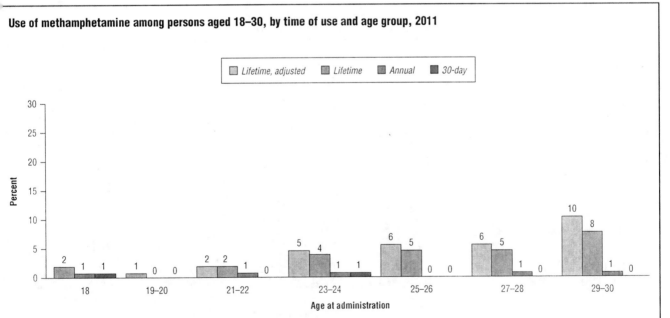

Use of methamphetamine among persons aged 18–30, by time of use and age group, 2011

Notes: Lifetime prevalence estimates were adjusted for inconsistency in self-reports of drug use over time.
Due to rounding some bars with the same number may have uneven height.
Questions about the use of methamphetamines were not included in the questionnaires for 35-, 40-, 45-, and 50-year-olds.

SOURCE: Lloyd D. Johnston et al., "Figure 4-5. Methamphetamine: Lifetime, Annual, and 30-Day Prevalence among Respondents of Modal Ages 18 through 30 by Age Group, 2011," in *Monitoring the Future National Survey Results on Drug Use, 1975–2011: Volume II, College Students and Adults Ages 19–50*, University of Michigan, Ann Arbor, Institute for Social Research, 2012, http://www.monitoringthefuture.org/pubs/monographs/mtf-vol2_2011.pdf (accessed February 13, 2013)

Cocaine produces a short but extremely powerful rush of energy and confidence. Because the pleasurable effects are so intense, cocaine can lead to severe mental dependency, destroying a person's life as the need for the drug supersedes any other considerations. Physically, cocaine users risk permanent damage to their nose by exposing the cartilage and dissolving the nasal septum (membrane), resulting in a collapsed nose. Cocaine significantly increases the risk of a heart attack in the first hour after use. Heavy use (0.1 of an ounce [2 g] or more per week) impairs memory, decision making, and manual dexterity.

Freebasing is the smoking of purified cocaine prepared using a method that frees the cocaine base from impurities. Freebase is prepared by mixing cocaine with ether and sodium hydroxide or baking powder (sodium bicarbonate). The salt base dissolves, leaving granules of pure cocaine. Next, these granules are collected, dried, and heated in a pipe that is filled with water or rum until they vaporize. The vapor is inhaled directly into the lungs, causing an immediate high that lasts about 10 minutes.

There is a danger of being badly burned if the open flame gets too close to the ether or the rum, causing it to flare up as it burns. After the actor-comedian Richard Pryor (1940–2005) set himself on fire while freebasing in 1980, many users began searching for a safer way to achieve the same high. The dangers inherent in freebasing may have been the catalyst for the development of crack cocaine.

**Crack Cocaine**

Cocaine hydrochloride, the powdered form of cocaine, is soluble in water, can be injected, and is fairly insensitive to heat. Crack cocaine is processed by mixing cocaine with baking soda and heating it to remove the hydrochloride. The resultant chips or rocks of pure cocaine are usually smoked in a pipe or added to a cigarette or marijuana joint. The name comes from the crackling sound that is made when the mixture is smoked.

Inhaling the cocaine fumes produces a rapid, intense and short-lived high. This incredible intensity is followed within minutes by an abnormally disconcerting and anxious crash, which leads almost inevitably to the need for more of the drug—and a great likelihood of addiction.

**Prevalence of Cocaine Use**

Figure 4.3 shows that between 0.5% and 1% of the population aged 12 years and older were current users of cocaine between 2002 and 2011. Narrowing the survey population from 18 to 50 years gives a clearer picture of actual use because most users are within this age range. Figure 4.8 shows that in 2011 between 1% and

**FIGURE 4.8**

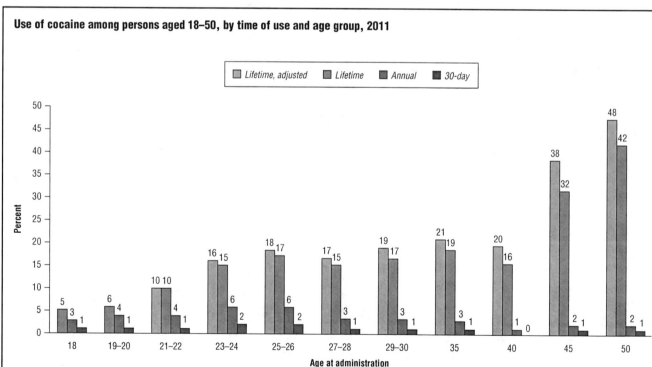

Use of cocaine among persons aged 18–50, by time of use and age group, 2011

Notes: Lifetime prevalence estimates were adjusted for inconsistency in self-reports of drug use over time.
Due to rounding some bars with the same number may have uneven height.

SOURCE: Lloyd D. Johnston et al., "Figure 4-7. Cocaine: Lifetime, Annual, and 30-Day Prevalence among Respondents of Modal Ages 18 through 50 by Age Group, 2011," in *Monitoring the Future National Survey Results on Drug Use, 1975–2011: Volume II, College Students and Adults Ages 19–50*, University of Michigan, Ann Arbor, Institute for Social Research, 2012, http://www.monitoringthefuture.org/pubs/monographs/mtf-vol2_2011.pdf (accessed February 13, 2013)

% of 18- to 30-year-olds were current users and between % and 6% were annual users. For 35- to 50-year-olds, 0% ) 1% were current users and 1% to 3% were annual users.

# HALLUCINOGENS

According to the NSDUH, after marijuana, psychotherapeutics, and cocaine, hallucinogenic drugs were the ext most used illicit drugs in 2011. (See Figure 4.3.) Hallucinogens, also known as psychedelics, are natural or ynthetic substances that distort the perceptions of reality. They cause excitation, which can vary from a sense of vell-being to severe depression. Time may appear to tand still, and forms and colors seem to change and take n new meaning. Typically, the heart rate increases, the blood pressure rises, and the pupils dilate. The experience may be pleasurable or extremely frightening. The effects f hallucinogens vary from use to use and cannot be predicted.

The most common danger of using hallucinogens is mpaired judgment, which can lead to rash decisions and ccidents. Long after hallucinogens have been eliminated rom the body, users may experience flashbacks, in the orm of perceived intensity of color, the apparent motion f fixed objects, or illusions that present one object when nother one is present. Some hallucinogens are present in plants (e.g., mescaline in the peyote cactus), whereas others (e.g., LSD) are synthetic.

## Mescaline and Peyote

Mescaline is a psychoactive alkaloid, or chemical compound, known for its hallucinogenic properties. Mescaline is found naturally in several species of cacti, notably the peyote cactus (*Lophophora williamsii*), which is a small, spineless plant native to Mexico and the U.S. Southwest. The top of the cactus, often called the crown, consists of disk-shaped buttons that can be cut off and dried. These buttons are generally chewed or soaked in water to produce an intoxicating liquid. A dose of 0.01 to 0.02 of an ounce (350 to 500 mg) produces hallucinations lasting from five to 12 hours. Mescaline can be extracted from peyote or other cacti or produced synthetically.

Peyote has long been used by Native Americans in religious ceremonies. The legality of the use of peyote in these ceremonies is decided by individual states.

## MDMA and Other Designer Drugs

Designer drugs are those that are produced in a laboratory by making minor modifications to the chemical structure of existing drugs, resulting in new substances with similar effects. DOM (4-methyl-2,5-dimethoxyamphetamine), DOB (4-bromo-2,5-dimethoxyamphetamine), MDA (3,4-methylenedioxyamphetamine), MDMA (3,4-methylenedioxy-methamphetamine), and other designer drugs are chemical variations of mescaline and amphetamine

that have been synthesized in the laboratory. Designer drugs differ from one another in speed of onset, duration of action, and potency. They are usually taken orally, but they can also be snorted or injected. Because they are produced illegally, designer drugs are seldom pure. Dosage quantity and quality vary considerably.

The most noted designer drug is MDMA (also called ecstasy). It acts as both a stimulant and a psychedelic and is known for enhancing a user's sense of touch. It was first banned by the U.S. Drug Enforcement Administration in 1985. The Anti-drug Abuse Act of 1986 made all designer drugs illegal. Widespread abuse placed MDMA in Schedule I of the CSA.

Designer drugs such as MDMA are often used at raves (large, all-night dance parties that are held in unusual places such as warehouses or railroad yards). Even though many raves have become mainstream events that are professionally organized and held at public venues, the underground culture of raves remains an alluring draw to many teenagers. Part of the allure is drug use. For this reason, such drugs are also called club drugs. (Club drugs include MDMA, Rohypnol, LSD, and methamphetamine, among others.)

Users of MDMA have been known to suffer serious psychological effects—including confusion, depression, sleep problems, drug craving, severe anxiety, and paranoia—both during and sometimes weeks after taking the drug. Physical symptoms include muscle tension, involuntary teeth clenching, nausea, blurred vision, rapid eye movement, faintness, and chills or sweating. MDMA can also interfere with the body's ability to regulate temperature, and severe dehydration, particularly among users who dance for hours while under the drug's influence, is a serious hazard.

According to Johnston et al., past-year MDMA use by high school seniors plummeted during the first half of the first decade of the 21st century, from 9.2% in 2001 to 3% in 2005. Thereafter, MDMA use among high school seniors began a steady climb, reaching 5.3% in 2011.

### LSD

LSD is one of the most potent mood-changing chemicals in existence. Odorless, colorless, and tasteless, it is produced from a substance derived from ergot fungus or from a chemical found in morning glory seeds. Both chemicals are found in Schedule III of the CSA, whereas LSD itself is a Schedule I substance.

LSD is usually sold in tablets, thin squares of gelatin, or impregnated paper. It can also be taken in a liquid form that is dropped on the tongue or in the eyes with an eye dropper. The effects of doses higher than 30 to 50 micrograms can persist for 10 to 12 hours, severely impairing judgment and decision making. Tolerance develops rapidly, and more of the drug is needed to achieve the desired effect. It is, however, nonaddictive.

Because of its structural similarity to a chemical that is present in the brain, LSD was originally used as a research tool to study the mechanism of mental illness. It was later adopted by the drug culture of the 1960s. LSD use dropped during the 1980s, showed a resurgence during the 1990s, and then dropped again through 2011. Johnston et al. note that the past-year use of LSD in 2011 was 2.7% for high school seniors, 2% for college students, and 1.7% for young adults.

### Phencyclidine and Related Drugs

Many drug-treatment professionals believe that phencyclidine (PCP) poses greater risks to the user than any other drug. In the United States most PCP is manufactured in clandestine laboratories and sold on the black market. This drug is sold under at least 50 different names, many of which reflect its bizarre and volatile effects. It is often sold to users who think they are buying mescaline or LSD.

PCP is an anesthetic, so it produces an inability to feel pain, which can lead to serious bodily injury. Unlike other hallucinogens, PCP produces depression in some individuals. Regular use often impairs memory, perception,

concentration, motor movement, and judgment. PCP can also produce a psychotic state that is in many ways indistinguishable from schizophrenia, or it can lead to hallucinations, mood swings, paranoia, and amnesia.

Because of the extreme psychic disorders that are associated with repeated use, or even with one dose, of PCP and related drugs, Congress passed the Psychotropic Substances Act of 1978. The penalties imposed for the manufacture or possession of these chemicals are the stiffest of any nonnarcotic violation under the CSA.

In its pure form PCP is a white crystalline powder that readily dissolves in water. It can be taken in tablet or capsule form. It can also be swallowed, snorted, smoked, or injected. It is commonly applied to a leafy material, such as parsley, mint, oregano, or marijuana, and smoked. According to Johnston et al., the past-year use of PCP in 2011 was 1.3% for high school seniors. For young adults the annual prevalence has historically fluctuated between 0.1% and 0.6%.

### Prevalence of Hallucinogen Use

According to the NSDUH, roughly 1 million people aged 12 years and older used hallucinogens in the past month in 2011. (See Figure 4.2.) In 2011 current users were concentrated among 18- to 22-year-olds, while annual use persisted through age 45. (See Figure 4.9.)

**FIGURE 4.9**

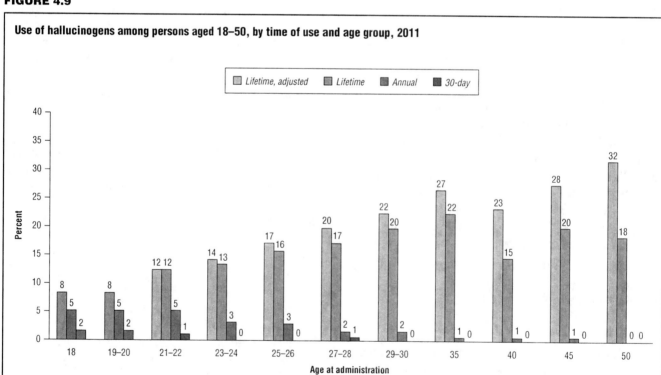

Use of hallucinogens among persons aged 18–50, by time of use and age group, 2011

Notes: Lifetime prevalence estimates were adjusted for inconsistency in self-reports of drug use over time.
Due to rounding some bars with the same number may have uneven height. Unadjusted for the possible underreporting of PCP.

SOURCE: Lloyd D. Johnston et al., "Figure 4-10. Hallucinogens: Lifetime, Annual, and 30-Day Prevalence among Respondents of Modal Ages 18 through 50 by Age Group, 2011," in *Monitoring the Future National Survey Results on Drug Use, 1975–2011: Volume II, College Students and Adults Ages 19–50*, University of Michigan, Ann Arbor, Institute for Social Research, 2012, http://www.monitoringthefuture.org/pubs/monographs/mtf-vol2_2011.pdf (accessed February 13, 2013)

hnston et al. indicate that the annual prevalence for hallucinogen use other than LSD in 2011 was 4.3% for high school seniors, 3.4% for college students, and 3.2% for young adults.

## INHALANTS

Inhalants were the least used group of illicit drugs in 2011, with the exception of heroin. (See Figure 4.2.) Inhalants are volatile liquids, such as cleaning fluids, glue, gasoline, paint, and turpentine, the vapors of which are inhaled. Sometimes the sprays of aerosols are inhaled, such as those of spray paints, spray deodorants, hair spray, or fabric protector spray. According to the NSDUH, an estimated 600,000 people tried inhalants for the first time in 2011. As in past years, this group was dominated by those aged 18 years and younger, representing 67.1% of new users. The NSDUH also reports that in 2011, 1% of people aged 12 to 13 years were current inhalant users. By the age of 26, only 0.1% were inhalant users.

## OTHER ILLICIT DRUGS

### Heroin

Heroin is a narcotic, as are oxycodone, hydrocodone, and morphine. Heroin, however, is not used as a medicine, so it is not included with the psychotherapeutics.

Heroin is extracted from morphine, which is extracted from opium. This drug was not used extensively until the Bayer Company of Elberfeld, Germany, began commercial production in 1898. It was widely used as a cough remedy and painkiller for years, with the medical profession largely unaware of its potential for addiction. However, by 1914 the Harrison Narcotic Act established control of heroin in the United States.

Pure heroin, a bitter white powder, is usually dissolved and injected. Street-quality heroin may vary in color from white to dark brown, depending on the amount of impurities left from the extraction process or the presence of additives, such as food coloring, cocoa, or brown sugar.

Black tar heroin is popular in the western United States. A crudely processed form of heroin, black tar is manufactured illegally in Mexico and derives its name from its sticky, dark brown or black appearance. Black tar is often sold on the street in its tar-like state and can be diluted with substances such as burned cornstarch or converted into a powder.

In the past heroin was usually injected—intravenously (the preferred method), subcutaneously (directly under the skin), or intramuscularly (directly into the muscle). However, the increased availability of high-purity heroin meant that users could snort or smoke the drug, which contributed to an increase in heroin use. Snorting or smoking is more appealing to users who fear contracting the human immunodeficiency virus (HIV) and hepatitis through needles that are shared with potentially infected users. Users who smoke or snort heroin also avoid the stigma that is attached to heroin use: the needle marks that are left on the user's skin. Once hooked, however, many abusers who started snorting or smoking heroin eventually shift to injecting it.

Symptoms and signs of heroin use include euphoria, drowsiness, respiratory depression, constricted pupils, and nausea. Withdrawal symptoms include watery eyes, runny nose, yawning, loss of appetite, tremors, panic, chills, sweating, nausea, diarrhea, muscle cramps, and insomnia. Elevations in blood pressure, pulse, respiratory rate, and temperature occur as withdrawal progresses. Because heroin abusers are often unaware of the actual strength of the drug and its true contents, they are at risk of overdose. Symptoms of overdose, which may result in death, include shallow breathing, clammy skin, convulsions, and coma. The NSDUH reports that 300,000 Americans aged 12 years and older were current heroin users in 2011. (See Figure 4.2.)

### Anabolic Steroids

Anabolic steroids are drugs that are derived from the male sex hormone testosterone. They are used illegally by some athletes, including weight lifters, bodybuilders, long-distance runners, and cyclists, who believe these drugs can give them a competitive advantage or improve their physical appearance. When used in combination with exercise training and a high-protein diet, anabolic steroids can lead to increased muscle size and strength, improved endurance, and shorter recovery time between workouts.

Steroids are taken orally or by intramuscular injection. Most are smuggled into the United States and sold at gyms and competitions or sold by mail-order companies. In 1991 concerns about anabolic steroids led Congress to place them into Schedule III of the CSA.

There is growing evidence that using anabolic steroids can result in serious health problems, including cardiovascular and liver damage and harm to reproductive organs. The U.S. Department of Justice and the Drug Enforcement Administration's Diversion Control Program list the effects of anabolic steroids in "Anabolic Steroids: Hidden Dangers" (March 2008, http://www .deadiversion.usdoj.gov/pubs/brochures/steroids/hidden/ hiddendangers.pdf). There are many types of physical side effects, including elevated LDL (bad) cholesterol levels and reduced HDL (good) cholesterol levels, severe acne, premature balding, mood swings, and atrophying of the testicles. Males may develop breasts, whereas females may experience a deepening of the voice, increased body-hair growth, fewer menstrual cycles, and diminished breast size. Some of these effects are irreversible. In adolescents, bone development may stop, causing stunted growth. Some users become violently aggressive.

By the turn of the 21st century a few professional sports agencies had begun to acknowledge that widespread steroid use was taking place in their ranks. For example, in 2005 Major League Baseball (MLB) initiated regular testing of players for steroid use. In 2009 New York Yankees third baseman Alex Rodriguez (1975–) was accused of using steroids back in 2003, when he played shortstop for the Texas Rangers. Rodriguez joined a long list of other record-breaking, award-winning MLB players who have been implicated in the use of performance-enhancing drugs, including Roger Clemens (1962–), Mark McGwire (1963–), and Barry Bonds (1964–).

One of the most far-reaching drug scandals in the history of international sports broke in 2012, when it was discovered that the celebrated American cyclist Lance Armstrong (1971–) had used a number of banned substances over the course of his career, including corticosteroids, testosterone, human growth hormone, and erythropoietin. In addition, the U.S. Anti-Doping Agency revealed that Armstrong had also coerced several of his teammates on the U.S. Postal Service cycling team to use performance-enhancing drugs. As a result, Armstrong was stripped of all seven of his Tour de France titles, in addition to being permanently banned from competitive cycling.

According to Amy Brittain and Mark Mueller, in "N.J. Doctor Supplied Steroids to Hundreds of Law Enforcement Officers, Firefighters" (NJ.com, December 12, 2010), a seven-month-long investigation by the *Star-Ledger* of Newark, New Jersey, revealed in December 2010 that over 200 police officers and firefighters had been using steroids. Brittain and Mueller note that the investigation implicated Joseph Colao, a Jersey City, New Jersey, physician, who died in 2007, and state that "in just over a year, records show, at least 248 officers and firefighters from 53 agencies used Colao's fraudulent practice to obtain muscle-building drugs, some of which have been linked to increased aggression, confusion and reckless behavior." Taxpayer dollars were allegedly used to fill the prescriptions. As of April 2013, an investigation was ongoing.

Steroid use is not limited to professional athletes and other public figures, however. Danice K. Eaton et al. report in "Youth Risk Behavior Surveillance—United States, 2011" (*Morbidity and Mortality Weekly Report*, vol. 61, no. SS04, June 8, 2012) that in 2011, 4.2% of male high school students and 2.9% of female students had used illegal steroids by the time they were seniors. Johnston et al. determine the annual prevalence rates for androstenedione, a precursor to anabolic steroids, which was available over the counter until early 2005: among male students, annual prevalence rates of this drug in 2011 were 0.5%, 0.9%, and 1.5% in eighth, 10th, and 12th grades, respectively. The rates among female students in 2011 were lower than among male students: 0.5%, 0.7%, and 0.1% in eighth, 10th, and 12th grades, respectively.

## ILLICIT DRUG USE DURING PREGNANCY

Illicit drug use during pregnancy places both the mother and the fetus (unborn child) at risk for serious health problems. For example, a fetus may become addicted to heroin in its mother's womb—provided the fetus reaches full term and is born (fetal death is a possibility). Cocaine use by the pregnant mother carries similar risks to the fetus and may kill the mother as well. LSD use may lead to birth defects. PCP users may have smaller-than-normal babies who later turn out to have poor muscle control. Learning disabilities are associated with children born to women using cocaine and MDMA while pregnant. Smoking marijuana may prevent an embryo from attaching to the uterine wall and halt pregnancy.

The NSDUH surveyed women regarding their illicit drug use. A smaller percentage of pregnant women took illicit drugs than did women who were not pregnant. However, illicit drug use among pregnant women did occur. In 2010–11, 5% of pregnant women took illicit drugs. (See Table 4.4.) The most prevalent illicit drug use during pregnancy was smoking marijuana and hashish—4.1% in 2010–11, up from 3.9% in 2008–09. Even though smoking marijuana may seem safe to some pregnant women, it is not. In "Neurobiological Consequences of Maternal Cannabis on Human Fetal Development and Its Neuropsychiatric Outcome" (*European Archives of Psychiatry and Clinical Neuroscience*, vol. 259, no. 7, October 2009), Didier Jutras-Aswad et al. note that there is growing scientific evidence that smoking marijuana during pregnancy has a long-term influence on the developing brain and other parts of the nervous system of the fetus, which affects behavior and mental health.

The next most used illicit drugs during pregnancy were psychotherapeutics, which were taken for nonmedical reasons. (See Table 4.4.) One percent of pregnant women took prescription drugs such as pain relievers, tranquilizers, stimulants, and sedatives in 2010–11, down from 1.1% of pregnant women in 2008–09. Of the psychotherapeutics, pain relievers were taken the most often. The percentage of pregnant women who used heroin, hallucinogens, or inhalants during their pregnancy was low.

## DRUG ABUSE ARRESTS

The Office of National Drug Policy reports in *National Drug Control Strategy: Data Supplement 2012* (May 2012, http://www.whitehouse.gov/sites/default/files/page/files/2012_data_supplement_final.pdf) that there were over 1.6 million arrests for drug abuse violations in 2010. As Table 4.5 shows, the estimated number of arrests for drug abuse violations gradually increased beginning in

**ercentage of past-month illicit drug use among females aged 15–44, by pregnancy status, 2008–09 and 2010–11**

| | Total[a] | | Pregnancy status | | | |
|---|---|---|---|---|---|---|
| | | | Pregnant | | Not pregnant | |
| rug | 2008–2009 | 2010–2011 | 2008–2009 | 2010–2011 | 2008–2009 | 2010–2011 |
| icit drugs[b] | 10.4 | 10.5 | 4.5 | 5.0 | 10.6 | 10.8 |
| arijuana and hashish | 7.7 | 8.0 | 3.9 | 4.1 | 7.9 | 8.2 |
| ocaine | 0.7 | 0.6 | 0.1 | 0.1 | 0.8 | 0.6 |
| Crack | 0.2 | 0.1 | * | 0.1 | 0.2 | 0.1 |
| eroin | 0.1 | 0.1 | 0.1 | 0.2 | 0.1 | 0.1 |
| allucinogens | 0.7 | 0.6 | 0.7 | 0.1 | 0.7 | 0.6 |
| LSD | 0.1 | 0.0 | 0.2 | * | 0.1 | 0.0 |
| PCP | 0.0 | 0.0 | 0.2 | 0.0 | 0.0 | 0.0 |
| Ecstasy | 0.4 | 0.4 | 0.7 | 0.1 | 0.4 | 0.4 |
| halants | 0.2 | 0.2 | 0.3 | 0.0 | 0.2 | 0.2 |
| onmedical use of psychotherapeutics[c, d] | 3.8 | 3.5 | 1.1 | 1.0 | 3.9 | 3.6 |
| Pain relievers | 2.7 | 2.4 | 0.9 | 0.9 | 2.8 | 2.5 |
| OxyContin® | 0.2 | 0.2 | 0.2 | 0.1 | 0.2 | 0.2 |
| Tranquilizers | 1.3 | 1.2 | 0.6 | 0.1 | 1.3 | 1.2 |
| Stimulants[d] | 0.7 | 0.6 | 0.2 | 0.2 | 0.7 | 0.6 |
| Methamphetamine[d] | 0.2 | 0.2 | 0.2 | * | 0.2 | 0.2 |
| Sedatives | 0.1 | 0.1 | 0.2 | 0.0 | 0.1 | 0.1 |
| licit drugs other than Marijuana[b] | 4.7 | 4.4 | 1.7 | 1.3 | 4.8 | 4.5 |

Low precision; no estimate reported.

ote: Some 2008–2009 estimates may differ from previously published estimates due to updates.

stimates in the total column are for all females aged 15 to 44, including those with unknown pregnancy status.

licit drugs include marijuana/hashish, cocaine (including crack), heroin, hallucinogens, inhalants, or prescription-type psychotherapeutics used nonmedically. Illicit drugs other than arijuana include cocaine (including crack), heroin, hallucinogens, inhalants, or prescription-type psychotherapeutics used nonmedically. The estimates for nonmedical use of sychotherapeutics, stimulants, and methamphetamine incorporated in these summary estimates do not include data from new methamphetamine items added in 2005 and 2006. lonmedical use of prescription-type psychotherapeutics includes the nonmedical use of pain relievers, tranquilizers, stimulants, or sedatives and does not include over-the-counter rugs.

stimates of nonmedical use of psychotherapeutics, stimulants, and methamphetamine in the designated rows include data from new methamphetamine items added in 2005 and 2006 nd are not comparable with estimates presented in NSDUH reports prior to the 2007 National Findings report.

OURCE: "Table 6.71B. Types of Illicit Drug Use in the Past Month among Females Aged 15 to 44, by Pregnancy Status: Percentages, Annual Averages Based n 2008–2009 and 2010–2011," in *Results from the 2011 National Survey on Drug Use and Health: Detailed Tables*, U.S. Department of Health and Human ervices, Substance Abuse and Mental Health Services Administration, September 2012, http://www.samhsa.gov/data/NSDUH/2011SummNatFindDetTables/ SDUH-DetTabsPDFWHTML2011/2k11DetailedTabs/Web/PDFW/NSDUH-DetTabsSect6peTabs71to78-2011.pdf (accessed February 13, 2013)

he early 1990s, peaked at 1.9 million in 2006, before teadily decreasing over the next four years. The report also eveals that drug arrests as a proportion of all arrests peaked t 13.1% in 2005 and 2006; by comparison, drug arrests ccounted for only 7.1% of all arrests in 1991. During this pan, the distribution of arrests for specific drug infractions hifted dramatically. For example, in 1989 arrests for heroin and cocaine possession represented over one-third 34.7%) of all drug arrests; by 2010 this figure had dropped o 16.4%. In contrast, marijuana possession accounted for ess than a quarter (23.1%) of all drug arrests in 1989. Two lecades later this figure had nearly doubled, with marijuana oossession accounting for 45.8% of all drug-related arrests n 2010.

Most people arrested for drug offenses are charged with possession (carrying some kind of drug) rather than with trafficking (the sale or manufacture of drugs). As Table 4.5 shows, in 2010 more than four-fifths (82%) of those arrested for drug law violations were for possession.

## ARRESTEE DRUG USE

The National Institute of Justice operated the Arrestee Drug Abuse Monitoring (ADAM) Program from 1987 to 2004 and published an annual report that summarized the previous year's data. The ADAM Program ended in 2004 in response to budgetary considerations and resumed in 2007 under the ONDCP.

In 2011 the ADAM Program surveyed arrestees in 10 urban sites about drug use in the past year and conducted urinalyses to determine if any of 10 drugs (amphetamine/ methamphetamine, barbiturates, benzodiazepines, cocaine, marijuana, methadone, opiates, oxycodone, PCP, and propoxyphene) had been used recently. According to the *ADAM II 2011 Annual Report* (May 2012, http://www .whitehouse.gov/sites/default/files/email-files/adam_ii_2011 _annual_rpt_web_version_corrected.pdf), in nine out of the 10 sites surveyed, urinalysis revealed that 60% or more of adult male arrestees in 2011 had used at least one of the 10 drugs. Over all sites, use ranged from a low of 64.1% of arrestees in Atlanta, Georgia, to a high of 81% in Sacramento, California. Many had used multiple drugs, ranging from 12.9% in Charlotte, North Carolina, to 38.2% in Sacramento.

### Arrests and Race

Enforcing the official public policy on drugs has a significant impact on the nation's justice system: the law

TABLE 4.5

**Drug arrests as percentage of total arrests, by drug category, 1989–2010**

| Year | Total arrests | Arrests for all drug abuse violations | | Distribution of arrests for drug abuse violations[a] | | | | | | | |
|------|---------------|--------|---------|------|------------|------|------------|------|------------|------|------------|
| | | | | Heroin/cocaine[b] | | Marijuana | | Synthetics | | Other drugs | |
| | | Number | Percent | Sale[c] | Possession | Sale[c] | Possession | Sale[c] | Possession | Sale[c] | Possession |
| 1989 | 14,340,900 | 1,361,700 | 9.4 | 19.1 | 34.7 | 6.2 | 23.1 | 0.7 | 1.4 | 6.3 | 8.4 |
| 1990 | 14,195,100 | 1,089,500 | 7.6 | 21.0 | 33.3 | 6.1 | 23.9 | 0.6 | 1.5 | 3.9 | 9.7 |
| 1991 | 14,211,900 | 1,010,000 | 7.1 | 22.5 | 32.8 | 6.1 | 22.4 | 0.8 | 1.4 | 4.0 | 10.1 |
| 1992 | 14,075,100 | 1,066,400 | 7.5 | 20.6 | 32.4 | 6.6 | 25.5 | 0.7 | 1.2 | 3.9 | 9.2 |
| 1993 | 14,036,300 | 1,126,300 | 8.0 | 19.2 | 31.1 | 6.2 | 27.6 | 0.6 | 1.2 | 3.7 | 10.4 |
| 1994 | 14,648,700 | 1,351,400 | 9.2 | 16.8 | 30.3 | 5.8 | 29.8 | 0.5 | 1.2 | 3.6 | 12.0 |
| 1995 | 15,119,800 | 1,476,100 | 9.7 | 14.7 | 27.8 | 5.8 | 34.1 | 0.7 | 1.5 | 3.7 | 11.8 |
| 1996 | 15,168,100 | 1,506,200 | 9.9 | 14.2 | 25.6 | 6.3 | 36.3 | 0.6 | 1.4 | 3.7 | 11.9 |
| 1997 | 15,284,300 | 1,583,600 | 10.3 | 10.3 | 25.4 | 5.6 | 38.3 | 0.8 | 1.8 | 3.9 | 14.0 |
| 1998 | 14,528,300 | 1,559,100 | 10.7 | 11.0 | 25.6 | 5.4 | 38.4 | 1.0 | 1.9 | 3.8 | 12.9 |
| 1999 | 14,031,070 | 1,532,200 | 10.9 | 10.0 | 24.5 | 5.5 | 40.5 | 1.2 | 1.9 | 2.9 | 13.5 |
| 2000 | 13,980,297 | 1,579,566 | 10.9 | 9.3 | 24.2 | 5.6 | 40.9 | 1.1 | 2.2 | 3.0 | 13.6 |
| 2001 | 13,699,254 | 1,586,902 | 11.5 | 9.7 | 23.1 | 5.2 | 40.4 | 1.4 | 2.7 | 3.1 | 14.4 |
| 2002 | 13,741,438 | 1,538,813 | 11.2 | 8.8 | 21.3 | 5.4 | 39.9 | 1.4 | 3.0 | 4.0 | 16.0 |
| 2003 | 13,639,479 | 1,678,192 | 12.3 | 8.8 | 21.5 | 5.5 | 39.5 | 1.5 | 3.1 | 3.6 | 16.6 |
| 2004 | 13,938,071 | 1,746,670 | 12.5 | 8.3 | 22.0 | 5.0 | 39.3 | 1.6 | 3.5 | 3.3 | 17.0 |
| 2005 | 14,094,186 | 1,846,351 | 13.1 | 8.0 | 22.2 | 4.9 | 37.7 | 1.4 | 3.4 | 4.0 | 18.3 |
| 2006 | 14,380,370 | 1,889,810 | 13.1 | 8.0 | 22.8 | 4.8 | 39.1 | 1.5 | 3.4 | 3.2 | 17.2 |
| 2007 | 14,209,365 | 1,841,182 | 13.0 | 7.9 | 21.5 | 5.3 | 42.1 | 1.5 | 3.3 | 2.8 | 15.6 |
| 2008 | 14,005,615 | 1,702,537 | 12.2 | 7.7 | 20.1 | 5.5 | 44.3 | 1.5 | 3.3 | 3.0 | 14.6 |
| 2009 | 13,687,241 | 1,663,582 | 12.2 | 7.1 | 17.7 | 6.0 | 45.6 | 1.7 | 3.7 | 3.5 | 14.6 |
| 2010 | 13,120,947 | 1,638,846 | 12.5 | 6.2 | 16.4 | 6.3 | 45.8 | 1.8 | 4.1 | 3.7 | 15.7 |

[a]Percentages may not add to 100 because of rounding.
[b]Includes heroin or cocaine and their derivatives.
[c]Includes sale/manufacture of drugs.

SOURCE: "Table 50. Total Estimated Arrests and Drug Arrests, 1989–2010," in *National Drug Control Strategy: Data Supplement 2012*, Executive Office of the President, Office of National Drug Policy, 2012, http://www.whitehouse.gov/sites/default/files/page/files/2012_data_supplement_final.pdf (accessed February 16, 2013)

enforcement agencies, the courts, and the state and federal corrections systems. A relatively small percentage of total users are arrested, but at increasing rates. Sentencing policies have changed to require mandatory incarceration of those who possess, not just those who sell, drugs. As a consequence, prison populations have swollen, thereby putting pressure on prison capacities. The number of people in state and federal correctional facilities for drug offenses escalated from 682,563 in 1989 to 1.6 million in 2010. (See Table 4.6.) Table 4.7 shows the sentenced prisoners by offense under state jurisdiction in 2009 alone. The 242,900 people who were incarcerated for drug offenses made up nearly 18% of the total state prison population of 1.4 million. E. Ann Carson and William J. Sabol of the Bureau of Justice Statistics (BJS) report in *Prisoners in 2011* (December 2012, http://bjs.gov/content/pub/pdf/p11.pdf) that in 2011 nearly half (48%) of all federal prisoners were serving time for drug offenses. This figure actually represented a decline from 2000 statistics, when 56.4% of all federal prisoners had been convicted on drug charges.

The proportion of state prison inmates incarcerated on drug charges differ for whites, African-Americans, and Hispanics. In 2009, 73,900 (out of 242,900, or 30.4%) of state drug offense arrestees were white, 122,600 (50.5%) were African-American, and 41,400 (17%) were Hispanic.

(See Table 4.7.) The remainder were people of other races and ethnicities.

## SENTENCING TRENDS

Table 4.8 shows that the duration of sentences fluctuated in the years between 1988 and 2010, increasing from 78 months in 1988 to 95.7 months in 1991, then generally decreasing to a low of 73.8 months in 2001, then steadily increasing again to 88.9 months in 2007, and finally dropping to 78.8 months in 2010.

### Convictions and Race

Carson and Sabol note that of the 237,000 drug offenders serving time in state prisons in 2010, 69,500 (29.3%) were white and 105,600 (44.6%) were African-American. According to the U.S. Census Bureau (May 2012, http://www.census.gov/popest/data/national/asrh/2011/tables/NC-EST2011-03.xls), in 2010 the U.S. population was 78.3% (242.3 million of 309.3 million) white and 13% (40.4 million) African-American. These figures reveal that a disproportionate number of African-Americans were serving time for drug offenses, relative to their overall proportion of the population.

The Human Rights Watch (HRW), an independent and nongovernmental organization that is dedicated to

ug offenders in state and federal prisons, 1989–2010

| ar | Inmates in custody | | | Estimated inmates in custody with drug offense as the most serious offense | | | |
| | State | Federal | Total | Number | | Percent of inmates | |
| | | | | State[a] | Federal[b] | State[a] | Federal[b] |
|---|---|---|---|---|---|---|---|
| 89 | 629,995 | 52,568 | 682,563 | 120,100 | 25,300 | 19.1 | 48.1 |
| 90 | 684,544 | 56,989 | 741,533 | 148,600 | 30,500 | 21.7 | 53.5 |
| 91 | 728,605 | 63,930 | 792,535 | 155,200 | 36,800 | 21.3 | 55.9 |
| 92 | 778,245 | 72,071 | 850,316 | 168,100 | 42,900 | 21.6 | 58.9 |
| 93 | 828,400 | 80,815 | 909,215 | 177,000 | 49,000 | 21.4 | 59.2 |
| 94 | 904,647 | 85,500 | 990,147 | 193,500 | 49,500 | 21.4 | 60.5 |
| 95 | 989,005 | 88,101 | 1,077,106 | 212,800 | 51,700 | 21.5 | 59.9 |
| 96 | 1,032,676 | 92,672 | 1,125,348 | 216,900 | 55,200 | 21.0 | 60.2 |
| 97 | 1,075,167 | 98,944 | 1,174,111 | 222,100 | 58,600 | 20.7 | 60.0 |
| 98 | 1,113,676 | 110,793 | 1,224,469 | 230,500 | 64,000 | 20.7 | 57.8 |
| 99 | 1,161,490 | 125,682 | 1,287,172 | 245,100 | 72,100 | 21.1 | 57.4 |
| 00 | 1,245,845 | 145,416 | 1,391,261 | 244,700 | 74,276 | 20.8 | 56.4 |
| 01 | 1,247,039 | 156,992 | 1,404,032 | 240,800 | 82,400 | 20.4 | 55.0 |
| 02 | 1,276,616 | 163,528 | 1,440,144 | 258,800 | 89,700 | 21.4 | 56.7 |
| 03 | 1,295,542 | 173,059 | 1,468,601 | 244,400 | 92,300 | 20.0 | 54.9 |
| 04 | 1,316,772 | 180,328 | 1,497,100 | 243,800 | 98,400 | 19.6 | 55.4 |
| 05 | 1,340,311 | 187,618 | 1,527,929 | 246,100 | 101,200 | 19.5 | 54.3 |
| 06 | 1,376,899 | 193,046 | 1,569,945 | 264,300 | 101,500 | 19.9 | 53.2 |
| 07 | 1,398,627 | 199,618 | 1,598,245 | 273,600 | 105,200 | 20.2 | 53.3 |
| 08 | 1,408,479 | 201,280 | 1,609,759 | 255,700 | 95,079 | 18.7 | 52.2 |
| 09 | 1,406,237 | 208,118 | 1,614,355 | 242,200 | 96,735 | 17.8 | 50.7 |
| 10 | 1,395,356 | 209,771 | 1,605,127 | NA | 97,472 | NA | 46.5 |

A = Data not yet available.

om 1989 to 1999, estimates for state prisoners held for drug offenses as the most serious crime were made using the Survey of Inmates in State Correctional Facilities, and adjusted to the custody population collected in the National Prisoner Statistics. After 1999, estimates for state prisoners held for drug offenses as the most serious crime were made using the tional Correctional Reporting Program and the National Prisoner Statistics.

ercent of federal drug offenders calculated using the Federal Justice Statistics Resource Center query system and applied to the federal custody count and rounded for an estimated imber of federal drug offenders.

ote: These estimates may not match previously published data. State and federal drug offender counts will differ from previous publications because custody rather than jurisdiction unts are used as denominators to enhance comparability to the 1989 to 1999 estimates.

URCE: "Table 51. Adult Drug Offenders in State or Federal Prisons, 1989–2010," in *National Drug Control Strategy: Data Supplement 2012*, Executive Office
the President, Office of National Drug Policy, 2012, http://www.whitehouse.gov/sites/default/files/page/files/2012_data_supplement_final.pdf (accessed
bruary 16, 2013)

rotecting the human rights of people around the world, ocuments racial disparities in the incarceration of state rug offenders. The HRW considers crime rates, law nforcement priorities, and sentencing legislation as actors that contribute to creating racial disparities in ncarceration. It contends that African-Americans have een disproportionately affected by the War on Drugs, vhich largely aims to arrest, prosecute, and imprison treet-level drug offenders from inner-city areas. Bolster-ig its claims, the HRW discusses in "Race, Drugs, and _aw Enforcement in the United States" (June 19, 2009, ttp://www.hrw.org/en/news/2009/06/19/race-drugs-and-aw-enforcement-united-states) these racial disparities nd notes that African-American males are arrested and ailed on drug charges at "significantly higher rates" than vhite males and that these "rates bear no relationship to ates of offending."

## HE BROADER RELATIONSHIP BETWEEN ILLICIT DRUGS AND CRIME

The relationship between illicit drugs and crime goes eyond the fact that illicit drug use is illegal. There are trong correlations between drug use and a variety of

nondrug crimes. There are usually three reasons given for this correlation:

- Drugs may reduce inhibitions or stimulate aggression and interfere with the ability to earn a legitimate income.

- People who develop a dependence on an illegal drug need a substantial income to pay for it and may commit crimes to fund their habit.

- Drug trafficking may lead to crimes such as extortion, aggravated assault, and homicide.

In *Drug Use and Dependence, State and Federal Prisoners, 2004* (October 2006, http://bjs.ojp.usdoj.gov/content/pub/pdf/dudsfp04.pdf), the most recent report on this topic as of April 2013, Christopher J. Mumola and Jennifer C. Karberg of the BJS discuss the drug use of state and federal prisoners by the type of offense they committed in 2004. Overall, more than half of state and federal prisoners (56% and 50.2%, respectively) reported using illicit drugs in the month before their offense. Unsurprisingly, a high percentage of those in state prison for drug offenses (71.9%) had used drugs in the month before their offense. The correlation between drug use

**TABLE 4.7**

## Number of sentenced offenders in state prisons, by race, gender, and offense, 2009

| Offense | All inmates | Male | Female | White[a] | Black[a] | Hispan |
|---|---|---|---|---|---|---|
| **Total** | 1,365,800 | 1,272,200 | 93,600 | 532,000 | 582,100 | 212,10 |
| **Violent** | 726,100 | 692,600 | 33,600 | 265,600 | 319,700 | 117,80 |
| Murder[b] | 179,000 | 168,800 | 10,200 | 55,700 | 84,000 | 32,30 |
| Manslaughter | 16,900 | 14,800 | 2,200 | 8,200 | 6,400 | 1,90 |
| Rape | 67,800 | 67,200 | 700 | 36,300 | 22,800 | 6,80 |
| Other sexual assault | 99,600 | 98,200 | 1,400 | 58,600 | 22,600 | 15,20 |
| Robbery | 185,700 | 177,700 | 8,000 | 45,300 | 110,000 | 26,60 |
| Assault | 138,100 | 130,000 | 8,200 | 46,600 | 58,400 | 28,00 |
| Other violent | 39,000 | 36,000 | 2,900 | 15,000 | 15,500 | 6,90 |
| **Property** | 261,900 | 234,100 | 27,700 | 132,000 | 88,500 | 34,40 |
| Burglary | 131,000 | 124,900 | 6,200 | 63,400 | 48,100 | 16,40 |
| Larceny | 49,900 | 41,600 | 8,300 | 24,700 | 18,100 | 5,90 |
| Motor vehicle theft | 19,800 | 18,300 | 1,500 | 8,500 | 4,300 | 6,10 |
| Fraud | 33,200 | 23,700 | 9,400 | 19,600 | 10,300 | 2,40 |
| Other property | 28,000 | 25,600 | 2,400 | 15,900 | 7,700 | 3,60 |
| **Drug** | 242,900 | 218,800 | 24,000 | 73,900 | 122,600 | 41,40 |
| **Public-order**[c] | 121,000 | 114,300 | 6,800 | 54,400 | 46,400 | 16,00 |
| **Other/unspecified**[d] | 13,900 | 12,400 | 1,400 | 6,000 | 4,900 | 2,50 |

Note: Counts based on prisoners with a sentence of more than 1 year. Detail may not add to total due to rounding.
[a]Excludes Hispanics and persons identifying as two or more races.
[b]Includes non-negligent manslaughter.
[c]Includes weapons, drunk driving, court offenses, commercialized vice, morals and decency offenses, liquor law violations, and other public-order offenses.
[d]Includes juvenile offenses and other unspecified offense categories.

SOURCE: Paul Guerino, Paige M. Harrison, and William J. Sabol, "Appendix Table 16B. Estimated Number of Sentenced Prisoners under State Jurisdiction, by Offense, Gender, Race, and Hispanic Origin, December 31, 2009," in *Prisoners in 2010*, U.S. Department of Justice, Office of Justice Programs, Bureau of Justice Statistics, December 2011, http://bjs.ojp.usdoj.gov/content/pub/pdf/p10.pdf (accessed February 13, 2013)

and nondrug crimes can be seen, however, in the fact that 64% of state prisoners who committed property offenses and 49.6% of those who committed violent offenses had used drugs in the month before their offense. The percentages for federal prisoners were lower but still substantial, with 57.3% of drug offenders, 49.1% of violent offenders, and 27.7% of property offenders reporting drug use in the month before their offense. Furthermore, more than a quarter of state and federal prisoners (32.1% and 26.4%, respectively) reported they were using illicit drugs at the time of their offense.

For state prisoners, the likelihood that they used drugs in the month before the offense stayed the same from 1997 to 2004, at approximately 56%. The likelihood that federal prisoners used drugs in the month before their offense rose from 44.8% in 1997 to 50.2% in 2004. For state prisoners, women were more likely than men to

have used drugs in the month before their offense in both years. Federal prisoners showed the opposite trend—men were more likely than women to have used drugs in the month before their offense in both years.

For both state and federal prisoners, people aged 24 years and younger were the most likely to have used drugs in the month before the offense in both years. The likelihood of drug use fell with age in both years and for both sets of prisoners. In general, whites were slightly more likely than African-Americans to have used drugs in the month before their offense in both years. Hispanics were the least likely of the three racial groups to have used drugs in the month before their offense. In 2004 the incidence of drug use was over half for whites (58.2%) and African-Americans (52.7%) in federal prison. Only 38.4% of Hispanic federal prisoners used drugs in the month before their offense.

entences for violations of drug laws, by type and length of sentence, U.S. District Courts, 1945–2010

| | | Type of sentence | | | | | | | | | Average sentence to imprisonment (in months)[d] | Average sentence to probation (in months)[e] |
|---|---|---|---|---|---|---|---|---|---|---|---|---|
| | | Imprisonment | | | | | | | | | | |
| | | Regular sentences[a] | | | | | | | | | | |
| | Total | Total regular | 1 through 12 months | 13 through 35 months | 36 through 60 months | Over 60 months | Life sentences | Other[b] | Probation | Fine and other[c] | | |
| 1945 | 861 | X | 308 | 360 | 140 | 53 | NA | X | 287 | 37 | 22.2 | NA |
| 1946 | 949 | X | 430 | 377 | 108 | 34 | NA | X | 369 | 20 | 18.7 | NA |
| 1947 | 1,128 | X | 471 | 452 | 161 | 44 | NA | X | 504 | 38 | 19.7 | NA |
| 1948 | 1,048 | X | 488 | 408 | 122 | 30 | NA | X | 411 | 23 | 18.6 | NA |
| 1949 | 1,187 | X | 541 | 451 | 152 | 43 | NA | X | 398 | 13 | 18.9 | NA |
| 1950 | 1,654 | X | 595 | 736 | 218 | 105 | NA | X | 471 | 11 | 21.9 | NA |
| 1951 | 1,659 | X | 473 | 671 | 328 | 187 | NA | X | 345 | 24 | 27.1 | NA |
| 1952 | 1,551 | X | 221 | 652 | 402 | 276 | NA | X | 312 | 6 | 35.2 | NA |
| 1953 | 1,586 | X | 108 | 789 | 358 | 331 | NA | X | 403 | 14 | 38.4 | NA |
| 1954 | 1,483 | X | 72 | 681 | 360 | 370 | NA | X | 411 | 16 | 41.3 | NA |
| 1955 | 1,457 | X | 47 | 648 | 360 | 402 | NA | X | 329 | 17 | 43.5 | NA |
| 1956 | 1,258 | X | 30 | 511 | 341 | 376 | NA | X | 250 | 13 | 45.8 | NA |
| 1957 | 1,432 | X | 16 | 326 | 248 | 842 | NA | X | 220 | 2 | 66.0 | NA |
| 1958 | 1,351 | X | 25 | 167 | 141 | 1,018 | NA | X | 282 | 8 | 69.4 | NA |
| 1959 | 1,151 | X | 43 | 126 | 95 | 887 | NA | X | 224 | 3 | 74.2 | NA |
| 1960 | 1,232 | X | 33 | 145 | 148 | 906 | NA | X | 271 | 3 | 72.8 | NA |
| 1961 | 1,258 | X | 42 | 126 | 105 | 985 | NA | X | 252 | 5 | 74.0 | NA |
| 1962 | 1,173 | X | 38 | 129 | 106 | 900 | NA | X | 217 | 13 | 70.5 | NA |
| 1963 | 1,085 | X | 39 | 144 | 113 | 789 | NA | X | 304 | 17 | 70.1 | NA |
| 1964 | 1,076 | X | 28 | 142 | 157 | 749 | NA | X | 309 | 23 | 63.7 | NA |
| 1965 | 1,257 | X | 53 | 186 | 197 | 821 | NA | X | 480 | 18 | 60.3 | NA |
| 1966 | 1,272 | X | 85 | 154 | 276 | 757 | NA | X | 589 | 13 | 61.3 | NA |
| 1967 | 1,180 | X | 83 | 139 | 245 | 713 | NA | X | 620 | 22 | 62.0 | NA |
| 1968 | 1,368 | X | 93 | 141 | 293 | 841 | NA | X | 728 | 33 | 64.4 | NA |
| 1969 | 1,581 | X | 110 | 179 | 500 | 892 | NA | X | 1,110 | 18 | 63.7 | NA |
| 1970 | 1,283 | X | 101 | 166 | 276 | 740 | NA | X | 1,156 | 22 | 64.8 | NA |
| 1971 | 1,834 | X | 249 | 300 | 428 | 857 | NA | X | 1,258 | 70 | 58.5 | NA |
| 1972 | 3,050 | X | 882 | 396 | 789 | 983 | NA | X | 2,068 | 130 | 46.4 | NA |
| 1973 | 5,097 | X | 1,445 | 744 | 1,343 | 1,565 | NA | X | 2,591 | 126 | 45.5 | NA |
| 1974 | 5,125 | X | 1,547 | 792 | 1,390 | 1,396 | NA | X | 3,039 | 81 | 43.7 | NA |
| 1975 | 4,887 | X | 1,366 | 706 | 1,441 | 1,374 | NA | X | 3,209 | 55 | 45.3 | NA |
| 1976 | 5,039 | X | 1,221 | 790 | 1,544 | 1,484 | NA | X | 2,927 | 75 | 47.6 | NA |
| 1977 | 5,223 | X | 1,505 | 886 | 1,366 | 1,466 | NA | X | 2,324 | 88 | 47.3 | NA |
| 1978 | 4,119 | 3,605 | 885 | 623 | 956 | 1,141 | NA | 514 | 1,630 | 68 | 51.3 | 38.6 |
| 1979 | 3,641 | 2,820 | 369 | 614 | 868 | 969 | NA | 821 | 1,379 | 47 | 50.8 | 37.8 |
| 1980 | 3,479 | 2,547 | 281 | 565 | 792 | 909 | NA | 932 | 1,232 | 38 | 54.5 | 38.7 |
| 1981 | 3,856 | 2,865 | 403 | 578 | 748 | 1,136 | NA | 991 | 1,371 | 119 | 55.5 | 36.6 |
| 1982 | 4,586 | 3,516 | 383 | 729 | 966 | 1,438 | NA | 1,070 | 1,617 | 133 | 61.4 | 34.1 |
| 1983 | 5,449 | 4,150 | 447 | 890 | 1,011 | 1,802 | NA | 1,299 | 1,893 | 148 | 63.8 | 33.7 |
| 1984 | 5,756 | 4,306 | 354 | 845 | 1,173 | 1,934 | NA | 1,450 | 1,584 | 119 | 65.7 | 43.2 |
| 1985 | 6,786 | 5,207 | 411 | 1,103 | 1,459 | 2,234 | NA | 1,579 | 2,039 | 238 | 64.8 | 36.2 |
| 1986 | 8,152 | 6,601 | 506 | 1,271 | 1,808 | 3,016 | NA | 1,551 | 2,353 | 259 | 70.0 | 38.7 |
| 1987 | 9,907 | 8,188 | 613 | 1,491 | 2,049 | 4,035 | NA | 1,719 | 2,680 | 112 | 73.0 | 39.9 |
| 1988 | 9,983 | 8,560 | 708 | 1,466 | 1,577 | 4,809 | NA | 1,423 | 3,042 | 137 | 78.0 | 33.4 |
| 1989 | 11,626 | 10,838 | 1,270 | 2,343 | 1,844 | 5,381 | NA | 788 | 2,358 | 155 | 73.8 | 32.8 |
| 1990 | 13,838 | 13,462 | 1,490 | 3,047 | 1,801 | 7,124 | NA | 376 | 2,135 | 215 | 79.3 | 32.3 |
| 1991 | 14,382[f] | 14,286 | 1,687 | 2,828 | 3,063 | 6,708 | 34 | 61 | 1,896 | 68 | 95.7 | 53.4 |
| 1992 | 16,040 | 15,775 | 1,810 | 3,423 | 3,397 | 7,145 | 80 | 185 | 2,011 | 194 | 87.8 | 38.7 |
| 1993 | 16,995[f] | 16,639 | 2,097 | 3,383 | 4,128 | 7,031 | 186 | 169 | 1,943 | 310 | 83.2 | 35.8 |
| 1994 | 15,623 | 15,130 | 1,836 | 3,074 | 3,798 | 6,422 | 238 | 255 | 1,908 | 73 | 84.3 | 34.4 |
| 1995 | 14,157 | 13,734 | 1,606 | 2,716 | 3,311 | 6,101 | 150 | 273 | 1,597 | 107 | 88.7 | 33.6 |
| 1996 | 18,333 | 16,684 | 1,643 | 3,334 | 4,025 | 7,113 | 197 | 372 | 1,534 | 112 | 82.5 | 35.0 |
| 1997 | 18,231[f] | 17,456 | 1,687 | 4,166 | 4,445 | 7,158 | 228 | 546 | 1,523 | 79 | 79.3 | 34.9 |
| 1998 | 19,809 | 19,062 | 2,100 | 4,443 | 4,517 | 8,002 | 180 | 567 | 1,629 | 91 | 78.0 | 34.9 |
| 1999 | 22,443[f] | 21,513 | 2,670 | 5,074 | 5,240 | 8,529 | 205 | 724 | 1,719 | 85 | 74.6 | 34.2 |
| 2000 | 23,120 | 22,207 | 2,523 | 5,095 | 5,452 | 9,137 | 148 | 765 | 1,591 | 75 | 75.7 | 35.1 |
| 2001 | 24,011 | 23,127 | 2,780 | 5,350 | 5,670 | 9,327 | 122 | 762 | 1,671 | 133 | 73.8 | 34.5 |
| 2002 | 25,031 | 23,838 | 2,825 | 5,250 | 5,727 | 10,036 | 168 | 1,025 | 1,947 | 148 | 75.9 | 33.4 |
| 2003 | 25,060 | 23,937 | 2,632 | 4,781 | 5,967 | 10,557 | 157 | 966 | 1,781 | 145 | 80.2 | 32.2 |
| 2004 | 23,920 | 22,984 | 2,581 | 4,181 | 5,553 | 10,669 | 146 | 790 | 1,598 | 184 | 82.5 | 28.4 |
| 2005 | 24,786 | 23,831 | 2,389 | 4,296 | 5,719 | 11,427 | 151 | 804 | 1,508 | 294 | 85.7 | 32.7 |
| 2006 | 26,488[g] | 25,437 | 2,035 | 4,438 | 6,159 | 12,805 | 195 | 853 | 1,548 | 275 | 87.9 | 31.8 |
| 2007 | 25,520 | 24,439 | 2,132 | 4,017 | 5,962 | 12,328 | 171 | 910 | 1,344 | 250 | 88.9 | 31.0 |
| 2008 | 25,305[f] | 24,055 | 2,131 | 4,124 | 5,940 | 11,860 | 157 | 1,092 | 1,389 | 226 | 86.0 | 34.5 |
| 2009 | 24,929 | 23,396 | 2,304 | 4,150 | 5,822 | 11,120 | 183 | 1,350 | 1,420 | 263 | 83.7 | 36.2 |
| 2010 | 26,491 | 23,402 | 2,388 | 4,542 | 5,961 | 10,511 | 114 | 1,316 | 1,468 | 191 | 78.8 | 34.8 |

**TABLE 4.8**

## Sentences for violations of drug laws, by type and length of sentence, U.S. District Courts, 1945–2010 [CONTINUED]

Note: Data for 1945–91 are reported for the 12-month period ending June 30. Beginning in 1992, data are reported for the Federal fiscal year, which is the 12-month period ending September 30. Between 1991 and 2004, defendants charged in two or more cases that were terminated during the year are counted only once. Beginning in 2005, defendants charged in two or more cases that were terminated during the year are counted separately for each case.

[a]Includes sentences of more than 6 months that are to be followed by a term of probation (mixed sentences). Beginning in 1991, includes sentences of at least 1 month that may be followed by a term of probation.

[b]From 1978–88, "other" includes split sentences, indeterminate sentences, and Youth Corrections Act and youthful offender sentences. In 1989 and 1990, the category includes split sentences and indeterminate sentences. Beginning in 1991, "other" includes deportation, suspended and sealed sentences, imprisonment of 4 days or less, and no sentence.

[c]Includes supervised release, probation of 4 days or less, suspended sentences, sealed sentences, and no sentence.

[d]From 1978–90, split sentences, Youth Corrections Act and youthful offender sentences, and life sentences were not included in computing average sentence. Beginning in 1991, life sentences, death sentences, deportation, suspended and sealed sentences, imprisonment of 4 days or less, and no sentence also are not included in computing average sentence.

[e]From 1986–90, split sentences, indeterminate sentences, and Youth Corrections Act and youthful offender sentences were not included in computing average sentence. Beginning in 1991, supervised release, probation of 4 days or less, suspended sentences, sealed sentences, and no sentence also are not included in computing average sentence.

[f]Includes one death sentence.

[g]Includes three death sentences.

SOURCE: Table 5.37.2010. Defendants Sentenced for Violation of Drug Laws in U.S. District Courts, by Type and Length of Sentence, 1945–2010," in *Sourcebook of Criminal Justice Statistics Online*, U.S. Department of Justice, Bureau of Justice Statistics, University at Albany School of Criminal Justice, Hindelang Criminal Justice Research Center, 2013, http://www.albany.edu/sourcebook/pdf/t5382010.pdf (accessed February 13, 2013)

## CHAPTER 5
# ALCOHOL, TOBACCO, ILLICIT DRUGS, AND YOUTH

In 2012, when teens were asked, "What is the most important problem facing people your age?" the most frequent answer was "drugs," which included tobacco and alcohol. The National Center on Addiction and Substance Abuse (CASA) at Columbia University has been asking this question in its national survey for many years. In *National Survey of American Attitudes on Substance Abuse XVII: Teens* (August 2012, http://www.casacolumbia.org/upload/2012/20120822teensurvey.pdf), CASA states that "every year, including this year, teens tell us that tobacco, alcohol and other drugs are the biggest problem facing teens their age."

According to CASA, 26% of teen respondents said that drugs (including alcohol and tobacco) are the most important problem facing them. The second-most important problem was social pressures (18%). These social pressures often include the pressure to drink, smoke, or use drugs. Furthermore, in the digital age social networking sites such as Facebook and Myspace can play a key role in influencing a teenager's decision whether or not to take drugs, drink alcohol, or smoke cigarettes. According to CASA, 75% of teens surveyed believe that viewing photos on social media pages of teens drinking alcohol or smoking marijuana encourages other teens to want to emulate that behavior. Almost half (47%) of teens surveyed reported that "it generally seems like the teens in the pictures are having a good time."

## PROBLEM BEHAVIORS BEGIN EARLY IN LIFE
### Risk and Protective Factors

Figure 5.1 shows the risk factors that are associated with drug addiction. The figure points out that drug addiction is not due to a single factor but to a variety of interacting factors. A person's heredity and environment act together to influence his or her behavior. More specifically, the National Institute on Drug Abuse (NIDA) explains in *Drugs, Brains, and Behavior: The Science of*

*Addiction* (August 2010, http://www.drugabuse.gov/sites/default/files/sciofaddiction.pdf) that genetic factors account for about half of an individual's risk for addiction. In addition, certain environmental factors, such as having parents or close friends who use drugs, being a victim of abuse, or being an underachiever in school, raise the risk that an individual will use and become addicted to drugs. Figure 5.1 notes that early use of drugs is also a risk factor for drug addiction.

Protective factors are those that lower the risk for drug addiction. According to the NIDA, these factors include positive relationships with peers and parents, success in schoolwork, self-control, and a strong neighborhood attachment.

### Early Use of Alcohol, Tobacco, and Marijuana

Danice K. Eaton et al. of the Centers for Disease Control and Prevention indicate in "Youth Risk Behavior Surveillance—United States, 2011" (*Morbidity and Mortality Weekly Report*, vol. 61, no. 4, June 8, 2012) that high school students were asked if they had drunk alcohol, smoked a whole cigarette, or tried marijuana before the age of 13 years. The results are shown in Table 5.1, Table 5.2, and Table 5.3.

As Table 5.1, Table 5.2, and Table 5.3 reveal, a higher percentage of younger students than older students reported having initiated cigarette, alcohol, or marijuana use before the age of 13 years. The most frequently reported behavior in 2011 was drinking alcohol before the age of 13 years. Over one-quarter (26.6%) of ninth graders reported they had done so, as had over one-fifth (21.1%) of 10th graders, over one-sixth (17.6%) of 11th graders, and more than one-seventh (15.1%) of 12th graders. (See Table 5.1.) Males (23.3%) throughout all grades were more likely to report having had a drink before the age of 13 years than females (17.4%). Of the groups surveyed, Hispanics (25.2%) were the most likely ethnic group to report having an alcoholic drink before the age of 13 years, followed by non-Hispanic African-Americans (21.8%) and non-Hispanic whites (18.1%).

Table 5.2 shows that the next most frequently reported behavior in 2011 was smoking an entire cigarette before the age of 13 years. Once again, males (12%) throughout all grades were more likely than females (8.4%) to report having smoked a cigarette before the age of 13 years. Hispanics (11.8%) were the most likely to report having smoked before their teens. Non-Hispanic whites (9.8%) and non-Hispanic African-Americans (8.8%) reported this behavior slightly less frequently.

**FIGURE 5.1**

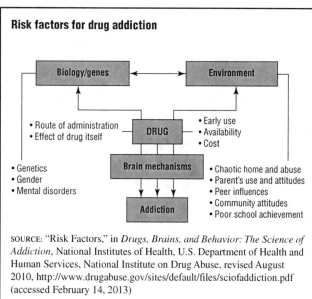

Risk factors for drug addiction

SOURCE: "Risk Factors," in *Drugs, Brains, and Behavior: The Science of Addiction*, National Institutes of Health, U.S. Department of Health and Human Services, National Institute on Drug Abuse, revised August 2010, http://www.drugabuse.gov/sites/default/files/sciofaddiction.pdf (accessed February 14, 2013)

The same pattern between males (10.4%) and female (5.7%) emerged with the least frequently reported behavior in 2011 of trying marijuana before the age of 13 years (See Table 5.3.) Non-Hispanic African-Americans (10.5%) and Hispanics (9.4%) were the most likely to report this early behavior, followed by non-Hispanic whites (6.5%).

## ALCOHOL AND YOUTH
### Age of First Use

The data in the previous section clearly show that the use of alcohol, tobacco, and marijuana often begins early in life, especially alcohol use. In *National Survey of American Attitudes on Substance Abuse XVII: Teens* CASA notes that teens who attend schools in which drugs are used, kept, or sold (what the center calls "drug-infected" schools) are two and a half times more likely to use alcohol than students who attend drug-free schools. CASA also reveals that nearly two-thirds (66%) of students at drug-infected schools are able to obtain alcohol within a day, compared with only 38% of students at drug-free schools. According to CASA, attending drug-infected schools places students at risk for early alcohol use.

The Substance Abuse and Mental Health Services Administration conducts the annual National Survey on Drug Use and Health (NSDUH), and its 2011 survey results are published in *Results from the 2011 National Survey on Drug Use and Health: Summary of National Findings* (September 2012, http://www.samhsa.gov/data/NSDUH/2k11Results/NSDUHresults2011.pdf). According to the NSDUH, 4.7 million people used alcohol for the first time in 2011. Approximately 82.9% of these first-time alcohol users were younger than the age of 21 years when they took their first drink.

**TABLE 5.1**

Percentage of high school students who ever drank alcohol, and who drank alcohol before age 13, by gender, ethnicity, and grade, 2011

| Category | Ever drank alcohol | | | Drank alcohol for the first time before age 13 years | | |
|---|---|---|---|---|---|---|
| | Female | Male | Total | Female | Male | Total |
| | % | % | % | % | % | % |
| **Race/ethnicity** | | | | | | |
| White* | 71.0 | 72.3 | 71.7 | 14.8 | 21.1 | 18.1 |
| Black* | 66.1 | 60.9 | 63.5 | 19.4 | 24.1 | 21.8 |
| Hispanic | 74.1 | 72.4 | 73.2 | 23.0 | 27.2 | 25.2 |
| **Grade** | | | | | | |
| 9 | 61.9 | 61.6 | 61.7 | 24.1 | 28.9 | 26.6 |
| 10 | 69.1 | 69.2 | 69.2 | 17.6 | 24.3 | 21.1 |
| 11 | 74.8 | 75.7 | 75.3 | 14.2 | 20.9 | 17.6 |
| 12 | 80.0 | 78.0 | 79.0 | 12.2 | 17.9 | 15.1 |
| **Total** | **70.9** | **70.6** | **70.8** | **17.4** | **23.3** | **20.5** |

Notes: Students had at least one drink of alcohol on at least 1 day during their life, but other than a few sips.
*Non-Hispanic.

SOURCE: Danice K. Eaton et al., "Table 41. Percentage of High School Students Who Ever Drank Alcohol and Who Drank Alcohol for the First Time before Age 13 Years, by Sex, Race/Ethnicity, and Grade—United States, Youth Risk Behavior Survey, 2011," in "Youth Risk Behavior Surveillance—United States, 2011," *Morbidity and Mortality Weekly Report*, vol. 61, no. 4, June 8, 2012, http://www.cdc.gov/mmwr/pdf/ss/ss6104.pdf (accessed February 14, 2013)

TABLE 5.2

Percentage of high school students who smoked cigarettes before age 13, and who currently smoke cigarettes, by gender, ethnicity, and grade, 2011

| | Smoked a whole cigarette before age 13 years | | | Current cigarette use | | |
|---|---|---|---|---|---|---|
| | Female | Male | Total | Female | Male | Total |
| Category | % | % | % | % | % | % |
| Race/ethnicity | | | | | | |
| White* | 8.4 | 11.2 | 9.8 | 18.9 | 21.5 | 20.3 |
| Black* | 6.6 | 11.1 | 8.8 | 7.4 | 13.7 | 10.5 |
| Hispanic | 8.7 | 14.7 | 11.8 | 15.2 | 19.5 | 17.5 |
| Grade | | | | | | |
| 9 | 9.2 | 14.8 | 12.1 | 10.9 | 15.1 | 13.0 |
| 10 | 8.5 | 11.5 | 10.1 | 15.1 | 16.1 | 15.6 |
| 11 | 8.7 | 10.9 | 9.8 | 17.2 | 21.2 | 19.3 |
| 12 | 6.8 | 9.6 | 8.2 | 22.2 | 28.0 | 25.1 |
| **Total** | **8.4** | **12.0** | **10.3** | **16.1** | **19.9** | **18.1** |

Note: Students smoked cigarettes on at least 1 day during the 30 days before the survey.
*Non-Hispanic.

SOURCE: Danice K. Eaton et al., "Table 29. Percentage of High School Students Who Smoked a Whole Cigarette for the First Time before Age 13 Years and Who Currently Smoked Cigarettes, by Sex, Race/Ethnicity, and Grade—United States, Youth Risk Behavior Survey, 2011," in "Youth Risk Behavior Surveillance—United States, 2011," *Morbidity and Mortality Weekly Report*, vol. 61, no. 4, June 8, 2012, http://www.cdc.gov/mmwr/pdf/ss/ss6104.pdf (accessed February 14, 2013)

TABLE 5.3

Percentage of high school students who ever used marijuana, and who used marijuana before age 13, by gender, ethnicity, and grade, 2011

| | Ever used marijuana[a] | | | Tried marijuana for the first time before age 13 years | | |
|---|---|---|---|---|---|---|
| | Female | Male | Total | Female | Male | Total |
| Category | % | % | % | % | % | % |
| Race/ethnicity | | | | | | |
| White[b] | 35.4 | 40.3 | 37.9 | 4.4 | 8.5 | 6.5 |
| Black[b] | 37.7 | 48.5 | 43.0 | 6.9 | 14.2 | 10.5 |
| Hispanic | 39.1 | 45.0 | 42.1 | 7.1 | 11.6 | 9.4 |
| Grade | | | | | | |
| 9 | 26.4 | 34.9 | 30.8 | 6.6 | 12.7 | 9.7 |
| 10 | 35.2 | 37.5 | 36.4 | 4.8 | 10.1 | 7.5 |
| 11 | 42.1 | 48.7 | 45.5 | 5.6 | 9.6 | 7.6 |
| 12 | 47.1 | 50.8 | 48.9 | 5.3 | 8.7 | 7.0 |
| **Total** | **37.2** | **42.5** | **39.9** | **5.7** | **10.4** | **8.1** |

[a]Used marijuana one or more times during their life.
[b]Non-Hispanic.

SOURCE: Danice K. Eaton et al., "Table 47. Percentage of High School Students Who Used Marijuana, by Sex, Race/Ethnicity, and Grade—United States, Youth Risk Behavior Survey, 2011," in "Youth Risk Behavior Surveillance—United States, 2011," *Morbidity and Mortality Weekly Report*, vol. 61, no. 4, June 8, 2012, http://www.cdc.gov/mmwr/pdf/ss/ss6104.pdf (accessed February 14, 2013)

## Influences on the Decision to Drink

According to the Century Council, a nonprofit organization that works against drunk driving and underage drinking but that is funded by the distilling industry, in "What Youth Say about Alcohol" (2013, http://www.centurycouncil.org/underage-drinking/what-youth-say-about-alcohol), a 2012 survey of youth aged 10 to 18 years revealed that 83% cited parents as the most influential factor in their decision on whether or not drink. By comparison, only 33% of the young people surveyed cited either friends or teachers as the most important influence, while another 24% cited siblings. In addition, the Century Council finds that young people were becoming increasingly responsive to their parents' efforts to talk to them about the risks involved with underage drinking. In 2003 only 26% of young people reported talking to their parents regularly about the hazards of underage drinking. By 2012 this figure had risen to 42%.

## How Do Adolescents Obtain Alcohol?

In "Youth Risk Behavior Surveillance—United States, 2011," Eaton et al. indicate that of high school students who drank alcohol in 2011, 40% were given the alcohol. In *National Survey of American Attitudes on Substance Abuse XVII: Teens*, CASA indicates that it supports the idea that alcohol is easy for youth to obtain. When asked by researchers "Which is easiest to *get*: cigarettes, marijuana, beer or prescription drugs?," over one-quarter (27%) of teens responded that cigarettes were easiest to obtain, but alcohol was a close second, cited by nearly one-quarter (24%) of teens.

The Century Council notes in "We Don't Serve Teens" (2013, http://www.centurycouncil.org/underage-drinking/we-dont-serve-teens) that 96% of parents do not think it is acceptable for another adult to provide alcohol to their teens. According to the NSDUH, in *Results from the 2011 National Survey on Drug Use and Health: Summary of National Findings*, however, more than one out of five (21.4%) underage drinkers acquired alcohol through "parents, guardians, or other adult family members." Indeed, many adults do not know that they can be held liable if they serve alcohol to a minor and if the minor is then killed or injured or kills or injures another person while under the influence of the alcohol that they served. Such laws vary from state to state and are called social liability laws.

## Current Use of Alcohol by High School Students

It is illegal for high school students to purchase alcoholic beverages, yet Eaton et al. indicate in "Youth Risk Behavior Surveillance—United States, 2011" that in 2011, 38.7% of high school students had consumed alcohol at least once in the 30 days before being surveyed. (See Table 5.4.) These students are considered current users. In addition, more than one-fifth (21.9%) of high school students had engaged in binge drinking—that is, consumed five or more drinks in the space of a couple of hours—at least once within the past 30 days.

Lloyd D. Johnston et al. of the Institute for Social Research at the University of Michigan, in *Monitoring the Future National Survey Results on Drug Use, 1975–2011, Volume I: Secondary School Students* (June 2012, http://www.monitoringthefuture.org/pubs/monographs/mtf-vol1_2011.pdf), provide data on current alcohol use among eighth, 10th, and 12th graders. Data from Johnston et al.'s survey and Eaton et al.'s survey overlap in current drinking data for 10th and 12th graders. Comparing the "Total" figures in Table 5.4 and Table 5.5 for these grades, Eaton et al. show a higher prevalence of current drinking for 12th graders (48.4% compared with 40% by Johnston et al.) and for 10th graders (35.7% compared with 27.2% by Johnston et al.).

The NSDUH also collected data on alcohol use in 2011. It reports that an estimated 9.7 million people aged 12 to 20 years (25.1% of this age group) used alcohol in the month before the survey. The NSDUH presents rates of current alcohol use in 2011 among various age groups: 2.5% among 12- to 13-year-olds (seventh and eighth grades), 11.3% of 14- to 15-year-olds (ninth and 10th grades), 25.3% of 16- to 17-year-olds (11th and 12th grades), and 46.8% of 18- to 20-year-olds. The peak age of current alcohol use was 21 to 25 years at 69.7% of this population.

What can be gleaned from all these studies? Looking at all the data presented here, each study shows 2011 current rates of alcohol use in high school students rising

**TABLE 5.4**

Percentage of high school students who drank alcohol, and who engaged in binge drinking, by gender, ethnicity, and grade, 2011

| Category | Current alcohol use[a] | | | Binge drinking[b] | | |
|---|---|---|---|---|---|---|
| | Female | Male | Total | Female | Male | Total |
| | % | % | % | % | % | % |
| **Race/ethnicity** | | | | | | |
| White[c] | 38.8 | 41.6 | 40.3 | 21.7 | 26.1 | 24.0 |
| Black[c] | 31.6 | 29.5 | 30.5 | 10.3 | 14.5 | 12.4 |
| Hispanic | 42.4 | 42.1 | 42.3 | 22.4 | 25.9 | 24.2 |
| **Grade** | | | | | | |
| 9 | 30.3 | 29.3 | 29.8 | 13.0 | 15.0 | 14.0 |
| 10 | 37.1 | 34.4 | 35.7 | 17.8 | 19.0 | 18.4 |
| 11 | 40.1 | 45.2 | 42.7 | 22.6 | 27.9 | 25.2 |
| 12 | 45.4 | 51.2 | 48.4 | 27.0 | 35.7 | 31.5 |
| **Total** | **37.9** | **39.5** | **38.7** | **19.8** | **23.8** | **21.9** |

[a]Had at least one drink of alcohol on at least 1 day during the 30 days before the survey.
[b]Had five or more drinks of alcohol in a row within a couple of hours on at least 1 day during the 30 days before the survey.
[c]Non-Hispanic.

SOURCE: Danice K. Eaton et al., "Table 43. Percentage of High School Students Who Drank Alcohol, by Sex, Race/Ethnicity, and Grade—United States, Youth Risk Behavior Survey, 2011," in "Youth Risk Behavior Surveillance—United States, 2011," *Morbidity and Mortality Weekly Report*, vol. 61, no. 4, June 8, 2012, http://www.cdc.gov/mmwr/pdf/ss/ss6104.pdf (accessed February 14, 2013)

## TABLE 5.5

**Last-month alcohol use by 8th, 10th, and 12th graders, 2011**

[Entries are percentages]

| Grade: | Alcohol | | | Been drunk[c] | | | Flavored alcoholic beverages[d, e] | | |
|---|---|---|---|---|---|---|---|---|---|
| | 8th | 10th | 12th | 8th | 10th | 12th | 8th | 10th | 12th |
| Total | 12.7 | 27.2 | 40.0 | 4.4 | 13.7 | 25.0 | 8.6 | 15.8 | 23.1 |
| **Gender** | | | | | | | | | |
| Male | 12.1 | 28.2 | 42.1 | 4.4 | 14.9 | 27.5 | 8.3 | 13.8 | 21.8 |
| Female | 12.8 | 26.0 | 37.5 | 4.2 | 12.4 | 22.0 | 8.6 | 17.7 | 24.6 |
| **College plans** | | | | | | | | | |
| None or under 4 years | 24.6 | 41.4 | 45.2 | 10.9 | 23.8 | 27.9 | 14.4 | 25.7 | 26.2 |
| Complete 4 years | 11.7 | 25.6 | 38.8 | 3.9 | 12.6 | 24.1 | 8.3 | 14.7 | 22.4 |
| **Region** | | | | | | | | | |
| Northeast | 8.8 | 31.5 | 46.3 | 2.9 | 16.6 | 31.5 | 5.4 | 17.5 | 25.7 |
| Midwest | 11.7 | 23.2 | 41.2 | 4.1 | 11.9 | 27.5 | 7.8 | 14.3 | 23.1 |
| South | 14.2 | 27.7 | 37.5 | 4.4 | 14.0 | 21.5 | 9.6 | 16.6 | 22.1 |
| West | 14.2 | 27.5 | 38.0 | 5.7 | 13.0 | 23.3 | 10.4 | 15.1 | 22.9 |
| **Population density** | | | | | | | | | |
| Large MSA | 11.5 | 26.5 | 41.1 | 3.5 | 12.9 | 23.8 | 6.4 | 15.3 | 25.3 |
| Other MSA | 13.1 | 27.7 | 41.1 | 4.8 | 14.1 | 26.9 | 9.7 | 15.8 | 23.8 |
| Non-MSA | 13.6 | 27.1 | 35.8 | 4.7 | 14.0 | 22.3 | 9.6 | 16.5 | 18.6 |
| **Parental education[a]** | | | | | | | | | |
| 1.0–2.0 (low) | 19.7 | 30.3 | 36.7 | 7.9 | 13.6 | 19.1 | 12.7 | 17.6 | 24.8 |
| 2.5–3.0 | 16.6 | 30.2 | 38.8 | 6.6 | 15.8 | 22.9 | 12.1 | 19.2 | 26.1 |
| 3.5–4.0 | 14.1 | 29.4 | 41.2 | 4.8 | 14.8 | 26.3 | 10.3 | 17.5 | 25.3 |
| 4.5–5.0 | 9.5 | 24.3 | 40.1 | 3.2 | 12.1 | 25.6 | 6.2 | 13.6 | 20.0 |
| 5.5–6.0 (high) | 9.3 | 24.0 | 41.9 | 2.7 | 13.1 | 27.5 | 6.2 | 12.3 | 20.5 |
| **Race/ethnicity (2-year average)[b]** | | | | | | | | | |
| White | 12.3 | 29.1 | 43.8 | 4.7 | 15.6 | 29.9 | 8.5 | 17.4 | 24.6 |
| African American | 11.6 | 20.8 | 30.1 | 2.9 | 8.3 | 14.2 | 7.7 | 14.0 | 20.0 |
| Hispanic | 18.0 | 31.8 | 39.7 | 5.6 | 13.8 | 20.0 | 11.4 | 22.6 | 25.5 |

[a]Parental education is an average score of mother's education and father's education reported on the following scale: (1) Completed grade school or less, (2) Some high school, (3) Completed high school, (4) Some college, (5) Completed college, (6) Graduate or professional school after college. Missing data were allowed on one of the two variables.

[b]To derive percentages for each racial subgroup, data for the specified year and the previous year have been combined to increase subgroup sample sizes and thus provide more stable estimates.

[c]12th grade only: Data based on two of six forms; population is two sixths of population indicated.

[d]8th and 10th grades only: Data based on one of four forms; population is one third of population indicated.

[e]12th grade only: Data based on one of six forms; population is one sixth of population indicated.

SOURCE: Adapted from Lloyd D. Johnston et al., "Table 4-7. Thirty-Day Prevalence of Use of Various Drugs by Subgroups for 8th, 10th, and 12th Graders, 2011," in Monitoring the Future National Survey Results on Drug Use, 1975–2011: Volume I, Secondary School Students, 2012, University of Michigan, Ann Arbor, Institute for Social Research http://www.monitoringthefuture.org/pubs/monographs/mtf-vol1_2011.pdf (accessed February 14, 2013)

with grade level. As students grew older, they drank more. Looking at the studies together, the percentage of 10th graders who were current alcohol users in 2011 ranged from about 11% to 35%. The percentage of 12th graders who were current alcohol users in 2011 ranged from about 25% to 48%.

Taken separately or together, data from these surveys present a picture of a high percentage of teens who use alcohol, which can cause bodily harm, diseases, and possibly death. Studies also show that binge drinking can inflict serious damage on the adolescent brain, which is particularly vulnerable because it is still in the process of developing. Michelle Trudeau reports in "Teen Drinking May Cause Irreversible Brain Damage" (January 25, 2010, http://www.npr.org/templates/story/story.php?storyId=122765890) that binge drinking has been shown to cause cognitive problems in high school students. Citing a study conducted by Susan Tapert of the University of California, San Diego, Trudeau reveals that binge drinking was linked to shorter attention spans in high school boys and to an inability to process spatial relationships in high school girls. In addition, brain scans revealed that binge drinking can cause damage to the nerve tissue, or "white matter," of the brain, which is responsible for relaying information between individual brain cells. Underage binge drinkers were also shown to have poor functioning in the hippocampus, the area of the brain responsible for storing memory.

Underage drinking can lead to other long-term negative consequences. In "Effects and Consequences of Underage Drinking" (Juvenile Justice Bulletin, September 2012), the Office of Justice Programs (OJP) of the U.S. Department of Justice indicates that drinking alcohol to excess can significantly compromise adolescents' decision making, leading them to engage in risky activities such as unprotected sex or driving under the influence. At the same time, many teens have little understanding of the limits of their body when it comes to binge drinking, putting them at risk for alcohol poisoning. According to the OJP, underage binge drinkers are also more likely to develop problems with alcoholism as adults.

Unfortunately, the tendency to binge drink comes all too naturally to adolescents. Ron Dahl, a brain specialist and pediatrician at the University of Pittsburgh, told Trudeau that the adolescent brain is wired to become "passionate about a particular activity, a particular sport, passionate about literature or changing the world or a particular religion." Dahl warned that "those same tendencies ... may also increase the likelihood of starting on negative pathways."

## Alcohol Use among College Students and Other Young Adults

The NSDUH indicates that 46.8% of 18- to 20-year-olds and 69.7% of 21- to 25-year-olds (the peak age group) were current alcohol users in 2011. These college-aged students and recent graduates are using a potentially dangerous drug, and those under the age of 21 years are using it illegally.

In *Monitoring the Future National Survey Results on Drug Use, 1975–2011, Volume II: College Students and Adults Ages 19–50* (July 2012, http://www.monitoringthe future.org/pubs/monographs/mtf-vol2_2011.pdf), Johnston et al. report the drug use results for college students and adults. Table 5.6 shows the annual prevalence of alcohol use by college students and other young adults who are one to four years beyond high school. The results indicate that both groups had a high annual prevalence of alcohol use in 2011 (77.4% for full-time college students and 75.8% for other young adults of the same age), but that college students had the higher rate of use. Female college students were more likely to have consumed alcohol

during the past year (78.1%) than male college student (76.2%). The same is true for other young adults one t four years beyond high school; females (75.9%) we slightly more likely than males (75.5%) to have consume alcohol during the past year.

Table 5.7 shows the trend of lifetime prevalence o alcohol use between 1991 and 2011 among those aged 1 to 28 years. In 1991 the annual prevalence of alcohol use for this group stood at slightly above 94%. Throughou the rest of the 1990s the annual prevalence fell slightly by 1999 the annual prevalence of alcohol use for this group was 90.2%. In 2011 the lifetime prevalence reached a low of 87.4%, which was a very slight decrease from the rate of 87.5% in 2010. The lifetime prevalence of drinking flavored alcoholic beverages (the data for which did not begin being gathered until the first decade of the 21st century) among 19- to 28-year-olds peaked a 84.6% in 2005, then dropped steadily to 81.4% by 2010 before climbing again slightly to 82.2% in 2011.

Table 5.8 shows the trend of lifetime prevalence of alcohol use among college students one to four years beyond high school. The lifetime prevalence of alcohol use in this group (80.5% in 2011) was lower than that for the 19- to 28-year-old group (87.4% in 2011).

## Heavy Drinking, Binge Drinking, and Drunkenness

*Merriam-Webster's Collegiate Dictionary* defines the term *drunk* as "having the faculties impaired by alcohol." According to Johnston et al., in *Monitoring the Future National Survey Results on Drug Use, 1975–2011, Volume I*, the rates of occurrences of drunkenness within the past 30 days among high school students generally declined between 2000 and 2011 after having increased during the 1990s. The highest rate for eighth graders occurred in 1996, when 9.6% reported having been drunk in the past 30 days. The highest rate for 10th graders came

**TABLE 5.6**

Annual prevalence of alcohol use by full-time college students vs. other young adults 1–4 years beyond high school, by gender, 2011

[Entries are percentages]

| | Total | | Males | | Females | |
|---|---|---|---|---|---|---|
| | Full-time college | Others | Full-time college | Others | Full-time college | Others |
| Alcohol | 77.4 | 75.8 | 76.2 | 75.5 | 78.1 | 75.9 |
| Been drunk[a] | 60.1 | 59.7 | 63.4 | 64.5 | 58.1 | 55.7 |
| Flavored alcoholic beverages[b] | 63.0 | 52.8 | 61.5 | 46.4 | 64.0 | 56.8 |
| Alcoholic beverages containing caffeine[c] | 33.6 | 32.8 | 38.9 | 37.1 | 30.1 | 29.2 |
| Approximate weighted population = | 1,230 | 720 | 480 | 310 | 750 | 410 |

[a]This drug was asked about in three of the six questionnaire forms. Total population in 2011 for college students is approximately 630.
[b]This drug was asked about in one of the six questionnaire forms. Total population in 2011 for college students is approximately 210.
[c]This drug was asked about in two of the six questionnaire forms. Total population in 2011 for college students is approximately 420.

SOURCE: Adapted from Lloyd D. Johnston et al., "Table 8-2. Annual Prevalence of Use for Various Types of Drugs, 2011: Full-Time College Students vs. Others among Respondents 1 to 4 Years beyond High School, by Gender," in *Monitoring the Future National Survey Results on Drug Use, 1975–2011: Volume II. College Students and Adults Ages 19–50*, University of Michigan, Ann Arbor, Institute for Social Research, 2012, http://www.monitoringthefuture.org/pubs/monographs/mtf-vol2_2011.pdf (accessed February 14, 2013)

TABLE 5.7

**Trends in lifetime prevalence of alcohol use among young adults aged 19–28, selected years 1991–2011**

[Entries are percentages]

| | 1991 | 1993 | 1995 | 1997 | 1999 | 2001 | 2003 | 2005 | 2007 | 2009 | 2010 | 2011 | 2010–2011 change |
|---|---|---|---|---|---|---|---|---|---|---|---|---|---|
| Approximate weighted population | 6,600 | 6,700 | 6,400 | 6,400 | 6,000 | 5,800 | 5,300 | 5,400 | 4,800 | 4,900 | 4,900 | 4,600 | |
| Alcohol[a] | 94.1 | 92.1 | 91.6 | 90.7 | 90.2 | 89.9 | 89.3 | 89.1 | 87.9 | 87.9 | 87.5 | 87.4 | −0.1 |
| Been drunk[b] | 82.9 | 81.4 | 82.1 | 81.4 | 81.6 | 81.1 | 80.9 | 79.9 | 80.1 | 78.2 | 79.0 | 78.9 | −0.1 |
| Flavored alcoholic beverages[c] | n/a | n/a | n/a | n/a | n/a | n/a | n/a | 84.6 | 84.0 | 83.5 | 81.4 | 82.2 | −0.8 |

Notes: Any apparent inconsistency between the change estimate and the prevalence estimates for the two most recent years is due to rounding.
n/a = date not available.
In 1993 and 1994, the question text was changed slightly in three of the six questionnaire forms to indicate that a drink meant more than just a few sips. Because this revision resulted in rather little change in reported prevalence in the surveys of high school graduates, the data for all forms combined are used in order to provide the most reliable estimate of change. After 1994 the new question text was used in all six of the questionnaire forms.
[b]This drug was asked about in three of the six questionnaire forms; population is three sixths of population indicated.
[c]This drug was asked about in one of the six questionnaire forms; population is one sixth of population indicated.

SOURCE: Adapted from Lloyd D. Johnston et al., "Table 5-1. Trends in Lifetime Prevalence of Various Types of Drugs among Respondents of Modal Ages 19–28," in *Monitoring the Future National Survey Results on Drug Use, 1975–2011: Volume II, College Students and Adults Ages 19–50*, University of Michigan, Ann Arbor, Institute for Social Research, 2012, http://www.monitoringthefuture.org/pubs/monographs/mtf-vol2_2011.pdf (accessed February 14, 2013)

TABLE 5.8

**Trends in lifetime prevalence of alcohol use among college students 1–4 years beyond high school, selected years 1991–2011**

[Entries are percentages]

| | 1991 | 1993 | 1995 | 1997 | 1999 | 2001 | 2003 | 2005 | 2007 | 2009 | 2010 | 2011 | 2010–2011 change |
|---|---|---|---|---|---|---|---|---|---|---|---|---|---|
| Approximate weighted population | 1,410 | 1,490 | 1,450 | 1,480 | 1,440 | 1,340 | 1,270 | 1,360 | 1,250 | 1,320 | 1,260 | 1,230 | |
| Alcohol[a] | 93.6 | 89.3 | 88.5 | 87.3 | 88.0 | 86.1 | 86.2 | 86.6 | 83.1 | 82.6 | 82.3 | 80.5 | −1.7 |
| Been drunk[b] | 79.6 | 76.4 | 76.6 | 77.0 | 75.1 | 76.1 | 74.9 | 72.9 | 71.6 | 69.1 | 70.5 | 67.9 | −2.7 |
| Flavored alcoholic beverages[c] | n/a | n/a | n/a | n/a | n/a | n/a | n/a | 84.5 | 80.6 | 78.1 | 77.4 | 76.7 | −0.8 |

n/a = date not available.
In 1993 and 1994, the question text was changed slightly in three of the six questionnaire forms to indicate that a drink meant more than just a few sips. Because this revision resulted in rather little change in reported prevalence in the surveys of high school graduates, the data for all forms combined are used in order to provide the most reliable estimate of change. After 1994 the new question text was used in all six of the questionnaire forms.
[b]This drug was asked about in three of the six questionnaire forms. Total population in 2011 is approximately 630.
[c]This drug was asked about in one of the six questionnaire forms. Total population in 2011 is approximately 210.

SOURCE: Adapted from Lloyd D. Johnston et al., "Table 9-1. Trends in Lifetime Prevalence of Various Types of Drugs among College Students 1 to 4 Years beyond High School," in *Monitoring the Future National Survey Results on Drug Use, 1975–2011: Volume II, College Students and Adults Ages 19–50*, University of Michigan, Ann Arbor, Institute for Social Research, 2012, http://www.monitoringthefuture.org/pubs/monographs/mtf-vol2_2011.pdf (accessed February 14, 2013)

in 2000, when the rate hit 23.5%. The highest rate for 12th graders was 34.2% in 1997. In 2011, 4.4% of eighth graders, 13.7% of 10th graders, and 25% of 12th graders reported being drunk during the previous month. (See Table 5.5.)

The National Institute on Alcohol Abuse and Alcoholism defines binge drinking as the consumption of five or more drinks (for men), or four or more drinks (for women), of alcoholic beverages in about two hours. Heavy drinking is an average of more than one drink per day for women and more than two drinks per day for men. (There is a male-female difference because the same amount of alcohol affects women more than it does men. Women's bodies have less water than men's bodies, so a given amount of alcohol becomes more highly concentrated in a woman's body than in a man's.)

According to Eaton et al., in "Youth Risk Behavior Surveillance—United States, 2011," 21.9% of high school students were current binge drinkers in 2011. The incidence of binge drinking increased with grade level: 14% in ninth grade, 18.4% in 10th grade, 25.2% in 11th grade, and 31.5% in 12th grade. (See Table 5.4.)

## Demographic Factors in Youth Alcohol Use

GENDER, RACIAL, AND ETHNIC DIFFERENCES. In 2011 high school males (39.5%) were slightly more likely to be current alcohol users than females (37.9%). (See Table 5.4.) At the same time, males (23.8%) were more likely than females (19.8%) to engage in binge drinking.

Similarly, Johnston et al. show in *Monitoring the Future National Survey Results on Drug Use, 1975–2011,*

*Volume I* that in 2011 eighth-grade girls (12.8%) were slightly more likely to have drunk alcohol in the past month than eighth-grade boys (12.1%). (See Table 5.5.) The data, however, indicate that 10th-grade boys (28.2%) were more likely to be current drinkers than 10th-grade girls (26%). This gap continued to widen among 12th-grade males (42.1%) and 12th-grade females (37.5%). The results that Johnston et al. report for being drunk are similar to the results that Eaton et al. report in "Youth Risk Behavior Surveillance—United States, 2011" for binge drinking: males in grades 10 (14.9%) and 12 (27.5%) were more likely than females in these grades (12.4% and 22%, respectively) to have been drunk. The data for eighth grade show that males (4.4%) were slightly more likely than females (4.2%) to have been drunk.

Johnston et al. also provide data for males and females among full-time college students and other young adults one to four years beyond high school. (See Table 5.6.) The 2011 annual prevalence rates for alcohol use show gender differences. Males of both groups were more likely than females to have been drunk. Full-time college females (64%) were more likely than full-time college males (61.5%) to drink flavored alcoholic beverages, while male college students (38.9%) were more likely than female college students (30.1%) to drink alcoholic beverages that contained caffeine. The same was true for other young adults in the same age group: females (56.8%) were more likely than males (46.4%) to drink flavored alcoholic beverages, while males (37.1%) were more likely than females (29.2%) to drink alcoholic beverages with caffeine. A female preference for flavored alcoholic drinks was also seen among eighth and 10th graders. (See Table 5.5.)

Johnston et al. also report that in 2011 Hispanic eighth graders and high school students were more likely to have consumed alcohol during their lifetime than non-Hispanic white or non-Hispanic African-American eighth graders and high school students. According to Johnston et al., in 2011, 43.8% of Hispanic eighth graders reported having drunk alcohol at some point during their life, compared with 35.3% of non-Hispanic African-Americans and 31.4% of non-Hispanic whites. By 12th grade, however, the gap between Hispanics (73.3%) and non-Hispanic whites (72%) who had drunk alcohol at some point during their life closed considerably. Among male high school students, non-Hispanic whites (26.1%) were slightly more likely to have engaged in binge drinking than Hispanics (25.9%); both groups were considerably more likely to have done so than non-Hispanic African-Americans (14.5%). (See Table 5.4.) Hispanic (42.3%) high school students were slightly more likely than non-Hispanic white (40.3%) high school students to be current drinkers in 2011, and non-Hispanic African-American (30.5%) high school students were much less likely than the other two groups to be current drinkers.

**WHERE STUDENTS LIVE.** In *Monitoring the Future National Survey Results on Drug Use, 1975–2011, Volume I,* Johnston et al. look at population density as a factor in student drinking patterns. (See Table 5.5.) They use the category metropolitan statistical area (MSA), which means the area contains at least one town that has more than 50,000 inhabitants. Large MSAs are the biggest cities in the United States, such as New York, New York; Los Angeles, California; Chicago, Illinois; Philadelphia, Pennsylvania; and Boston, Massachusetts. In 2011 a smaller proportion of eighth graders who lived in large MSAs were current drinkers (11.5%) than eighth graders who lived in other MSAs (13.1%) or non-MSAs (13.6%). By 10th grade, there was little difference in the proportion of students who were current drinkers in any of these three population density areas. The proportion was approximately 27%. Twelfth graders in large MSAs and other MSAs had the greatest proportion of current drinkers, with both at 41.1%, compared with 35.8% of 12th graders who lived in non-MSAs. Tenth- and 12th-grade high school students who lived in the Northeast were more likely to be current alcohol users than same-aged students who lived in other parts of the country, while eighth graders who lived in the South and West were more likely to be current alcohol users than their peers in other parts of the country.

**PARENTAL EDUCATION.** Table 5.5 shows an inverse relationship between current alcohol use in eighth and 10th graders and parental education: the less parental education, the more likely eighth and 10th graders were to drink. Among 12th graders, in contrast, students whose parents had the highest education level were the most likely to be current alcohol users, at 41.9%. In addition, students in all three grades who had no college plans were more likely to be current drinkers, to have been drunk in the past 30 days, and to drink flavored alcoholic beverages than those with plans to complete four years of college.

### Perception of Harmfulness of Alcohol Use

The NSDUH reports in *Results from the 2011 National Survey on Drug Use and Health: Summary of National Findings* that nearly two-thirds (64.8%) of young people aged 12 to 17 years believed that binge drinking "nearly every day" posed a "great risk" to their health; another 40.7% perceived great risk in binge drinking once a week. The same study reveals that young people aged 12 to 17 years who perceived "moderate," "slight," or "no risk" in consuming five or more alcoholic drinks once or twice a week were more than twice as likely to have engaged in binge drinking at some point in the past 30 days as those who perceived great risk in such activities.

Easy access to alcohol increases the probability that adolescents and teenagers will drink. Eaton et al. show in "Youth Risk Behavior Surveillance—United States, 2011" that female high school students (45.7%) were

ercentage of high school students who drank alcohol on school property and who usually obtained their alcohol by someone giving it to em, by gender, ethnicity, and grade, 2011

| | Drank alcohol on school property | | | Someone gave alcohol to them | | |
|---|---|---|---|---|---|---|
| | Female | Male | Total | Female | Male | Total |
| tegory | % | % | % | % | % | % |
| ce/ethnicity | | | | | | |
| hite* | 3.8 | 4.2 | 4.0 | 43.9 | 34.4 | 38.8 |
| ack* | 3.8 | 6.5 | 5.1 | 50.6 | 39.1 | 44.9 |
| spanic | 6.6 | 7.9 | 7.3 | 46.9 | 33.1 | 39.8 |
| ade | | | | | | |
| | 5.2 | 5.6 | 5.4 | 49.4 | 29.4 | 39.3 |
| | 4.5 | 4.2 | 4.4 | 42.8 | 41.8 | 42.3 |
| | 4.9 | 5.4 | 5.2 | 43.7 | 32.9 | 37.9 |
| | 3.8 | 6.4 | 5.1 | 47.3 | 36.3 | 41.3 |
| Total | 4.7 | 5.4 | 5.1 | 45.7 | 35.0 | 40.0 |

otes: Student had at least one drink of alcohol on at least 1 day during the 30 days before the survey. Students who obtained their alcohol by someone giving it to them, among the 3.7% of students nationwide who currently drank alcohol during the 30 days before the survey.
Jon-Hispanic.

ource: Danice K. Eaton et al., "Table 45. Percentage of High School Students Who Drank Alcohol on School Property and Who Usually Obtained the Alcohol hey Drank by Someone Giving It to Them, by Sex, Race/Ethnicity, and Grade—United States, Youth Risk Behavior Survey, 2011," in "Youth Risk Behavior urveillance—United States, 2011," *Morbidity and Mortality Weekly Report*, vol. 61, no. 4, June 8, 2012, http://www.cdc.gov/mmwr/pdf/ss/ss6104.pdf ccessed February 14, 2013)

onsiderably more likely than male high school students 35%) to drink alcohol that was given to them by some-ne else. (See Table 5.9.) Among gender and ethnic roups, female African-American high school students 50.6%) were the most likely to drink alcohol given to hem by someone else, while male Hispanic high school tudents (33.1%) were the least likely to consume alcohol btained for them by someone else.

### Drinking and Young Drivers

In *Traffic Safety Facts, 2010 Data: Young Drivers* May 2012, http://www-nrd.nhtsa.dot.gov/Pubs/811622 pdf), the National Highway Traffic Safety Administra-ion (NHTSA) reports that a total of 1,963 drivers aged 5 to 20 years were involved in fatal crashes in 2010, vhich was a 16% decrease from the 2,343 drivers in that ge group who were involved in fatal crashes in 2009. Overall, traffic fatalities among drivers aged 15 to 20 ears old fell by 46% between 2000 and 2010. In 2010, 25% of the drivers aged 15 to 20 years who were killed in rashes were intoxicated (had a blood alcohol level of 0.08 grams per deciliter [g/dL] or higher).

As of July 2004, all 50 states, the District of Columbia, and Puerto Rico had lowered the legal blood alcohol con-entration (BAC) limit for driving to 0.08 g/dL. The NHTSA estimates that between 1975 and 2010 the mini-num drinking age laws reduced traffic fatalities involving drivers aged 18 to 20 years by 13%, saving approximately 28,230 lives. All 50 states and the District of Columbia have zero-tolerance laws for drinking drivers under the age of 21 years. It is illegal for drivers under the age of 21 years o drive with BAC levels of 0.02 g/dL or greater.

## TOBACCO AND YOUTH

### Health Consequences of Early Tobacco Use

In "Polyphenol Associated-DNA Adducts in Lung and Blood Mononuclear Cells from Lung Cancer Patients" (*Cancer Letters*, vol. 236, no. 1, May 8, 2006), Andrea Várkonyi et al. indicate that the age at which smoking is initiated is a significant factor in the risk of developing lung cancer. Smoking during the teen years appears to cause permanent genetic changes in the lungs, increasing the risk of lung cancer—even if the smoker quits. The younger a person starts smoking, the more lasting damage is done to his or her lungs. Such damage is less likely among smokers who start in their 20s.

*Preventing Tobacco Use among Young People: A Report of the Surgeon General* (1994, http://profiles .nlm.nih.gov/NN/B/C/L/Q/_/nnbclq.pdf) indicates that cigarette smoking during adolescence seems to retard lung growth and reduce maximum lung function. As a result, young smokers are less likely than their nonsmok-ing peers to be physically fit and more likely to experi-ence shortness of breath, coughing spells, wheezing, and overall poorer health. These health problems pose a clear risk for developing other chronic conditions in adulthood, such as chronic obstructive pulmonary disease, including emphysema and chronic bronchitis. Early smoking is also linked to an increased risk of cardiovascular diseases, such as high cholesterol and triglyceride levels, athero-sclerosis (a hardening of the walls of the arteries caused by the buildup of fatty deposits on the inner walls of the arteries that interferes with blood flow), and early onset of heart disease.

The surgeon general's report also points out that the use of smokeless tobacco has undesirable health effects on young users. Adolescent use is linked to the development of periodontal disease, soft-tissue damage, and oral cancers. In addition, young people who use smokeless tobacco are more likely than their nonusing peers to become cigarette smokers.

## Tobacco Regulation and Youth

In June 2009 President Barack Obama (1961–) signed the Family Smoking Prevention and Tobacco Control Act, which granted the U.S. Food and Drug Administration the power to regulate the production and marketing of tobacco products. In the fact sheet "The Family Smoking Prevention and Tobacco Control Act of 2009" (June 22, 2009, http://www.whitehouse.gov/the _press_office/Fact-sheet-and-expected-attendees-for-todays-Rose-Garden-bill-signing/), the White House lists key points of the law. After October 2009 cigarette manufacturers were no longer allowed to produce fruit- and candy-flavored cigarettes, which appealed to adolescents and teens. In June 2010 provisions went into effect that banned marketing tactics that appealed to young smokers, such as advertising cigarettes at sporting events, giving away clothing with cigarette company logos, and distributing free samples of tobacco products to youth.

## Age of First Use

Even though the health effects of early tobacco use are known, most cigarette smokers begin their habit early in life. According to Johnston et al., in *Monitoring the Future National Survey Results on Drug Use, 1975–2011, Volume 1*, 6.1% of the eighth graders surveyed in 2011 said they had their first cigarette in the fifth grade,

and 10% said they had their first cigarette by the sixth grade. By contrast, just 6% of the 12th graders who were surveyed said they had their first cigarette by the sixth grade.

Johnston et al. reveal that smokeless tobacco use begins early in life as well. Smokeless tobacco is chewing tobacco or finer-cut tobacco that is inhaled (snuff). The highest rates of initiation in smokeless tobacco use are in grades seven to 11. In 2011, 4.1% of the eighth graders surveyed reported they began using smokeless tobacco by the sixth grade, and another 5.6% started by the eighth grade.

## Current Use of Tobacco by High School Students

The NSDUH indicates that in 2011, 10% of students aged 12 to 17 years used various tobacco products in the month before the survey; that is, they were current users. The use of tobacco products among this age group declined from 15.2% in 2002. This decline was due primarily to the decrease in the use of cigarettes. In 2002, 13% of students aged 12 to 17 years were current cigarette smokers, and by 2011, 7.8% were. Use of other tobacco products (cigars, smokeless tobacco, and pipe tobacco) remained relatively steady. In 2011, 3.4% of students aged 12 to 17 years were current cigar smokers, 2.1% were smokeless tobacco users, and 0.7% were pipe tobacco users.

In "Youth Risk Behavior Surveillance—United States, 2011," Eaton et al. focus on students in grades nine to 12, not on students aged 12 to 17 years as the NSDUH does. The researchers note that 23.4% of high school students in 2011 reported current tobacco use. (See Table 5.10.) The NSDUH results are lower (10%

**TABLE 5.10**

Percentage of high school students who smoked cigars and who used tobacco, by gender, ethnicity, and grade, 2011

| Category | Current cigar use | | | Current tobacco use | | |
|---|---|---|---|---|---|---|
| | Female | Male | Total | Female | Male | Total |
| | % | % | % | % | % | % |
| **Race/ethnicity** | | | | | | |
| White* | 7.5 | 19.0 | 13.5 | 21.2 | 31.5 | 26.5 |
| Black* | 8.5 | 15.1 | 11.8 | 12.3 | 18.8 | 15.4 |
| Hispanic | 9.1 | 17.2 | 13.3 | 16.3 | 24.4 | 20.5 |
| **Grade** | | | | | | |
| 9 | 5.5 | 12.3 | 9.0 | 12.4 | 19.7 | 16.1 |
| 10 | 8.1 | 15.4 | 11.9 | 17.2 | 25.3 | 21.5 |
| 11 | 8.4 | 20.4 | 14.5 | 19.8 | 31.6 | 25.8 |
| 12 | 10.2 | 23.9 | 17.3 | 25.4 | 37.1 | 31.4 |
| **Total** | **8.0** | **17.8** | **13.1** | **18.5** | **28.1** | **23.4** |

Notes: Students who smoked cigars, cigarillos, or little cigars on at least 1 day during the 30 days before the survey.
Also includes current cigarette use, current smokeless tobacco use, or current cigar use.
*Non-Hispanic.

SOURCE: Danice K. Eaton et al., "Table 39. Percentage of High School Students Who Currently Smoked Cigars and Who Currently Used Tobacco, by Sex, Race/Ethnicity, and Grade—United States, Youth Risk Behavior Survey, 2011," in "Youth Risk Behavior Surveillance—United States, 2011," *Morbidity and Mortality Weekly Report*, vol. 61, no. 4, June 8, 2012, http://www.cdc.gov/mmwr/pdf/ss/ss6104.pdf (accessed February 14, 2013)

f 12- to 17-year-olds), but it includes younger students, who are less likely to use tobacco, and it does not include 18-year-olds, who are more likely to use tobacco and who re likely present in Eaton et al.'s cohort of high school seniors. In their report, Eaton et al. find that 13.1% of igh school students in 2011 were current cigar smokers the NSDUH reports 3.4%), and that 7.7% used smoke-ess tobacco (the NSDUH reports 2.1%). Eaton et al.'s results also show that, in general, tobacco use increases with grade level.

## Trends in Prevalence of Cigarette Use by High School Students

In "Youth Risk Behavior Surveillance—United States, 2011," Eaton et al. look for trends in the prevalence of cigarette smoking by high school students between 1991 and 2011. Their results reveal that in 2011, 18.1% of high school students were current cigarette smokers. This rate was down from 27.5% in 1991. Current cigarette smoking rates rose from 1991 to 1997, however, to a high of 36.4% in 1997 before falling in ensuing years to the 2011 level. In 2011, 4.9% of high school students smoked on school property. (See Table 5.11.) Male high school students (5.7%) were more likely than female high school students (4.1%) to smoke on school grounds. As Table 5.11 shows, male high school students (17.1%) were also more likely than female high school students (10.2%) to purchase cigarettes in a store or gas station.

What are the causes of the general decrease in current smoking rates among high school students after 1997? In *Monitoring the Future National Survey Results on Drug Use, 1975–2011, Volume I*, Johnston et al.

provide a possible answer to this question: "We think that the extensive adverse publicity generated by the President, Congress, and the state attorneys general in the debate over a possible legal settlement with the tobacco companies contributed importantly to this turnaround by influencing youth attitudes toward cigarette companies and their products. Substantial price increases, the removal of some forms of advertising (such as billboard advertising and the Joe Camel campaign), the implementation of vigorous antismoking advertising (particularly that launched by the American Legacy Foundation and some of the states), and strong prevention programs in some states all may have contributed."

According to Eaton et al., lifetime cigarette use among high school students was also lower in 2011 (44.7%) than in 1991. In 1991, 70.1% of all high school students had tried smoking. The lifetime rates did not begin to fall, however, until 2000. The percentage of high school students who were current, frequent users of cigarettes in 2011 (6.4%) was also down from 1991 (12.7%), as was the percentage of students who smoked more than 10 cigarettes per day (7.8% in 2011 versus 18% in 1991).

## Tobacco Use among College Students and Other Young Adults

In *Monitoring the Future National Survey Results on Drug Use, 1975–2011, Volume II*, Johnston et al. report on the prevalence of drug use for college students and adults aged 19 to 50 years. In 2011 the rates of current cigarette smoking for young adults was lowest for 18-year-olds (19%) and 19- to 20-year-olds (18%). Figures for current smokers were slightly higher for the

**TABLE 5.11**

**Percentage of high school students who smoked cigarettes on school property, and who purchased their own cigarettes at a store or gas station, by gender, ethnicity, and grade, 2011**

| | Smoked cigarettes on school property | | | Bought cigarettes in a store or gas station | | |
|---|---|---|---|---|---|---|
| | Female | Male | Total | Female | Male | Total |
| Category | % | % | % | % | % | % |
| **Race/ethnicity** | | | | | | |
| White[a] | 5.0 | 5.7 | 5.4 | 9.8 | 17.5 | 13.9 |
| Black[a] | 1.8 | 4.3 | 3.0 | —[b] | — | 13.7 |
| Hispanic | 3.1 | 5.5 | 4.4 | 7.5 | 20.8 | 14.9 |
| **Grade** | | | | | | |
| 9 | 2.2 | 3.4 | 2.8 | 6.5 | 10.3 | 8.7 |
| 10 | 4.2 | 4.6 | 4.4 | 6.6 | 16.1 | 11.8 |
| 11 | 5.2 | 6.7 | 5.9 | 13.4 | 22.4 | 18.3 |
| 12 | 4.7 | 8.5 | 6.6 | 15.5 | 20.8 | 18.1 |
| **Total** | **4.1** | **5.7** | **4.9** | **10.2** | **17.1** | **14.0** |

Notes: Students who smoked cigarettes on school property on at least 1 day during the 30 days before the survey. Students who purchased their own cigarettes at a store or gas station during the 30 days before the survey, among the 14.2% of students nationwide who currently smoked cigarettes and who were aged <18 years.
[a]Non-Hispanic.
[b]Not available.

SOURCE: Danice K. Eaton et al., "Table 33. Percentage of High School Students Who Smoked Cigarettes on School Property and Who Usually Obtained Their Own Cigarettes by Buying Them at a Store or Gas Station, by Sex, Race/Ethnicity, and Grade—United States, Youth Risk Behavior Survey, 2011," in "Youth Risk Behavior Surveillance—United States, 2011," *Morbidity and Mortality Weekly Report*, vol. 61, no. 4, June 8, 2012, http://www.cdc.gov/mmwr/pdf/ss/ss6104.pdf (accessed February 14, 2013)

21- to 30-year-old range—20% to 23%. Johnston et al. note that beginning in around 2004 smoking rates began to fall steadily among both college students and young adults. The decline was slightly more notable among college students. In 2004, 24.3% of college students were current smokers; by 2011 this figure had dropped to 15.2%. By comparison, current smoking rates among young adults fell from 29.2% to 21.3% during this same span.

## Demographic Factors in Youth Tobacco Use

GENDER, RACIAL, AND ETHNIC DIFFERENCES. In 2011 high school males (28.1%) were much more likely to currently use various tobacco products than females (18.5%). (See Table 5.10.) According to Eaton et al., in "Youth Risk Behavior Surveillance—United States, 2011," report, they were also much more likely to be current cigar smokers (17.8% for males versus 8% for females) and current smokeless tobacco users (12.8% for males versus 2.2% for females). According to Johnston et al., in *Monitoring the Future National Survey Results on Drug Use, 1975–2011, Volume I*, there were similar differences in current smokeless tobacco use in 2011 between males and females in grades eight (4.9% for males versus 1.9 for females), 10 (11.5% versus 1.9%), and 12 (14.2% versus 1.8%).

Looking at current cigarette use alone, Johnston et al. indicate that even though the gender gap was considerably narrower than with smokeless tobacco, male rates of cigarette smoking were higher than that of females in all three grades: eighth grade (6.2% for males versus 5.7% for females), 10th grade (13.4% versus 10%), and 12th grade (21.5% versus 15.1%).

Johnston et al. note in *Monitoring the Future National Survey Results on Drug Use, 1975–2011, Volume II* that in 2011 male college students (16%) had a slightly higher rate of current cigarette smoking than females (15%), but it has not always been that way. From 1980 to 1994 female college students were more likely to be current smokers than male college students. In 1994 their current rates of smoking were roughly the same—just under 25%. The rates for both increased during the mid- to late 1990s, with males generally leading females, but then both rates dropped to the 1994 level again in 2005, and dropped even further by 2011.

Eaton et al. note that non-Hispanic white (26.5%) high school students were more likely than Hispanic (20.5%) or non-Hispanic African-American (15.4%) high school students to be current tobacco users in 2011. (See Table 5.10.) They also report that this pattern persisted with current smokeless tobacco use (15.6% of non-Hispanic whites, 8.7% of Hispanics, and 5.4% of non-Hispanic African-Americans). Non-Hispanic white high school students (13.5%) had roughly the same prevalence of current cigar smoking as Hispanic high school students

(13.3%), both of which were higher than the prevalence among non-Hispanic African-American students (11.8%) (See Table 5.10.)

WHERE STUDENTS LIVE. In *Monitoring the Future National Survey Results on Drug Use, 1975–2011, Volume 1*, Johnston et al. look at population density as a factor in student patterns of tobacco use. Eighth, 10th, and 12th graders who lived in the largest cities in the United States in 2011 (large MSAs such as Boston, Los Angeles, and New York) were the least likely to be current smokers. Those who lived in smaller cities (other MSAs) were somewhat more likely to be current smokers, and those who lived in rural areas (non-MSAs) were the most likely to be current smokers. Mark P. Doescher et al. determine in "Prevalence and Trends in Smoking: A National Rural Study" (*Journal of Rural Health*, vol. 22, no. 2, Spring 2006) that "the higher prevalence of smoking in rural areas compared to urban areas . . . can be explained, in part, by lower levels of income and education attainment among rural residents and by the greater likelihood of rural residents being white or American Indian; both groups have high rates of smoking. Additionally, people with lower levels of income and education who reside in rural counties smoke at slightly higher rates than their urban counterparts."

PARENTAL EDUCATION. Johnston et al. note in *Monitoring the Future National Survey Results on Drug Use, 1975–2011, Volume I* an inverse relationship between current daily cigarette use among high school students and parental education: the less parental education, the more likely eighth, 10th, and 12th graders were to be current daily smokers in 2011. In addition, students in all three grades who had no college plans or had plans to complete less than four years of college were much more likely to be current smokers and to have used smokeless tobacco than those students who had plans to complete four years of college.

## Perception of Harmfulness of Tobacco Use

According to the *Pride Surveys: Questionnaire Report for Grades 6 to 12, National Summary Statistics for 2009–10* (September 27, 2010, http://www.pridesurveys.com/customercenter/us09ns.pdf), 69.5% of sixth graders perceived the use of tobacco as "very harmful." The perception of tobacco being very harmful decreased with increasing grade level to grade nine. Between 63.3% and 65% of ninth, 10th, 11th, and 12th graders perceived tobacco use as being very harmful. Even though the perception of risk of tobacco use stayed relatively steady in grades nine to 12, the use of tobacco increased in these grades as the grade level increased. (See Table 5.10.) In addition, Table 5.11 shows that as the grade level increased, a higher proportion of students bought cigarettes in a store or gas station, from 8.7% of ninth graders to approximately 18% of 11th and 12th graders, in 2011.

# ILLICIT DRUGS AND YOUTH

## Age of First Use

The use of alcohol and tobacco often begins early in life; the initiation data are presented previously in this chapter. Regarding the initiation of other drugs, Johnston et al. reveal in *Monitoring the Future National Survey Results on Drug Use, 1975–2011, Volume I* that inhalants and marijuana are the drugs next most likely to be initiated early in life. Peak initiation rates for illicit drugs other than marijuana generally do not occur until grades nine to 11 in high school, and initiation rates for hallucinogens, amphetamines, and tranquilizers tend to be in grades 10 to 12. Johnston et al. state:

Of all 12th graders who reported prior use of a drug, the proportion reporting their initial use of that drug *by the end of grade 9* is presented here. This listing is generally a good indicator of the order of grade-level initiation:

- cigarettes (60%)
- alcohol (54%)
- inhalants (53%)
- steroids (50%)
- heroin (50%)
- smokeless tobacco (50%)

- been drunk (45%)
- marijuana (44%)
- tranquilizers (43%)
- cigarettes (daily) (42%)
- sedatives (barbiturates) (40%)
- narcotics other than heroin (37%)
- crack (37%)
- amphetamines (36%)
- cocaine (33%)
- cocaine powder (33%)
- hallucinogens (28%)
- hallucinogens other than LSD (26%)
- LSD (23%)

## Trends in Annual Prevalence of Drug Use in Youth

TRENDS ACROSS FIVE POPULATIONS. Annual prevalence means that a person has tried a particular drug at least once during the year before being surveyed about its use. Figure 5.2 compares trends in the annual prevalence of drug use across five populations: eighth-, 10th-, and

**FIGURE 5.2**

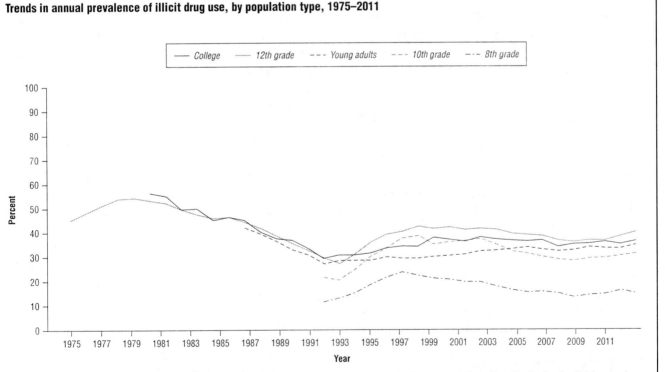

Trends in annual prevalence of illicit drug use, by population type, 1975–2011

Notes: Illicit drug use index includes any use of marijuana, LSD, other hallucinogens, crack, other cocaine, or heroin; or any use of narcotics other than heroin which is not under a doctor's orders, stimulants, sedatives (barbiturates), methaqualone (excluded since 1990), or tranquilizers. Beginning in 1982, the question about stimulant use (i.e., amphetamines) was revised to get respondents to exclude the inappropriate reporting of nonprescription stimulants. The prevalence rate dropped slightly as a result of this methodological change.

SOURCE: Lloyd D. Johnston et al., "Figure 2-1. Trends in Annual Prevalence of an Illicit Drug Use Index across 5 Populations," in *Monitoring the Future National Survey Results on Drug Use, 1975–2011: Volume II, College Students and Adults Ages 19–50*, University of Michigan, Ann Arbor, Institute for Social Research, 2012, http://www.monitoringthefuture.org/pubs/monographs/mtf-vol2_2011.pdf (accessed February 14, 2013)

12th-grade students; full-time college students aged 19 to 22 years; and all young adults through the age of 28 years who are high school graduates (a group that includes college students). During the early to mid-1980s the rates of drug use decreased, and college students had roughly the same rate of drug use as high school seniors. During the late 1980s, when data for young adults were added, the annual prevalence rates of drug use in all three groups declined dramatically. The annual prevalence of drug use by college students and 12th graders was about the same during those years, and the annual prevalence of drug use by young adults was slightly lower.

In 1991 data for eighth and 10th graders were added. The annual prevalence of drug use rose dramatically for high school students for several years, peaking during the second half of the 1990s. The increase was somewhat less dramatic for college students. The annual prevalence of drug use increase for young adults was also relatively minor. Indeed, by 1997 the annual prevalence of drug use for 10th and 12th graders was higher than the annual prevalence for college students and young adults. Around 1998, however, the annual prevalence of drug use for 12th graders began to slowly decline. It dropped, then rose, then dropped again for 10th graders, and it dropped dramatically for eighth graders. Nevertheless, the annual prevalence rates continued to slowly climb for young adults and eventually dropped somewhat for college students. In 2005 the annual prevalence rate of drug use was the highest for 12th graders at nearly 40%, followed by college students at about 38%, young adults at about 33%, 10th graders at about 30%, and eighth graders at about 17%. By 2009 the rates for all three groups of high school students had dropped somewhat from the 2005 rates, whereas the rates for college students and young adults had increased slightly. Between 2009 and 2011, however, annual prevalence of drug use rose across all age groups, although drug use among eighth graders dropped slightly after 2010.

**TRENDS IN INHALANT USE IN HIGH SCHOOL STUDENTS.** Inhalants have a high early initiation rate. According to Johnston et al., in *Monitoring the Future National Survey Results on Drug Use, 1975–2011, Volume I*, of all the 12th graders who reported prior use of any drug in 2011, 53% reported an initial use of inhalants by the end of the ninth grade. Inhalants are volatile liquids, such as cleaning fluids, glue, gasoline, paint, and turpentine, the vapors of which are inhaled. Sometimes the sprays of aerosols are inhaled, such as those of spray paints, spray deodorants, hair spray, or fabric protector spray. These products may be purchased legally and are easily accessible.

Figure 5.3 shows trends in annual prevalence of inhalant use for eighth, 10th, and 12th graders. Since 1991, when data collection began for all three of these grade levels, eighth graders have had the highest annual prevalence of inhalant use, followed by 10th graders and

then 12th graders. Between 1991 and 1995 the annual prevalence of inhalant use rose by more than one-third among eighth graders to reach 12.8% and among 10th graders to reach 9.6%, and rose by about one-fifth among 12th graders to reach 8%. The annual prevalence rates for inhalant use then fell through 2002 for eighth graders to 7.7%, and through 2003 for 10th graders to 5.4% and for 12th graders to 3.9%. Rates rose quite steeply for eighth graders from 2002 until 2004, reaching 9.6%, then dropping to 7% by 2011. Rates rose relatively less dramatically through 2005, for 10th graders to 6% and for 12th graders to 5%. Rates overall fell for both grades between 2007 and 2011. The decline was more dramatic for 10th graders, which saw rates of annual inhalant use fall from 6.6% in 2007 to 4.5% in 2011; annual prevalence of inhalant use among 12th graders, in contrast, experienced a more modest decline, from 3.7% in 2007 to 3.2% in 2011.

**TRENDS IN MARIJUANA USE IN HIGH SCHOOL STUDENTS.** Besides inhalants, marijuana is one of the first drugs tried by high school students. Johnston et al. note in *Monitoring the Future National Survey Results on Drug Use, 1975–2011, Volume I* that perceptions concerning the risks involved with marijuana use drop considerably as high school students become older. In 2011, 43% of eighth graders viewed even occasional marijuana use to pose a "great risk of harm"; this figure dropped to less than one-third (30%) among 10th graders and to less than one-quarter (23%) among 12th graders.

Figure 5.4 shows trends in annual prevalence rates of marijuana use for eighth, 10th, and 12th graders. Since 1991, when data collection began for all three of these grade levels, 12th graders have had the highest annual prevalence of marijuana use, followed by 10th graders and then eighth graders. The annual prevalence rate of marijuana use for eighth graders rose from 1991 to 1996 reaching 18.3%. The rate then dropped steadily to 11.8% in 2004 and to 10.3% in 2007 but rose again to 12.5% in 2011. For 10th graders the annual prevalence rates of marijuana use rose to 34.8% between 1992 and 1997 and for 12th graders in the same period the annual prevalence rates of marijuana use rose to 38.5%. The rates for both held relatively steady from 1998 to 2001 and then dropped to the 2007 levels of 24.6% and 31.7%, respectively. In 2011 the rates for 10th graders rose to 28.8% and for 12th graders climbed to 36.4%.

**TRENDS IN TRANQUILIZER USE IN HIGH SCHOOL STUDENTS.** In *Monitoring the Future National Survey Results on Drug Use, 1975–2011, Volume I*, Johnston et al. state that of all the 12th graders who reported prior use of any drug in 2011, 43% reported an initial use of tranquilizers by the end of the ninth grade. Tranquilizers are drugs that are prescribed by a physician to relieve a patient's tension and anxiety. Drugs such as diazepam, chlordiazepoxide, and alprazolam are tranquilizers. This

## FIGURE 5.3

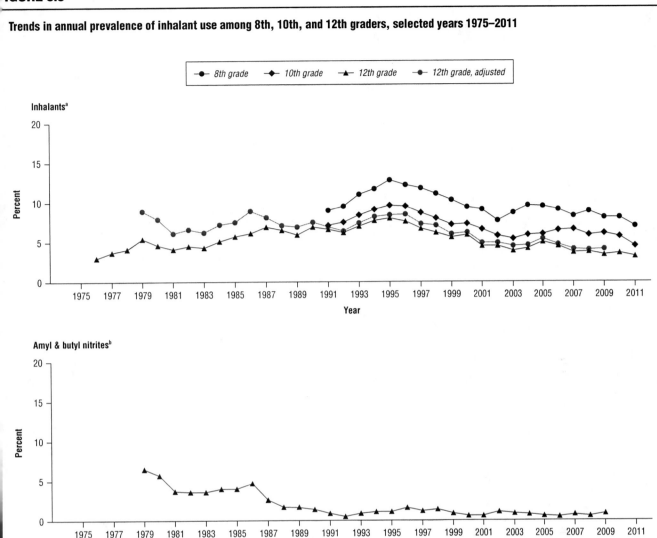

Trends in annual prevalence of inhalant use among 8th, 10th, and 12th graders, selected years 1975–2011

[Legend] ● 8th grade  ◆ 10th grade  ▲ 12th grade  ● 12th grade, adjusted

Inhalants[a]

Amyl & butyl nitrites[b]

[a]Adjusted for underreporting of amyl and butyl nitrites.
[b]Eighth and 10th graders are not asked about nitrite use. Beginning in 2010, questions on nitrite use were omitted from the 12th-grade questionnaires.

SOURCE: Lloyd D. Johnston et al., "Figure 5-4c. Inhalants and Amyl/Butyl Nitrites: Trends in Annual Prevalence in Grades 8, 10, and 12," in *Monitoring the Future National Survey Results on Drug Use, 1975–2011: Volume I, Secondary School Students*, University of Michigan, Ann Arbor, Institute for Social Research, 2012, http://www.monitoringthefuture.org/pubs/monographs/mtf-vol1_2011.pdf (accessed February 14, 2013)

type of illicit drug does not have a high rate of early initiation as inhalants and marijuana do.

Figure 5.5 shows trends in annual prevalence rates of illicit tranquilizer use for eighth, 10th, and 12th graders. Since 1991, when data collection began for all three of these grade levels, 10th and 12th graders have had the highest prevalence of use. Eighth graders have had a lower annual prevalence rate of tranquilizer use. The annual prevalence rate for eighth graders rose slowly from 1.8% in 1991 to 3.3% in 1996. The rate declined slightly to 2.9% in 1997 and then leveled off. The 2011 annual prevalence rate for tranquilizer use by eighth graders was 2%.

For 10th graders the annual prevalence rate remained fairly steady from 1991 to 1994. (See Figure 5.5.) The

rate proceeded to rise steadily from 3.3% in 1994 to 7.3% in 2001, then declined to 4.8% in 2005. In 2011 the annual prevalence rate of tranquilizer use in 10th graders was 4.5%. For 12th graders the annual prevalence rate fell from 3.6% in 1991 to 2.8% in 1992. The rate then rose steadily, reaching 7.7% in 2002. It declined in 2003, rose in 2004, and declined again in 2005. The 2011 annual prevalence rate of tranquilizer use in 12th graders was 5.6%.

**TRENDS IN AMPHETAMINE USE IN HIGH SCHOOL STUDENTS.** Johnston et al. explain in *Monitoring the Future National Survey Results on Drug Use, 1975–2011, Volume I* that of all the 12th graders who reported prior use of any drug in 2011, 36% reported an initial use

**FIGURE 5.4**

**Trends in annual prevalence of marijuana use among 8th, 10th, and 12th graders, selected years 1975–2011**

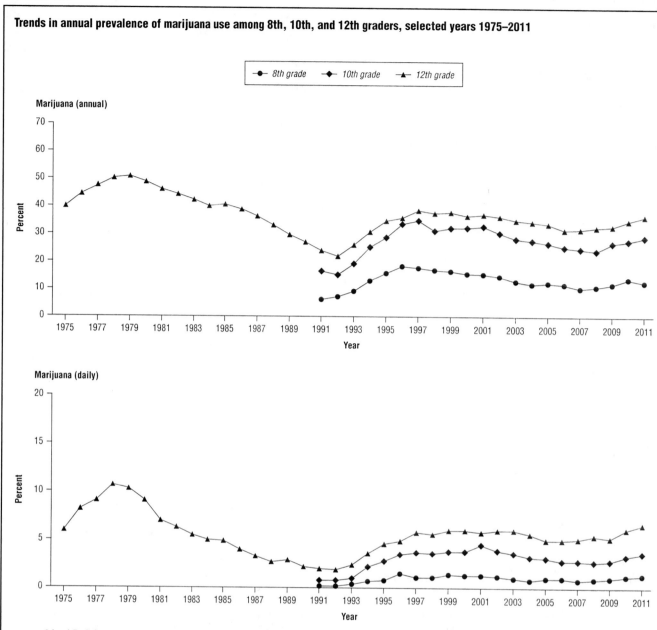

SOURCE: Lloyd D. Johnston et al., "Figure 5-4a. Marijuana: Trends in 30-Day Prevalence and 30-Day Prevalence in Daily Use in Grades 8, 10, and 12," in *Monitoring the Future National Survey Results on Drug Use, 1975–2011: Volume I, Secondary School Students*, University of Michigan, Ann Arbor, Institute for Social Research, 2012, http://www.monitoringthefuture.org/pubs/monographs/mtf-vol1_2011.pdf (accessed February 14, 2013).

of amphetamines by the end of the ninth grade. Amphetamines are stimulants (uppers), drugs that produce a sense of euphoria or wakefulness. They are used to increase alertness, boost endurance and productivity, and suppress the appetite. Other stimulants include caffeine, nicotine, methamphetamine, and cocaine.

Figure 5.6 shows trends in annual prevalence rates of amphetamine use for eighth, 10th, and 12th graders. Since 1991, when data collection began for all three of these grade levels, 10th and 12th graders have had the highest rate of use. From 1992 to 2001, 10th-grade annual prevalence rates were higher than 12th-grade

rates. From 1991 to 2011, eighth-grade annual prevalence rates were consistently lower than those of their older classmates.

The annual prevalence rate of amphetamine use for eighth graders rose from 6.2% in 1991 to 9.1% in 1996. (See Figure 5.6.) The rate then declined to 6.9% in 1999 and then declined in short plateaus to 3.5% in 2011. For 10th graders the annual prevalence rate rose from 8.2% in 1991 to 11.7% in 2001, and then declined to 6.6% in 2011. For 12th graders the annual prevalence rate of amphetamine use generally rose throughout the 1990s and after 2000 in a slight up-and-down fashion, from

**Trends in annual prevalence of tranquilizer use among 8th, 10th, and 12th graders, selected years 1975–2011**

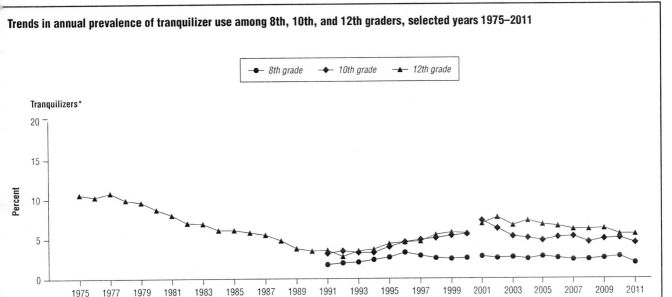

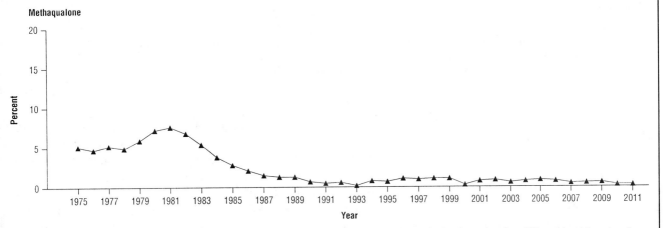

*Beginning in 2001, a revised set of questions on tranquilizer use was introduced in which Xanax replaced Miltown in the list of examples. From 2001 on data points are based on the revised question.

SOURCE: Lloyd D. Johnston et al., "Figure 5-4d. Tranquilizers and Methaqualone: Trends in Annual Prevalence in Grades 8, 10, and 12," in *Monitoring the Future National Survey Results on Drug Use, 1975–2011: Volume I, Secondary School Students*, University of Michigan, Ann Arbor, Institute for Social Research, 2012, http://www.monitoringthefuture.org/pubs/monographs/mtf-vol1_2011.pdf (accessed February 14, 2013)

8.2% in 1991 to 11.1% in 2002. After 2002 the annual prevalence rate of amphetamine use in 12th graders declined to 6.6% by 2009, before seeing a notable rise to 8.2% in 2011.

**TRENDS IN HALLUCINOGEN USE IN HIGH SCHOOL STUDENTS.** In *Monitoring the Future National Survey Results on Drug Use, 1975–2011, Volume I*, Johnston et al. note that of all the 12th graders who reported prior use of any drug in 2011, 28% reported an initial use of hallucinogens by the end of the ninth grade, and 26% reported the use of hallucinogens other than lysergic acid diethylamide (LSD) by the end of the ninth grade. Hallucinogens, also known as psychedelics, distort the perception of reality. They cause excitation, which can vary from a sense of well-being to severe depression. The

experience may be pleasurable or quite frightening. The effects of hallucinogens vary from use to use and cannot be predicted.

Figure 5.7 shows trends in the annual prevalence rates of hallucinogen use for eighth, 10th, and 12th graders. Since 1991, when data collection began for all three of these grade levels, 12th graders have had the highest annual prevalence of hallucinogen use, followed by 10th graders and then eighth graders.

The annual prevalence rate of hallucinogen use for eighth graders rose from 1.9% in 1991 to 4.1% in 1996. (See Figure 5.7.) The rate declined to 2.2% in 2004 and then slightly rose to 2.4% in 2005. The rate then remained relatively steady, hovering around 2%; in

FIGURE 5.6

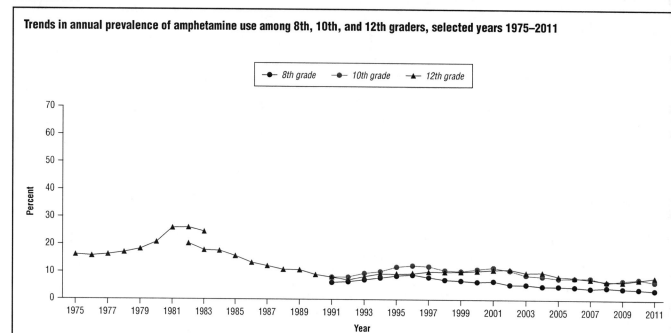

Trends in annual prevalence of amphetamine use among 8th, 10th, and 12th graders, selected years 1975–2011

Note: Beginning in 1982, the lines connect percentages that result if nonprescription stimulants are excluded.

SOURCE: Lloyd D. Johnston et al., "Figure 5-4b. Amphetamines: Trends in Annual Prevalence in Grades 8, 10, and 12," in *Monitoring the Future National Survey Results on Drug Use, 1975–2011: Volume I, Secondary School Students*, 2012, University of Michigan, Ann Arbor, Institute for Social Research, http://www.monitoringthefuture.org/pubs/monographs/mtf-vol1_2011.pdf (accessed February 14, 2013)

2011 it was 2.2%. The trend patterns of annual prevalence rates of hallucinogen use for 10th and 12th graders were similar to that of eighth graders and to each other. The annual prevalence rates rose from 4% in 1991 to 7.8% in 1996 for 10th graders and from 5.8% in 1991 to 10.1% in 1996 for 12th graders. The rates for both grades then declined through 2003 to 4.1% for 10th graders and 5.9% for 12th graders. For 10th graders the rate stayed relatively steady through 2011, which was also 4.1% that year. For 12th graders the rate rose slightly in 2004, dipping to its lowest rate, 4.7%, in 2009. The rate of annual prevalence of hallucinogen use among 12th graders then rose to 5.5% in 2010, before dropping slightly to 5.2% in 2011.

**TRENDS IN MDMA USE IN HIGH SCHOOL STUDENTS.** MDMA (3,4-methylenedioxy-methamphetamine), or ecstasy, is a mind-altering drug with hallucinogenic properties. It is related to amphetamine and is created in laboratories by making minor modifications in the chemical structure of this drug. Thus, it is called a designer drug and is one of the most popular of this type of drug.

Figure 5.8 shows trends in the annual prevalence rates of ecstasy use for eighth, 10th, and 12th graders. Since 1996, when data collection began for this drug, 12th graders have had the highest annual prevalence of ecstasy use, followed by 10th graders and then eighth graders.

The annual prevalence rate of MDMA use for eighth graders declined initially from 2.3% in 1996 and 1997 to 1.7% in 1999. (See Figure 5.8.) The rate then peaked in 2001 at 3.5% but then dropped significantly through 2006 to 1.4%, and rose to 1.7% in 2008. In 2009 the rate dropped to 1.3%, before rising again to 2.4% in 2010. In 2011 the rate declined to 1.7%. The trend patterns of annual prevalence rates of MDMA use for 10th and 12th graders were similar to that of eighth graders and to each other, with an initial drop, a sharp peak in 2001, a drop through 2004 and 2005, and then an increase through 2007. After a drop in 2008, the rate for 10th graders was 4.5% in 2011 and for 12th graders was 5.3%. The peak annual prevalence rate for MDMA use for 10th graders was 6.2% and for 12th graders was 9.2%, both in 2001.

**ABUSE OF NONPRESCRIPTION COUGH AND COLD MEDICINES.** In 2006 the Monitoring the Future study added dextromethorphan to its questionnaires for eighth, 10th, and 12th graders. Dextromethorphan is a cough suppressant that is found in over-the-counter (nonprescription) cough and cold remedies. Students were asked how often they took cough or cold medicines to get high. In *Monitoring the Future National Survey Results on Drug Use, 1975–2011, Volume I*, Johnston et al. note that 4.2% of eighth graders, 5.3% of 10th graders, and 6.9% of 12th graders were current abusers of this drug in 2006. In 2011 the rates were similar, at 3%, 6%, and 5%, respectively.

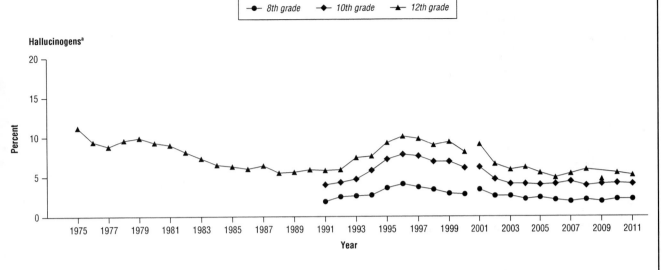

Trends in annual prevalence of hallucinogen use among 8th, 10th, and 12th graders, selected years 1975–2011

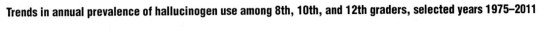

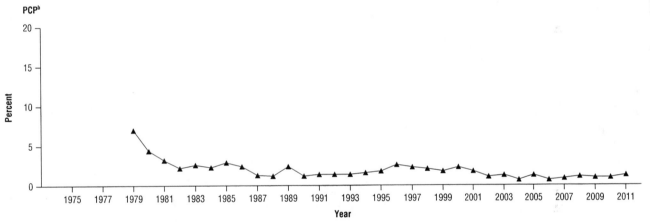

[a]In 2001, a revised set of questions on other hallucinogen use was introduced. Other psychedelics was changed to other hallucinogens and shrooms was added to the list of examples. Data for hallucinogens were affected by these changes. From 2001 on, data points are based on the revised question.
[b]Eighth and 10th graders are not asked about PCP use.

SOURCE: Lloyd D. Johnston et al., "Figure 5-4f. Hallucinogens and PCP: Trends in Annual Prevalence in Grades 8, 10, and 12," in *Monitoring the Future National Survey Results on Drug Use, 1975–2011: Volume I, Secondary School Students*, 2012, University of Michigan, Ann Arbor, Institute for Social Research, http://www.monitoringthefuture.org/pubs/monographs/mtf-vol1_2011.pdf (accessed February 14, 2013).

**NEW DRUGS.** Each decade, new and potentially harmful drugs gain popularity among young people. As data about use of these drugs emerge, Johnston et al. include the information in their annual survey. For instance, Adderall, a stimulant that is used in the treatment of attention-deficit/hyperactivity disorder, is sometimes used for nonprescription purposes among high school students. Johnston et al. first began surveying high school students concerning annual prevalence of Adderall use in 2009. That year, 10th graders (5.7%) were the most likely to have taken Adderall in the previous year, followed by 12th graders (5.4%) and eighth graders (2%). In 2011 annual prevalence of Adderall use had risen to 6.5% among 12th graders, while dropping among both 10th (4.6%) and eighth (1.7%) graders.

The NIDA notes in "DrugFacts: Salvia" (December 2012, http://www.drugabuse.gov/publications/drugfacts/salvia) that salvia is an herb, indigenous to southern Mexico and Central and South America, and is known to induce hallucinations, sensory disorientation, and in some cases psychotic episodes when chewed or smoked. Johnston et al. began monitoring salvia use among 12th graders in 2009, and among eighth and 10th graders the following year. In 2011 annual prevalence of salvia use among eighth, 10th, and 12th graders was 1.6%, 3.9%, and 5.9%, respectively. According to the NIDA, as of 2012 the U.S. Drug Enforcement Administration had categorized salvia as a "drug of concern" and was considering classifying the drug as a Schedule I substance (as

FIGURE 5.8

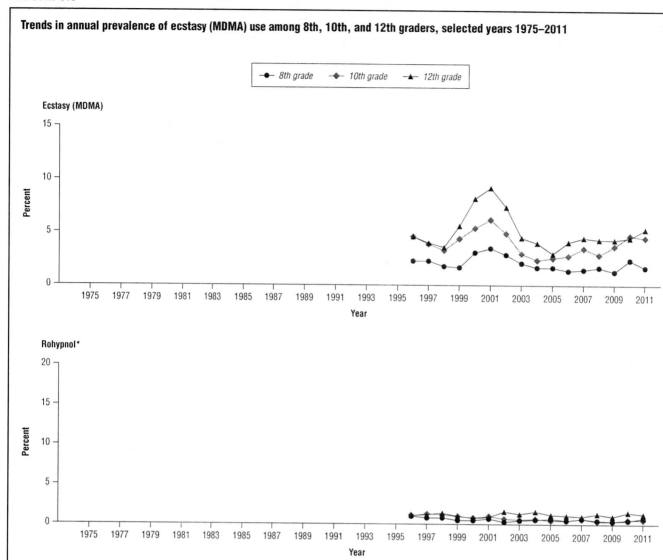

**Trends in annual prevalence of ecstasy (MDMA) use among 8th, 10th, and 12th graders, selected years 1975–2011**

*For 12th graders only, Rohypnol data for 2001 are not comparable with data for 2002 due to changes in the questionnaire forms.

SOURCE: Lloyd D. Johnston et al., "Figure 5-4l. Ecstasy (MDMA) and Rohypnol: Trends in Annual Prevalence in Grades 8, 10, and 12," in *Monitoring the Future National Survey Results on Drug Use, 1975–2011: Volume I, Secondary School Students*, University of Michigan, Ann Arbor, Institute for Social Research, 2012, http://www.monitoringthefuture.org/pubs/monographs/mtf-vol1_2011.pdf (accessed February 14, 2013)

LSD and marijuana are classified). In 2011 Johnston et al. also began to track annual prevalence of synthetic marijuana use among 12th graders, which was 11.4% that year. Synthetic marijuana consists of natural herbs that are sprayed with synthetic cannabinoids, and then are legally marketed as "herbal incense" or "herbal smoke."

Another potentially dangerous drug, generally known as "bath salts," first began gaining popularity around 2010. Powerful stimulants that are legally marketed under brand names such as Cloud Nine and Drone, bath salts have been known to cause hallucinations, panic attacks, and in some cases heart failure. In spite of these hazards, high school students remain particularly at risk for experimenting with bath salts. Johnston et al. planned to add data concerning the use of bath salts in their 2012 survey.

### Current, Past-Year, and Lifetime Use of Illicit Drugs in Youth

The NSDUH indicates that young people had the highest rate of current illicit drug use in the U.S. population in 2011. The rate of current drug use starting with 12-year-olds increased with age, peaking with 18- to 20-year-olds, who had a current drug use rate of 23.8%. The rate of illicit drug use then generally declined with age.

The NSDUH also compares age groups 12 to 17, 18 to 25, and 26 and older regarding their past-month (current), past-year, and lifetime prevalence of drug use. Those aged 18 to 25 years showed the highest rates of illicit drug use in all categories in both 2010 and 2011. (See Table 4.1 in Chapter 4.) Those aged 12 to 17 years ad the next highest prevalence rate for past-month and ast-year drug use, also in both 2010 and 2011.

## Youth Phenomenon

In *Monitoring the Future National Survey Results on rug Use, 1975–2011, Volume I*, Johnston et al. sum up e situation of drugs and youth quite well:

> Young people are often at the leading edge of social change, and this has been particularly true of drug use. The massive upsurge in illicit drug use during the last 35 to 40 years has proven to be a youth phenomenon, and MTF [Monitor the Future] documented that the relapse in the drug epidemic in the early 1990s initially occurred almost exclusively among adolescents. Adolescents and adults in their 20s fall into the age groups at highest risk for illicit drug use; moreover, for some drug users, use that begins in adolescence continues well into adulthood. The original epidemic of illicit drug use began on the nation's college campuses and then spread downward in age, but the more recent relapse phase first manifested itself among secondary school students and then started moving upward in age as those cohorts matured.

## CHAPTER 6
# DRUG TREATMENT

## DRUG ABUSE AND ADDICTION

### Psychiatric Definition

Even though not all experts agree on a single definition of drug addiction, the American Psychiatric Association's (APA) *Diagnostic and Statistical Manual of Mental Disorders-IV Text Revision* (*DSM-IV-TR*; 2000) is the most widely used reference for diagnosing and treating mental illness and substance-related disorders. In the *DSM-IV-TR*, the APA draws a distinction between the terms *substance abuse* and *substance dependence*. It stresses that these terms should not be used interchangeably.

As mentioned in Chapter 1, the *DSM-IV-TR* requires that at least one of the following conditions be met within the year prior before a person can be diagnosed as a substance abuser:

- The person has repeatedly failed to live up to major obligations, such as on the job, at school, or in the family, because of drug use

- The person has used the substance in dangerous situations, such as before driving

- The person has had multiple legal problems because of drug use

- The person continues to use drugs in the face of interpersonal problems, such as arguments or fights caused by substance use

The *DSM-IV-TR* requires that at least three of the following conditions be met during the previous year before a person can be said to be substance dependent (drug addicted):

- Increased tolerance, withdrawal symptoms, loss of control over the quantity or duration of use

- An ongoing wish or inability to decrease use

- Inordinate amounts of time spent procuring or consuming drugs or recovering from substance use

- Important goals or activities given up because of substance use

- Substance use continued despite knowledge experiencing damaging effects

### The National Institute on Drug Abuse Definition

In *Drugs, Brains, and Behavior: The Science of Addiction* (August 2010, http://www.drugabuse.gov/sites/default/files/sciofaddiction.pdf), the National Institute on Drug Abuse (NIDA) answers the question "What is drug addiction?" the following way: "Addiction is defined as a chronic, relapsing brain disease that is characterized by compulsive drug seeking and use, despite harmful consequences. It is considered a brain disease because drugs change the brain—they change its structure and how it works. These brain changes can be long lasting, and can lead to the harmful behaviors seen in people who abuse drugs.... Addiction is similar to other diseases, such as heart disease. Both disrupt the normal, healthy functioning of the underlying organ, have serious harmful consequences, are preventable, treatable, and if left untreated, can last a lifetime."

### Disease Model of Addiction

Beginning in the 1980s advances in neuroscience led to a new understanding of how people become addicted to drugs and why they stay that way. As reflected in the NIDA definition, most psychiatric and medical researchers espouse the disease model of addiction. Addicts, they say, respond to drugs differently than people who are not addicted. Much of the difference is associated with differences in brain functioning and can be linked to genetic factors. According to George R. Uhl et al., in "Molecular Genetics of Addiction and Related Heritable Phenotypes" (*Annals of the New York Academy of Sciences*, vol. 1141, October 2008), drug addiction is a disease that is linked to the effects of many genes as well as to environmental factors. Approaches to treatment emphasize that addiction must be treated in the same way as other chronic diseases.

In "Evidence-Based Treatments of Addiction" (*Philosophical Transactions of the Royal Society*, vol. 363, no. 1507, October 12, 2008), Charles P. O'Brien of the University of Pennsylvania points out that modern definitions of addiction (such as the NIDA definition) emphasize "uncontrolled drug use rather than tolerance and physiological dependence as essential features of the disorder." He adds that "it is generally recognized that addiction has strong hereditary influences and once established, it behaves as a chronic brain disorder with relapses and remissions over the long term." To help understand this pattern of compulsive behavior and its importance, O'Brien suggests that one only need to think of a friend, relative, or acquaintance who has tried to give up smoking only to relapse at some later time, and probably multiple times, into compulsive smoking behavior while knowing full well the health consequences of his or her actions.

## An Integrated Approach to Treatment

The modern approach to treatment has come to reflect the complexity of the drug abuse-addiction spectrum and combines medical approaches, behavior modification, education, and social support functions that are intended to redress imbalances in the patient's total environment. The components of a comprehensive drug treatment approach are shown in Figure 6.1. Arrayed in the center are categories of treatment used alone or in combination and, on the periphery, social service functions that may have to be deployed to solve some of the patient's problems that led to drug use or addiction in the first place.

## HOW MANY PEOPLE ARE BEING TREATED? N-SSATS Data

The Substance Abuse and Mental Health Services Administration (SAMHSA) has been collecting data on substance abuse facilities since 1976. One of its current programs is the National Survey of Substance Abuse Treatment Services (N-SSATS). The N-SSATS numbers represent a snapshot of the treatment units on a particular

**FIGURE 6.1**

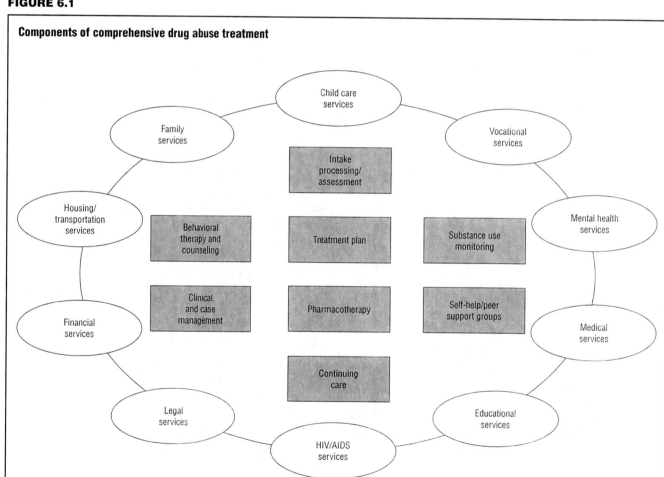

SOURCE: "Components of Comprehensive Drug Abuse Treatment," in *Principles of Drug Addiction Treatment: A Research-Based Guide*, 3rd ed., National Institutes of Health, National Institute on Drug Abuse, December 2012, http://www.drugabuse.gov/sites/default/files/podat_1.pdf (accessed February 14, 2013)

iy and do not indicate how many people are being eated over the course of an entire year.

SAMHSA reports in *National Survey of Substance buse Treatment Services (N-SSATS): 2011, Data on ibstance Abuse Treatment Facilities* (November 2012, tp://www.samhsa.gov/data/DASIS/2k11nssats/NSSATS )11Web.pdf) that as of March 31, 2011, the number of eople in the treatment facilities that responded to the -SSATS stood at over 1.2 million. (See Table 6.1.)

## SDUH Data

To collect data from people who seek and receive ibstance abuse treatment, SAMHSA included questions oout treatment in its 2011 National Survey on Drug Use nd Health (NSDUH) and published its findings in *esults from the 2011 National Survey on Drug Use nd Health: Summary of National Findings* (September 012, http://www.samhsa.gov/data/NSDUH/2k11Results/ ISDUHresults2011.pdf). Figure 6.2 shows the results of sking recipients where they received treatment for sub- tance use in the past year at any location. People could eport receiving treatment at more than one location. (This efinition of treatment location is different from the spe- ific treatment facilities that reported to SAMHSA for the I-SSATS.) As Figure 6.2 shows, 2.1 million recipients eported receiving treatment through self-help groups in 011, the most of any category of substance abuse treat- 1ent location. Large numbers of respondents also reported eeking treatment at outpatient rehabilitation facilities 1.5 million), outpatient mental health centers (just over million), and inpatient rehabilitation facilities (1 million). ewer than half a million recipients (435,000) reported eceiving treatment for addiction in jail or prison.

The NSDUH also asked substance abusers why they lid not receive the treatment they needed. Based on ombined data from 2008 to 2011, among people who leeded but did not receive treatment, most (37.3%) ited financial reasons for not receiving treatment. See Figure 6.3.) Just over a quarter (25.5%) admitted hey were not yet ready to give up drugs.

## Treatment Episode Data Set Data

Another source of data for the drug-treatment popu- ation comes from SAMHSA's Treatment Episode Data et (TEDS). This program counts admissions over the period of a year rather than the number of people in reatment on a particular day during the year. When the ame person is admitted two or more times during the ame year, he or she is counted for each of those admis- ions, whereas the N-SSATS counts individuals only mce. SAMHSA reports in *Treatment Episode Data Set TEDS) 2000–2010: National Admissions to Substance Abuse Treatment Services* (June 2012, http://www.samhsa gov/data/2k12/TEDS2010N/TEDS2010NWeb.pdf) that here were 1.8 million TEDS admissions in 2010.

## CHARACTERISTICS OF THOSE ADMITTED

TEDS data from 2000 to 2010 on admissions by sex, age, race, and ethnicity are presented in Table 6.2 and Table 6.3.

### Gender

Males represented most of those who were admitted for drug and/or alcohol treatment, although the percent- age of men dropped slightly between 2000 and 2010 (from 69.9% to 67.6%) and that of women increased (from 30.1% to 32.4%). (See Table 6.2.) The number of males admitted for treatment in 2010 was over 1.2 mil- lion versus 588,764 female admissions. These results and data reflect that a greater proportion of men than women abuse drugs in the United States. According to Table 4.1 in Chapter 4, 11.2% of males were past-month (current) users in 2010 and 11.1% in 2011, compared with 6.8% of females in 2010 and 6.5% in 2011.

### Age

In 2000, 35- to 39-year-olds (17.9% of total) accounted for the largest percentage receiving substance abuse treatment, followed by those aged 30 to 34 years (15.2%). (See Table 6.2.) Ten years later the two largest groups receiving treatment were those aged 25 to 29 years (15.6%) and 20 to 24 years (15.3%). Those aged 65 years and older were the least represented, accounting for just under 0.7% in both 2000 and 2010.

### Race and Ethnicity

Most of those admitted to substance abuse treatment facilities in 2010 were non-Hispanic white (60.8%), and non-Hispanic whites were admitted in the greatest numbers (1.1 million). (See Table 6.3.) They were followed by non- Hispanic African-Americans at 20.1% (363,500). Com- pared with data from 2000, non-Hispanic whites increased slightly from 58.2% and increased in number from just over 1 million, and non-Hispanic African-Americans decreased in percentage, from 25.1%, and in number, from 434,545. Hispanics increased their proportion of admissions to drug treatment facilities from 12.1% (210,633) in 2000 to 13% (234,806) in 2010. Native Americans or Alaskan Natives rose in share of those treated from 2.2% (37,551) to 2.4% (42,830) during this period. Asian-Americans or Pacific Islanders increased from 0.8% (14,618) of the total admis- sions in 2000 to 1% (18,587) in 2010.

## TYPES OF TREATMENT

The disease model of addiction described at the begin- ning of this chapter, which views drug addiction as a chronic disease, views long-term treatment as necessary. O'Brien notes that "as is the case with other chronic diseases, when the treatment is ended, relapse eventually occurs in most cases."

## TABLE 6.1

### Persons admitted into substance abuse treatment, by state or region and type of care received, as of March 31, 2011

Number of clients — Type of care received

| State or jurisdiction* | Total | Total out-patient | Outpatient Regular | Intensive | Day treatment or partial hospitalization | Detox | Methadone maintenance | Total residential | Residential (non-hospital) Short-term | Long-term | Detox | Total hospital inpatient | Hospital inpatient Treatment | Detox |
|---|---|---|---|---|---|---|---|---|---|---|---|---|---|---|
| Total | 1,224,127 | 1,095,897 | 617,715 | 141,964 | 23,338 | 13,450 | 299,430 | 112,827 | 29,164 | 74,337 | 9,326 | 15,403 | 9,224 | 6,179 |
| Alabama | 15,924 | 14,882 | 1,859 | 5,050 | 237 | 41 | 7,695 | 998 | 428 | 513 | 57 | 44 | 19 | 25 |
| Alaska | 2,840 | 2,455 | 1,738 | 443 | 114 | 9 | 151 | 381 | 55 | 311 | 15 | 4 | — | 4 |
| Arizona | 31,514 | 29,595 | 19,355 | 3,664 | 286 | 251 | 6,039 | 1,547 | 462 | 992 | 93 | 372 | 264 | 108 |
| Arkansas | 3,401 | 2,658 | 1,555 | 364 | 52 | 132 | 555 | 698 | 201 | 458 | 39 | 45 | 20 | 25 |
| California | 132,562 | 115,928 | 66,382 | 15,591 | 3,733 | 3,216 | 27,006 | 15,806 | 2,497 | 12,300 | 1,009 | 828 | 446 | 382 |
| Colorado | 38,927 | 37,060 | 31,784 | 2,267 | 496 | 133 | 2,380 | 1,795 | 339 | 1,090 | 366 | 72 | 42 | 30 |
| Connecticut | 25,914 | 24,294 | 9,663 | 2,341 | 391 | 252 | 11,647 | 1,338 | 338 | 983 | 17 | 282 | 148 | 134 |
| Delaware | 4,607 | 4,368 | 1,928 | 175 | 84 | 5 | 2,176 | 186 | 10 | 176 | — | 53 | 5 | 48 |
| District of Columbia | 4,166 | 3,655 | 1,006 | 671‡ | 45‡ | ‡ | 1,933 | 475 | 255‡ | 193 | 27‡ | 36‡ | 25‡ | 11‡ |
| Fed. of Micronesia | | | | | | | | | | | | | | |
| Florida | 51,201 | 44,044 | 24,974 | 2,870 | 1,753 | 760 | 13,687 | 6,478 | 1,578 | 4,312 | 588 | 679 | 388 | 291 |
| Georgia | 21,804 | 19,027 | 6,907 | 2,623 | 1,700 | 347 | 7,450 | 2,245 | 436 | 1,680 | 129 | 532 | 322 | 210 |
| Guam | 297 | 245 | 189 | 41 | 15 | — | — | 52 | 1 | 47 | 4 | — | — | — |
| Hawaii | 4,464 | 4,065 | 2,101 | 1,173 | 129 | 23 | 639 | 399 | 40 | 341 | 18 | 213 | 110 | 103 |
| Idaho | 5,171 | 4,731 | 3,084 | 1,376 | 16 | 10 | 245 | 227 | 84 | 137 | 6 | 270 | 97 | 173 |
| Illinois | 43,971 | 40,687 | 22,427 | 5,863 | 749 | 273 | 11,375 | 3,014 | 1,113 | 1,713 | 188 | 324 | 176 | 148 |
| Indiana | 25,186 | 24,169 | 13,085 | 4,380 | 278 | 457 | 5,969 | 693 | 234 | 434 | 25 | 173 | 6 | 167 |
| Iowa | 8,977 | 8,062 | 6,489 | 1,023 | 60 | 14 | 490 | 742 | 379 | 286 | 77 | 22 | 3 | 19 |
| Kansas | 11,381 | 10,608 | 7,550 | 1,056 | 6 | 14 | 1,982 | 751 | 215 | 470 | 66 | 22 | 3 | 19 |
| Kentucky | 20,481 | 18,260 | 14,451 | 1,731 | 95 | 139 | 1,844 | 1,831 | 275 | 1,409 | 147 | 390 | 275 | 115 |
| Louisiana | 11,180 | 9,466 | 4,381 | 1,541 | 294 | 174 | 3,076 | 1,590 | 492 | 1,009 | 89 | 124 | 84 | 40 |
| Maine | 10,769 | 10,293 | 5,924 | 673 | 152 | 8 | 3,536 | 429 | 53 | 358 | 18 | 47 | 11 | 36 |
| Maryland | 38,792 | 35,993 | 16,302 | 3,760 | 127 | 432 | 15,372 | 2,326 | 459 | 1,739 | 128 | 473 | 374 | 99 |
| Massachusetts | 46,891 | 41,986 | 23,084 | 1,545 | 952 | 1,315 | 15,090 | 4,027 | 1,660 | 2,123 | 244 | 878 | 390 | 488 |
| Michigan | 45,147 | 39,526 | 28,884 | 2,287 | 271 | 652 | 7,432 | 5,381 | 1,461 | 2,251 | 1,669 | 240 | 175 | 65 |
| Minnesota | 17,354 | 12,071 | 4,200 | 3,465 | 493 | 38 | 3,875 | 5,244 | 1,937 | 3,168 | 139 | 39 | 19 | 20 |
| Mississippi | 5,807 | 4,406 | 3,905 | 237 | 63 | 1 | 200 | 1,060 | 315 | 684 | 61 | 341 | 230 | 111 |
| Missouri | 21,455 | 19,903 | 10,044 | 6,240 | 880 | 101 | 2,638 | 1,426 | 875 | 440 | 111 | 126 | 48 | 78 |
| Montana | 9,885 | 9,513 | 8,624 | 720 | 52 | 17 | 100 | 346 | 273 | 64 | 9 | 26 | 1 | 25 |
| Nebraska | 6,354 | 5,534 | 4,285 | 638 | 75 | 34 | 502 | 806 | 256 | 519 | 31 | 14 | 12 | 2 |
| Nevada | 7,218 | 6,417 | 4,085 | 855 | 30 | 446 | 1,001 | 718 | 109 | 493 | 116 | 83 | 34 | 49 |
| New Hampshire | 5,931 | 5,350 | 3,017 | 330 | 5 | 61 | 1,937 | 575 | 98 | 210 | 267 | 6 | — | 6 |
| New Jersey | 31,777 | 28,811 | 10,497 | 5,416 | 1,310 | 297 | 11,291 | 2,448 | 627 | 1,768 | 53 | 518 | 335 | 183 |
| New Mexico | 12,664 | 11,621 | 8,479 | 1,128 | 83 | 199 | 1,732 | 896 | 273 | 345 | 278 | 147 | 113 | 34 |
| New York | 122,929 | 108,856 | 55,634 | 12,728 | 3,530 | 279 | 36,685 | 12,034 | 1,887 | 9,491 | 656 | 2,039 | 1,110 | 929 |
| North Carolina | 36,312 | 33,297 | 18,524 | 3,074 | 452 | 171 | 11,076 | 2,271 | 371 | 1,641 | 259 | 744 | 531 | 213 |
| North Dakota | 2,457 | 1,827 | 1,403 | 264 | 159 | 1 | — | 580 | 121 | 433 | 26 | 50 | 38 | 12 |
| Ohio | 37,238 | 34,466 | 23,872 | 5,366 | 431 | 491 | 4,306 | 2,181 | 436 | 1,657 | 88 | 591 | 446 | 145 |
| Oklahoma | 14,858 | 13,409 | 9,479 | 849 | 18 | 319 | 2,744 | 1,329 | 325 | 980 | 24 | 120 | 57 | 63 |
| Oregon | 23,166 | 21,487 | 13,301 | 3,868 | 195 | 172 | 3,951 | 1,671 | 408 | 1,082 | 181 | 8 | — | 8 |
| Palau | 105 | 104 | 104 | — | — | — | — | — | — | — | — | 1 | — | 1 |
| Pennsylvania | 53,377 | 47,688 | 20,769 | 8,833 | 999 | 338 | 16,749 | 4,736 | 1,924 | 2,276 | 536 | 953 | 584 | 369 |
| Puerto Rico | 16,166 | 10,720 | 2,089 | 282 | 220 | 122 | 8,007 | 4,860 | 259 | 4,304 | 297 | 586 | 501 | 85 |
| Rhode Island | 9,742 | 9,373 | 5,782 | 280 | 55 | 78 | 3,178 | 318 | 41 | 277 | — | 51 | 7 | 44 |

## TABLE 6.1

**Persons admitted into substance abuse treatment, by state or region and type of care received, as of March 31, 2011** [CONTINUED]

| | | | | | Number of clients | | | | | | | | | |
|---|---|---|---|---|---|---|---|---|---|---|---|---|---|---|
| | | | Type of care received | | | | | | | | | | | |
| | | | Outpatient | | | | | | Residential (non-hospital) | | | | Hospital inpatient | |
| State or jurisdiction* | Total | Total out-patient | Regular | Intensive | Day treatment or partial hospitalization | Detox | Methadone maintenance | Total residential | Short-term | Long-term | Detox | Total hospital inpatient | Treatment | Detox |
| South Carolina | 14,217 | 13,387 | 7,893 | 1,372 | 115 | 78 | 3,929 | 613 | 297 | 293 | 23 | 217 | 70 | 147 |
| South Dakota | 2,987 | 2,343 | 1,727 | 589 | 17 | 10 | — | 583 | 215 | 335 | 33 | 61 | 59 | 2 |
| Tennessee | 16,590 | 14,368 | 6,809 | 1,930 | 152 | 20 | 5,457 | 2,075 | 781 | 1,088 | 206 | 147 | 41 | 106 |
| Texas | 36,875 | 29,730 | 14,526 | 4,953 | 483 | 117 | 9,651 | 5,728 | 1,600 | 3,726 | 402 | 1,417 | 966 | 451 |
| Utah | 12,470 | 10,873 | 7,151 | 1,143 | 219 | 198 | 2,162 | 1,501 | 333 | 1,077 | 91 | 96 | 68 | 28 |
| Vermont | 4,182 | 3,932 | 2,844 | 314 | 103 | 15 | 656 | 130 | 51 | 78 | 1 | 120 | 75 | 45 |
| Virgin Islands | 96 | 75 | 54 | — | — | — | 21 | 21 | — | 21 | — | — | — | — |
| Virginia | 21,731 | 20,203 | 12,956 | 1,845 | 358 | 225 | 4,819 | 1,194 | 340 | 753 | 101 | 334 | 229 | 105 |
| Washington | 41,097 | 38,778 | 21,575 | 10,041 | 423 | 192 | 6,547 | 2,111 | 1,199 | 751 | 161 | 208 | 128 | 80 |
| West Virginia | 10,711 | 9,823 | 4,163 | 335 | 5 | 416 | 4,904 | 786 | 378 | 286 | 122 | 102 | 81 | 21 |
| Wisconsin | 19,413 | 18,430 | 12,660 | 1,487 | 377 | 366 | 3,540 | 841 | 299 | 512 | 30 | 142 | 51 | 91 |
| Wyoming | 3,396 | 3,045 | 2,162 | 874 | 1 | 5 | 3 | 336 | 71 | 260 | 5 | 15 | 10 | 5 |

*Facilities operated by Federal agencies are included in the States in which the facilities are located.
†No facilities in this category.
—Quantity is zero.

SOURCE: "Table 6.27a. Clients in Treatment, according to Type of Care Received, by State or Jurisdiction: March 31, 2011, Number," in *National Survey of Substance Abuse Treatment Services (N-SSATS): 2011 Data on Substance Abuse Treatment Facilities*, U.S. Department of Health and Human Services, Substance Abuse and Mental Health Services Administration, November 2012. http://www.samhsa.gov/data/DASIS/2k11nssats/NSSATS2011Web.pdf (accessed February 14, 2013)

**FIGURE 6.2**

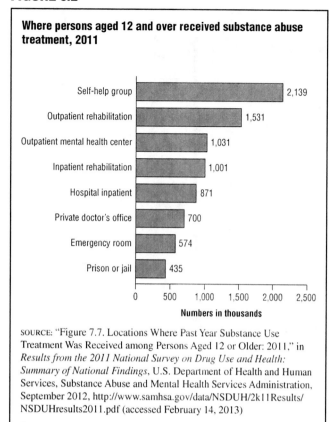

Where persons aged 12 and over received substance abuse treatment, 2011

SOURCE: "Figure 7.7. Locations Where Past Year Substance Use Treatment Was Received among Persons Aged 12 or Older: 2011," in *Results from the 2011 National Survey on Drug Use and Health: Summary of National Findings*, U.S. Department of Health and Human Services, Substance Abuse and Mental Health Services Administration, September 2012, http://www.samhsa.gov/data/NSDUH/2k11Results/NSDUHresults2011.pdf (accessed February 14, 2013)

**FIGURE 6.3**

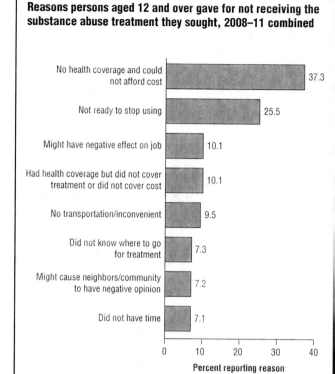

Reasons persons aged 12 and over gave for not receiving the substance abuse treatment they sought, 2008–11 combined

SOURCE: "Figure 7.11. Reasons for Not Receiving Substance Use Treatment among Persons Aged 12 or Older Who Needed and Made an Effort to Get Treatment but Did Not Receive Treatment and Felt They Needed Treatment: 2008–2011 Combined," in *Results from the 2011 National Survey on Drug Use and Health: Summary of National Findings*, U.S. Department of Health and Human Services, Substance Abuse and Mental Health Services Administration, September 2012, http://www.samhsa.gov/data/NSDUH/2k11Results/NSDUHresults2011.pdf (accessed February 14, 2013)

Detoxification is usually a precursor to rehabilitation because that process cannot begin until the individual's body has been cleared of the drug and a certain physiological equilibrium has been established. Drug rehabilitation refers to processes that assist a drug-addicted person in discontinuing drug use and returning to a drug-free life.

**Detoxification**

Drug-addicted individuals must usually undergo medical detoxification (detox) in an outpatient facility, a residential center, or a hospital. Medical help, including sedation, is provided to manage the painful physical and psychological symptoms of withdrawal. The detox of many drugs can be achieved with minimal discomfort by replacing the drug of dependence with a less risky drug in the same pharmacological category (e.g., replacing heroin with methadone) and gradually reducing the dose. People addicted to nicotine can accomplish detox on their own by using gradually decreasing doses of nicotine patches. Rehabilitation usually follows detox.

**Rehabilitation**

Rehabilitation (rehab) has many forms, but it is always designed to change the behavior of the drug abuser. Changed behavior (achieving independence of drugs or alcohol) requires understanding the circumstances that led to dependence, building the confidence that the individual can succeed, and changing the individual's lifestyle so that the individual avoids occasions that produce drug-using behavior. Individual counseling, interaction with support groups, and formal education are used in combination with close supervision, incentives, and disincentives. Certain individuals require a new socialization that is achieved by living for an extended period in a structured and supportive environment in which new life skills can be acquired. Treatment may involve guiding the individual to seek help from other social agencies to reorder his or her life. (See Figure 6.1.)

Some individuals may be mentally ill and will then receive, as part of drug rehab, mental health services in outpatient or hospital settings. Most treatment takes place in outpatient settings, with the individual reporting daily, weekly, or less frequently for periodic treatment and assessment.

**Distribution of Patients**

On March 31, 2011, nearly 1.1 million (89.5%) out of 1.2 million patients were receiving outpatient care. (See Table 6.1.) Of the remainder, 112,827 (9.2%) were in residential facilities and 15,403 (1.3%) were receiving

**TABLE 6.2**

## Number of persons admitted into substance abuse treatment, by gender and age at admission, 2000–10

[Number and average age at admission. Based on administrative data report to TEDS by all reporting states and jurisdictions, excluding Puerto Rico.]

| Gender and age at admission | 2000 | 2001 | 2002 | 2003 | 2004 | 2005 | 2006 | 2007 | 2008 | 2009 | 2010 |
|---|---|---|---|---|---|---|---|---|---|---|---|
| **Total** | 1,749,726 | 1,767,833 | 1,886,241 | 1,858,530 | 1,805,109 | 1,891,509 | 1,907,593 | 1,912,300 | 2,010,165 | 1,989,706 | 1,818,900 |
| **Gender** | | | | | | | | | | | |
| Male | 1,224,001 | 1,233,505 | 1,317,194 | 1,284,569 | 1,235,488 | 1,290,251 | 1,297,511 | 1,295,952 | 1,361,411 | 1,353,137 | 1,229,530 |
| Female | 522,301 | 532,123 | 568,524 | 573,571 | 568,910 | 600,770 | 609,669 | 615,814 | 648,390 | 636,130 | 588,764 |
| **No. of admissions** | 1,746,302 | 1,765,628 | 1,885,718 | 1,858,140 | 1,804,398 | 1,891,021 | 1,907,180 | 1,911,766 | 2,009,801 | 1,989,267 | 1,818,294 |
| **Age at admission** | | | | | | | | | | | |
| 12 to 17 years | 137,770 | 145,412 | 157,839 | 157,041 | 146,389 | 145,069 | 143,220 | 142,449 | 154,291 | 153,070 | 132,850 |
| 18 to 19 years | 72,815 | 73,476 | 77,638 | 76,484 | 75,543 | 77,618 | 77,252 | 77,006 | 82,690 | 83,994 | 74,389 |
| 20 to 24 years | 204,744 | 221,466 | 245,777 | 249,379 | 254,031 | 271,807 | 275,275 | 274,006 | 290,916 | 296,126 | 277,519 |
| 25 to 29 years | 206,712 | 201,529 | 214,035 | 216,382 | 223,507 | 250,571 | 267,410 | 276,405 | 297,710 | 302,699 | 283,177 |
| 30 to 34 years | 266,270 | 257,711 | 259,469 | 244,492 | 225,350 | 224,567 | 216,151 | 213,650 | 227,291 | 231,833 | 224,070 |
| 35 to 39 years | 313,170 | 302,055 | 304,884 | 281,981 | 257,139 | 257,043 | 249,164 | 238,140 | 233,587 | 215,564 | 186,835 |
| 40 to 44 years | 257,134 | 262,477 | 281,809 | 279,912 | 268,615 | 274,742 | 265,316 | 254,718 | 250,302 | 230,637 | 199,905 |
| 45 to 49 years | 155,890 | 163,623 | 185,730 | 188,203 | 186,827 | 202,629 | 211,723 | 218,921 | 229,842 | 224,548 | 199,814 |
| 50 to 54 years | 75,109 | 80,702 | 92,249 | 95,810 | 98,605 | 110,502 | 118,388 | 127,482 | 141,796 | 144,663 | 135,961 |
| 55 to 59 years | 33,517 | 33,284 | 39,245 | 41,079 | 41,814 | 47,338 | 53,422 | 56,863 | 65,263 | 67,845 | 66,609 |
| 60 to 64 years | 14,762 | 15,077 | 16,419 | 16,630 | 16,520 | 18,160 | 18,805 | 20,833 | 23,579 | 25,377 | 25,134 |
| 65 years and older | 11,833 | 11,021 | 11,147 | 11,137 | 10,769 | 11,463 | 11,467 | 11,827 | 12,898 | 13,350 | 12,637 |
| **No. of admissions** | 1,749,726 | 1,767,833 | 1,886,241 | 1,858,530 | 1,805,109 | 1,891,509 | 1,907,593 | 1,912,300 | 2,010,165 | 1,989,706 | 1,818,900 |
| **Average age at admission** | 33.9 yrs | 33.8 yrs | 33.9 yrs | 34.0 yrs | 34.0 yrs | 34.1 yrs | 34.2 yrs | 34.3 yrs | 34.3 yrs | 34.2 yrs | 34.2 yrs |

TEDS = Treatment Episode Data Set.

SOURCE: "Table 1.3a. Admissions Aged 12 and Older, by Gender and Age at Admission: 2000–2010. Number and Average Age at Admission," in *Treatment Episode Data Set (TEDS) 2000–2010. National Admissions to Substance Abuse Treatment Services*, U.S. Department of Health and Human Services, Substance Abuse and Mental Health Services Administration, June 2012, http://www.samhsa.gov/data/2k12/TEDS2010N/TEDS2010NWeb.pdf (accessed February 14, 2013)

## TABLE 6.3

**Number and percentage distribution of persons admitted into substance abuse treatment, by race/ethnicity, 2000–10**

[Number and percent distribution. Based on administrative data reported to TEDS by all reporting states and jurisdictions, excluding Puerto Rico.]

| Race/ethnicity | 2000 | 2001 | 2002 | 2003 | 2004 | 2005 | 2006 | 2007 | 2008 | 2009 | 2010 | U.S. pop. 2010 (000s)[a] |
|---|---|---|---|---|---|---|---|---|---|---|---|---|
| **Total** | **1,749,726** | **1,767,833** | **1,886,241** | **1,858,530** | **1,805,109** | **1,891,509** | **1,907,593** | **1,912,300** | **2,010,165** | **1,989,706** | **1,818,900** | |
| | | | | | | | Number | | | | | |
| White (non-Hispanic) | 1,009,008 | 1,029,513 | 1,095,077 | 1,081,247 | 1,068,108 | 1,105,774 | 1,135,320 | 1,139,424 | 1,188,390 | 1,162,112 | 1,100,072 | 168,115 |
| Black (non-Hispanic) | 434,545 | 431,719 | 454,746 | 443,024 | 409,261 | 419,055 | 403,695 | 393,178 | 409,444 | 401,620 | 363,500 | 26,699 |
| Hispanic origin | 210,633 | 214,366 | 240,221 | 236,815 | 230,262 | 254,775 | 258,585 | 254,266 | 264,346 | 257,968 | 234,806 | 30,552 |
| Mexican | 80,307 | 80,808 | 97,703 | 95,215 | 95,351 | 100,487 | 106,219 | 107,969 | 111,291 | 105,724 | 79,380 | n/a |
| Puerto Rican | 78,521 | 82,561 | 81,926 | 76,492 | 69,391 | 74,191 | 70,357 | 67,964 | 71,117 | 69,273 | 65,108 | n/a |
| Cuban | 4,632 | 4,198 | 5,448 | 7,070 | 5,564 | 9,482 | 8,155 | 3,794 | 4,296 | 4,330 | 3,743 | n/a |
| Other/not specified | 47,173 | 46,799 | 55,144 | 58,038 | 59,956 | 70,615 | 73,854 | 74,539 | 77,642 | 78,641 | 86,575 | n/a |
| Other | 79,731 | 77,302 | 82,535 | 83,840 | 85,508 | 90,417 | 99,735 | 105,535 | 110,923 | 108,537 | 109,861 | 14,425 |
| American Indian/Alaska Native | 37,551 | 37,538 | 39,283 | 35,478 | 35,835 | 39,044 | 42,067 | 44,067 | 45,199 | 44,355 | 42,830 | 1,812 |
| Asian/Pacific Islander | 14,618 | 14,079 | 16,429 | 17,719 | 16,058 | 19,033 | 18,374 | 17,782 | 18,935 | 18,404 | 18,587 | 11,597 |
| Other | 27,562 | 25,685 | 26,823 | 30,643 | 33,615 | 32,340 | 39,294 | 43,686 | 46,789 | 45,778 | 48,444 | 1,017 |
| **No. of admissions** | **1,733,917** | **1,752,900** | **1,872,579** | **1,844,926** | **1,793,139** | **1,870,021** | **1,897,335** | **1,892,403** | **1,973,103** | **1,930,237** | **1,808,239** | **239,791** |
| | | | | | | | Percent distribution | | | | | |
| White (non-Hispanic) | 58.2 | 58.7 | 58.5 | 58.6 | 59.6 | 59.1 | 59.1 | 60.2 | 60.2 | 60.2 | 60.8 | 70.1 |
| Black (non-Hispanic) | 25.1 | 24.6 | 24.3 | 24.0 | 22.8 | 22.4 | 21.3 | 20.8 | 20.8 | 20.8 | 20.1 | 11.1 |
| Hispanic origin | 12.1 | 12.2 | 12.8 | 12.8 | 12.8 | 13.6 | 13.6 | 13.4 | 13.4 | 13.4 | 13.0 | 12.7 |
| Mexican | 4.6 | 4.6 | 5.2 | 5.2 | 5.3 | 5.4 | 5.6 | 5.7 | 5.6 | 5.5 | 4.4 | n/a |
| Puerto Rican | 4.5 | 4.7 | 4.4 | 4.1 | 3.9 | 4.0 | 3.7 | 3.6 | 3.6 | 3.6 | 3.6 | n/a |
| Cuban | 0.3 | 0.2 | 0.3 | 0.4 | 0.3 | 0.5 | 0.4 | 0.2 | 0.2 | 0.2 | 0.2 | n/a |
| Other/not specified | 2.7 | 2.7 | 2.9 | 3.1 | 3.3 | 3.8 | 3.9 | 3.9 | 3.9 | 4.1 | 4.8 | n/a |
| Other | 4.6 | 4.4 | 4.4 | 4.5 | 4.8 | 4.8 | 5.3 | 5.6 | 5.6 | 5.6 | 6.1 | 6.0 |
| American Indian/Alaska Native | 2.2 | 2.1 | 2.1 | 1.9 | 2.0 | 2.1 | 2.2 | 2.3 | 2.3 | 2.3 | 2.4 | 0.8 |
| Asian/Pacific Islander | 0.8 | 0.8 | 0.9 | 1.0 | 0.9 | 1.0 | 1.0 | 0.9 | 1.0 | 1.0 | 1.0 | 4.8 |
| Other | 1.6 | 1.5 | 1.4 | 1.7 | 1.9 | 1.7 | 2.1 | 2.3 | 2.4 | 2.4 | 2.7 | 0.4 |
| **Total** | **100.0** | **100.0** | **100.0** | **100.0** | **100.0** | **100.0** | **100.0** | **100.0** | **100.0** | **100.0** | **100.0** | **100.0** |

[a]Resident population aged 12 and older. The population calculations exclude the population of the states and jurisdictions that did not report data to TEDS in 2010 (District of Columbia, Georgia, and Mississippi).

TEDS = Treatment Episode Data Set.

n/a = Not available.

SOURCE: "Table 1.4. Admissions Aged 12 and Older by Race/Ethnicity: TEDS 2000–2010 and U.S. Population Aged 12 and Older by Race/Ethnicity: TEDS 2000–2010 and U.S. Population Aged 12 and Older 2010, Number and Percent Distribution," in *Treatment Episode Data Set (TEDS) 2000–2010. National Admissions to Substance Abuse Treatment Services*, U.S. Department of Health and Human Services, Substance Abuse and Mental Health Services Administration, June 2012, http://www.samhsa.gov/data/2k12/TEDS2010N/TEDS2010NWeb.pdf (accessed February 14, 2013)

ospital inpatient treatment. Of those under outpatient treatment but not in detox, the majority were receiving what SAMHSA calls regular, or nonintensive, treatment.

Of the total treatment population, 28,955 individuals (2.4% of all patients) were undergoing detox, most in outpatient settings (13,450) and the rest in residential facilities (9,326) and hospitals (6,179). (See Table 6.1.) Among all patients under treatment, 299,430 (24.5%) were receiving methadone.

## STATISTICS ON ADMITTED PATIENTS
### Admissions by Substance

Data on admissions by the primary substance of abuse provided by TEDS for 2010 are shown in Table 6.4. In that year alcohol alone or in combination with a secondary substance accounted for the largest number of people receiving treatment (744,087, or 40.9% of all admissions), followed by opiates (413,427, or 22.7%, mainly heroin), marijuana (335,833, or 18.4%), cocaine (148,151, or 8.1%), and methamphetamine/amphetamines (112,473, or 6.2%).

The 2010 admissions for alcohol abuse (either alone or in combination with a secondary substance) of 40.9% were down from 46.3% reported by TEDS in 2000. (See Table 6.4.) Total alcohol-related admissions declined annually through 2005, reaching a low of 39%, largely accounting for the decreasing trend in total admissions. Alcohol-related admissions climbed steadily after 2005, reaching 41.6% of all admissions in 2009, before dropping to 40.9% in 2010.

The category showing the largest growth in admissions is methamphetamine/amphetamines. In 2000 these stimulant drugs accounted for approximately 4.6% of all admissions, whereas in 2010 they accounted for 6.2%. (See Table 6.4.) Marijuana-related admissions had the second-most-rapid growth, representing 18.4% of cases in 2010, up from 14.3% in 2000.

Opiate-related admissions have been growing, whereas cocaine-related admissions have been declining. In 2000 opiate-related admissions were 17% and cocaine-related admissions were 13.6% of the total; 10 years later opiates accounted for 22.7% and cocaine for 8.1% of admissions. (See Table 6.4.)

### Demographics by Substance

A detailed examination of admissions in 2010 is provided in Table 6.4, which shows the distribution of people at admission by major drug categories, gender, race, and ethnicity.

GENDER. As noted previously in this chapter, the total male admissions (69.9%) were higher than the total female admissions (30.1%) in 2010. (See Table 6.2.) This trend held in all but one substance category: sedatives

(51.3% females versus 32.5% males; the total does not add to 100% because the "all other" category does not show gender). (See Table 6.4.) The tranquilizer category was about equal in 2010: 46.5% females versus 47.8% males. The greatest male-female differences were noted in marijuana-related admissions (65.9% males versus 23.2% females), alcohol admissions with a secondary drug (67.5% males versus 25.7% females), alcohol-only admissions (67% males versus 25.9% females), and heroin admissions (61.9% males versus 30.9% females).

RACE AND ETHNICITY. In 2010 non-Hispanic whites made up 60.7% of the substance abuse treatment admissions; non-Hispanic African-Americans, 20%; Hispanics, 8.1%; Native Americans or Alaskan Natives, 2.4%; and Asian-Americans or Pacific Islanders, 1%. (See Table 6.4.) Non-Hispanic whites had the highest admission rates for all drug categories except smoked cocaine and phencyclidine (PCP). Non-Hispanic African-Americans had the highest smoked-cocaine admissions (53.5%) and PCP-related admissions (61.6%). Non-Hispanic African-Americans were second in admission rates for alcohol only, alcohol with a secondary drug, heroin, other opiates, cocaine other than smoked, marijuana, sedatives, hallucinogens, inhalants, and other. Hispanics were second in admission rates for methamphetamine/amphetamines. It should be noted that the Hispanics category is treated as an ethnicity rather than as a race and includes both white and African-American individuals of Hispanic origin.

It is important, however, to consider these rates of substance abuse treatment by race in the context of the overall racial composition of the United States. The 2010 TEDS data indicate that the total U.S. population consisted of 70.1% non-Hispanic whites, 12.7% Hispanics, and 11.1% non-Hispanic African-Americans in that year. (See Table 6.3.) When substance abuse treatment rates are compared with these population statistics, non-Hispanic whites were underrepresented in treatment (60.8% in treatment versus 70.1% of the U.S. population), the proportion of Hispanics in treatment was comparable to Hispanics in the population (13% in treatment versus 12.7% of the U.S. population), and non-Hispanic African-Americans were disproportionately admitted for treatment (20.1% in treatment versus 11.1% of the U.S. population).

AGE AT ADMISSION. The 2010 TEDS data show that 57.3% of people admitted for alcohol-only abuse that year were between the ages of 18 and 44 years. The average age of admission for alcohol-only abuse was 40 years. Crack (smoked) cocaine treatment recipients were primarily aged 35 years and older (74.6%) and had an average age of 41 years. In contrast, 61.2% of those admitted for using inhalants were aged 12 to 29 years and had an average age of 28 years. Those being

# TABLE 6.4

## Percentage of persons admitted into substance abuse treatment, by gender, ethnicity, and primary substance abused, 2010

[Column percent distribution. Based on administrative data reported to TEDS by all reporting states and jurisdictions.]

| Selected race/ethnicity/ gender/age group | All admissions | Alcohol: Alcohol only | Alcohol: With secondary drug | Opiates: Heroin | Opiates: Other opiates | Cocaine: Smoked cocaine | Cocaine: Other route | Marijuana/ hashish | Methamphetamine/ amphetamines | Tranquilizers | Sedatives | Hallucinogens | PCP | Inhalants | Other/ none specified |
|---|---|---|---|---|---|---|---|---|---|---|---|---|---|---|---|
| Total | 1,820,737 | 411,388 | 332,699 | 256,256 | 157,171 | 104,564 | 43,587 | 335,833 | 112,473 | 15,707 | 4,117 | 1,675 | 4,501 | 1,449 | 39,317 |
| White (non-Hisp.) male | 39.4 | 47.7 | 41.9 | 38.9 | 47.9 | 17.9 | 29.7 | 33.2 | 35.5 | 41.0 | 37.3 | 49.3 | 8.2 | 43.0 | 36.8 |
| White (non-Hisp.) female | 21.3 | 20.2 | 17.4 | 22.6 | 40.3 | 17.2 | 17.8 | 13.5 | 32.2 | 42.4 | 46.8 | 18.7 | 6.0 | 25.3 | 23.8 |
| Black (non-Hisp.) male | 14.4 | 9.7 | 17.3 | 11.7 | 1.7 | 32.6 | 21.2 | 23.4 | 2.1 | 2.7 | 2.8 | 12.5 | 36.7 | 6.1 | 16.2 |
| Black (non-Hisp.) female | 5.6 | 2.9 | 5.3 | 5.6 | 1.7 | 20.9 | 7.7 | 7.4 | 1.3 | 2.2 | 2.8 | 5.0 | 24.9 | 3.7 | 7.1 |
| Mexican-orig. male | 3.2 | 3.9 | 2.6 | 2.5 | 0.7 | 0.9 | 2.7 | 4.6 | 7.3 | 0.4 | 0.8 | 1.6 | 2.5 | 3.4 | 0.8 |
| Mexican-orig. female | 1.2 | 0.9 | 0.9 | 0.8 | 0.6 | 0.5 | 0.7 | 1.3 | 5.5 | 0.4 | 0.6 | 0.5 | 2.2 | 3.5 | 0.4 |
| Puerto Rican-orig. male | 3.0 | 1.7 | 2.9 | 8.2 | 0.6 | 2.1 | 5.4 | 2.8 | 0.2 | 3.1 | 0.6 | 1.9 | 6.3 | 0.8 | 1.3 |
| Puerto Rican-orig. female | 0.7 | 0.4 | 0.6 | 1.5 | 0.3 | 1.0 | 1.4 | 0.8 | 0.2 | 1.1 | 0.3 | 0.3 | 2.8 | 0.6 | 0.5 |
| American Indian/Alaska Native male | 1.5 | 2.9 | 2.2 | 0.3 | 0.7 | 0.4 | 0.4 | 1.1 | 1.0 | 0.3 | 0.6 | 1.2 | 0.3 | 2.2 | 0.9 |
| American Indian/Alaska Native female | 0.9 | 1.2 | 1.3 | 0.3 | 1.1 | 0.5 | 0.4 | 0.6 | 1.4 | 0.3 | 0.5 | 0.5 | 0.2 | 2.8 | 0.7 |
| Asian/Pacific Islander male | 0.7 | 1.1 | 0.6 | 0.3 | 0.3 | 0.4 | 0.5 | 0.8 | 2.0 | 0.3 | 0.4 | 1.0 | 0.3 | 0.8 | 0.4 |
| Asian/Pacific Islander female | 0.3 | 0.3 | 0.2 | 0.1 | 0.2 | 0.2 | 0.2 | 0.3 | 1.0 | 0.1 | 0.3 | 0.2 | 0.1 | 0.4 | 0.3 |
| All other | 7.7 | 7.1 | 7.0 | 7.2 | 4.0 | 5.4 | 12.0 | 10.1 | 10.2 | 5.7 | 6.3 | 7.4 | 9.4 | 7.4 | 11.0 |

SOURCE: Adapted from "Table 2.3a. Admissions Aged 12 and Older by Selected Race/Ethnicity/Gender/Age Groups, according to Primary Substance of Abuse: 2010 Column Percent Distribution," in *Treatment Episode Data Set (TEDS) 2000–2010. National Admissions to Substance Abuse Treatment Services*, U.S. Department of Health and Human Services, Substance Abuse and Mental Health Services Administration, June 2012, http://www.samhsa.gov/data/2k12/TEDS2010N/TEDS2010NWeb.pdf (accessed February 14, 2013)

eated for marijuana abuse were another young group. More than seven out of 10 (71.2%) were between the ges of 15 and 29 years. The marijuana treatment group ad an average age of 25 years.

## ype of Treatment

In 2010, 62.9% of those admitted to treatment were dmitted into ambulatory (nonresidential) treatment cilities; of the remainder, 20% went into residential-pe (24-hour) detox and 17.1% went into residential cilities. (See Table 6.5.)

Among those going into residential-type detox, the rgest percentages were admitted for tranquilizers 6.1%), heroin (32.5%), and alcohol only (28.7%). ee Table 6.5.) Those using marijuana had the highest ercentage entering ambulatory care (84.7%). The largest roportion of substance abusers assigned to some form of esidential treatment were heroin users (50.7%).

## eferring Source

Table 6.6 shows the source of referral of patients to ubstance abuse treatment in 2010. Nearly one-third 33.1%) of all people admitted came to get treatment on leir own volition. The largest referral source (sending 6.9% of individuals) was the criminal justice system. luch of the remaining one-third of all referrals came rom substance abuse care providers and other health care roviders (9.9% and 6.4% of referrals, respectively). )ther referrals came from schools, employers, and com-lunity agencies.

Regarding the source of referral based on the drug of buse, most heroin users (55%) and other opiate users 49.6%) sought treatment on their own accord. (See able 6.6.) The criminal justice system sent over half of larijuana users (53.6%) and methamphetamine/amphet-mine users (51.8%), along with nearly half of PCP users 46.4%), to treatment.

## IOW EFFECTIVE IS TREATMENT?

During the 1960s there was an opioid epidemic in the Jnited States, and the federal government released sub-tantial funds to substance abuse treatment programs. his funding has continued over the decades and is sup-lemented by state governments and private sources. according to the Office of National Drug Control Policy, n *FY 2013 Budget and Performance Summary: Compan-on to the National Drug Control Strategy* (April 2013, ttp://www.whitehouse.gov/sites/default/files/ondcp/fy2013 _drug_control_budget_and_performance_summary.pdf), he 2013 federal budget request for drug abuse treatment vas $9.2 billion, and the request for treatment prevention vas $1.4 billion.

With so much money devoted to substance abuse reatment, there has been considerable research conducted on the effectiveness of the programs. The bulk of this research began during the late 1960s and extended into the 1990s.

In the press release "New Research Documents Success of Drug Abuse Treatments" (December 15, 1997, http://www.nih.gov/news/pr/dec97/nida-15.htm), the National Institutes of Health notes that the first major study of drug-treatment effectiveness was the Drug Abuse Reporting Program (DARP), which studied more than 44,000 clients in 52 treatment centers between 1969 and 1973. Program staff then studied a smaller group of these clients six and 12 years after their treatment. A second important study was the Treatment Outcome Prospective Study (TOPS), which followed 11,000 clients admitted to 41 treatment centers between 1979 and 1981. Both the DARP and the TOPS found major reductions in both drug abuse and criminal activity after treatment.

### Services Research Outcomes Study

SAMHSA's Services Research Outcomes Study (SROS; September 1998, http://www.oas.samhsa.gov/sros/toc.htm) confirmed that both drug use and criminal behavior are reduced after drug treatment. Because it conducted a five-year follow-up on initial data in the Drug Services Research Survey (DSRS; http://www.oas .samhsa.gov/dsrs.htm), the SROS provided the first nationally representative data to answer the question: Does treatment work? This study, although now over 15 years old and reporting on even older data, has not been repeated.

In this nationally representative sample, alcohol use decreased by 14% and drug use declined by 21%. Decreases varied from drug to drug, with heroin use decreasing the least.

Results by type of treatment were variable. On aver-age, the best results for decreasing use of all drugs, especially cocaine and marijuana, were achieved with treatment that lasted six months or more. Long-term drug treatment appears to be necessary due to the chronic nature of addiction and its tendency to recur when treat-ment is stopped.

The SROS also showed that treatment for substance abuse can significantly reduce crime. Criminal activities such as breaking and entering, drug sales, prostitution, driving under the influence, and theft/larceny decreased between 23% and 38% after drug treatment.

### Current Principles of Effective Treatment

Even though no comprehensive research survey to rival the scope of the SROS has emerged, a number of important studies that evaluate the effectiveness of cer-tain substance abuse treatment and prevention programs have been published since the late 1990s. For example,

# TABLE 6.5

## Percentage of persons admitted into substance abuse treatment, by primary substance of abuse and type of care received, 2010

[Percent distribution. Based on administrative data reported to TEDS by all reporting states and jurisdictions.]

| Type of service at admission and medication-assisted opioid therapy | All admissions | Alcohol | | Opiates | | Cocaine | | Marijuana/hashish | Methamphetamine/amphetamines | Tranquilizers | Sedatives | Hallucinogens | PCP | Inhalants | Other/none specified |
|---|---|---|---|---|---|---|---|---|---|---|---|---|---|---|---|
| | | Alcohol only | With secondary drug | Heroin | Other opiates | Smoked cocaine | Other route | | | | | | | | |
| **Total** | 1,820,737 | 411,388 | 332,699 | 256,256 | 157,171 | 104,564 | 43,587 | 335,833 | 112,473 | 15,707 | 4,117 | 1,675 | 4,501 | 1,449 | 39,317 |
| **Type of service at admission** | | | | | | | | | | | | | | | |
| Ambulatory | 62.9 | 59.2 | 58.6 | 49.3 | 59.8 | 53.9 | 67.5 | 84.7 | 64.8 | 42.3 | 63.2 | 61.7 | 64.0 | 60.0 | 71.9 |
| Outpatient | 49.8 | 47.9 | 45.5 | 38.9 | 46.3 | 40.1 | 53.9 | 68.4 | 49.0 | 31.8 | 50.3 | 44.7 | 42.6 | 46.6 | 65.3 |
| Intensive outpatient | 12.0 | 10.1 | 12.8 | 7.2 | 11.1 | 13.7 | 13.5 | 16.3 | 15.7 | 9.9 | 12.0 | 17.0 | 21.4 | 12.9 | 6.1 |
| Detoxification | 1.0 | 1.2 | 0.4 | 3.2 | 2.4 | 0.2 | 0.2 | 0.1 | 0.1 | 0.6 | 1.0 | — | b | 0.6 | 0.5 |
| Rehabilitation/residential | 17.1 | 12.1 | 18.2 | 18.2 | 19.0 | 30.0 | 22.5 | 12.9 | 26.8 | 21.6 | 19.4 | 27.0 | 29.8 | 23.3 | 10.8 |
| Short-term (<31 days) | 9.2 | 7.3 | 10.6 | 9.4 | 11.3 | 15.4 | 11.8 | 6.5 | 9.8 | 14.5 | 12.7 | 14.4 | 15.2 | 14.1 | 5.3 |
| Long-term (31+ days) | 7.6 | 4.3 | 7.1 | 8.5 | 7.2 | 14.1 | 10.3 | 6.3 | 16.8 | 6.5 | 6.3 | 12.2 | 14.4 | 8.6 | 4.9 |
| Hospital (non-detox) | 0.4 | 0.4 | 0.5 | 0.3 | 0.6 | 0.4 | 0.3 | 0.1 | 0.2 | 0.6 | 0.5 | 0.3 | 0.1 | 0.6 | 0.7 |
| Detoxification (24-hour service) | 20.0 | 28.7 | 23.2 | 32.5 | 21.1 | 16.1 | 10.0 | 2.3 | 8.4 | 36.1 | 17.4 | 11.3 | 6.2 | 16.7 | 17.3 |
| Free-standing residential | 16.2 | 23.8 | 17.3 | 25.1 | 17.6 | 15.2 | 8.8 | 2.2 | 8.3 | 23.8 | 14.2 | 11.0 | 5.5 | 16.3 | 15.6 |
| Hospital inpatient | 3.8 | 4.9 | 5.8 | 7.4 | 3.5 | 0.9 | 1.3 | 0.2 | 0.1 | 12.3 | 3.2 | 0.3 | 0.7 | 0.4 | 1.6 |
| **Total** | 100.0 | 100.0 | 100.0 | 100.0 | 100.0 | 100.0 | 100.0 | 100.0 | 100.0 | 100.0 | 100.0 | 100.0 | 100.0 | 100.0 | 100.0 |
| No. of admissions | 1,820,737 | 411,388 | 332,699 | 256,256 | 157,171 | 104,564 | 43,587 | 335,833 | 112,473 | 15,707 | 4,117 | 1,675 | 4,501 | 1,449 | 39,317 |
| **Medication-assisted opioid therapy[a]** | | | | | | | | | | | | | | | |
| Yes | 6.1 | 0.5 | 0.7 | 27.9 | 19.8 | 0.6 | 1.0 | 0.3 | 0.3 | 3.0 | 4.4 | 2.0 | 0.3 | 2.7 | 2.9 |
| No | 93.9 | 99.5 | 99.3 | 72.1 | 80.2 | 99.4 | 99.0 | 99.7 | 99.7 | 97.0 | 95.6 | 98.0 | 99.7 | 97.3 | 97.1 |
| **Total** | 100.0 | 100.0 | 100.0 | 100.0 | 100.0 | 100.0 | 100.0 | 100.0 | 100.0 | 100.0 | 100.0 | 100.0 | 100.0 | 100.0 | 100.0 |
| No. of admissions | 1,779,412 | 401,662 | 326,720 | 251,737 | 153,389 | 103,031 | 42,818 | 328,853 | 108,600 | 15,429 | 4,034 | 1,644 | 4,486 | 1,427 | 35,582 |

[a]Therapy with methadone or buprenorphine is part of client's treatment plan.
[b]Less than 0.05 percent.
TEDS = Treatment Episode Data Set.
—Quantity is zero.

SOURCE: "Table 2.7. Admissions Aged 12 and Older, by Type of Service and Medication-Assisted Opioid Therapy according to Primary Substance of Abuse: 2010 Percent Distribution," in *Treatment Episode Data Set (TEDS) 2000–2010. National Admissions to Substance Abuse Treatment Services*, U.S. Department of Health and Human Services, Substance Abuse and Mental Health Services Administration, June 2012, http://www.samhsa.gov/data/2k12/TEDS2010N/TEDS2010NWeb.pdf (accessed February 14, 2013)

# TABLE 6.6

## Percentage of persons admitted into substance abuse treatment, by primary substance of abuse and source of referral, 2010

[Percent distribution. Based on administrative data reported to TEDS by all reporting states and jurisdictions.]

| Treatment referral source and detailed criminal justice referral[a] | All admissions | Alcohol | | Opiates | | Cocaine | | Marijuana/ hashish | Methamphetamine/ amphetamines | Tranquilizers | Sedatives | Hallucinogens | PCP | Inhalants | Other/none specified |
|---|---|---|---|---|---|---|---|---|---|---|---|---|---|---|---|
| | | Alcohol only | With secondary drug | Heroin | Other opiates | Smoked cocaine | Other route | | | | | | | | |
| **Total** | 1,820,737 | 411,388 | 332,699 | 256,256 | 157,171 | 104,564 | 43,587 | 335,833 | 112,473 | 15,707 | 4,117 | 1,675 | 4,501 | 1,449 | 39,317 |
| **Treatment referral source** | | | | | | | | | | | | | | | |
| Criminal justice/DUI (see detail, below) | 36.9 | 42.5 | 35.7 | 16.3 | 19.9 | 28.2 | 39.0 | 53.6 | 51.8 | 21.5 | 24.5 | 37.3 | 46.4 | 22.8 | 31.3 |
| Self or individual | 33.1 | 29.5 | 31.7 | 55.0 | 49.6 | 36.1 | 27.5 | 16.0 | 24.4 | 44.0 | 44.2 | 33.8 | 23.2 | 43.5 | 39.5 |
| Substance abuse care provider | 9.9 | 7.9 | 10.9 | 15.8 | 12.5 | 14.2 | 11.5 | 5.7 | 5.7 | 13.5 | 10.2 | 9.2 | 9.0 | 7.8 | 6.3 |
| Other health care provider | 6.4 | 8.2 | 7.6 | 4.8 | 8.0 | 6.8 | 5.6 | 4.1 | 3.4 | 9.8 | 8.8 | 6.2 | 4.2 | 10.3 | 7.0 |
| School (educational) | 1.2 | 0.6 | 0.7 | a | 0.2 | 0.1 | 0.2 | 4.1 | 0.3 | 0.6 | 1.0 | 2.2 | 0.1 | 3.5 | 4.4 |
| Employer/EAP | 0.5 | 0.7 | 0.5 | 0.1 | 0.4 | 0.2 | 0.9 | 0.7 | 0.2 | 0.4 | 0.6 | 0.2 | 0.2 | 0.1 | 0.5 |
| Other community referral | 12.1 | 10.6 | 12.9 | 7.9 | 9.3 | 14.4 | 15.3 | 16.0 | 14.1 | 10.4 | 10.6 | 11.2 | 16.9 | 11.9 | 10.9 |
| **Total** | 100.0 | 100.0 | 100.0 | 100.0 | 100.0 | 100.0 | 100.0 | 100.0 | 100.0 | 100.0 | 100.0 | 100.0 | 100.0 | 100.0 | 100.0 |
| No. of admissions | 1,791,732 | 405,375 | 327,611 | 252,211 | 155,243 | 103,462 | 42,937 | 331,037 | 110,844 | 15,533 | 4,039 | 1,638 | 4,409 | 1,416 | 35,977 |
| **Detailed criminal justice referral[b]** | | | | | | | | | | | | | | | |
| **Total** | 660,577 | 172,349 | 117,003 | 41,041 | 30,969 | 29,138 | 16,742 | 177,315 | 57,461 | 3,333 | 990 | 611 | 2,044 | 323 | 11,258 |
| Probation/parole | 34.6 | 18.6 | 31.7 | 42.4 | 34.7 | 43.3 | 44.0 | 42.9 | 44.0 | 31.6 | 31.5 | 41.0 | 54.0 | 27.9 | 42.0 |
| State/federal court | 14.7 | 11.1 | 16.3 | 16.3 | 19.9 | 16.5 | 17.9 | 16.8 | 10.9 | 19.6 | 15.4 | 18.5 | 10.4 | 19.6 | 10.6 |
| Formal adjudication | 14.5 | 16.0 | 14.9 | 12.6 | 20.3 | 13.2 | 10.0 | 12.4 | 15.1 | 23.2 | 29.9 | 10.7 | 7.6 | 22.4 | 19.6 |
| Other legal entity | 8.4 | 12.1 | 6.9 | 6.3 | 5.6 | 6.9 | 7.2 | 9.3 | 3.0 | 7.9 | 6.3 | 5.6 | 6.6 | 14.2 | 13.1 |
| DUI/DWI | 10.8 | 27.8 | 14.9 | 1.6 | 3.8 | 1.1 | 2.4 | 2.5 | 0.7 | 7.0 | 4.5 | 1.6 | 1.3 | 4.6 | 4.0 |
| Diversionary program | 2.5 | 0.9 | 1.7 | 6.9 | 4.2 | 3.8 | 4.0 | 3.2 | 0.6 | 3.0 | 1.3 | 2.7 | 4.8 | 0.5 | 2.1 |
| Prison | 2.4 | 1.1 | 2.5 | 4.9 | 3.7 | 4.1 | 4.6 | 2.3 | 2.5 | 2.3 | 4.2 | 5.6 | 3.8 | 0.9 | 2.2 |
| Other | 12.1 | 12.3 | 11.1 | 9.0 | 7.8 | 11.1 | 9.9 | 10.5 | 23.1 | 5.4 | 6.9 | 14.2 | 11.4 | 10.0 | 6.2 |
| **Total** | 100.0 | 100.0 | 100.0 | 100.0 | 100.0 | 100.0 | 100.0 | 100.0 | 100.0 | 100.0 | 100.0 | 100.0 | 100.0 | 100.0 | 100.0 |
| No. of admissions | 476,540 | 120,019 | 81,050 | 33,167 | 20,996 | 21,209 | 12,483 | 126,991 | 50,640 | 2,579 | 638 | 373 | 1,640 | 219 | 4,536 |

Primary substance at admission

a Less than 0.05 percent.

b "Detailed criminal justice referral" is a supplemental data set item. Not all supplemental data set items are reported by all states and jurisdictions.

TEDS = Treatment Episode Data Set.

SOURCE: "Table 2.6. Admissions Aged 12 and Older, by Treatment Referral Source and Detailed Criminal Justice Referral according to Primary Substance of Abuse: 2010 Percent Distribution," in *Treatment Episode Data Set (TEDS) 2000–2010. National Admissions to Substance Abuse Treatment Services*, U.S. Department of Health and Human Services, Substance Abuse and Mental Health Services Administration, June 2012. http://www.samhsa.gov/data/2k12/TEDS2010N/TEDS2010NWeb.pdf (accessed February 14, 2013)

Ted R. Miller and Delia Hendrie provide in *Substance Abuse Prevention Dollars and Cents: A Cost-Benefit Analysis* (2008, http://store.samhsa.gov/shin/content/SMA07-4298/SMA07-4298.pdf) a detailed analysis of existing substance abuse treatment programs (including school-based programs for minors) and of the various social and economic costs that are associated with addiction. The NIDA offers an overview of some recent findings in "DrugFacts: Lessons from Prevention Research" (August 2011, http://www.drugabuse.gov/publications/drugfacts/lessons-prevention-research). Drawing from a range of scholarly papers, the NIDA outlines 16 key "principles" of effective treatment methods, including the role of "protective factors" (such as family and community support) in sustaining effective substance abuse treatment and the importance of tailoring prevention programs to address the unique needs of particular communities and social groups. The NIDA cites several valuable research studies concerning the efficacy (the ability of an intervention to produce the intended diagnostic or therapeutic effect in optimal circumstances) of certain approaches to drug treatment, among them E. Michael Foster, Allison E. Olchowski, and Carolyn H. Webster-Stratton's "Is Stacking Intervention Components Cost-Effective? An Analysis of the Incredible Years Program" (*Journal of the American Academy of Child and Adolescent Psychology*, vol. 46, no. 11, November 2007) and J. David Hawkins et al.'s "Results of a Type 2 Translational Research Trial to Prevent Adolescent Drug Use and Delinquency: A Test of Communities That Care" (*Archives of Pediatrics and Adolescent Medicine*, vol. 163, no. 9, September 2009).

Additionally, the NIDA notes that treatment should be readily available and address issues in a person's life—not just the addiction. According to the NIDA principles, effective treatment should include counseling, behavioral therapies, appropriate medications, and drug use monitoring. Drug-addicted individuals often have other illnesses, such as mental illnesses or infectious diseases that were contracted by needle-sharing or other risky practices, and the NIDA suggests that these illnesses should also be treated. The NIDA adds that one single treatment is not appropriate for everyone and that any drug treatment plan should be periodically reevaluated and adjusted, depending on a patient's progress and needs.

### The Development of Antidrug Vaccines

Medications can help drug-addicted individuals not only by suppressing drug withdrawal symptoms but also by helping reestablish proper brain function and reducing drug cravings during treatment. Antidrug vaccines, which were under development as of April 2013, may help drug-addicted individuals in the future. In "Anti-drug Vaccines to Treat Substance Abuse" (*Immunology and Cell Biology*, vol. 87, no. 4, May–June 2009), Berma M. Kinsey, David C. Jackson, and Frank M. Orson review the status of the development of these vaccines for treating addictions. The researchers explain that antidrug vaccines work by triggering the development of antibodies against particular drugs in vaccinated individuals. The antibodies bind to the drug in the bloodstream before it is able to get to the brain. Thus, the vaccinated individual receives no drug effects by taking a drug, such as cocaine or methamphetamine; that is, the pleasure centers of the brain are not stimulated because the drug never reaches the brain. Because the person does not experience any "reward" for taking the drug, the craving sensations for the drug eventually subside.

In reality, however, antidrug vaccines do not work perfectly. For example, if an individual's body does not respond well to the vaccine by developing a substantial amount of antibodies, then only some of the drug is bound in the bloodstream and some enters the brain. To get a desired drug effect, a drug addict will have to increase the doses of a drug. Thus, Kinsey, Jackson, and Orson suggest that counseling and behavior therapy will also be needed for antidrug vaccines to be effective.

Kinsey, Jackson, and Orson surmise that antinicotine vaccines are the ones most likely to be available first to the public because their development is the furthest along. Vaccines are also under development for cocaine, morphine, and methamphetamine addictions.

## DRUG COURTS

Drug courts are programs that use the court's authority to offer certain drug-addicted offenders to have their charges dismissed or their sentences reduced if they participate in drug court substance abuse treatment programs. Drug court programs vary across the nation, but most programs offer a range of treatment options and generally require one year of commitment from the defendant.

Randall T. Brown of the University of Wisconsin School of Medicine and Public Health describes drug courts and reviews their effect in "Systematic Review of the Impact of Adult Drug-Treatment Courts" (*Translational Research*, vol. 155, no. 6, June 2010). Brown notes that drug courts vary in the number of individuals they serve annually, with the typical range being between 80 and 120. Courts in large urban areas often serve hundreds more. He explains that drug courts use rewards and sanctions to motivate individuals to comply with their treatment. Rewards include praise from the judge, fewer court appearances, and gift cards to local stores. Those who adhere to the rules and remain drug free for a sustained period (48% on average) graduate from treatment and are provided with a ceremony that is attended by family and friends. Sanctions include admonitions from the judge, community service, increased drug screening, and incarceration. Brown's review of the literature on the effect of drug courts "points toward benefit versus traditional adjudication in averting future criminal behavior and in reducing future substance use, at least in the short term."

The National Drug Court Institute (NDCI), which is supported by the Office of National Drug Control Policy and the U.S. Department of Justice's Office of Justice Programs, studied its own drug court system, and its findings were reported by West Huddleston and Douglas B. Marlowe in *Painting the Current Picture: A National Report on Drug Courts and Other Problem-Solving Court Programs in the United States* (July 2011, http://www.ndci.org/sites/default/files/nadcp/PCP%20Report%20FINAL.PDF). Huddleston and Marlowe indicate that drug courts decrease criminal recidivism (relapse into criminal activity), save money, increase retention in treatment, and provide affordable treatment. The researchers note that between 2005 and 2009 the total number of drug courts in the United States rose from 1,756 to 2,459, an increase of 40%.

## WHERE TO GO FOR HELP

Many organizations provide assistance for addicts, their families, and their friends. Most of the self-help groups are based on the Twelve Step program of Alcoholics Anonymous (AA). Whereas AA is a support group for problem drinkers, Al-Anon/Alateen is for friends and families of alcoholics. Families Anonymous provides support for family members and friends who are concerned about a loved one's problems with drugs and/or alcohol. Other organizations include Adult Children of Alcoholics, Cocaine Anonymous, and Narcotics Anonymous. For an addict, many of these organizations can provide immediate help. For families and friends, they can provide knowledge, understanding, and support. For contact information for some of these organizations, see the Important Names and Addresses section at the back of this book.

## CHAPTER 7
# HOW ALCOHOL, TOBACCO, AND DRUG USE AFFECT ECONOMICS AND GOVERNMENT

The alcohol and tobacco industries play large roles in the U.S. economy. Both industries not only provide jobs and income for those involved in growing, manufacturing, and selling these products, but also contribute significant tax revenues to the federal, state, and local governments. The U.S. economy also feels the effects of alcohol, tobacco, and illicit drug use in other, less beneficial, ways. All these drugs can have significant health consequences, with associated health care costs. There are also costs in the form of loss of productivity—work that was never performed because of poor health, death, or imprisonment. The cost of enforcing drug laws and incarcerating those convicted of breaking such laws are also significant.

## U.S. ALCOHOL SALES AND CONSUMPTION

Retail sales of alcoholic beverages are divided into three groups: beer, wine, and distilled spirits (liquor). According to the Economic Research Service (October 1, 2012, http://www.ers.usda.gov/datafiles/Food_Expenditures/Food_Expenditures/table4.xls), Americans spent $162.9 billion on alcoholic beverages in 2011. More than half ($86.5 billion, or 53.1%) of this money was spent on alcoholic beverages to be consumed at home, while more than one-third (35.6%) of all alcoholic beverage expenditures were made at restaurants and bars.

### Beer

Michael B. Sauter writes in "10 States That Sell the Most Beer Are Surprising" (USAToday.com, October 11, 2012) that Americans drank roughly 6.3 billion gallons (6.1 billion liters [L]) of beer in 2011, or 28.3 gallons (6.1 billion L) per person who was of legal drinking age. The Beer Institute reports in *Brewer's Almanac 2013* (March 2013, http://www.beerinstitute.org/assets/uploads/Brewers_Almanac-_20131.xlsx) that, per capita (per person), Americans consumed 20.3 gallons (76.8 L) of beer 2011. This figure marked a notable decline from 2007,

when Americans drank 21.8 gallons (82.5 L) per capita. At 31.9 gallons (120.8 L) per capita, New Hampshire was the state with the highest beer consumption in 2011, followed by North Dakota (30.6 gallons [115.8 L]) and Montana (29.8 gallons [112.8 L]). Utah (12.3 gallons [46.6 L]), Connecticut (15.9 gallons [60.2 L]), and New Jersey (16.3 gallons [61.7 L]) were the states with the lowest per capita consumption of beer that year. The Beer Institute notes that there were a total 2,751 breweries in the United States in 2012.

### Wine

The Wine Institute reports in "Wine Consumption in the U.S." (March 14, 2013, http://www.wineinstitute.org/resources/statistics/article86) that Americans consumed 856 million gallons (3.2 billion L) of wine in 2012. This figure encompasses a range of wine products, including table wine, sparkling wine, dessert wine, and vermouth. The Wine Institute indicates that wine consumption rose steadily during the first decade of the 21st century, from 2.01 gallons (7.6 L) per capita in 2000 to 2.73 gallons (10.3 L) per capita in 2012. In "2012 California and U.S. Wine Sales" (2013, http://www.wineinstitute.org/resources/statistics/article697), the Wine Institute states that 360.1 million cases of wine were sold in the United States in 2012, with a total retail value of roughly $34.6 billion. This volume of wine sales represented an increase of 2% over the previous year and the 19th consecutive year of growth for the U.S. domestic wine market. Of these sales, California accounted for 207.7 million cases sold domestically, or 57.7% of total U.S. wine sales 2011. In addition, California wines accounted for 90% of the nation's wine exports, selling more than 47.2 million cases to overseas markets.

### Distilled Spirits

The Distilled Spirits Council of the United States (DIS-CUS) indicates in "Apparent Consumption of Distilled

Spirits by State, in Wine Gallons" (December 2011, http://www.discus.org/assets/1/7/December_2011_Final.pdf) that Americans drank 478.8 million gallons (1.8 billion L) of distilled spirits in 2011. This figure represented 3.6% growth over 2010 totals, when 462.1 million gallons (1.7 billion L) of spirits were consumed in the United States. Among individual states, California consumed the largest amount of distilled spirits in 2011, at 54.4 million gallons (205.9 million L), followed by Florida (37.1 million gallons [140.4 million L]), Texas (29.8 million gallons [112.8 million L]), and New York (29 million gallons [109.8 million L]).

Chris Mercer reports in "US: Spirits Sales Increase Momentum in 2011—Figures" (Just-Drinks.com, January 31, 2012, http://www.just-drinks.com/news/spirits-sales-increase-momentum-in-2011-figures_id106168.aspx) that sales of distilled spirits in the United States topped $19.9 billion in 2011, a 4% increase over the previous year. The industry also enjoyed record export figures that year, shipping roughly $1.3 billion worth of distilled spirits overseas, an increase of 16.5% over 2010 totals. In "Spirits Sales Steal Share from Beer" (Bloomberg.com, January 30, 2012), Duane D. Stanford notes that in 2011 distilled liquor accounted for more than one-third (33.6%) of the U.S. alcoholic beverage market.

## How Much Do Individuals and Families Spend on Alcohol?

The Bureau of Labor Statistics (BLS) reports in *Consumer Expenditures Midyear Update—July 2011 through June 2012 Average* (March 27, 2013, http://www.bls.gov/cex/22012/midyear/cucomp.pdf) that the average American family (or other consumer unit) spent $554 on alcoholic beverages between midyear 2011 and midyear 2012. This figure represented 0.8% of the average American family's expenditures over that period.

The amount spent on alcohol varied depending on the characteristics of the household. On average, single parents with at least one child under the age of 18 years spent only $242 on alcoholic beverages during the 12-month period, or about 0.6% of their total expenditures. Married couples with no children spent $682 on average, which was 1.1% of their total expenditures from midyear 2011 to midyear 2012. Single people spent an average of $403 on alcoholic beverages, which was 1.1% of their total expenditures over the period.

## U.S. TOBACCO PRODUCTION AND CONSUMPTION

### Farming Trends

In 1881 James A. Bonsack (1859–1924) invented the cigarette-making machine, which made cigarettes cheaper and faster to manufacture. Tom Capehart of the ERS notes in "Trends in U.S. Tobacco Farming" (November 2004, http://usda.mannlib.cornell.edu/usda/ers/TBS/2000s/2004/TBS-11-08-2004_Special_Report.pdf) that tobacco production in the United States grew from 300 million pounds (136,000 metric tons [t]) during the mid-1860s to over 1 billion pounds (454,000 t) in 1909. In 1946, at the end of World War II (1939–1945), tobacco production was above 2 billion pounds (907,000 t).

During the 1960s changes in tobacco preparation and the introduction of new machinery increased the amount of tobacco production per acre. Nonetheless, the number of tobacco farms dropped dramatically from about 512,000 in 1954 to 56,977 in 2002. In general, the amount of land devoted to cultivating tobacco, the value of production, and the production of tobacco decreased as well. Table 7.1 shows that the acreage devoted to tobacco declined steadily during the first half of the first decade of the 21st century, reaching a low of 297,080 acres (120,224 hectares [ha]) in 2005. Tobacco crop acreage

**TABLE 7.1**

Tobacco crops by area, yield, production, price, and value, 2001–10

| Year | Area harvested | Yield per acre | Production* | Marketing year average price per pound received by farmers | Value of production |
|------|----------------|----------------|-------------|-----------------------------------------------------------|---------------------|
| | *Acres* | *Pounds* | *1,000 pounds* | *Dollars* | *1,000 dollars* |
| 2001 | 432,490 | 2,292 | 991,293 | 1.956 | 1,938,892 |
| 2002 | 427,310 | 2,039 | 871,122 | 1.936 | 1,686,809 |
| 2003 | 411,150 | 1,952 | 802,560 | 1.964 | 1,576,436 |
| 2004 | 408,050 | 2,161 | 881,875 | 1.984 | 1,749,856 |
| 2005 | 297,080 | 2,171 | 645,015 | 1.642 | 1,059,324 |
| 2006 | 339,000 | 2,147 | 727,897 | 1.665 | 1,211,885 |
| 2007 | 356,000 | 2,213 | 787,653 | 1.693 | 1,329,235 |
| 2008 | 354,490 | 2,258 | 800,504 | 1.859 | 1,488,069 |
| 2009 | 354,040 | 2,323 | 822,581 | 1.837 | 1,511,196 |
| 2010 | 337,500 | 2,130 | 718,883 | 1.747 | 1,253,884 |

*Production figures are on farm-sales-weight basis.

SOURCE: "Table 2-37. Tobacco: Area, Yield, Production, Price, and Value, United States, 2001–2010," in *Agricultural Statistics 2011*, U.S. Department of Agriculture, National Agricultural Statistics Service, 2011, http://www.nass.usda.gov/Publications/Ag_Statistics/2011/2011_Final.pdf (accessed February 15, 2013)

creased again beginning in 2006, reaching 356,000 acres (144,068 ha) in 2007, before falling to 337,500 acres (136,581 ha) by 2010. The value of production declined by almost $1 billion between 2001 and 2005, then climbed steadily to $1.5 billion in 2009. In 2010 the value of production dropped to $1.3 billion. The overall production of tobacco also fell at decade's end, from 422.6 million pounds (373.1 million t) in 2009 to 718.9 million pounds (326.1 million t) in 2010.

In 2010 North Carolina led all U.S. states in tobacco production, accounting for 49.9% of total tobacco growing acreage in the United States; it was followed by Kentucky, Tennessee, Virginia, South Carolina, and Georgia. (See Table 7.2.) Tobacco plays a major role in the agricultural economies of these leading tobacco-producing states.

## Manufacturing

The Centers for Disease Control and Prevention (CDC) reports in "Economic Facts about U.S. Tobacco Production and Use" (November 15, 2012, http://www.cdc.gov/tobacco/data_statistics/fact_sheets/economics/econ_facts/) that in 2010 over 303 billion cigarettes were sold in the United States. Three companies—Philip Morris USA Inc., Reynolds American Inc., and Lorillard Inc.—accounted for almost 85% of total sales. In addition, 122.6 million pounds (55,600 t) of smokeless tobacco and 13.3 billion cigars were purchased in the United States in 2011.

## Tobacco Consumption

In *Trends in Tobacco Use* (July 2011, http://www.lung.org/finding-cures/our-research/trend-reports/Tobacco-Trend-Report.pdf), the American Lung Association (ALA)

monitors shifts in U.S. cigarette consumption from 1900 to 2007. Cigarette consumption peaked in 1963, when it reached 4,345 cigarettes annually per American aged 18 years and older. As information concerning the dangers of smoking became more widespread, cigarette smoking began a long and steady decline, and by 2006 annual cigarette consumption fell to 1,691 per person aged 18 years and older.

The ALA states that in 2009, 46.6 million American adults aged 18 years and older were current cigarette smokers. This was 20.6% of the adult U.S. population that year. A majority of regular cigarette smokers (57.6%) smoked fewer than 15 cigarettes per day in 2009; 32.7% smoked between 15 and 24 cigarettes a day, and 9% smoked more than 24 cigarettes per day. In addition, the ALA finds that in 2009, 6.1% of Americans aged 18 to 25 years were current smokeless tobacco users and 11.4% were cigar smokers. For Americans aged 26 years and older the percentages were lower: 3.1% were smokeless tobacco users and 4.4% smoked cigars.

### Consumer Spending on Tobacco

Table 7.3 shows that the average American family (or other consumer unit) spent $317 on tobacco products and smoking supplies in 2008, $380 in 2009, and $362 in 2010. The BLS reports in *Consumer Expenditures Mid-year Update—July 2011 through June 2012 Average* that the average American family (or other consumer unit) spent $313 on tobacco products and smoking supplies in the period between July 2011 and June 2012. This figure represents 0.5% of the average annual expenditures for the American family.

The amount spent on tobacco products and smoking supplies varied during the 12 months reported on by the BLS, depending on the characteristics of the household.

**TABLE 7.2**

**Area, yield, and production of tobacco, by tobacco-growing state, 2008–10**

| State | Area harvested | | | Yield per harvested acre | | | Production | | |
|---|---|---|---|---|---|---|---|---|---|
| | 2008 | 2009 | 2010 | 2008 | 2009 | 2010 | 2008 | 2009 | 2010 |
| | Acres | Acres | Acres | Pounds | Pounds | Pounds | 1,000 pounds | 1,000 pounds | 1,000 pounds |
| CT | 2,600 | 1,900 | 2,600 | 1,352 | 1,277 | 1,665 | 3,516 | 2,426 | 4,329 |
| GA | 16,000 | 13,800 | 11,400 | 2,100 | 2,030 | 2,400 | 33,600 | 28,014 | 27,360 |
| KY | 87,800 | 88,700 | 85,200 | 2,345 | 2,333 | 2,133 | 205,850 | 206,900 | 181,760 |
| MA | 690 | 390 | 950 | 1,403 | 1,500 | 1,768 | 968 | 585 | 1,680 |
| MO* | 1,500 | — | — | 2,240 | — | — | 3,360 | — | — |
| NC | 174,300 | 177,400 | 168,300 | 2,240 | 2,389 | 2,095 | 390,360 | 423,856 | 352,625 |
| OH | 3,400 | 3,400 | 2,500 | 2,050 | 2,000 | 2,050 | 6,970 | 6,800 | 5,125 |
| PA | 7,900 | 8,200 | 8,500 | 2,232 | 2,276 | 2,349 | 17,630 | 18,660 | 19,965 |
| SC | 19,000 | 18,500 | 16,000 | 2,100 | 2,100 | 2,250 | 39,900 | 38,850 | 36,000 |
| TN | 21,800 | 21,600 | 22,300 | 2,403 | 2,313 | 2,051 | 52,380 | 49,960 | 45,740 |
| VA | 19,500 | 20,150 | 19,750 | 2,357 | 2,309 | 2,243 | 45,970 | 46,530 | 44,299 |
| US | 354,490 | 354,040 | 337,500 | 2,258 | 2,323 | 2,130 | 800,504 | 822,581 | 718,883 |

*Estimates discontinued in 2009.

SOURCE: "Table 2-38. Tobacco: Area, Yield, and Production, by State and United States, 2008–2010," in *Agricultural Statistics 2011*, U.S. Department of Agriculture, National Agricultural Statistics Service, 2011, http://www.nass.usda.gov/Publications/Ag_Statistics/2011/2011_Final.pdf (accessed February 15, 2013)

How Alcohol, Tobacco, and Drug Use Affect Economics and Government

**TABLE 7.3**

**Average annual consumer spending and percentage changes, by category, 2007–10**

| Item | 2007 | 2008 | 2009 | 2010 | Percent change 2007–2008 | 2008–2009 | 2009–201. |
|---|---|---|---|---|---|---|---|
| Number of consumer units (in thousands) | 120,171 | 120,770 | 120,847 | 121,107 | | | |
| Average income before taxes | $63,091 | $63,563 | $62,857 | $62,481 | 0.7 | −1.1 | −0.6 |
| Averages: | | | | | | | |
| Age of reference person | 48.8 | 49.1 | 49.4 | 49.4 | | | |
| Number of persons in consumer unit | 2.5 | 2.5 | 2.5 | 2.5 | | | |
| Number of earners | 1.3 | 1.3 | 1.3 | 1.3 | | | |
| Number of vehicles | 1.9 | 2.0 | 2.0 | 1.9 | | | |
| Percent homeowner | 67 | 66 | 66 | 66 | | | |
| Average annual expenditures | $49,638 | $50,486 | $49,067 | $48,109 | 1.7 | −2.8 | −2.0 |
| Food | 6,133 | 6,443 | 6,372 | 6,129 | 5.1 | −1.1 | −3.8 |
| Food at home | 3,465 | 3,744 | 3,753 | 3,624 | 8.1 | 0.2 | −3.4 |
| Cereals and bakery products | 460 | 507 | 506 | 502 | 10.2 | −0.2 | −0.8 |
| Meats, poultry, fish, and eggs | 777 | 846 | 841 | 784 | 8.9 | −0.6 | −6.8 |
| Dairy products | 387 | 430 | 406 | 380 | 11.1 | −5.6 | −6.4 |
| Fruits and vegetables | 600 | 657 | 656 | 679 | 9.5 | −0.2 | 3.5 |
| Other food at home | 1,241 | 1,305 | 1,343 | 1,278 | 5.2 | 2.9 | −4.8 |
| Food away from home | 2,668 | 2,698 | 2,619 | 2,505 | 1.1 | −2.9 | −4.4 |
| Alcoholic beverages | 457 | 444 | 435 | 412 | −2.8 | −2.0 | −5.3 |
| Housing | 16,920 | 17,109 | 16,895 | 16,557 | 1.1 | −1.3 | −2.0 |
| Shelter | 10,023 | 10,183 | 10,075 | 9,812 | 1.6 | −1.1 | −2.6 |
| Utilities, fuels, and public services | 3,477 | 3,649 | 3,645 | 3,660 | 4.9 | −0.1 | 0.4 |
| Household operations | 984 | 998 | 1011 | 1,007 | 1.4 | 1.3 | −0.4 |
| Housekeeping supplies | 639 | 654 | 659 | 612 | 2.3 | 0.8 | −7.1 |
| Household furnishings and equipment | 1,797 | 1,624 | 1,506 | 1,467 | −9.6 | −7.3 | −2.6 |
| Apparel and services | 1,881 | 1,801 | 1,725 | 1,700 | −4.3 | −4.2 | −1.4 |
| Transportation | 8,758 | 8,604 | 7,658 | 7,677 | −1.8 | −11 | 0.2 |
| Vehicle purchases (net outlay) | 3,244 | 2,755 | 2,657 | 2,588 | −15.1 | −3.6 | −2.6 |
| Gasoline and motor oil | 2,384 | 2,715 | 1,986 | 2,132 | 13.9 | −26.9 | 7.4 |
| Other vehicle expenses | 2,592 | 2,621 | 2,536 | 2,464 | 1.1 | −3.2 | −2.8 |
| Public transportation | 538 | 513 | 479 | 493 | −4.6 | −6.6 | 2.9 |
| Healthcare | 2,853 | 2,976 | 3,126 | 3,157 | 4.3 | 5.0 | 1.0 |
| Entertainment | 2,698 | 2,835 | 2,693 | 2,504 | 5.1 | −5.0 | −7.0 |
| Personal care products and services | 588 | 616 | 596 | 582 | 4.8 | −3.2 | −2.3 |
| Reading | 118 | 116 | 110 | 100 | −1.7 | −5.2 | −9.1 |
| Education | 945 | 1,046 | 1,068 | 1,074 | 10.7 | 2.1 | 0.6 |
| Tobacco products and smoking supplies | 323 | 317 | 380 | 362 | −1.9 | 19.9 | −4.7 |
| Miscellaneous | 808 | 840 | 816 | 849 | 4.0 | −2.9 | 4.0 |
| Cash contributions | 1,821 | 1,737 | 1,723 | 1,633 | −4.6 | −0.8 | −5.2 |
| Personal insurance and pensions | 5,336 | 5,605 | 5,471 | 5,373 | 5.0 | −2.4 | −1.8 |
| Life and other personal insurance | 309 | 317 | 309 | 318 | 2.6 | −2.5 | 2.9 |
| Pensions and social security | 5,027 | 5,288 | 5,162 | 5,054 | 5.2 | −2.4 | −2.1 |

SOURCE: "Table A. Average Annual Expenditures by Major Category of All Consumer Units and Percent Changes, Consumer Expenditure Survey, 2007–2010," in *Consumer Expenditures in 2010: Lingering Effects of the Great Recession*, U.S. Department of Labor, U.S. Bureau of Labor Statistics, August 2012, http://www.bls.gov/cex/csxann10.pdf (accessed February 15, 2013)

On average, married couples with no children spent $277, which was 0.5% of their average annual expenditures. The percentage that other groups spent on tobacco and smoking supplies varied within a range of 0.3% to 0.8%, except for the "single person and other consumer units" group, which spent an average 1% of their annual income on tobacco and tobacco-related products.

## Exports

In *Illicit Tobacco: Various Schemes Are Used to Evade Taxes and Fees* (March 2011, http://www.gao.gov/new.items/d11313.pdf), the U.S. Government Accountability Office (GAO) estimates that American tobacco companies generated $373 million from cigarette exports in 2010. This figure marked a dramatic decline from 2000, when U.S. cigarette exports topped $3.3 billion. According to the GAO, much of this slowdown could be attributed to the leading tobacco companies themselves, many of which had divested their overseas holdings during the first decade of the 21st century to concentrate on the U.S. market. Japan remained the biggest foreign market for American cigarettes, accounting for 83% of U.S. export sales in 2010.

## WORLD TOBACCO MARKETS

Michael Eriksen, Judith Mackay, and Hana Ross report in *The Tobacco Atlas, Fourth Edition* (2012, http://www.tobaccoatlas.org/uploads/Images/PDFs/Tobacco_Atlas_2ndPrint.pdf) that global tobacco production peaked in 1997, when 9.9 million tons (9 million t) of tobacco was cultivated worldwide. Tobacco crop production then began to decrease steadily, falling to 7.8 million tons (7.1 million t) in 2009. In 2009 China harvested nearly 3.4 million tons (3.1 million t) of tobacco, accounting for

3% of global production. The world's other leading tobacco producers in 2009 included Brazil (951,382 tons [863,079 t]), India (683,433 tons [620,000 t]), the United States (411,647 tons [373,440 t]), and Malawi (229,451 tons [208,155 t]). According to Eriksen, Mackay, and Ross, tobacco cultivation accounted for 9.4 million acres (3.8 million ha) of arable land, and was grown in 124 countries worldwide in 2009.

Even as overall tobacco production fell, cigarette manufacturing increased. Eriksen, Mackay, and Ross note that in 2010 tobacco companies worldwide produced nearly 6 trillion cigarettes. This figure represented a 12% increase over the total number of cigarettes produced in 2000. China was the world's largest cigarette manufacturer in 2010, producing 2.4 trillion cigarettes, or 41% of total global production. The Russian Federation was the second-leading cigarette manufacturer that year, producing 402.7 billion cigarettes. Other leading cigarette producers in 2010 were the United States (338.2 billion), Germany (225 billion), Indonesia (180.5 billion), and Japan (158.5 billion).

Eriksen, Mackay, and Ross reveal that China was the single-largest consumer of cigarettes in 2009, accounting for 2.3 trillion, or 38%, of all the cigarettes smoked worldwide. The Russian Federation was the next-largest cigarette market, consuming 390 billion cigarettes that year, followed by the United States (315.7 billion), Indonesia (260.8 billion), and Japan (233.9 billion). Smoking rates in 2009 were highest in Serbia, which consumed 2,861 cigarettes per capita. Bulgaria had the second-highest smoking rate that year, consuming 2,822 cigarettes per capita; it was followed by Greece (2,795 cigarettes per capita), the Russian Federation (2,786), and Moldova (2,479). In 2009 the United States consumed 1,028 cigarettes per capita.

## World Tobacco Control Treaty

On February 27, 2005, the world's first tobacco control treaty, the WHO Framework Convention on Tobacco Control (2005, http://www.who.int/tobacco/framework/WHO_FCTC_english.pdf), became law in the 40 countries that ratified it (became bound by it). According to the World Health Organization (WHO), in "Parties to the WHO Framework Convention on Tobacco Control" (December 7, 2012, http://www.who.int/fctc/signatories_parties/en/), the United States signed the measure in May 2004, but as of December 2012 it had still not ratified the treaty. The goal of the treaty is to improve global health by reducing tobacco consumption. Nations that ratified the treaty obligated themselves to raise taxes on tobacco products, ban tobacco advertising, pass laws requiring smoke-free workplaces and public places, and provide stronger health warnings about the dangers of smoking to their residents. (For further information on this effort and its progress, see Chapter 3.)

## ALCOHOL AND TOBACCO ADVERTISING

### Alcohol Advertising

The Center for Science in the Public Interest (CSPI) indicates in "Alcoholic-Beverage Advertising Expenditures" (October 2008, http://www.cspinet.org/booze/FactSheets/AlcAdExp.pdf), the most recent publication on this topic as of April 2013, that the beer industry spent approximately $978.9 million on advertising in 2007, down from over $1 billion spent each year between 2002 and 2006. The liquor industry spent $547 million in 2007, continuing a decade-long trend of increasing expenditures. The wine industry spent approximately $120.5 million in 2007, which was within its general range of advertising expenditures during the previous decade.

According to the CSPI, in 2007 the beer industry focused most (74.1%) of its advertising dollars on television. The wine industry targeted print media (magazines, newspapers, and billboards) with 79.9% of its spending. Wine industry spending for television advertising was down 69.9% from 1998, and accounted for only 15.3% of industry advertising in 2007. The liquor industry focused its advertising primarily on print media (75%) as well, but its spending on television advertising accounted for a larger share (22%) than the wine industry. Furthermore, the liquor industry's television advertising expenditures rose substantially (3,947.3%) between 1999 and 2007, as a result of the industry's 1996 decision to lift its self-imposed ban on advertising on television so that it could compete with the wine and beer industries.

After the liquor industry lifted its ban, the National Broadcasting Company (NBC) also ended its ban on hard liquor advertising and became the first television network to do so. NBC's 2001 decision was met with nearly universal derision, and a short time later the broadcaster returned to its ban on hard liquor advertisements. As a response, the liquor industry developed guidelines to restrict advertising to publications or television programs with at least 70% of readers or viewers being aged 21 years and older, which resulted in an underage reader or viewer threshold of 30%. In 2003 the wine and beer industries agreed to these guidelines as well.

Stuart Elliott reports in "Thanks to Cable, Liquor Ads Find a TV Audience" (NYTimes.com, December 15, 2003) that by the end of 2003 hard liquor was being advertised on two dozen national cable networks, 140 local cable systems, and 420 local broadcast stations. In "In a First, CNN Runs a Liquor Commercial" (NYTimes.com, March 2, 2005), Elliott notes that in March 2005 CNN became the first national cable news network to air advertisements for hard liquor, with a commercial for Grey Goose vodka. According to Paul J. Chung et al., in "Association between Adolescent Viewership and Alcohol Advertising on Cable Television" (*American*

*Journal of Public Health*, vol. 100, no. 3, March 2010), cable television has become the largest source of alcohol advertisements for youth.

**ALCOHOL ADVERTISING AND YOUTH.** In "Exposure to Alcohol Advertising and Teen Drinking" (*Preventive Medicine*, vol. 52, no. 2, February 1, 2011), Matthis Morgenstern et al. test whether there is an association between exposure to alcohol advertisements and the use of alcohol in adolescents. The researchers acknowledge that the results of many studies show that exposure to alcohol advertisements encourages youth to drink alcoholic beverages, to drink more if they already drink, and to develop favorable attitudes toward drinking. Morgenstern et al. go a step further, however, by testing whether an association exists between youth drinking and alcohol advertisements in particular, or between youth drinking and any type of advertisements in general. The researchers conclude that a positive association exists between exposure to alcohol advertising and certain youth drinking behaviors, such as current and binge drinking, but that no association exists between these behaviors and advertisements in general. These findings suggest that attempts to reduce youth drinking must involve limiting or changing alcohol advertising to lessen its effect on youth and/or countering alcohol advertising with public health campaigns to reduce youth drinking.

Is alcohol advertising targeted to youth or do young people just happen to watch advertising that is aimed at those aged 21 years and older? Chung et al. research this question and conclude that "across the vast majority of time slots, adolescent viewers, especially girls, were exposed to more beer, spirits, and alcopop [flavored alcoholic beverage] ads on cable television than would be expected through incidental exposure." The researchers comment that "the underage viewership threshold of 30% adopted by the various industries has been ineffective in reducing adolescent exposure to advertisements. Moreover, the wine industry's relative success in reaching young adults while avoiding adolescents suggests that more-careful discrimination between the two groups may be possible."

The Center on Alcohol Marketing and Youth notes in *Youth Exposure to Alcohol Advertising on Television, 2001–2009* (December 15, 2010, http://www.camy.org/bin/u/r/CAMYReport2001_2009.pdf) that "industry compliance with the 30 percent threshold remained uneven. In 2009, 7.5 percent of all alcohol product ad placements (23,718 ads) and 9 percent of all alcohol product ad placements on cable (16,283 ads) were on programming with underage audiences greater than 30 percent." The center also states that "the National Research Council and Institute of Medicine, as well as 20 state attorneys general, have suggested that a 15 percent standard, roughly proportionate to the percentage of the population between the ages of 12 and 20, would be more appropriate."

One effort to reduce alcohol advertising that is seen by youth is the CSPI's Campaign for Alcohol-Free Sports TV. Joshua Robinson observes in "N.C.A.A. Is Criticized for Beer Advertising" (NYTimes.com, January 16, 2009) that between 2005 and early 2009, 16 National Collegiate Athletic Association–member athletic conferences and 372 colleges had signed the campaign's pledge to remove beer advertisements from sports games and broadcasts. Signing the pledge does not mean that schools are required to take action on the pledge, however. As of January 2009, beer advertisements had been eliminated in the Chick-fil-A Bowl and on the Big Ten Network.

## Tobacco Advertising

According to the Federal Trade Commission (FTC), in *Cigarette Report for 2009 and 2010* (2012, http://www.ftc.gov/os/2012/09/120921cigarettereport.pdf), U.S. cigarette sales fell 3% between 2009 and 2010, from 290.2 billion cigarettes to 281.6 billion cigarettes. Advertising expenditures decreased as well, from $8.5 billion in 2009 to a little over $8 billion in 2010, a decline of nearly 6%.

The tobacco industry is forbidden by law to advertise on radio, television, and billboards. Where do the industry's advertising dollars go? In 2010 the largest share ($6.5 billion or 80.7%) of the $8 billion spent was used for price discounts, which are paid to cigarette retailers or wholesalers to discount the price of the cigarettes to consumers. About $780.6 million was paid in promotional allowances to retailers, wholesalers, and other entities involved in the distribution of cigarettes, and $235.8 million was devoted to coupons. These were all considered promotional activities and were the primary ways in which cigarettes were advertised.

In March 2010 the U.S. Food and Drug Administration (FDA) announced that it would restrict tobacco companies' marketing practices—especially the ones that targeted youth—using the power given it under a new tobacco control law that was passed in 2009. Lyndsey Layton notes in "New FDA Rules Will Greatly Restrict Tobacco Advertising and Sales" (WashingtonPost.com, March 19, 2010) that tobacco companies will no longer be able to sell cigarettes to people under the age of 18 years; sponsor sporting and entertainment events; give away cigarettes or other items with the purchase of tobacco products, such as tiny purses, wristbands, and cell phone jewelry for women and girls; offer fewer than 20 cigarettes per package (larger packages are less affordable and less likely to be purchased by youth); or sell cigarettes in vending machines to which young people have access. These new rules went into effect in June 2010.

**TOBACCO ADVERTISING AND YOUTH.** In *The Role of the Media in Promoting and Reducing Tobacco Use* (June 2008, http://cancercontrol.cancer.gov/tcrb/mono

aphs/19/m19_complete.pdf), the National Cancer Institute NCI) examines how the marketing efforts of the tobacco dustry affect adolescent tobacco use. The NCI concludes at "much tobacco advertising targets the psychological eeds of adolescents, such as popularity, peer acceptance, nd positive self-image. Advertising creates the perception at smoking will satisfy these needs." It cites "strong and onsistent evidence" that "exposure to cigarette advertising fluences nonsmoking adolescents to initiate smoking and move toward regular smoking." The NCI also discusses igarette product placement in movies and concludes that eeing people smoke in films can influence attitudes toward moking in positive ways, not only among adolescents but lso among adults. Furthermore, based on a variety of sci-ntific studies, the NCI determines that there is "a causal elationship between exposure to movie smoking depictions nd youth smoking initiation."

## LCOHOL AND TOBACCO TAXATION

Taxation is an age-old method by which the govern-ment raises money. Alcoholic beverages have been taxed since colonial times, and tobacco products have been taxed since 1863. The alcohol and tobacco industries contribute a great deal of tax money to federal, state, and local governments.

### Alcohol Taxes

According to DISCUS, in "Increasing Alcohol Taxes Punishes the Entire Hospitality Industry" (2013, http://www.discus.org/policy/taxes/), hard liquor is among the most highly taxed consumer products in the nation. DIS-CUS estimates that direct and indirect local, state, and federal taxes and fees account for 54% of the typical bottle price. Even though the beer and wine industries are taxed at lower levels, they still contribute a significant amount of tax revenue.

In fiscal year (FY) 2012, the federal government col-lected approximately $10.1 billion in excise taxes (monies paid on purchases of specific goods) on alcoholic bever-ages. (See Table 7.4.) Federal excise taxes on distilled spirits during this span amounted to approximately half (53.5%) that total—about $5.4 billion, which included

**ABLE 7.4**

ederal government tax collections on alcohol and tobacco, October 2011–September 2012

n thousands of dollars]

| evenue source | 1st quarter | 2nd quarter | 3rd quarter | 4th quarter | Cumulative 2012 | Cumulative 2011 |
|---|---|---|---|---|---|---|
| xcise tax, total | $6,078,968 | $5,965,136 | $7,035,277 | $7,300,356 | $26,379,737 | $26,316,457 |
| lcohol tax, total | $2,403,247 | $2,254,587 | $2,684,040 | $2,777,487 | $10,119,361 | $9,818,986 |
| Distilled spirits tax, total | $1,362,338 | $1,185,563 | $1,442,415 | $1,428,405 | $5,418,721 | $5,182,949 |
| Domestic | $1,010,080 | $831,799 | $1,074,789 | $1,087,601 | $4,004,269 | $3,779,850 |
| Imported* | $352,258 | $353,764 | $367,626 | $340,804 | $1,414,452 | $1,403,099 |
| Wine tax, total | $285,490 | $242,896 | $250,593 | $257,303 | $1,036,282 | $983,640 |
| Domestic | $196,446 | $156,895 | $168,253 | $178,424 | $700,018 | $684,750 |
| Imported* | $89,044 | $86,001 | $82,340 | $78,879 | $336,264 | $298,890 |
| Beer tax, total | $755,419 | $826,128 | $991,032 | $1,091,779 | $3,664,358 | $3,652,397 |
| Domestic | $655,993 | $699,293 | $843,694 | $949,064 | $3,148,044 | $3,126,091 |
| Imported* | $99,426 | $126,835 | $147,338 | $142,715 | $516,314 | $526,306 |
| obacco tax, total | $3,562,136 | $3,595,285 | $4,215,320 | $4,372,150 | $15,744,891 | $16,150,708 |
| Domestic | | | | | | |
| Regular | $3,380,697 | $3,438,342 | $4,011,689 | $4,175,144 | $15,005,872 | $15,518,459 |
| Floor stocks | $404 | $1,695 | $3,136 | $707 | $5,942 | $5,220 |
| Imported* | $181,035 | $155,248 | $200,495 | $196,299 | $733,077 | $627,029 |
| nclassified alcohol and tobacco tax (domestic), total | $320 | $200 | $49 | $294 | $863 | $2,501 |
| irearms and ammunition tax, total | $113,265 | $115,064 | $135,868 | $150,425 | $514,622 | $344,262 |
| pecial (occupational) tax, total | $8 | $4 | $122 | $114 | $248 | $268 |
| **Total imports (U.S. Customs)*** | **$721,763** | **$721,848** | **$797,799** | **$758,697** | **$3,000,107** | **$2,855,324** |
| **Total TTB tax collections** | **$5,357,213** | **$5,243,292** | **$6,237,600** | **$6,541,773** | **$23,379,878** | **$23,461,401** |
| **Total tax collections** | **$6,078,976** | **$5,965,140** | **$7,035,399** | **$7,300,470** | **$26,379,985** | **$26,316,725** |

All "imported" tax collection figures are obtained from U.S. Customs data.
TB = Alcohol and Tobacco Tax and Trade Bureau.
Jotes: This is an unofficial report. Official revenue collection figures are stated in the TTB Chief Financial Officer Annual Report. Addition of current fiscal year prior quarter figures year nay not agree with cumulative figures reported on this report for current fiscal year due to rounding. Cumulative figures for current fiscal year adjusted to reflect classification of nclassified alcohol and tobacco tax collections previously reported and to reflect collection adjustments for prior tax periods. Source for other tax collection figures on this report is a TB database that records tax collection data by tax return period. This data is summarized on this report by the quarter in which an incurred tax liability is satisfied. Unclassified Alcohol nd Tobacco Tax is tax collected, but not yet posted to a taxpayer account due to missing Employer Identification Number (EIN), permit number, and/or other taxpaper identify nformation.

OURCE: "Tax Collections TTB S 5630–FY–2012 Cumulative Summary Fiscal Year 2012 Final," in *Alcohol and Tobacco Tax and Trade Bureau Statistical Release*, U.S. Department of the Treasury, Alcohol and Tobacco Tax and Trade Bureau, December 3, 2012, http://www.ttb.gov/statistics/final12.pdf (accessed February 15, 2013)

taxes on both domestic and imported distilled spirits. Distilled spirits are taxed by the proof gallon, which is a standard U.S. gallon of 231 cubic inches (3,785 cubic cm) containing 50% ethyl alcohol by volume, or 100 proof.

Excise taxes on wine and beer made up the other half of the excise taxes that were collected on alcoholic beverages in FY 2012. The calculation of wine taxes depends on several variables, such as alcohol content and the size of the winery. In FY 2012 federal excise taxes on wine totaled just over $1 billion. (See Table 7.4.) Total beer excise taxes were much higher, at $3.7 billion. According to the Alcohol and Tobacco Tax and Trade Bureau (TTB), in "Brewery Audit Tutorial: Common Compliance and Tax Issues" (May 17, 2012, http://www.ttb.gov/beer/beer-tutorial.shtml), brewers who produce fewer than 2 million barrels (1 barrel equals 31 gallons [117.3 L]) get a reduced excise tax rate of $7 per barrel on the first 60,000 barrels, and pay $18 per barrel on all subsequent barrels produced. Those who produce more than 2 million barrels pay an excise tax of $18 per barrel on all barrels produced.

Besides the federal excise taxes, the states levy sales taxes on alcohol. In *State Government Tax Collections Summary Report: 2011* (April 12, 2012, http://www2.census.gov/govs/statetax/2011stcreport.pdf), Rudy Telles, Sheila O'Sullivan, and Jesse Willhide of the U.S. Census Bureau indicate that the state sales taxes collected on alcoholic beverages totaled $5.7 billion in FY 2011. This amounted to about 0.8% of all state taxes collected that fiscal year ($757.3 billion).

## Tobacco Taxes

Telles, O'Sullivan, and Willhide report that state sales taxes on tobacco products amounted to $17.3 billion in FY 2011. States have raised their excise taxes on cigarettes to help defray health care costs that are associated with tobacco, to discourage young people from starting to smoke, and to motivate smokers to stop. Figure 7.1 shows state cigarette excise tax rates in 2012. New York had the highest state excise tax on cigarettes at $4.35 per pack. Rhode Island was second with $3.50 per pack. Missouri had the lowest excise tax of $0.17 per pack. Ann Boonn of the Campaign for Tobacco-Free Kids indicates in the fact sheet "State Cigarette Excise Tax Rates and Rankings" (December 13, 2012, http://www.tobaccofreekids.org/research/factsheets/pdf/0097.pdf) that the average cigarette tax in 2012 was $1.48 per pack nationwide. Rates were considerably lower in the major tobacco-producing states, where the average tax was $0.485 per pack.

Besides state taxes on tobacco, the federal government imposes taxes on cigarettes and other tobacco products. In February 2009 President Barack Obama (1961–) signed into law the State Children's Health Insurance Plan bill, which includes an increase in the federal tobacco tax. According to the National Conference of State Legislatures, in "2009–2010 Proposed State Legislation for Tobacco Tax Increases" (May 19, 2010, http://www.ncsl.org/programs/health/tobacco_tax_bill09.htm), the federal excise tax on cigarettes increased to $1.01 per pack effective April 1, 2009.

## GOVERNMENT REGULATION OF ALCOHOL AND TOBACCO

Besides taxation, the alcohol and tobacco industries are subject to federal and state laws that regulate factors such as sales, advertising, and shipping.

### Alcohol Regulation

The best-known pieces of legislation regarding alcohol are the 18th and 21st Amendments to the U.S. Constitution. The 18th Amendment prohibited the manufacture, sale, and importation of alcoholic beverages. Ratified in 1919, it took effect in 1920 and ushered in a period in U.S. history known as Prohibition. After 13 years, during which it failed to stop the manufacture and sale of alcohol, Prohibition was repealed in 1933 by the 21st Amendment.

Most interpretations of the 21st Amendment hold that the amendment gives individual states the power to regulate and control alcoholic beverages within their own borders. Consequently, every state has its own alcohol administration and enforcement agency. "Control states" directly control the sale and distribution of alcoholic beverages within their borders. According to the TTB, in "Alcohol Beverage Control Boards" (2013, http://www.ttb.gov/wine/state-ABC.shtml), there were 18 control states in 2013: Alabama, Idaho, Iowa, Maine, Michigan, Mississippi, Montana, New Hampshire, North Carolina, Ohio, Oregon, Pennsylvania, Utah, Vermont, Virginia, Washington, West Virginia, and Wyoming. Montgomery County in Maryland acted as a control state as well. Some critics of this policy question whether such state monopolies violate antitrust laws. The other 32 states were licensure states and allowed only licensed businesses to operate as wholesalers and retailers.

DIRECT SHIPMENTS: RECIPROCITY OR FELONY? Controversy has developed over the direct shipment of alcoholic beverages from one state directly to consumers or retailers in another state. Under the U.S. Constitution's interstate commerce clause, Congress has the power to regulate trade between states. Nevertheless, the 21st Amendment gives states the authority to regulate the sale and distribution of alcoholic beverages. Furthermore, it allows states to set their own laws governing the sale of alcohol within their borders.

Because the laws of the states are not uniform, several states have passed reciprocity legislation that allows specific states to exchange direct shipments, thus eliminating the state-licensed wholesalers from the exchange. Wholesalers and retailers charge that reciprocity and direct

## FIGURE 7.1

### State cigarette tax rates, 2012

Average state cigarette tax: $1.48 per pack
Average cigarette tax in major tobacco states: 48.5 cents per pack
Average cigarette tax in non-tobacco states: $1.61 per pack

Map shows state cigarette tax rates in effect now.* The three states that have not increased their cigarette tax rate since 1999 or earlier are marked in bold. Currently, 30 states, DC, Puerto Rico, the Northern Marianas, and Guam have cigarette tax rates of $1.00 per pack or higher; 14 states, DC, Puerto Rico, and Guam have cigarette tax rates of $2.00 per pack or higher; five states and Guam have cigarette tax rates of $3.00 per pack or higher; and one state (NY) has a cigarette tax rate more than $4.00 per pack. The state averages listed above do not include Puerto Rico (with a population larger than those in 20 states) or any of the U.S. territories (such as Guam). The major tobacco states with extensive tobacco farming and, often, cigarette manufacturing, are NC, KY, VA, SC, TN, & GA. Federal cigarette tax is $1.01 per pack. Not shown are the special taxes or fees some states place on cigarettes made by Non-Participating Manufacturers (NPMs), the companies that have not joined the Master Settlement Agreement (MSA) between the states and the major cigarette companies. Some local governments also have their own cigarette taxes, such as Chicago (68¢), Cook County, IL ($3.00), New York City ($1.50), and Anchorage, K ($2.206). The U.S. Centers for Disease Control & Prevention estimates that smoking-caused health costs and productivity losses total $10.47 per pack sold.

*Previous versions of this factsheet listed cigarette tax rates for Washington, DC and Minnesota that included the per-pack cigarette sales tax rates that are collected at the wholesale level with the excise tax. Now the listed tax rates are purely the excise tax portion, exclusive of the sales tax. This is not a change in the actual excise tax rates, just the way that the rates are listed.

SOURCE: Ann Boonn, "Map of State Cigarette Tax Rates," Campaign for Tobacco-Free Kids, December 5, 2012, http://www.tobaccofreekids.org/research/factsheets/pdf/0222.pdf (accessed February 15, 2013)

shipment are violations of the 21st Amendment. They fear being bypassed in the exchange, as do states that prohibit direct shipments of alcohol. Other stakeholders in this issue are consumers and wine producers who want the right to deal directly with each other.

**ALCOHOL SALES AND THE INTERNET.** In January 2001 the 21st Amendment Enforcement Act became law. This legislation makes it difficult for companies to sell alcohol over the Internet or through mail-order services. It allows attorneys general in states that ban direct alcohol sales to seek federal injunctions against companies that violate their liquor sales laws.

Within a month of the passage of this act, the high-tech community voiced its concern regarding such legislation, suggesting that if states could ban Internet alcohol sales they might restrict other electronic commerce as well. Senator Orrin G. Hatch (1934–; R-UT) said he crafted the bill to take other e-commerce concerns into account and insisted that the measure is narrowly tailored to deal only with alcohol.

In May 2005 the U.S. Supreme Court ruled on three cases that had been consolidated under the name *Granholm v. Heald* (544 U.S. 460). At issue were state laws in Michigan and New York that prohibited out-of-state wineries from selling their products over the Internet directly to Michigan and New York residents, but that allowed in-state wineries to make such sales. The Michigan and New York state governments argued that these laws were permissible under the 21st Amendment. A group of wineries and business advocates argued that the state laws were unconstitutional restrictions of interstate trade. In a 5–4 decision, the court agreed that the state laws were unconstitutional, stating, "States have broad power to regulate liquor under §2 of the Twenty-First Amendment. This power, however, does not allow States to ban, or severely limit, the direct shipment of out-of-state wine while simultaneously authorizing direct shipment by in-state producers. If a State chooses to allow direct shipment of wine, it must do so on evenhanded terms." It should be noted that this ruling only applies to state laws that prohibit out-of-state Internet alcohol sales and not to the 21st Amendment Enforcement Act.

## Tobacco Regulation and Legislation

Federal tobacco legislation has covered everything from unproved advertising claims and warning label requirements to the development of cigarettes and little cigars that are less likely to start fires. In the past the FDA prohibited the claim that Fairfax cigarettes prevented respiratory and other diseases (1953) and denied the claim that tartaric acid, which was added to Trim Reducing-Aid cigarettes, helped promote weight loss (1959).

The FTC has also been given jurisdiction over tobacco issues in several areas. As early as 1942 the FTC issued a cease-and-desist order in reference to Kool cigarettes' claim that smoking Kools gave extra protection against or cured colds. In January 1964 the FTC proposed a rule to strictly regulate cigarette advertisements and to prohibit explicit or implicit health claims by cigarette companies.

The tobacco industry had avoided some other forms of federal regulation by being exempted from many federal health and safety laws. In the Hazardous Substances Act of 1960, the term *hazardous substance* does not include tobacco and tobacco products, nor does the term *consumer product* in the Consumer Product Safety Act of 1972. Tobacco was similarly exempted from regulation under the Fair Packaging and Labeling Act of 1966 and the Toxic Substance Control Act of 1976.

Some of the legislation of the late 1980s included requiring four alternating health warnings to be printed on tobacco packaging, prohibiting smokeless tobacco advertising on television and radio, and banning smoking on domestic airline flights. In 1992 the Synar Amendment was passed. The amendment said that states must have laws that ban the sale of tobacco products to people under 18 years of age.

In 1993 the U.S. Environmental Protection Agency released its final risk assessment on secondhand smoke and classified it as a known human carcinogen (cancer-causing agent). In 1994 the Occupational Safety and Health Administration proposed regulations that would prohibit smoking in workplaces, except in smoking rooms that are separately ventilated. As of April 2013, the United States did not have federal smoking control legislation, but many states and municipalities did have legislation that banned smoking in a variety of public places and workplaces. However, the Family Smoking Prevention and Tobacco Control Act of 2009 did give the FDA the authority to regulate the production and marketing of tobacco products within limits, such as banning certain flavored cigarettes that appealed to youth and strengthening the warnings on cigarette packages.

TOBACCO SALES AND THE INTERNET. In the early 21st century it became apparent that some online tobacco vendors were not following the same rules as conventional tobacco retailers. For example, some vendors did not indicate that sales to minors were prohibited on their site. Many required that a user simply state that he or she was of legal age, making no attempt to verify the information. In addition, many did not collect and pay cigarette sales taxes.

As a response to these problems, Congress passed the Prevent All Cigarette Trafficking (PACT) Act of 2009. The law affects Internet sales of tobacco products in that it ensures the collection of federal, state, and local taxes on cigarettes and smokeless tobacco by requiring online vendors of tobacco products to register with the states in which their customers reside and by imposing strong penalties against those who do not comply. Paying these taxes is important not only for government revenues but also to ensure that the price of cigarettes remains high to discourage their use, especially by youth.

To further safeguard illegal sales to youth, the PACT Act also bars Internet vendors of tobacco products from shipping these products via the U.S. Postal Service (USPS). The USPS does not have the means to verify the age and identification of the person receiving the products. According to the Campaign for Tobacco-Free Kids, in the fact sheet "Preventing Illegal Internet Sales f Cigarettes and Smokeless Tobacco" (March 31, 2010, ttp://www.tobaccofreekids.org/research/factsheets/pdf/ 361.pdf), "the PACT Act will stop such Internet sales of igarettes and smokeless tobacco to kids by requiring the ellers to verify the age of their customers prior to sale by hecking against available government and commercial D databases, and by requiring sellers to use a method of elivery that will verify the age and ID of the person ccepting the final delivery of the cigarettes or smokeless obacco prior to handing them over."

**FDA REGULATION OF TOBACCO PRODUCTS.** In 1994 he FDA investigated the tobacco industry to determine vhether nicotine is an addictive drug that should be egulated like other addictive drugs. Weeks of testimony efore Congress indicated that tobacco companies may ave been aware of the addictive effects of nicotine and he likely connection between smoking and cancer as arly as the mid-1950s.

In August 1995 the FDA ruled that the nicotine in obacco products is a drug and, therefore, is liable to FDA egulation. However, the tobacco, advertising, and con- enience store industries filed a lawsuit against the FDA, laiming it did not have the authority to regulate tobacco s an addictive drug. After conflicting decisions in the ower courts, the Supreme Court ruled 5–4 in *FDA v. Brown and Williamson Tobacco Corp.* (529 U.S. 120 2000]) that the FDA lacked this authority. Even though he ruling did not allow the FDA to regulate tobacco, state laws regarding selling cigarettes to minors were not affected.

In March 2005 bipartisan bills were introduced in the U.S. House of Representatives and the U.S. Senate to grant the FDA the authority to regulate tobacco products. The bills never became law during that session of Con- gress, but similar legislation was introduced again in 2009. The Family Smoking Prevention and Tobacco Control Act was passed by the House and the Senate and was subsequently signed into law by President Obama in June 2009. This law gives the FDA the author- ity to control tobacco advertising and sales to children, require changes in tobacco products to make them less harmful, prohibit health claims that have no scientific backing, and require the contents and health dangers of tobacco products to be listed on the packaging.

## THE SOCIETAL COSTS OF SUBSTANCE USE

Few reports are available on the economic costs of alcohol, tobacco, and drug use, and many are outdated. As of April 2013, the most recent report that calculated the economic costs of alcohol was *Updating Estimates of the Economic Costs of Alcohol Abuse in the United States: Estimates, Update Methods, and Data* (2000, http://pubs.niaaa.nih.gov/publications/economic-2000/ alcoholcost.PDF) by the Lewin Group for the National

Institute on Alcohol Abuse and Alcoholism (NIAAA). This report estimates that national costs related to alcohol abuse and dependence were approximately $185 billion in 1998. More research has ensued in subse- quent years on the costs of drug abuse and tobacco use.

### Costs of Drug Abuse

The U.S. Department of Justice's National Drug Intelligence Center (NDIC) discusses the costs that are associated with illegal drug use in *The Economic Impact of Illicit Drug Use on American Society, 2011* (April 2011, http://www.justice.gov/archive/ndic/pubs44/44731/ 44731p.pdf). As Table 7.5 shows, in 2007 illicit drug use resulted in total economic losses of $193.1 billion.

The NDIC divides the costs of drug abuse into three major cost components: productivity, crime, and health. The largest cost component in 2007 was productivity. (See Table 7.5.) In this case, productivity means lost productivity. It is an indirect cost that reflects losses such as work that was never performed because of poor health, premature death, or incarceration. In 2007 lost produc- tivity accounted for $120.3 billion, or over 62%, of the total costs associated with illicit drug use that year.

The second-largest cost component was crime, which includes drug-related crime costs such as the operation of prisons, state and local police protection, and victim costs. These costs totaled $61.4 billion in 2007.

The third-largest cost component associated with illicit drug use in 2007 was health care. These costs include expenses associated with specialty treatment, hospital care, and other costs. In 2007 these costs totaled $11.4 billion.

Table 7.6 and Table 7.7 chart drug-related deaths, by age, among male and female segments of the U.S. pop- ulation between 1968 and 2007. A total of 255,991 male individuals died from drug-induced deaths during this span, compared with 143,987 female deaths. The highest number of drug-related deaths for both men and women occurred among those aged 40 to 44 years, whereas the lowest number of deaths for both males and females occurred among those aged five to nine years. As Table 7.6 and Table 7.7 reveal, beyond the age of 45 years the number of drug-induced deaths declines stead- ily with age for both gender groups, but with a small spike among those over 80 years of age.

In 2009 Rosalie Liccardo Pacula et al. published *Issues in Estimating the Economic Cost of Drug Abuse in Consuming Nations* (http://www.rand.org/content/dam/ rand/pubs/technical_reports/2009/RAND_TR709.pdf), which was developed for the European Commission by the Rand Corporation. Pacula et al. analyze studies undertaken in various developed countries to try to quantify the economic costs of drug abuse and observe

**TABLE 7.5**

## Economic impact of illicit drug use on criminal justice system, health care industry, and overall productivity, 2007

| Crime | | a | b |
|---|---|---|---|
| Criminal justice system | | $56,373,254 | $56,373,254 |
| Crime victim | | $1,455,555 | $1,455,555 |
| Personal | $134,864 | | |
| Property | $1,320,691 | | |
| Other | | $3,547,885 | $3,547,885 |
| Productivity | | $0 | $51,900,922 |
| **Subtotal** | | **$61,376,694** | **$113,277,616** |

| Health | | a | b |
|---|---|---|---|
| Specialty treatment | | $3,723,338 | $3,723,338 |
| State | $3,368,564 | | |
| Federal | $354,774 | | |
| Hospital and emergency department | | | |
| Non-homicide | | $5,684,248 | $5,684,248 |
| Hospital | $5,523,189 | | |
| Emergency department | $161,059 | | |
| Homicide | | $12,938 | $12,938 |
| Hospital | $12,700 | | |
| Emergency department | $238 | | |
| Insurance administration | $544 | $544 | $544 |
| Other | | $1,995,164 | $1,995,164 |
| Federal prevention | $803,761 | | |
| Federal research | $569,340 | | |
| AIDS | $622,063 | | |
| **Subtotal** | | **$11,416,232** | **$11,416,232** |

| Productivity | | a | b |
|---|---|---|---|
| Labor participation | | $49,237,777 | $49,237,777 |
| Males | $34,998,122 | | |
| Females | $14,239,655 | | |
| Specialty treatment (state) | | $2,828,207 | $2,828,207 |
| Males | $1,981,428 | | |
| Females | $846,779 | | |
| Specialty treatment (federal) | | $44,830 | $44,830 |
| Males | $43,252 | | |
| Females | $1,578 | | |
| Hospitalization | | $287,260 | $287,260 |
| Males | $178,016 | | |
| Females | $109,244 | | |
| Incarceration | | $48,121,949 | $0 |
| Males | $44,048,432 | | |
| Females | $4,073,517 | | |
| Premature mortality (non-homicide) | | $16,005,008 | $16,005,008 |
| Males | $11,710,119 | | |
| Females | $4,294,889 | | |
| Premature mortality (homicide) | | $3,778,973 | $0 |
| Males | $3,089,080 | | |
| Females | $689,893 | | |
| **Subtotal** | | **$120,304,004** | **$68,403,082** |
| **Total** | | **$193,096,930** | **$193,096,930** |

[a]Incarceration and homicide components of Productivity not included in Crime.
[b]Incarceration and homicide components of Productivity included in Crime.

SOURCE: Adapted from "Statistical Summary," in *The Economic Impact of Illicit Drug Use on American Society, 2011*, U.S. Department of Justice, National Drug Intelligence Center, April 2011, http://www.justice.gov/archive/ndic/pubs44/44731/44731p.pdf (accessed February 15, 2013)

that they use a range of approaches and methods, which makes it impossible to compare results across countries. The researchers also note that "the pitfalls and assumptions necessary to construct a comparable estimate across countries are quite significant and described in detail throughout this report. We conclude that it is not possible at this time to develop a meaningful comparative estimate of the cost of drug use across countries or to aggregate these costs to the regional or global level."

Likewise, a coalition of drug abuse agencies came together in Canada to develop an international model for estimating the costs of substance abuse, and its findings were published by Eric Single of the University of Toronto in "Why We Should Still Estimate the Costs of Substance Abuse Even if We Needn't Pay Undue Attention to the Bottom Line" (*Drug and Alcohol Review*, vol. 28, no. 2, March 2009). Single indicates that studies carried out in various countries use differing methods, so they cannot be compared. He also notes that the results of cost studies in general are uncertain due to problems such as incomplete data and "a layering of multiple assumptions." Nonetheless, the coalition promotes the idea of conducting cost studies and improving their methods to help target problems and develop policies, to determine which policies and programs are most effective, and to develop national research agendas.

### Costs of Tobacco Use

In 2008 the CDC published "Smoking-Attributable Mortality, Years of Potential Life Lost, and Productivity Losses—United States, 2000–2004" (*Morbidity and Mortality Weekly Report*, vol. 57, no. 45, November 14, 2008), which included data on the economic costs of tobacco use. As of April 2013, this was the CDC's most recent report on this topic. The CDC estimates the economic cost of smoking-attributable lost productivity at $96.8 billion annually between 2000 and 2004. The CDC suggests, however, that with smoking-attributable health care expenditures added to this figure, the annual economic cost of cigarette smoking was approximately $193 billion per year. Andrew Fenelon and Samuel H. Preston of the University of Pennsylvania report in "Estimating Smoking-Attributable Mortality in the United States" (*Demography*, vol. 49, no. 3, August 2012) that in 2004 smoking accounted for roughly 21% of all deaths among U.S. males, and 17% of all deaths among females.

### TOBACCO COMPANIES AND RESPONSIBILITY FOR THE COSTS OF TOBACCO USE

Between 1960 and 1988 approximately 300 lawsuits sought damages from tobacco companies for smoking-related illnesses; courts, though, consistently held that people who choose to smoke are responsible for the health consequences of that decision. This changed in 1988, when a tobacco company was ordered to pay damages for the first time. A federal jury in Newark, New Jersey, ordered Liggett Group, Inc. to pay $400,000 to the family of Rose Cipollone, a longtime smoker who died of lung cancer in 1984. The case was overturned on appeal, but the Supreme Court ruled in favor of the Cipollone family in *Cipollone v. Liggett Group, Inc.* (505 U.S. 504 [1992]). In a 7–2 ruling, the court broadened a smoker's right to sue cigarette makers in cancer cases. The justices decided that the Federal Cigarette Labeling and Advertising Act of

**TABLE 7.6**

**Drug-induced deaths among male population, by age group, 1968–2007**

| Year | 0–4 | 5–9 | 10–14 | 15–19 | 20–24 | 25–29 | 30–34 | 35–39 | 40–44 | 45–49 | 50–54 | 55–59 | 60–64 | 65–69 | 70–74 | 75–79 | 80+ | Total |
|---|---|---|---|---|---|---|---|---|---|---|---|---|---|---|---|---|---|---|
| 1968 | 24 | 1 | 7 | 168 | 310 | 238 | 174 | 163 | 139 | 109 | 103 | 111 | 63 | 48 | 45 | 26 | 24 | 1,753 |
| 1969 | 18 | 2 | 10 | 240 | 414 | 272 | 174 | 154 | 118 | 110 | 90 | 91 | 74 | 55 | 51 | 28 | 23 | 1,924 |
| 1970 | 17 | 2 | 13 | 345 | 622 | 317 | 231 | 163 | 166 | 128 | 99 | 73 | 64 | 66 | 41 | 24 | 36 | 2,407 |
| 1971 | 20 | 1 | 13 | 470 | 943 | 462 | 240 | 207 | 166 | 166 | 111 | 91 | 63 | 60 | 50 | 28 | 33 | 3,124 |
| 1972 | 20 | 0 | 16 | 392 | 834 | 502 | 254 | 228 | 178 | 134 | 74 | 84 | 80 | 30 | 40 | 32 | 42 | 2,940 |
| 1973 | 16 | 2 | 7 | 261 | 703 | 476 | 256 | 164 | 147 | 121 | 79 | 82 | 68 | 43 | 35 | 36 | 30 | 2,526 |
| 1974 | 12 | 1 | 6 | 244 | 710 | 538 | 318 | 181 | 144 | 98 | 88 | 58 | 45 | 49 | 28 | 33 | 16 | 2,569 |
| 1975 | 9 | 2 | 3 | 206 | 886 | 695 | 372 | 194 | 135 | 112 | 82 | 55 | 43 | 39 | 35 | 29 | 27 | 2,924 |
| 1976 | 9 | 2 | 7 | 142 | 669 | 660 | 326 | 194 | 140 | 102 | 71 | 57 | 52 | 40 | 27 | 28 | 22 | 2,548 |
| 1977 | 7 | 1 | 4 | 80 | 327 | 357 | 215 | 117 | 77 | 70 | 63 | 49 | 48 | 40 | 33 | 19 | 24 | 1,531 |
| 1978 | 7 | 2 | 4 | 80 | 280 | 320 | 219 | 116 | 68 | 70 | 59 | 34 | 33 | 29 | 33 | 21 | 23 | 1,398 |
| 1979 | 18 | 1 | 2 | 114 | 434 | 656 | 436 | 234 | 194 | 141 | 133 | 100 | 79 | 56 | 52 | 33 | 28 | 2,711 |
| 1980 | 14 | 4 | 2 | 96 | 392 | 671 | 495 | 296 | 203 | 153 | 115 | 116 | 57 | 55 | 43 | 31 | 34 | 2,777 |
| 1981 | 15 | 4 | 7 | 65 | 350 | 642 | 559 | 329 | 220 | 152 | 118 | 82 | 65 | 50 | 33 | 23 | 33 | 2,747 |
| 1982 | 10 | 0 | 6 | 79 | 317 | 759 | 714 | 387 | 192 | 170 | 113 | 95 | 43 | 39 | 29 | 37 | 42 | 3,032 |
| 1983 | 12 | 0 | 4 | 61 | 299 | 651 | 709 | 447 | 259 | 174 | 123 | 91 | 70 | 45 | 45 | 37 | 43 | 3,070 |
| 1984 | 10 | 0 | 7 | 63 | 271 | 628 | 804 | 531 | 311 | 166 | 123 | 119 | 59 | 53 | 46 | 24 | 42 | 3,257 |
| 1985 | 7 | 0 | 3 | 62 | 297 | 710 | 999 | 788 | 356 | 219 | 148 | 102 | 76 | 49 | 42 | 31 | 32 | 3,921 |
| 1986 | 14 | 1 | 7 | 78 | 289 | 747 | 1,136 | 949 | 477 | 243 | 193 | 109 | 73 | 50 | 47 | 28 | 36 | 4,477 |
| 1987 | 19 | 4 | 5 | 65 | 240 | 579 | 948 | 930 | 462 | 273 | 153 | 124 | 99 | 57 | 40 | 33 | 47 | 4,078 |
| 1988 | 5 | 0 | 3 | 78 | 271 | 584 | 1,096 | 1,057 | 617 | 352 | 174 | 134 | 86 | 66 | 38 | 34 | 52 | 4,647 |
| 1989 | 14 | 2 | 10 | 99 | 246 | 578 | 961 | 1,098 | 617 | 317 | 188 | 135 | 79 | 57 | 36 | 30 | 48 | 4,515 |
| 1990 | 12 | 3 | 4 | 72 | 195 | 461 | 778 | 928 | 610 | 290 | 172 | 121 | 81 | 54 | 44 | 35 | 49 | 3,909 |
| 1991 | 17 | 2 | 7 | 70 | 216 | 477 | 748 | 877 | 731 | 311 | 199 | 132 | 89 | 61 | 39 | 44 | 55 | 4,075 |
| 1992 | 11 | 1 | 10 | 73 | 257 | 573 | 922 | 1,246 | 969 | 459 | 248 | 130 | 109 | 64 | 41 | 30 | 64 | 5,207 |
| 1993 | 11 | 8 | 6 | 83 | 297 | 595 | 1,079 | 1,473 | 1,348 | 595 | 259 | 141 | 107 | 57 | 49 | 30 | 53 | 6,201 |
| 1994 | 21 | 3 | 8 | 75 | 284 | 583 | 1,122 | 1,381 | 1,387 | 759 | 323 | 164 | 93 | 56 | 37 | 33 | 53 | 6,376 |
| 1995 | 15 | 3 | 5 | 87 | 341 | 629 | 1,083 | 1,574 | 1,507 | 888 | 390 | 174 | 103 | 53 | 40 | 26 | 60 | 6,977 |
| 1996 | 13 | 4 | 8 | 127 | 330 | 578 | 1,010 | 1,402 | 1,491 | 1,048 | 399 | 189 | 95 | 80 | 47 | 39 | 42 | 6,902 |
| 1997 | 13 | 5 | 8 | 132 | 376 | 614 | 1,033 | 1,532 | 1,648 | 1,164 | 478 | 240 | 106 | 61 | 55 | 43 | 46 | 7,554 |
| 1998 | 15 | 5 | 6 | 155 | 440 | 633 | 1,057 | 1,498 | 1,798 | 1,331 | 584 | 237 | 127 | 65 | 53 | 31 | 62 | 8,097 |
| 1999 | 14 | 3 | 11 | 237 | 639 | 999 | 1,455 | 2,265 | 2,841 | 2,378 | 1,183 | 513 | 243 | 139 | 79 | 43 | 60 | 13,102 |
| 2000 | 19 | 3 | 10 | 261 | 760 | 974 | 1,373 | 2,176 | 2,755 | 2,494 | 1,347 | 507 | 244 | 108 | 70 | 48 | 62 | 13,211 |
| 2001 | 27 | 1 | 18 | 340 | 863 | 1,031 | 1,396 | 2,159 | 2,850 | 2,662 | 1,607 | 622 | 272 | 141 | 75 | 57 | 69 | 14,190 |
| 2002 | 15 | 3 | 17 | 400 | 1,038 | 1,204 | 1,672 | 2,465 | 3,229 | 3,039 | 2,008 | 846 | 363 | 150 | 90 | 66 | 78 | 16,683 |
| 2003 | 25 | 3 | 11 | 416 | 1,294 | 1,346 | 1,739 | 2,501 | 3,379 | 3,393 | 2,299 | 1,049 | 403 | 212 | 92 | 64 | 76 | 18,302 |
| 2004 | 22 | 3 | 18 | 554 | 1,391 | 1,592 | 1,711 | 2,384 | 3,296 | 3,566 | 2,603 | 1,268 | 458 | 204 | 104 | 74 | 63 | 19,310 |
| 2005 | 23 | 2 | 15 | 413 | 1,228 | 1,462 | 1,532 | 1,921 | 2,862 | 3,156 | 2,379 | 1,220 | 487 | 173 | 91 | 52 | 88 | 17,104 |
| 2006 | 33 | 6 | 21 | 583 | 1,825 | 2,178 | 2,199 | 2,659 | 3,668 | 4,138 | 3,483 | 1,890 | 645 | 295 | 131 | 68 | 93 | 23,915 |
| 2007 | 28 | 4 | 18 | 498 | 1,527 | 1,820 | 1,866 | 2,290 | 3,265 | 3,647 | 2,931 | 1,555 | 566 | 234 | 111 | 60 | 91 | 20,510 |
| Total | 605 | 90 | 329 | 7,566 | 21,878 | 27,971 | 33,545 | 39,368 | 41,755 | 35,251 | 22,461 | 11,435 | 5,444 | 3,049 | 2,006 | 1,428 | 1,810 | 255,991 |

SOURCE: Adapted from "Table 3.17. Age at Death for Males: Drug-Induced (without ICD–10 Correction)," in *The Economic Impact of Illicit Drug Use on American Society, 2011*, U.S. Department of Justice, National Drug Intelligence Center, April 2011, http://www.justice.gov/archive/ndic/pubs44/44731/44731p.pdf (accessed February 15, 2013)

## TABLE 7.7

### Drug-induced death among female population, by age group, 1968–2007

| Year | 0–4 | 5–9 | 10–14 | 15–19 | 20–24 | 25–29 | 30–34 | 35–39 | 40–44 | 45–49 | 50–54 | 55–59 | 60–64 | 65–69 | 70–74 | 75–79 | 80+ | Total |
|---|---|---|---|---|---|---|---|---|---|---|---|---|---|---|---|---|---|---|
| 1968 | 11 | 1 | 3 | 59 | 102 | 128 | 143 | 174 | 215 | 217 | 213 | 196 | 146 | 90 | 68 | 57 | 44 | 1,867 |
| 1969 | 13 | 0 | 10 | 114 | 157 | 180 | 135 | 182 | 205 | 243 | 237 | 195 | 152 | 121 | 89 | 62 | 42 | 2,137 |
| 1970 | 16 | 2 | 10 | 143 | 226 | 175 | 151 | 168 | 191 | 224 | 220 | 198 | 176 | 118 | 90 | 55 | 52 | 2,215 |
| 1971 | 27 | 3 | 11 | 182 | 296 | 207 | 154 | 194 | 230 | 248 | 218 | 174 | 142 | 117 | 104 | 47 | 51 | 2,405 |
| 1972 | 10 | 4 | 22 | 118 | 264 | 258 | 164 | 154 | 184 | 222 | 172 | 190 | 184 | 110 | 62 | 46 | 68 | 2,232 |
| 1973 | 16 | 2 | 8 | 104 | 262 | 188 | 159 | 130 | 167 | 175 | 191 | 149 | 124 | 103 | 83 | 64 | 48 | 1,973 |
| 1974 | 10 | 1 | 9 | 121 | 252 | 222 | 141 | 133 | 143 | 171 | 174 | 141 | 123 | 102 | 77 | 57 | 38 | 1,915 |
| 1975 | 8 | 3 | 4 | 88 | 280 | 249 | 158 | 103 | 160 | 168 | 136 | 133 | 97 | 98 | 65 | 45 | 48 | 1,843 |
| 1976 | 6 | 1 | 7 | 89 | 263 | 235 | 160 | 105 | 139 | 132 | 120 | 109 | 108 | 92 | 64 | 52 | 46 | 1,728 |
| 1977 | 11 | 2 | 5 | 50 | 203 | 176 | 134 | 98 | 116 | 121 | 115 | 125 | 93 | 89 | 72 | 54 | 48 | 1,512 |
| 1978 | 12 | 0 | 3 | 43 | 152 | 193 | 133 | 104 | 101 | 131 | 103 | 113 | 68 | 77 | 55 | 39 | 40 | 1,367 |
| 1979 | 24 | 1 | 9 | 83 | 244 | 299 | 287 | 260 | 196 | 215 | 235 | 178 | 166 | 111 | 91 | 55 | 65 | 2,519 |
| 1980 | 11 | 4 | 4 | 69 | 216 | 280 | 273 | 222 | 200 | 173 | 183 | 174 | 128 | 102 | 67 | 66 | 65 | 2,237 |
| 1981 | 9 | 5 | 9 | 83 | 171 | 255 | 270 | 197 | 192 | 196 | 180 | 233 | 130 | 101 | 71 | 50 | 53 | 2,205 |
| 1982 | 16 | 1 | 4 | 80 | 185 | 281 | 280 | 246 | 186 | 164 | 193 | 161 | 130 | 88 | 79 | 53 | 80 | 2,227 |
| 1983 | 10 | 4 | 14 | 56 | 173 | 283 | 293 | 238 | 195 | 168 | 181 | 152 | 119 | 88 | 87 | 75 | 81 | 2,217 |
| 1984 | 6 | 1 | 1 | 63 | 149 | 261 | 323 | 240 | 199 | 184 | 161 | 141 | 134 | 89 | 79 | 51 | 85 | 2,167 |
| 1985 | 6 | 2 | 19 | 62 | 151 | 257 | 364 | 262 | 193 | 188 | 128 | 129 | 106 | 89 | 75 | 72 | 72 | 2,175 |
| 1986 | 6 | 2 | 7 | 75 | 146 | 273 | 390 | 360 | 237 | 187 | 160 | 129 | 134 | 95 | 72 | 77 | 61 | 2,415 |
| 1987 | 5 | 2 | 3 | 86 | 124 | 267 | 393 | 354 | 242 | 151 | 165 | 142 | 101 | 103 | 73 | 67 | 83 | 2,361 |
| 1988 | 4 | 2 | 14 | 87 | 138 | 256 | 382 | 398 | 282 | 186 | 131 | 127 | 145 | 87 | 80 | 55 | 88 | 2,462 |
| 1989 | 10 | 3 | 16 | 89 | 117 | 278 | 385 | 371 | 307 | 204 | 128 | 141 | 94 | 95 | 58 | 69 | 83 | 2,448 |
| 1990 | 9 | 2 | 16 | 59 | 108 | 212 | 308 | 354 | 278 | 190 | 147 | 149 | 95 | 104 | 76 | 60 | 77 | 2,244 |
| 1991 | 10 | 3 | 13 | 61 | 119 | 186 | 314 | 390 | 309 | 227 | 137 | 129 | 122 | 93 | 63 | 54 | 71 | 2,301 |
| 1992 | 14 | 2 | 15 | 68 | 96 | 196 | 357 | 429 | 349 | 252 | 159 | 98 | 107 | 97 | 78 | 59 | 86 | 2,462 |
| 1993 | 14 | 6 | 17 | 55 | 124 | 203 | 388 | 467 | 429 | 258 | 176 | 121 | 101 | 81 | 70 | 49 | 97 | 2,656 |
| 1994 | 11 | 4 | 14 | 59 | 107 | 225 | 384 | 482 | 452 | 294 | 193 | 143 | 105 | 69 | 67 | 52 | 103 | 2,764 |
| 1995 | 13 | 0 | 9 | 53 | 124 | 186 | 374 | 495 | 504 | 322 | 189 | 102 | 84 | 61 | 70 | 45 | 78 | 2,700 |
| 1996 | 13 | 4 | 9 | 52 | 124 | 230 | 375 | 526 | 552 | 406 | 206 | 125 | 97 | 68 | 61 | 58 | 85 | 3,000 |
| 1997 | 7 | 7 | 8 | 57 | 102 | 236 | 361 | 538 | 616 | 423 | 261 | 154 | 91 | 77 | 64 | 57 | 72 | 3,131 |
| 1998 | 10 | 7 | 5 | 66 | 124 | 224 | 384 | 613 | 703 | 462 | 315 | 178 | 89 | 77 | 66 | 53 | 95 | 3,470 |
| 1999 | 9 | 6 | 4 | 87 | 194 | 323 | 577 | 945 | 1,059 | 840 | 490 | 209 | 123 | 86 | 68 | 81 | 106 | 5,205 |
| 2000 | 9 | 4 | 13 | 100 | 200 | 327 | 552 | 937 | 1,185 | 942 | 510 | 294 | 123 | 79 | 73 | 44 | 98 | 5,488 |
| 2001 | 8 | 3 | 8 | 111 | 250 | 327 | 580 | 1,030 | 1,311 | 1,060 | 702 | 288 | 159 | 85 | 76 | 53 | 97 | 6,146 |
| 2002 | 6 | 1 | 9 | 133 | 344 | 403 | 693 | 1,145 | 1,628 | 1,523 | 862 | 424 | 213 | 134 | 90 | 74 | 127 | 7,825 |
| 2003 | 22 | 5 | 7 | 154 | 396 | 471 | 741 | 1,212 | 1,717 | 1,654 | 1,054 | 519 | 234 | 138 | 86 | 92 | 115 | 8,611 |
| 2004 | 16 | 7 | 23 | 165 | 425 | 531 | 770 | 1,210 | 1,890 | 1,892 | 1,228 | 623 | 281 | 140 | 93 | 82 | 121 | 9,496 |
| 2005 | 15 | 7 | 15 | 127 | 381 | 502 | 658 | 991 | 1,506 | 1,645 | 1,194 | 572 | 263 | 136 | 86 | 66 | 113 | 8,269 |
| 2006 | 11 | 3 | 17 | 199 | 544 | 767 | 842 | 1,319 | 2,005 | 2,324 | 1,772 | 945 | 353 | 194 | 96 | 72 | 159 | 11,638 |
| 2007 | 27 | 3 | 16 | 163 | 463 | 635 | 750 | 1,155 | 1,756 | 1,985 | 1,483 | 759 | 308 | 165 | 91 | 69 | 136 | 9,954 |
| **Total** | **485** | **112** | **410** | **3,713** | **8,496** | **11,385** | **14,680** | **18,931** | **22,529** | **20,767** | **14,822** | **9,262** | **5,748** | **4,049** | **3,035** | **2,388** | **3,177** | **143,987** |

SOURCE: Adapted from "Table 3.24. Age at Death for Females: Drug-Induced (without ICD–10 Correction)," in *The Economic Impact of Illicit Drug Use on American Society, 2011*, U.S. Department of Justice, National Drug Intelligence Center, April 2011, http://www.justice.gov/archive/ndic/pubs44/44731/44731p.pdf (accessed February 15, 2013)

965, which required warnings on tobacco products, did not preempt damage suits. Despite the warnings on tobacco packaging, people could still sue on the grounds that tobacco companies purposely concealed information about the risks of smoking.

## The Master Settlement Agreement

Following the Supreme Court's decision, the tobacco industry was faced with the possibility of never-ending lawsuits and massive damage awards. Many state governments began lawsuits against major cigarette companies, seeking to recover the costs the states had incurred in caring for those with smoking-related health problems. The tobacco industry responded by negotiating with the states and offering money and changes in its business practices in exchange for an end to the lawsuits and protection from future lawsuits.

In November 1998 the attorneys general from 46 states (Florida, Minnesota, Mississippi, and Texas were excluded because they had already concluded previous settlements), five territories, and the District of Columbia signed an agreement with the five largest cigarette companies (Philip Morris, R. J. Reynolds, Brown and Williamson, Lorillard, and Liggett Group) to settle all the state lawsuits brought to recover the Medicaid costs of treating smokers. The Master Settlement Agreement (MSA; http://ag.ca.gov/tobacco/msa.php) required the tobacco companies to make annual payments totaling $206 billion over 25 years, beginning in 2000. It also placed restrictions on how the companies could advertise, market, and promote tobacco products. Since the original signing, more than 30 additional tobacco firms have signed the MSA, and Philip Morris has contributed more than half of the payments received by the states under the agreement. Even though the MSA settles all the state and local government lawsuits, the tobacco industry is still subject to class-action and individual lawsuits.

The four states that negotiated their own lawsuit settlements began receiving payments from the tobacco companies in 1998. "Up-front" payments to other states began in 1999, prior to the beginning of the annual payments in 2000. In the fact sheet "Actual Tobacco Settlement Payments Received by the States, 2002–2012" (October 5, 2012, http://www.tobaccofreekids.org/research/factsheets/pdf/0365.pdf), the Campaign for Tobacco-Free Kids details the amount of money that the states received between 2002 and 2012. (See Table 7.8.) According to the terms of the MSA, these payments were scheduled to continue through 2025.

### HOW ARE STATES USING THE SETTLEMENT FUNDS?
The MSA did not place any restrictions on how state governments are to use the funds they receive under the agreement. Antismoking and public health organizations argue that the most appropriate use for MSA money is to fund smoking prevention and cessation programs. Since the November 1998 tobacco settlement, the Campaign for Tobacco-Free Kids, the American Lung Association, the American Cancer Society, and the American Heart Association have published an annual report to monitor how states are handling the settlement funds. The FY 2013 report *Broken Promises to Our Children: The 1998 State Tobacco Settlement 14 Years Later* (December 6, 2012, http://www.tobaccofreekids.org/content/what_we_do/state_local_issues/settlement/FY2013/1.%202012%20State%20Report%20-%20Full.pdf) notes that states have fallen far short in their efforts to adequately fund tobacco prevention and cessation programs and that "there is more evidence than ever that tobacco prevention and cessation programs work."

According to the report, in FY 2013 Alaska was the only state to fund tobacco prevention and cessation programs at the minimum levels recommended by the CDC. (See Table 7.9.) Only four other states were funding these programs at half the recommended level or more: North Dakota, Delaware, Wyoming, and Hawaii. The remaining 45 states and the District of Columbia funded tobacco prevention and cessation programs at less than half the CDC-recommended amount. Table 7.10 shows each state's tobacco prevention spending versus tobacco company spending for marketing in each state. On average, tobacco companies outspend the states 18.5 to 1 in marketing versus prevention spending.

What have states done with the tobacco settlement funds not allocated to tobacco prevention and cessation programs? The answer to this question varies with each state; in general, states have used settlement monies to fund other health- and youth-related programs, capital projects (e.g., building hospitals), medical research, medical education, enforcement of tobacco control laws, and expansion of health clinics for low-income citizens. Some states also used part of the money to pay down their debt or to help balance their budgets.

## TOBACCO QUOTA SYSTEM ENDED
In 1938 federal tobacco marketing quota and price support loan programs were established during the Great Depression under the Agricultural Adjustment Act of 1933. The act provided funding for farmers who left part of their fields unplanted, which reduced crop sizes and crop surpluses and caused prices to rise. This approach helped stabilize crop prices and raise their value so that American farmers would remain or become profitable.

For decades prices for tobacco were supported through this system of quotas that limited supply and raised market prices to a federally guaranteed price. If the guaranteed price of tobacco was not reached in the marketplace, tobacco farmers were given the guaranteed price, called a nonrecourse loan price.

TABLE 7.8

## Tobacco settlement payments, by state, 2002–12

[Millions of dollars]

| State | 1998–2001 Total | 2002 | 2003 | 2004 | 2005 | 2006 | 2007 | 2008 | 2009 | 2010 | 2011 | 2012 | Total payments 1998–2012 | State tobacco prevention* |
|---|---|---|---|---|---|---|---|---|---|---|---|---|---|---|
| Alabama | $267.8 | $114.4 | $92.7 | $100.7 | $103.0 | $94.3 | $98.1 | $106.1 | $116.6 | $97.2 | $92.0 | $93.8 | $1,376.9 | $0.0 |
| Alaska | $56.2 | $23.7 | $19.6 | $21.2 | $21.8 | $19.9 | $20.7 | $34.7 | $37.3 | $31.5 | $29.4 | $30.0 | $345.9 | $10.8 |
| Arizona | $239.0 | $105.4 | $85.8 | $91.6 | $94.0 | $86.0 | $89.5 | $115.6 | $125.6 | $105.4 | $99.1 | $101.1 | $1,338.0 | $18.0 |
| Arkansas | $140.1 | $57.4 | $47.5 | $51.5 | $52.8 | $48.3 | $50.3 | $57.3 | $62.7 | $52.4 | $49.5 | $50.5 | $720.3 | $7.4 |
| California | $2,051.7 | $912.7 | $743.4 | $793.5 | $813.7 | $744.5 | $774.8 | $832.1 | $914.4 | $762.5 | $721.5 | $735.8 | $10,800.5 | $70.0 |
| Colorado | $225.5 | $95.0 | $78.6 | $85.2 | $87.4 | $80.0 | $83.2 | $103.6 | $112.8 | $94.6 | $89.1 | $90.8 | $1,225.7 | $6.5 |
| Connecticut | $298.4 | $132.7 | $108.1 | $115.4 | $118.4 | $108.3 | $112.7 | $141.3 | $153.8 | $129.0 | $121.4 | $123.8 | $1,663.4 | $0.0 |
| Delaware | $63.6 | $28.3 | $23.0 | $24.6 | $25.2 | $23.1 | $24.0 | $30.5 | $33.2 | $28.4 | $26.2 | $26.7 | $356.7 | $9.0 |
| DC | $99.9 | $42.1 | $34.8 | $37.7 | $38.7 | $35.4 | $36.9 | $43.6 | $47.6 | $39.2 | $37.6 | $38.3 | $531.8 | $0.0 |
| Florida | $2,477.8 | $765.7 | $546.4 | $363.9 | $378.3 | $389.7 | $396.4 | $398.0 | $388.0 | $361.2 | $366.1 | $365.4 | $7,200.9 | $62.3 |
| Georgia | $350.9 | $170.0 | $140.7 | $152.6 | $156.5 | $143.2 | $149.0 | $159.5 | $175.4 | $146.2 | $138.4 | $141.1 | $2,023.4 | $2.0 |
| Hawaii | $83.8 | $43.0 | $35.1 | $37.4 | $38.4 | $35.1 | $36.5 | $56.1 | $60.4 | $50.9 | $47.7 | $48.6 | $572.9 | $10.7 |
| Idaho | $51.9 | $25.2 | $20.8 | $22.6 | $23.2 | $21.2 | $22.1 | $28.5 | $31.0 | $26.0 | $24.4 | $24.9 | $321.7 | $0.9 |
| Illinois | $665.4 | $322.4 | $266.9 | $289.3 | $296.7 | $271.5 | $282.5 | $310.0 | $340.2 | $283.9 | $268.4 | $273.7 | $3,870.9 | $9.5 |
| Indiana | $291.6 | $141.3 | $117.0 | $126.8 | $130.0 | $119.0 | $123.8 | $147.4 | $161.0 | $134.7 | $127.0 | $129.5 | $1,749.2 | $10.1 |
| Iowa | $124.3 | $60.2 | $49.9 | $54.1 | $55.4 | $50.7 | $52.8 | $75.5 | $81.6 | $68.7 | $64.4 | $65.7 | $803.2 | $3.3 |
| Kansas | $119.2 | $57.7 | $47.8 | $51.8 | $53.1 | $48.6 | $50.6 | $66.3 | $72.0 | $60.5 | $56.9 | $58.0 | $742.6 | $1.0 |
| Kentucky | $245.2 | $125.9 | $102.6 | $109.5 | $112.3 | $102.7 | $106.9 | $115.1 | $126.5 | $105.5 | $99.8 | $101.8 | $1,453.8 | $2.2 |
| Louisiana | $322.4 | $156.2 | $129.3 | $140.2 | $143.8 | $131.5 | $136.9 | $160.6 | $175.5 | $146.8 | $138.5 | $141.2 | $1,923.1 | $8.4 |
| Maine | $110.0 | $53.3 | $44.1 | $47.8 | $49.0 | $44.9 | $46.7 | $58.2 | $63.4 | $53.1 | $50.0 | $51.0 | $671.6 | $9.4 |
| Maryland | $323.3 | $156.6 | $129.6 | $140.5 | $144.1 | $131.8 | $137.2 | $166.2 | $181.2 | $151.8 | $143.0 | $145.8 | $1,951.2 | $4.3 |
| Massachusetts | $562.4 | $288.8 | $235.2 | $251.1 | $257.5 | $235.6 | $245.2 | $288.5 | $315.2 | $263.7 | $248.7 | $253.6 | $3,445.4 | $4.2 |
| Michigan | $605.9 | $311.2 | $253.5 | $270.5 | $277.4 | $253.8 | $264.2 | $290.2 | $318.4 | $265.7 | $251.2 | $256.2 | $3,618.2 | $1.8 |
| Minnesota | $1,139.0 | $377.9 | $260.2 | $168.5 | $175.5 | $180.8 | $183.9 | $182.0 | $179.9 | $164.7 | $169.4 | $169.8 | $3,348.5 | $19.5 |
| Mississippi | $772.5 | $229.0 | $169.6 | $112.5 | $116.9 | $120.5 | $122.6 | $121.3 | $120.1 | $112.4 | $113.0 | $106.8 | $2,105.2 | $9.9 |
| Missouri | $387.8 | $159.6 | $130.4 | $141.4 | $145.0 | $132.7 | $138.1 | $153.3 | $168.1 | $140.3 | $132.6 | $135.2 | $1,964.5 | $0.1 |
| Montana | $60.7 | $29.4 | $24.4 | $26.4 | $27.1 | $24.7 | $25.8 | $34.6 | $37.5 | $31.5 | $29.6 | $30.2 | $382.0 | $4.7 |
| Nebraska | $85.1 | $41.2 | $34.1 | $37.0 | $37.9 | $34.7 | $36.1 | $42.9 | $46.8 | $39.2 | $36.9 | $37.7 | $509.6 | $2.4 |
| Nevada | $87.2 | $42.3 | $35.0 | $37.9 | $38.9 | $35.6 | $37.0 | $46.0 | $50.1 | $42.0 | $39.5 | $40.3 | $531.6 | $0.0 |
| New Hampshire | $95.2 | $46.1 | $38.2 | $41.4 | $42.5 | $38.8 | $40.4 | $48.4 | $52.8 | $44.2 | $41.7 | $42.5 | $572.3 | $0.0 |
| New Jersey | $638.3 | $267.9 | $221.7 | $240.4 | $246.5 | $225.5 | $234.7 | $262.2 | $287.4 | $240.0 | $226.8 | $231.3 | $3,322.9 | $1.2 |
| New Mexico | $85.3 | $41.3 | $34.2 | $37.1 | $38.0 | $34.8 | $36.2 | $44.9 | $48.9 | $40.9 | $38.6 | $39.3 | $519.4 | $5.9 |
| New York | $1,777.0 | $912.5 | $743.3 | $793.4 | $813.6 | $744.4 | $774.7 | $834.5 | $916.8 | $764.6 | $723.5 | $737.7 | $10,535.8 | $41.4 |
| North Carolina | $324.7 | $166.8 | $135.8 | $145.0 | $148.7 | $136.0 | $141.6 | $160.0 | $175.2 | $146.4 | $138.3 | $141.0 | $1,959.3 | $17.3 |
| North Dakota | $52.3 | $25.4 | $21.0 | $22.8 | $23.3 | $21.3 | $22.2 | $36.5 | $39.2 | $33.1 | $30.9 | $31.5 | $359.5 | $8.1 |
| Ohio | $720.2 | $348.9 | $288.8 | $313.1 | $321.1 | $293.8 | $305.8 | $334.3 | $366.9 | $306.1 | $289.5 | $295.2 | $4,183.9 | $0.0 |
| Oklahoma | $148.1 | $71.8 | $59.4 | $64.4 | $66.1 | $60.4 | $62.9 | $89.0 | $96.2 | $81.0 | $75.9 | $77.4 | $952.6 | $21.2 |
| Oregon | $159.8 | $82.1 | $66.8 | $71.3 | $73.2 | $66.9 | $69.7 | $90.3 | $98.1 | $82.3 | $77.4 | $78.9 | $1,016.9 | $8.3 |
| Pennsylvania | $800.8 | $410.9 | $334.7 | $357.3 | $366.4 | $335.2 | $348.8 | $382.0 | $419.2 | $349.8 | $330.8 | $337.4 | $4,773.4 | $13.9 |
| Rhode Island | $102.8 | $49.8 | $41.2 | $44.7 | $45.8 | $41.9 | $43.6 | $53.2 | $58.0 | $48.6 | $45.8 | $46.7 | $622.3 | $0.4 |
| South Carolina | $168.2 | $81.5 | $67.4 | $73.1 | $76.0 | $68.6 | $71.4 | $83.5 | $91.2 | $76.3 | $72.0 | $73.4 | $1,002.6 | $5.0 |
| South Dakota | $49.9 | $24.2 | $20.0 | $21.7 | $22.2 | $20.4 | $21.2 | $27.6 | $30.0 | $25.2 | $23.7 | $24.1 | $310.1 | $4.0 |
| Tennessee | $406.7 | $169.1 | $140.0 | $151.7 | $155.6 | $142.4 | $148.2 | $157.3 | $173.0 | $144.2 | $136.5 | $139.2 | $2,063.7 | $0.2 |
| Texas | $3,211.0 | $1,004.5 | $719.0 | $479.9 | $498.6 | $516.1 | $524.4 | $525.2 | $512.6 | $477.8 | $483.5 | $474.6 | $8,945.4 | $5.5 |
| Utah | $63.6 | $30.8 | $25.5 | $27.7 | $28.4 | $25.9 | $27.0 | $42.1 | $45.2 | $38.2 | $35.7 | $36.4 | $426.6 | $5.5 |
| Vermont | $57.3 | $29.4 | $23.9 | $25.6 | $26.2 | $24.0 | $25.0 | $39.9 | $42.9 | $32.6 | $33.9 | $34.5 | $398.7 | $7.2 |
| Virginia | $292.3 | $141.6 | $117.2 | $127.1 | $130.4 | $119.3 | $124.1 | $132.7 | $145.9 | $121.6 | $115.1 | $117.4 | $1,684.8 | $3.3 |
| Washington | $293.5 | $142.2 | $117.7 | $127.6 | $130.9 | $119.8 | $124.6 | $173.0 | $187.2 | $157.5 | $147.8 | $150.7 | $1,872.6 | $8.4 |
| West Virginia | $126.7 | $61.4 | $50.8 | $55.1 | $56.5 | $51.7 | $53.8 | $73.0 | $79.1 | $66.5 | $62.5 | $63.7 | $800.8 | $0.8 |
| Wisconsin | $288.5 | $148.2 | $120.7 | $128.8 | $132.1 | $120.9 | $125.8 | $149.2 | $162.9 | $136.3 | $128.6 | $131.1 | $1,772.9 | $5.7 |
| Wyoming | $34.6 | $17.8 | $14.5 | $15.4 | $15.8 | $14.5 | $15.1 | $21.4 | $23.1 | $19.5 | $18.2 | $18.6 | $228.4 | $5.4 |

**TABLE 7.8**

**Tobacco settlement payments, by state, 2002–12** [CONTINUED]

[Millions of dollars]

| State | 1998–2001 Total | 2002 | 2003 | 2004 | 2005 | 2006 | 2007 | 2008 | 2009 | 2010 | 2011 | 2012 | Total payments 1998–2012 | State tobacco prevention* |
|---|---|---|---|---|---|---|---|---|---|---|---|---|---|---|
| Am. Samoa | $2.1 | $1.1 | $0.9 | $0.9 | $1.0 | $0.89 | $0.9 | $2.4 | $2.5 | $2.1 | $2.0 | $2.0 | $18.8 | NA |
| Guam | $3.1 | $1.6 | $1.3 | $1.4 | $1.4 | $1.28 | $1.3 | $2.8 | $3.0 | $2.5 | $2.3 | $2.4 | $24.3 | NA |
| No. Mariana | $1.0 | $0.4 | $0.6 | $0.5 | $0.5 | $0.49 | $0.5 | $2.0 | $2.0 | $1.8 | $1.6 | $1.6 | $13.1 | NA |
| Puerto Rico | $134.3 | $54.6 | $83.9 | $70.0 | $71.5 | $65.4 | $68.1 | $82.6 | $90.1 | $75.4 | $71.1 | $72.5 | $939.4 | NA |
| Virgin Islands | $2.1 | $0.8 | $1.3 | $1.1 | $1.1 | $1.10 | $1.1 | $2.5 | $2.7 | $2.3 | $2.1 | $2.1 | $20.2 | NA |
| **MSA total** | **$14.7 bill.** | **$7.0 bill.** | **$5.8 bill.** | **$6.2 bill.** | **$6.4 bill.** | **$5.8 bill.** | **$6.1 bill.** | **$7.0 bill.** | **$7.6 bill.** | **$6.4 bill.** | **$6.0 bill.** | **$6.2 bill.** | **$85.9 bill.** | **$0.36 bill.** |
| **Ind. state total** | **$7.6 bill.** | **$2.4 bill.** | **$1.7 bill.** | **$1.1 bill.** | **$1.2 bill.** | **$1.2 bill.** | **$1.2 bill.** | **$1.2 bill.** | **$1.2 bill.** | **$1.1 bill.** | **$1.1 bill.** | **$1.1 bill.** | **$20.9 bill.** | **$0.10 bill.** |
| **National total** | **$22.3 bill.** | **$9.4 bill.** | **$7.5 bill.** | **$7.3 bill.** | **$7.5 bill.** | **$7.0 bill.** | **$7.3 bill.** | **$8.2 bill.** | **$8.8 bill.** | **$7.5 bill.** | **$7.2 bill.** | **$7.3 bill.** | **$106.8 bill.** | **$0.46 bill.** |

MSA = Master settlement agreement.

Note: The Non-Participating Manufacturer (NPM) adjustment issue is being resolved through arbitration and the courts. States that win will get all the withheld payments plus interest.

*State tobacco prevention spending is for fiscal year 2012 and only includes state funds.

SOURCE: "Actual Tobacco Settlement Payments Received by the States, 2002–2012," Campaign for Tobacco–Free Kids, October 5, 2012, http://www.tobaccofreekids.org/research/factsheets/pdf/0365.pdf (accessed February 15, 2013)

How Alcohol, Tobacco, and Drug Use Affect Economics and Government

**TABLE 7.9**

### Rankings of funding for state tobacco prevention programs, fiscal year (FY) 2013

[Annual funding amounts only include state funds]

| State | Fiscal year 2013 current annual funding ($millions) | CDC annual recommendation (millions) | Fiscal year 2013 percent of CDC's recommendation | Current rank |
|---|---|---|---|---|
| Alaska | $10.9 | $10.7 | 101.6% | 1 |
| North Dakota[a] | $8.2 | $9.3 | 88.4% | 2 |
| Delaware | $9.0 | $13.9 | 64.9% | 3 |
| Wyoming | $5.4 | $9.0 | 60.0% | 4 |
| Hawaii | $8.9 | $15.2 | 58.8% | 5 |
| Arkansas | $17.8 | $36.4 | 48.9% | 6 |
| Oklahoma | $19.7 | $45.0 | 43.8% | 7 |
| Colorado | $22.6 | $54.4 | 41.5% | 8 |
| Maine | $7.5 | $18.5 | 40.7% | 9 |
| Vermont | $4.0 | $10.4 | 38.2% | 10 |
| South Dakota | $4.0 | $11.3 | 35.4% | 11 |
| Minnesota | $19.6 | $58.4 | 33.6% | 12 |
| Montana | $4.6 | $13.9 | 33.1% | 13 |
| Florida | $64.3 | $210.9 | 30.5% | 14 |
| Utah | $7.0 | $23.6 | 29.8% | 15 |
| New Mexico | $5.9 | $23.4 | 25.3% | 16 |
| Mississippi | $9.7 | $39.2 | 24.7% | 17 |
| Arizona | $15.2 | $68.1 | 22.3% | 18 |
| West Virginia | $5.7 | $27.8 | 20.5% | 19 |
| Oregon | $7.5 | $43.0 | 17.5% | 20 |
| New York | $41.4 | $254.3 | 16.3% | 21 |
| California | $62.1 | $441.9 | 14.1% | 22 |
| Connecticut | $6.0 | $43.9 | 13.7% | 23 |
| Louisiana | $7.2 | $53.5 | 13.4% | 24 |
| Idaho | $2.2 | $16.9 | 13.0% | 25 |
| Indiana | $9.3 | $78.8 | 11.8% | 26 |
| Nebraska | $2.4 | $21.5 | 11.1% | 27 |
| Pennsylvania | $14.2 | $155.5 | 9.1% | 28 |
| Iowa | $3.2 | $36.7 | 8.7% | 29 |
| Wisconsin | $5.3 | $64.3 | 8.2% | 30 |
| Virginia | $8.4 | $103.2 | 8.1% | 31 |
| South Carolina | $5.0 | $62.2 | 8.0% | 32 |
| Illinois | $11.1 | $157.0 | 7.1% | 33 |
| Maryland | $4.2 | $63.3 | 6.6% | 34 |
| District of Columbia | $495,000 | $10.5 | 4.7% | 35 |
| Massachusetts | $4.2 | $90.0 | 4.6% | 36 |
| Kentucky | $2.1 | $57.2 | 3.7% | 37 |
| Washington | $2.5 | $67.3 | 3.7% | 37 |
| Kansas | $1.0 | $32.1 | 3.1% | 39 |
| Rhode Island | $376,437 | $15.2 | 2.5% | 40 |
| Texas | $6.5 | $266.3 | 2.4% | 41 |
| Michigan | $1.8 | $121.2 | 1.5% | 42 |
| Georgia | $750,000 | $116.5 | 0.6% | 43 |
| Nevada | $150,000 | $32.5 | 0.5% | 44 |
| Tennessee | $222,267 | $71.7 | 0.3% | 45 |
| Missouri | $61,785 | $73.2 | 0.1% | 46 |
| New Hampshire | $0.0 | $19.2 | 0.0% | 50 |
| New Jersey | $0.0 | $119.8 | 0.0% | 50 |
| North Carolina | $0.0 | $106.8 | 0.0% | 50 |
| Ohio | $0.0 | $145.0 | 0.0% | 50 |
| Alabama[b] | NA | $56.7 | NA | NA |

CDC = Centers for Disease Control and Prevention.

[a]North Dakota currently funds tobacco prevention programs at the CDC-recommended levels if both state and federal funding is counted.

[b]As in fiscal year 2012, Alabama's tobacco prevention program budget for fiscal year 2013 was not available when this report went to press. In fiscal year 2011, Alabama budgeted $860,000, which is just 1.5 percent of the CDC's recommendation.

SOURCE: "FY2013 Rankings of Funding for State Tobacco Prevention Programs," Campaign for Tobacco-Free Kids, 2013, http://www.tobaccofreekids.org/content/what_we_do/state_local_issues/settlement/FY2013/3.%20FY2013%20Rankings%20of%20Funding%20for%20State%20Tobacco%20Prevention%20Programs%2011-19-12.pdf (accessed February 15, 2013).

In 2004 the Fair and Equitable Tobacco Reform Act ended the quota program and in 2005 established the Tobacco Transition Payment Program, which provided 10 years of transitional payments to farmers previously holding quota contracts. The USDA's Farm Service Program reports in "Tobacco Transition Payment Program" (October 2009, http://www.fsa.usda.gov/Internet/FSA_File/ttpp09.pdf) that "payments are funded through assessments of approximately $10 billion on tobacco product manufacturers and importers."

**Tobacco prevention spending, fiscal year 2013, vs. tobacco company marketing, 2010, by state**

[All amounts are annual and in millions of dollars per year, except where otherwise indicated]

| State | Annual smoking caused health costs in state | Fiscal year 2013 total tobacco prevention spending | 2010 tobacco company marketing in state | Percentage of tobacco company marketing that state spends on tobacco prevention | Ratio of tobacco company marketing to state tobacco prevention spending |
|---|---|---|---|---|---|
| Total | $96.7 bill. | $459.5 | $8.49 bill. | 5.4% | 18.5 to 1 |
| Alabama | $1.49 bill. | NA | $180.8 | NA | NA |
| Alaska | $169 | $10.9 | $17.0 | 64.0% | 1.6 to 1 |
| Arizona | $1.3 bill. | $15.2 | $95.6 | 15.9% | 6.3 to 1 |
| Arkansas | $812 | $17.8 | $98.6 | 18.1% | 5.5 to 1 |
| California | $9.14 bill. | $62.1 | $535.7 | 11.6% | 8.6 to 1 |
| Colorado | $1.31 bill. | $22.6 | $113.1 | 20.0% | 5.0 to 1 |
| Connecticut | $1.63 bill. | $6.0 | $71.7 | 8.4% | 12.0 to 1 |
| Delaware | $284 | $9.0 | $43.5 | 20.7% | 4.8 to 1 |
| DC | $243 | $495,000 | $8.0 | 6.2% | 16.2 to 1 |
| Florida | $6.32 bill. | $64.3 | $516.7 | 12.4% | 8.0 to 1 |
| Georgia | $2.25 bill. | $750,000 | $291.0 | 0.3% | 388.0 to 1 |
| Hawaii | $336 | $8.9 | $24.7 | 36.1% | 2.8 to 1 |
| Idaho | $319 | $2.2 | $39.4 | 5.6% | 17.9 to 1 |
| Illinois | $4.10 bill. | $11.1 | $321.8 | 3.4% | 29.0 to 1 |
| Indiana | $2.08 bill. | $9.3 | $249.5 | 3.7% | 26.8 to 1 |
| Iowa | $1.01 bill. | $3.2 | $82.7 | 3.9% | 25.9 to 1 |
| Kansas | $927 | $1.0 | $64.9 | 1.5% | 64.9 to 1 |
| Kentucky | $1.50 bill. | $2.1 | $248.9 | 0.9% | 117.2 to 1 |
| Louisiana | $1.47 bill. | $7.2 | $197.6 | 3.6% | 27.6 to 1 |
| Maine | $602 | $7.5 | $37.6 | 20.0% | 5.0 to 1 |
| Maryland | $1.96 bill. | $4.2 | $110.3 | 3.8% | 26.6 to 1 |
| Massachusetts | $3.54 bill. | $4.2 | $123.7 | 3.4% | 29.8 to 1 |
| Michigan | $3.40 bill. | $1.8 | $253.6 | 0.7% | 138.6 to 1 |
| Minnesota | $2.06 bill. | $19.6 | $151.2 | 13.0% | 7.7 to 1 |
| Mississippi | $719 | $9.7 | $111.5 | 8.7% | 11.5 to 1 |
| Missouri | $2.13 bill. | $61,785 | $301.8 | 0.0% | 4,884.5 to 1 |
| Montana | $277 | $4.6 | $24.9 | 18.5% | 5.4 to 1 |
| Nebraska | $537 | $2.4 | $54.0 | 4.4% | 22.7 to 1 |
| Nevada | $565 | $150,000 | $68.2 | 0.2% | 454.7 to 1 |
| New Hampshire | $564 | $0.0 | $67.6 | 0.0% | NA |
| New Jersey | $3.17 bill. | $0.0 | $158.0 | 0.0% | NA |
| New Mexico | $461 | $5.9 | $31.1 | 19.1% | 5.2 to 1 |
| New York | $8.17 bill. | $41.4 | $196.0 | 21.1% | 4.7 to 1 |
| North Carolina | $2.46 bill. | $0.0 | $321.3 | 0.0% | NA |
| North Dakota | $247 | $8.2 | $25.7 | 32.0% | 3.1 to 1 |
| Ohio | $4.37 bill. | $0.0 | $362.5 | 0.0% | NA |
| Oklahoma | $1.16 bill. | $19.7 | $147.2 | 13.4% | 7.5 to 1 |
| Oregon | $1.11 bill. | $7.5 | $99.6 | 7.6% | 13.2 to 1 |
| Pennsylvania | $5.19 bill. | $14.2 | $396.0 | 3.6% | 27.8 to 1 |
| Rhode Island | $506 | $376,437 | $21.2 | 1.8% | 56.3 to 1 |
| South Carolina | $1.09 bill. | $5.0 | $178.9 | 2.8% | 35.8 to 1 |
| South Dakota | $274 | $4.0 | $19.7 | 20.3% | 4.9 to 1 |
| Tennessee | $2.16 bill. | $222,267 | $251.6 | 0.1% | 1,132.1 |
| Texas | $5.83 bill. | $6.5 | $538.5 | 1.2% | 83.5 to 1 |
| Utah | $345 | $7.0 | $34.0 | 20.7% | 4.8 to 1 |
| Vermont | $233 | $4.0 | $16.9 | 23.5% | 4.2 to 1 |
| Virginia | $2.08 bill. | $8.4 | $296.9 | 2.8% | 35.5 to 1 |
| Washington | $1.95 bill. | $2.5 | $80.8 | 3.1% | 32.6 to 1 |
| West Virginia | $690 | $5.7 | $110.6 | 5.2% | 19.4 to 1 |
| Wisconsin | $2.02 bill. | $5.3 | $133.7 | 4.0% | 25.2 to 1 |
| Wyoming | $136 | $5.4 | $22.0 | 24.5% | 4.1 to 1 |

SOURCE: Adapted from "Spending vs. Tobacco Company Marketing," Campaign for Tobacco-Free Kids, 2013, http://www.tobaccofreekids.org/content/what_we_do/state_local_issues/settlement/FY2013/10.%20State%20Tobacco%20Prevention%20Spending%20vs.%20Tob.%20Co.%20Marketing%2011-27-12.pdf (accessed February 15, 2013)

Since the termination of the federal tobacco program with the 2005 crop, the USDA Economic Research Service no longer maintains an active tobacco market analysis program. Thus, many annual tobacco-related publications are no longer being produced.

# CHAPTER 8
# DRUG TRAFFICKING

Trafficking in drugs refers to commercial activity: the buying and selling of illegal and controlled substances without a permit to do so—a permit that, for example, a physician, pharmacist, or researcher would have. Illegal drugs are those with no currently accepted medical use in the United States, such as heroin, lysergic acid diethylamide (LSD), and marijuana. It is illegal to buy, sell, possess, and use these drugs except for research purposes. (Some states and local jurisdictions have decriminalized certain uses of specific amounts of marijuana, but federal laws supersede these state and local marijuana decriminalization laws. For a more detailed discussion on the legalization of marijuana, see Chapter 9.)

Legal drugs are those whose sale, possession, and use as intended are not forbidden by law. However, the use of legal psychoactive (mood- or mind-altering) drugs, which have the potential for abuse, is restricted. These drugs, which include narcotics, depressants, and stimulants, are available only with a prescription. They are called controlled substances. Drug trafficking includes all commercial activities that are integral to the buying and selling of illegal and controlled substances, including their manufacture, production, preparation, importation, exportation, supply, distribution, or transportation.

## CRIMINAL PENALTIES FOR TRAFFICKING
### Federal Penalties

The Controlled Substances Act of 1970 provides penalties for the unlawful trafficking in controlled substances, based on the schedule (rank) of the drug or substance. (For definitions of the schedules, see Table 1.3 in Chapter 1.) Generally, the more dangerous the drug and the larger the quantity involved, the stiffer the penalty. The trafficking of heroin, cocaine, LSD, and phencyclidine (PCP), all Schedule I or II drugs, includes mandatory jail time and fines. For example, a person caught selling at least 18 ounces (500 grams [g]) but less than 11 pounds (5 kilograms [kg]) of cocaine powder will receive a minimum of five years in prison and may be fined up to $5 million for a first offense. (See Table 8.1.) The same penalty is imposed for the sale of between 1 ounces and 9.8 ounces (28 to 279 g) of cocaine base (crack).

Following the second offense, penalties double to a minimum of 10 years in prison and up to $8 million in fines. When higher quantities are involved (11 or more pounds [5 or more kg] of cocaine powder, 9.8 ounces or more [280 g or more] of crack, and so on), penalties for the first offense are a minimum of 10 years in prison and fines up to $4 million may be levied. For the second offense, a minimum of 20 years and up to $20 million in fines are given, and the third offense results in mandatory life imprisonment. These examples are for an individual. Higher penalties apply if an organized group is involved or if a death or injury is associated with the arrest event.

These penalties also apply to the sale of fentanyl (a powerful painkiller medicine) or similar-acting drugs, heroin, LSD, methamphetamine, and PCP. The smallest amount, which can earn someone a minimum sentence of five years in prison and a fine of up to $2 million, involves trafficking in LSD, in which an amount of 0.03 ounces (1 g) carries a five-year-minimum sentence in prison.

Punishments for marijuana, hashish, and hashish oil are shown in Table 8.2. Special penalties exist for marijuana trafficking because it may be traded in large quantities or grown in substantial amounts. The lower the amounts sold or the fewer the plants grown, the lower the sentence. A person cultivating one to 49 plants or selling less than 110 pounds (50 kg) of marijuana mixture, 22 pounds (10 kg) or less of hashish, or 2.2 pounds (1 kg) or less of hashish oil may get a maximum sentence of five years in prison and a maximum fine of $250,000.

**TABLE 8.1**

## Federal drug trafficking penalties, excluding marijuana

| Schedule | Substance/quantity | Penalty | Substance/quantity | Penalty |
|---|---|---|---|---|
| II | Cocaine<br>500–4,999 grams mixture | **First offense:** Not less than 5 yrs. and not more than 40 yrs. If death or serious bodily injury, not less than 20 yrs. or more than life. Fine of not more than $5 million if an individual, $25 million if not an individual. | Cocaine<br>5 kilograms or more mixture | **First offense:** Not less than 10 yrs. and not more than life. If death or serious bodily injury, not less than 20 yrs. or more than life. Fine of not more than $10 million if an individual, $50 million if not an individual. |
| II | Cocaine base<br>28–279 grams mixture | | Cocaine base<br>280 grams or more mixture | |
| IV | Fentanyl<br>40–399 grams mixture | | Fentanyl<br>400 grams or more mixture | |
| I | Fentanyl analogue<br>10–99 grams mixture | **Second offense:** Not less than 10 yrs. and not more than life. If death or serious bodily injury, life imprisonment. Fine of not more than $8 million if an individual, $50 million if not an individual. | Fentanyl analogue<br>100 grams or more mixture | **Second offense:** Not less than 20 yrs, and not more than life. If death or serious bodily injury, life imprisonment. Fine of not more than $20 million if an individual, $75 million if not an individual. |
| I | Heroin<br>100–999 grams mixture | | Heroin<br>1 kilogram or more mixture | |
| I | LSD<br>1–9 grams mixture | | LSD<br>10 grams or more mixture | **2 or more prior offenses:** Life imprisonment. Fine of not more than $20 million if an individual, $75 million if not an individual. |
| II | Methamphetamine<br>5–49 grams pure or<br>50–499 grams mixture | | Methamphetamine<br>50 grams or more pure or<br>500 grams or more mixture | |
| II | PCP<br>10–99 grams pure or<br>100–999 grams mixture | | PCP<br>100 grams or more pure or 1 kilogram or more mixture | |

| Substance/quantity | Penalty |
|---|---|
| Any amount of other schedule I & II substances<br>Any drug product containing gamma hydroxybutyric acid<br>Flunitrazepam (Schedule IV) 1 gram | **First offense:** Not more than 20 yrs. If death or serious bodily injury, not less than 20 yrs. or more than Life. Fine $1 million if an individual, $5 million if not an individual.<br>**Second offense:** Not more than 30 yrs. If death or serious bodily injury, life imprisonment. Fine $2 million if an individual, $10 million if not an individual. |
| Any amount of other Schedule III drugs | **First offense:** Not more than 10 yrs. If death or serious bodily injury, not more that 15 yrs. Fine not more than $500,000 if an individual, $2.5 million if not an individual.<br>**Second offense:** Not more than 20 yrs. If death or serious injury, not more than 30 yrs. Fine not more than $1 million if an individual, $5 million if not an individual. |
| Any amount of all other Schedule IV drugs (other than one gram or more of Flunitrazepam) | **First offense:** Not more than 5 yrs. Fine not more than $250,000 if an individual, $1 million if not an individual.<br>**Second offense:** Not more than 10 yrs. Fine not more than $500,000 if an individual, $2 million if other than an individual. |
| Any amount of all Schedule V drugs | **First offense:** Not more than 1 yr. Fine not more than $100,000 if an individual, $250,000 if not an individual.<br>**Second offense:** Not more than 4 yrs. Fine not more than $200,000 if an individual, $500,000 if not an individual. |

SOURCE: "Federal Trafficking Penalties for Schedules I, II, III, IV, and V (Except Marijuana)," U.S. Department of Justice, U.S. Drug Enforcement Administration, 2013, http://www.justice.gov/dea/druginfo/ftp_chart1.pdf (accessed February 15, 2013)

---

**TABLE 8.2**

## Federal marijuana trafficking penalties

| Drug | Quantity | First offense | Second offense |
|---|---|---|---|
| Marijuana | 1,000 kilograms or more marijuana mixture or 1,000 or more marijuana plants | • Not less than 10 yrs. or more than life<br>• If death or serious bodily injury, not less than 20 yrs., or more than life<br>• Fine not more than $10 million if an individual $50 million if other than an individual | • Not less than 20 yrs. or more than life<br>• If death or serious bodily injury, life imprisonment<br>• Fine not more than $20 million if an individual $75 million if other than an individual |
| Marijuana | 100 to 999 kilograms marijuana mixture or 100 to 999 marijuana plants | • Not less than 5 yrs. or more than 40 yrs.<br>• If death or serious bodily injury, not less than 20 yrs. or more than life<br>• Fine not more than $5 million if an individual, $25 million if other than an individual. | • Not less than 10 yrs. or more than life<br>• If death or serious bodily injury, life imprisonment<br>• Fine not more than $8 million if an individual $50 million if other than an individual |
| Marijuana<br>Hashish<br>Hashish oil | 50 to 99 kilograms marijuana mixture<br>50 to 99 marijuana plants<br>More than 10 kilograms<br>More than 1 kilogram | • Not more than 20 yrs.<br>• If death or serious bodily injury, not less than 20 yrs. or more than life<br>• Fine $1 million if an individual $5 million if other than an individual | • Not more than 30 yrs.<br>• If death or serious bodily injury, life imprisonment<br>• Fine $2 million if an individual $10 million if other than an individual |
| Marijuana<br><br><br>Hashish<br>Hashish oil | Less than 50 kilograms marijuana (but does not include 50 or more marijuana plants regardless of weight)<br>1 to 49 marijuana plants<br>10 kilograms or less<br>1 kilogram or less | • Not more than 5 yrs.<br>• Fine not more than $250,000, $1 million if other than an individual | • Not more than 10 yrs.<br>• Fine $500,000 if an individual, $2 million if other than individual |

SOURCE: "Federal Trafficking Penalties for Marijuana, Hashish and Hashish Oil, Schedule I Substances," U.S. Department of Justice, U.S. Drug Enforcement Administration, 2013, http://www.justice.gov/dea/druginfo/ftp_chart2.pdf (accessed February 15, 2013)

entences for second offenses involving large amounts of marijuana may earn the trafficker up to life imprisonment.

## State Laws

States have the discretionary power to make their own drug laws. The possession of marijuana may be a misdemeanor in one state but a felony in another. Prison sentences can also vary for the same charges in different states—the distribution of 18 ounces (500 g) of cocaine as a Class C felony may specify 10 to 50 years in one state and 24 to 40 years in another. Most states follow the model of the Controlled Substances Act and enforce laws that facilitate the seizure of drug trafficking profits, specify greater penalties for trafficking, and promote user accountability by punishing drug users.

## IS THE PROFIT WORTH THE RISK?

Despite the possibility of long prison terms (up to life imprisonment), many drug dealers evidently consider the enormous potential profits of drug trafficking worth the risk. The media often report drug busts and indictments of people involved in multimillion- or billion-dollar operations. Paying fines of hundreds of thousands of dollars, or even millions of dollars, becomes part of doing business when the profits are so high.

## THE WORLD'S POPULATION AND ILLICIT DRUGS

The United Nations Office on Drugs and Crime estimates in *World Drug Report 2012* (June 2012, http://www.unodc.org/documents/data-and-analysis/WDR2012/WDR_2012_web_small.pdf) that between 153 million and 300 million people (3.4% to 6.6% of the world's population aged 15 to 64 years) were users of illicit drugs in 2010. Between 10% and 13% of these illicit drug users— roughly 27 million people—were classified as problem drug users, many of whom were addicted to drugs. In 2010, 119.4 million to 224.5 million people used cannabis, 26.4 million to 36.1 million used opioids, 14.3 million to 52.5 million people used amphetamine-type stimulants, 13.2 million to 19.5 million people used cocaine, and 10.5 million to 28 million used drugs from the "ecstasy group."

## WORLD PRODUCTION OF PLANT-DERIVED (ORGANIC) DRUGS

In *International Narcotics Control Strategy Report: Volume I, Drug and Chemical Control* (March 2012, http://www.state.gov/documents/organization/184314.pdf), the Bureau of International Narcotics and Law Enforcement Affairs (INL), an element of the U.S. Department of State, provides data on the amount of land that is cultivated to raise opium poppy, the source of heroin and other opioids; coca leaf, from which cocaine is derived; and

cannabis, the hemp plant from which marijuana and hashish are derived. The INL cautions that these are estimates, based on satellite observations and other sources of intelligence, and that there are countries and areas of countries that were not studied.

According to the INL, the largest amount of cultivated land was dedicated to the production of coca leaf, followed by opium poppy and cannabis. (See Table 8.3.) In 2009, the most recent year for which data were complete, coca was cultivated on 472,000 acres (191,000 hectares [ha]). The largest producer was Colombia. Opium poppy was cultivated on 419,100 acres (169,600 ha) of land, a 13.6% decrease from 2008. The largest producer was Afghanistan. Cannabis cultivation took place on 43,200 acres (17,500 ha) in 2009. (Cultivation within the United States was excluded from this calculation.) This figure was three times greater than the amount of land used to cultivate cannabis in 2005, when the total was 13,800 acres (5,600 ha); however, the amount of land dedicated to cannabis cultivation was expected to drop in 2010. (See Table 8.4). Over the five-year period from 2005 to 2009, reported coca leaf cultivation was higher than poppy cultivation in 2005, 2006, and 2009, but lower than poppy cultivation in 2007 and 2008. Reported cannabis cultivation was a distant third.

## ILLICIT DRUG MOVEMENT INTO AND WITHIN THE UNITED STATES

Illicit drug cultivation takes place primarily outside the United States. Even though each drug type has its own method and route of entering the United States, the most common method is overland smuggling and subsequent transportation via the interstate highway system.

The National Drug Intelligence Center (NDIC) provides in *National Drug Threat Assessment, 2011* (August 2011, http://www.justice.gov/archive/ndic/pubs44/44849/44849p.pdf) data on the seizures of drugs in transit within the United States. As Figure 8.1 reveals, the vast majority of illegal drug movement into the United States in fiscal year (FY) 2010 occurred along the nation's southwest border with Mexico. That year, out of all drug seizures made at U.S. borders and points of entry, trafficking along the southwest border accounted for 96% of all marijuana seizures, 80% of all methamphetamine seizures, 64% of all cocaine seizures, and 58% of all heroin seizures.

Table 8.5 shows drug seizures along the southwest and northern borders of the United States, and within the United States (away from the borders), between FYs 2006 and 2010. Cocaine seizures declined by 36.7%, from 153,355 pounds (69,561 kg) in 2006 to 97,142 pounds (44,063 kg) in 2010. In contrast, marijuana seizures increased from 2.8 million pounds (1.3 million kg)

**TABLE 8.3**

## Illicit drug production worldwide, by crop and country, 2005–10

[In hectares]

| | 2005 | 2006 | 2007 | 2008 | 2009 | 2010 |
|---|---|---|---|---|---|---|
| **Poppy** | | | | | | |
| Afghanistan | 107,400 | 172,600 | 202,000 | 157,000 | 131,000 | 119,00• |
| Burma | 40,000 | 21,000 | 21,700 | 22,500 | 17,000 | In process |
| Colombia | | 2,300 | 1,000 | | 1,100 | In process |
| Guatemala | 100 | | | | | |
| Laos | 5,600 | 1,700 | 1,100 | 1,900 | 1,000 | In process |
| Mexico | 3,300 | 5,000 | 6,900 | 15,000 | 19,500 | In process |
| Pakistan | See note below | | | | | |
| **Total poppy** | **156,400** | **202,600** | **232,700** | **196,400** | **169,600** | |
| **Coca** | | | | | | |
| Bolivia | 26,500 | 25,800 | 29,500 | 32,000 | 35,000 | In process |
| Colombia | 144,000 | 157,000 | 167,000 | 119,000 | 116,000 | In process |
| Peru | 34,000 | 42,000 | 36,000 | 41,000 | 40,000 | In process |
| **Total coca** | **204,500** | **224,800** | **232,500** | **192,000** | **191,000** | |
| **Cannabis** | | | | | | |
| Mexico | 5,600 | 8,600 | 8,900 | 12,000 | 17,500 | In process |
| **Total cannabis** | **5,600** | **8,600** | **8,900** | **12,000** | **17,500** | |

Notes on Colombia poppy cultivation: The 2008 and 2005 surveys could not be conducted due to cloud cover. Partial survey in 2007 due to cloud cover.
Note on Laos poppy cultivation: A partial survey of only the Phongsali growing area was conducted in 2009.
Notes on Pakistan poppy cultivation: There are no United States Government (USG) countrywide numbers for Pakistan.
Notes on Colombia coca cultivation: Survey areas were expanded greatly in 2005 and to a lesser extent in 2006 and 2007.
Notes on Peru cultivation: In the 2006 survey, the Cusco growing area could not be completed; the value for that area is an average of the 2005 and 2007 estimates. The 2005 cultivation estimate was revised in 2007.

SOURCE: "Worldwide Illicit Drug Cultivation: 2005–2010," in *International Narcotics Control Strategy Report: Volume I, Drug and Chemical Control*, U.S. Department of State, Bureau of International Narcotics and Law Enforcement Affairs, March 2012, http://www.state.gov/documents/organization/184314.pdf (accessed February 15, 2013)

**TABLE 8.4**

## Potential illicit drug production worldwide, by crop and country, 2005–10

[In hectares]

| | 2005 | 2006 | 2007 | 2008 | 2009 | 2010 |
|---|---|---|---|---|---|---|
| **Poppy** | | | | | | |
| Afghanistan | 107,400 | 172,600 | 202,000 | 157,000 | 131,000 | 119,000 |
| Burma | 40,000 | 21,000 | 21,700 | 22,500 | 17,000 | In process |
| Colombia | | 2,300 | 1,000 | | 1,100 | |
| Guatemala | 100 | | | | | |
| Laos | 5,600 | 1,700 | 1,100 | 1,900 | 1,000 | In process |
| Mexico | 3,300 | 5,100 | 6,900 | 15,000 | 19,500 | 14,000 |
| Pakistan | See note below | | | | | |
| **Total poppy** | **156,400** | **202,700** | **232,700** | **196,400** | **169,600** | |
| **Coca** | | | | | | |
| Bolivia | 26,500 | 25,800 | 29,500 | 32,000 | 35,000 | 34,500 |
| Colombia | 144,000 | 157,000 | 167,000 | 119,000 | 116,000 | 100,000 |
| Peru | 34,000 | 42,000 | 36,000 | 41,000 | 40,000 | 53,000 |
| **Total coca** | **204,500** | **224,800** | **232,500** | **192,000** | **191,000** | **187,500** |
| **Cannabis** | | | | | | |
| Mexico | 5,600 | 8,600 | 8,900 | 12,000 | 17,500 | 16,500 |
| **Total cannabis** | **5,600** | **8,600** | **8,900** | **12,000** | **17,500** | **16,500** |

Notes on Colombia poppy: The 2008 and 2005 surveys could not be conducted due to cloud cover. Partial survey in 2007 due to cloud cover.
Note on Laos poppy cultivation: A partial survey of only the Phongsali growing area was conducted.
Notes on Pakistan poppy cultivation: There are no United States Government (USG) countrywide numbers for Pakistan.

SOURCE: "Worldwide Potential Illicit Drug Production: 2005–2010," in *International Narcotics Control Strategy Report: Volume I, Drug and Chemical Control*, U.S. Department of State, Bureau of International Narcotics and Law Enforcement Affairs, March 2012, http://www.state.gov/documents/organization/184314.pdf (accessed February 15, 2013)

FIGURE 8.1

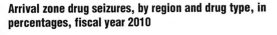

**Arrival zone drug seizures, by region and drug type, in percentages, fiscal year 2010**

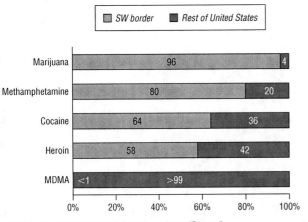

MDMA = 3,4-methylenedioxymyethamphetamine or "Ecstasy"
Notes: Totals include only seizures made at and between points of entry (POEs).
Seizures for "Rest of United States" include seizures made in Puerto Rico and the U.S. Virgin Islands.

SOURCE: "Figure 1. Arrival Zone Drug Seizures along the Southwest Border Compared with Arrival Zone Drug Seizures for the Rest of the United States, FY2010," in *National Drug Threat Assessment, 2011*, U.S. Department of Justice, National Drug Intelligence Center, August 2011, http://www.justice.gov/archive/ndic/pubs44/44849/44849p.pdf (accessed February 15, 2013)

to 4 million pounds (1.8 million kg) over this same period. These seizures are an indication of the relative quantity of the flow of drugs along these borders; seizures along the southwest border area far outstripped those along the northern border, with the exception of MDMA (3,4-methylenedioxy-methamphetamine), which arrived primarily across the northern border. Although the majority of some drugs were seized in "rest of U.S.," this does not necessarily mean they originated within the United States; in many cases these drugs were successfully smuggled past the border only to be seized later.

Table 8.6 indicates the seven major Mexican drug cartels that were primarily responsible for smuggling illicit drugs into, and within, the United States in 2011. All the cartels conducted operations in the U.S. Southwest, and all but one also operated in the Southeast. Most of the cartels were active in at least one other region. All seven of the cartels smuggled marijuana and cocaine. The Sinaloa Cartel had the most extensive drug smuggling operation in the United States, both in terms of regions of operation and the variety of drugs that were smuggled.

## Greatest Drug Threat

The NDIC surveyed state and local law enforcement agencies nationwide in 2010 to determine what they believed to be the greatest drug threat in the United States. As Figure 8.2 reveals, methamphetamine was perceived to

be the greatest drug threat among law enforcement agencies in the Southwest, along the West Coast, and in the West Central region of the country. In the Southeast, Florida, Great Lakes, and mid-Atlantic regions, cocaine was perceived to be the greatest threat, while heroin was viewed as the most serious drug threat by law enforcement agencies in New England, New York, and New Jersey.

As Figure 8.3 shows, in 2010 marijuana was the most readily available illegal drug in every region of the country, while controlled prescription drugs were the second-most readily available drug. Ice methamphetamine was the third-most readily available drug in the Pacific and Southwest regions; by contrast, in the West Central region powder methamphetamine was the third-most available illicit drug. In the eastern portion of the United States, crack cocaine was the third-most readily available illegal drug in every region except New England, where the third-most readily available drug was heroin.

## Federal Interdiction Efforts

As drug smuggling into the Southwest from Mexico increased, federal law enforcement agencies developed an aggressive interdiction strategy that was aimed at curbing the movement of illegal drugs across U.S. borders. Much of the responsibility for implementing this strategy lies with U.S. Customs and Border Protection (CBP), a law enforcement division that was founded as part of the Homeland Security Act (HSA) of 2003. James F. Tomsheck of the CBP said in a statement before the U.S. Senate Committee on Homeland Security and Governmental Affairs, Ad Hoc Subcommittee on State, Local, and Private Sector Preparedness and Integration (March 11, 2010, http://www.hsdl.org/?view&did=14472) that by 2010 the CBP was the largest single law enforcement agency in the nation, with more than 58,000 employees, including 20,000 border patrol agents. The Office of National Drug Control Policy (ONDCP) notes in *FY 2013 Budget and Performance Summary: Companion to the National Drug Control Strategy* (April 2012, http://www.whitehouse.gov/sites/default/files/ondcp/fy2013_drug_control_budget_and_performance_summary.pdf) that the federal government designated $3.7 billion toward interdiction efforts in FY 2013, an increase of 2.5% over the interdiction budget for FY 2012.

Although the federal government has made considerable investment in forceful interdiction measures to curtail drug trafficking, many people question its effectiveness in curbing the flow of illegal drugs into the United States. Writing for the Council on Foreign Relations, David A. Shirk of the University of San Diego states in *The Drug War in Mexico: Confronting a Shared Threat* (March 2011, http://i.cfr.org/content/publications/attachments/Mexico_CSR60.pdf) that U.S. interdiction activities along the Mexican border have ultimately

TABLE 8.5

**Total drug seizures, by region and drug type, fiscal years 2006–10**

[In kilograms. Includes seizures made in the United States and U.S. territories.]

| | 2006 | 2007 | 2008 | 2009 | 2010 |
|---|---|---|---|---|---|
| **Cocaine** | | | | | |
| Southwest border area[a] | 27,361 | 24,780 | 17,459 | 18,737 | 17,830 |
| Northern border | 2 | <1 | <1 | 18 | 23 |
| Rest of U.S. | 42,198 | 33,177 | 28,547 | 29,629 | 26,210 |
| **Total U.S.** | **69,561** | **57,957** | **46,006** | **48,384** | **44,063** |
| **Methamphetamine** | | | | | |
| Southwest border area | 2,706 | 2,128 | 2,221 | 3,278 | 4,486 |
| Northern border | <1 | 1 | 135 | 0 | 11 |
| Rest of U.S. | 2,872 | 3,100 | 3,696 | 3,323 | 4,202 |
| **Total U.S.** | **5,578** | **5,229** | **6,052** | **6,601** | **8,699** |
| **Heroin** | | | | | |
| Southwest border area | 449 | 358 | 496 | 737 | 905 |
| Northern border | 5 | <1 | 0 | 28 | 20 |
| Rest of U.S. | 1,719 | 1,631 | 1,404 | 1,485 | 1,637 |
| **Total U.S.** | **2,173** | **1,989** | **1,900** | **2,250** | **2,562** |
| **Marijuana** | | | | | |
| Southwest border area | 1,046,419 | 1,459,162 | 1,242,758 | 1,730,344 | 1,545,138 |
| Northern border | 5,455 | 3,084 | 2,369 | 3,784 | 2,194 |
| Rest of U.S. | 237,330 | 263,904 | 227,948 | 241,000 | 262,164 |
| **Total U.S.** | **1,289,204** | **1,726,150** | **1,473,075** | **1,975,128** | **1,809,496** |
| **MDMA[b]** | | | | | |
| Southwest border area | 17 | 43 | 69 | 77 | 216 |
| Northern border | 271 | 316 | 440 | 506 | 557 |
| Rest of U.S. | 1,150 | 1,444 | 2,069 | 1,896 | 1,351 |
| **Total U.S.** | **1,438** | **1,803** | **2,578** | **2,479** | **2,124** |

[a]The Southwest border area includes seizures made by federal, state, and local law enforcement officers at and between U.S. points of entry along the U.S.-Mexico border, as well as seizures made within 150 miles of the border.
[b]MDMA (3,4-methylenedioxymethamphetamine or Ecstasy) seizures in kilograms include seizures of powder as well as dosage units (tablets). MDMA dosage units vary in size and weight depending on the manufacturing process, the type of pill press used, and the amount of adulterants incorporated into the tablets. National Drug Intelligence Center (NDIC) uses the conversion ration of 7,143 tablets to 1 kilogram of MDMA powder.

SOURCE: "Table B3. Total U.S. Seizures, by Drug, in Kilograms, FY2006–2010," in *National Drug Threat Assessment, 2011*, U.S. Department of Justice, National Drug Intelligence Center, August 2011, http://www.justice.gov/archive/ndic/pubs44/44849/44849p.pdf (accessed February 15, 2013)

proven "inconsequential" in stemming the activities of the Mexican drug cartels, while unintentionally resulting in "the expansion and increased sophistication of cross-border smuggling operations, and greater U.S. vulnerability to attacks and even infiltration by traffickers." (Federal drug interdiction efforts are discussed in further detail in Chapter 9.)

## METHAMPHETAMINE

Methamphetamine (meth) is made in laboratories from precursor drugs rather than directly from plant material. The drug was first synthesized in 1919 and has been a factor on the drug market since the 1960s. The Substance Abuse and Mental Health Services Administration (SAMHSA) reveals in *Results from the 2011 National Survey on Drug Use and Health: Summary of National Findings* (September 2012, http://www.samhsa.gov/data/NSDUH/2k11Results/NSDUHresults2011.pdf) that 439,000 people were current users of methamphetamine in 2011. In addition, 133,000 people aged 12 years and older used methamphetamine for the first time that year.

### Methamphetamine Production

Like other synthetics, such as LSD or MDMA, methamphetamine appeals to small and large criminal enterprises alike because it frees them from dependence on vulnerable crops such as coca or opium poppy. Even a small organization can control the whole process, from manufacture to sale on the street, of methamphetamine. The drug can be made almost anywhere and can generate large profit margins. The NDIC indicates in *National Drug Threat Assessment, 2011* that in FY 2010 most methamphetamine in the United States was produced in Mexico, but it was also widely produced at clandestine labs within the United States.

Clandestine methamphetamine laboratories in the United States are usually operated as temporary facilities. Drug producers make a batch, tear down the lab, and either store the lab and equipment for later use or rebuild it at another site. This constant assembling and disassembling of laboratories is necessary to avoid detection by law enforcement authorities.

The ingredients for making methamphetamine are lithium (available from batteries), acetone (e.g., from

**:tivities of Mexican Transnational Crime Organizations (TCOs),
drug type and U.S. region, 2011**

| O | Primary drugs | Primary regions |
|---|---|---|
| naloa rtel | Cocaine<br>Heroin<br>Marijuana<br>MDMA<br>Methamphetamine | Florida/Caribbean<br>Great Lakes<br>Mid-Atlantic<br>New England<br>New York/New Jersey<br>Pacific<br>Southeast<br>Southwest<br>West Central |
| s tas | Cocaine<br>Marijuana | Florida/Caribbean<br>Great Lakes<br>Southeast<br>Southwest |
| ılf rtel | Cocaine<br>Marijuana | Florida/Caribbean<br>Mid-Atlantic<br>New England<br>New York/New Jersey<br>Southeast<br>Southwest |
| árez rtel | Cocaine<br>Marijuana | Great Lakes<br>New York/New Jersey<br>Pacific<br>Southeast<br>Southwest<br>West Central |
| _O | Cocaine<br>Heroin<br>Marijuana | Southeast<br>Southwest |
| FM | Cocaine<br>Heroin<br>Marijuana<br>Methamphetamine | Southeast<br>Southwest |
| juana rtel | Cocaine<br>Heroin<br>Marijuana<br>Methamphetamine | Great Lakes<br>Pacific<br>Southwest |

LO = Beltrán-Leyva Organization.
FM = La Familia Michoacana.

ɔURCE: "Table 1. Concentrated Activities by Mexican-Based TCOs in the ine OCDETF Regions," in *National Drug Threat Assessment, 2011*, U.S. epartment of Justice, National Drug Intelligence Center, August 2011, ttp://www.justice.gov/archive/ndic/pubs44/44849/44849p.pdf (accessed ebruary 16, 2013)

aint thinner), lye (a widely used chemical), and ephe-drine/pseudoephedrine (found in cold medicines). Anhy-lrous ammonia, which is used as a fertilizer, can be used o dry the drug and cut the production cycle by 10 hours. Vlaking methamphetamine creates a horrible odor, forc-ng producers into remote areas to avoid arousing the uspicion of those living downwind; explosions and fires re also common.

Ephedrine, a stimulant, appetite suppressant, and lecongestant, is the key ingredient for making metham-ɔhetamine. In 1989 the Chemical Diversion and Traffick-ng Act gave the U.S. Drug Enforcement Administration DEA) authority to regulate the bulk sales of ephedrine, ɔut over-the-counter (without a prescription) sales were ıot included. As a result, meth manufacturers simply

bought ephedrine-containing products at drugstores and then used it to manufacture methamphetamine.

The passage of the Domestic Chemical Diversion Control Act of 1993 made it illegal to sell ephedrine over the counter as well, but pseudoephedrine, a substitute, was not included in the ban. The Comprehensive Meth-amphetamine Control Act of 1996 made it illegal to knowingly possess ephedrine and pseudoephedrine (called precursor chemicals) and doubled the possible penalty for manufacturing and/or distributing metham-phetamine from 10 to 20 years. The Methamphetamine Trafficking Penalty Enhancement Act of 1998 further increased penalties for trafficking in methamphetamine. The Combat Methamphetamine Epidemic Act of 2005 placed restrictions on the amount of ephedrine, pseudo-ephedrine, and phenylpropanolamine (another precursor drug to methamphetamine) that can be sold to an individual in one day or over a 30-day period, required vendors to verify the identity of purchasers of these drugs, and required vendors to keep these products inac-cessible to customers without vendor help. Because of these restrictions on the purchase and sale of ephedrine and pseudoephedrine, the drug ephedra is often used as a substitute. Ephedra, also known as ma huang in tradi-tional Chinese medicine, contains both ephedrine and pseudoephedrine. In addition, drug traffickers circumvent the law on restrictive sales by having many individuals purchase the drugs up to the daily and monthly limit, a practice that is called "smurfing."

For a brief period after the precursors ephedrine and pseudoephedrine became difficult to get in large quanti-ties in the United States due to restrictive laws, the number of methamphetamine laboratory seizures fell dra-matically throughout the country. In 2005 law enforce-ment officials seized 6,019 meth labs nationwide; by 2007 this total fell by nearly half, to 3,101. (See Table 8.7.) During this period, methamphetamine and its precursors flowed into the United States from other countries, primarily Mexico. By 2008, however, the num-ber of meth lab seizures once again began to climb rapidly, reaching 6,768 labs seized in 2010. According to the NDIC, in *National Drug Threat Assessment, 2011*, of the labs seized, the large majority (5,738, or 84.8%) had a production capacity of only 2 ounces (56.7 g) or fewer of methamphetamine per batch. The assessment also states that seizures of methamphetamine labs in Mexico increased dramatically, from 51 labs in 2008 to 221 labs in 2009. Increasing seizures of labs in both countries indicates that production of methamphetamine was on the rise.

### Methamphetamine Prices, Purities, and Supply

The prices and purity of illicit drugs play an impor-tant role in understanding and analyzing drug markets.

**FIGURE 8.2**

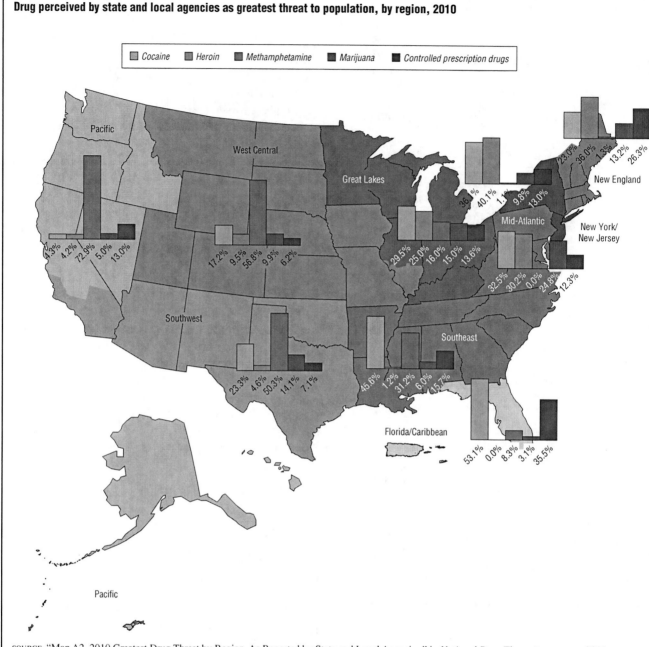

**Drug perceived by state and local agencies as greatest threat to population, by region, 2010**

☐ Cocaine   ☐ Heroin   ☐ Methamphetamine   ☐ Marijuana   ☐ Controlled prescription drugs

SOURCE: "Map A2. 2010 Greatest Drug Threat by Region, As Reported by State and Local Agencies," in *National Drug Threat Assessment, 2011*, U.S. Department of Justice, National Drug Intelligence Center, August 2011, http://www.justice.gov/archive/ndic/pubs44/44849/44849p.pdf (accessed February 16, 2013)

The purity of a drug refers to the extent to which it is diluted (mixed) with other substances. Determining the prices and purities of illicit drugs accurately is challenging because illicit drugs are not sold in standard quantities and are generally sold at varying purities. In addition, data can be collected only from seizures and purchases by undercover agents. Thus, the data gleaned from the samples collected must be used to estimate these factors for the total drug supply for that year.

Figure 8.4 shows the average price and purity of methamphetamine between January 2007 and September 2010. Drug prices fluctuate with supply and demand. As with other products, when supply outpaces demand, the price drops. Conversely, when the demand outpaces supply, the price rises. In addition, the purity of drugs may drop if demand outpaces supply; it is a way for drug traffickers to stretch the drug resources they have.

The price per gram of methamphetamine rose in 2007, then declined steadily between 2008 and 2010 as production increased in both Mexico and the United States. (See Figure 8.4.) The highest price was $286.36 per gram in late 2007, which was nearly three times the

FIGURE 8.3

**Drug availability by region, as reported by state and local agencies, 2010**

SOURCE: "Map A5. Drug Availability by Region—Percentage of State and Local Agencies Reporting High Availability," in *National Drug Threat Assessment, 2011*, U.S. Department of Justice, National Drug Intelligence Center, August 2011, http://www.justice.gov/archive/ndic/pubs44/44849/44849p .pdf (accessed February 16, 2013)

price per gram in 2010 of $105.49. In addition, the purity of methamphetamine more than doubled during this same span, from 40.4% pure in 2007 to 82.7% pure in September 2010.

**Distribution of Methamphetamine**

In *National Drug Threat Assessment, 2011*, the NDIC explains that as of 2011 Mexican drug trafficking organizations (DTOs) controlled most of the wholesale

distribution of both the powder and ice forms of methamphetamine in the United States, and were the greatest organized crime threat to the country. Mexican DTOs exist throughout the United States. These groups, which were often Mexican criminal groups as well, supplied midlevel distributors in at least 230 U.S. cities. Table 8.5 shows that more than half of all the methamphetamine that was smuggled into the United States entered along the southwest border.

TABLE 8.7

**Methamphetamine laboratory seizures, by region, 2005–10**

|  | 2005 | 2006 | 2007 | 2008 | 2009 | 2010 |
|---|---|---|---|---|---|---|
| Florida/Caribbean | 200 | 104 | 108 | 97 | 257 | 24? |
| Great Lakes | 1,343 | 951 | 800 | 1,012 | 1,796 | 2,01? |
| Mid-Atlantic | 182 | 108 | 55 | 66 | 82 | 13? |
| New England | 17 | 10 | 6 | 2 | 9 | 1? |
| New York/New Jersey | 22 | 35 | 12 | 15 | 12 | 2? |
| Pacific | 582 | 259 | 168 | 127 | 124 | 11? |
| Southeast | 1,705 | 1,362 | 1,061 | 1,545 | 2,030 | 2,52? |
| Southwest | 529 | 366 | 202 | 295 | 575 | 43? |
| West Central | 1,439 | 788 | 689 | 811 | 1,147 | 1,25? |
| **Grand total** | **6,019** | **3,983** | **3,101** | **3,970** | **6,032** | **6,76?** |

Note: Data as of July 7, 2011.

SOURCE: "Table 6. Reported Methamphetamine Laboratory Seizures by OCDETF Region, 2005–2010," in *National Drug Threat Assessment, 2011*, U.S. Department of Justice, National Drug Intelligence Center, August 2011, http://www.justice.gov/archive/ndic/pubs44/44849/44849p.pdf (accessed February 16, 2013)

---

**FIGURE 8.4**

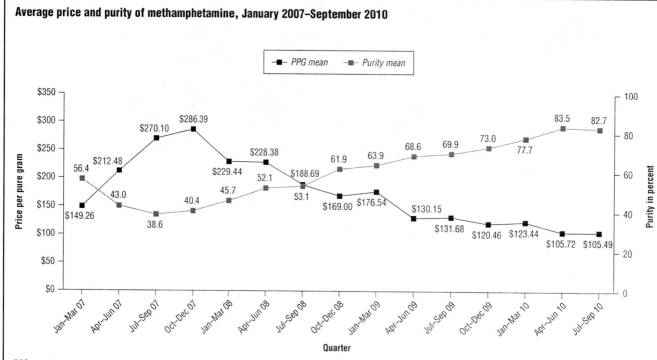

**Average price and purity of methamphetamine, January 2007–September 2010**

PPG = price per pure gram.
Note: From July 2007 through September 2010, the price per pure gram of methamphetamine decreased 60.9%, from $270.10 to $105.49, while the purity increased 114.1%, from 39% to 83%.

SOURCE: "Figure 11. Methamphetamine Price and Purity Data," in *National Drug Threat Assessment, 2011*, U.S. Department of Justice, National Drug Intelligence Center, August 2011, http://www.justice.gov/archive/ndic/pubs44/44849/44849p.pdf (accessed February 16, 2013)

---

# COCAINE

## Production and Distribution

The coca plant, from which cocaine is produced, is grown primarily in the Andean region of Colombia, Peru, and Bolivia, with Colombia being the largest producer. The first step in the production of cocaine is to mix the coca leaves with sulfuric acid in a plastic-lined hole in the ground. The leaves are then pounded to create an acidic juice. When this juice is filtered and neutralized, it forms a paste. The paste is purified into cocaine base by the addition of more chemicals and filtering. This cocaine base includes coca paste, freebase cocaine, and crack cocaine. It is typically transported from the jungles where it was produced to southern Colombia, where it is processed into cocaine hydrochloride (white powder) at clandestine drug laboratories. Small, independent Bolivian and Peruvian trafficking groups also process some cocaine. It takes 660 to 1,100 pounds (300 to 500 kg) of coca leaf to make 2.2 pounds (1 kg) of cocaine.

After processing, cocaine is shipped to the United States and Europe. Mexico and other Caribbean and Central American countries serve as transit countries for the shipment of drugs into the United States. Drug traffickers shift routes according to law enforcement and interdiction pressures but, as with most drugs, cocaine is primarily smuggled into the United States across the southwest border. The NDIC also indicates that substantial amounts enter the country at New York City and Miami via maritime and commercial air smuggling.

## Cocaine Prices, Purities, and Supply

According to the NDIC, in *National Drug Threat Assessment, 2011*, the availability of cocaine in the United States decreased between FYs 2007 and 2010. The NDIC cites a number of reasons for the decline, including fighting between drug cartels, successful interdiction efforts, increased smuggling to other markets instead of the United States, and decreased cocaine production in Colombia.

Figure 8.5 shows the average price and purity of cocaine between January 2007 and September 2010. The average price per gram of cocaine increased by 68.8% ($97.71 to $164.91) during that period. Similarly, the average purity decreased by 30% (67.2% pure to 47% pure) over the same period. A rise in the price of a drug

with a concurrent drop in purity is evidence of its decreased availability.

## MARIJUANA
### Production, Availability, and Distribution

Marijuana is made from the flowering tops and leaves of the cannabis plant; these are collected, trimmed, dried, and then most often smoked in a pipe or as a cigarette. Many users smoke "blunts," named after the inexpensive blunt cigars from which they are made. Blunt cigars are approximately 5 inches (12.7 cm) long and can be purchased at any store that sells tobacco products. A marijuana blunt is made from the emptied cigar casing, which is then stuffed with marijuana or a marijuana-tobacco mixture. A blunt may contain as much marijuana as six regular marijuana cigarettes. In some cases blunt users add crack cocaine or PCP to the mixture to make it more potent.

According to the NDIC, in *National Drug Threat Assessment, 2011*, marijuana was widely available in the United States in 2010. Estimated marijuana production in Mexico, a major source of marijuana in the United States, more than doubled between 2005 and 2008, from 11,100 tons (10,100 metric tons [t]) to 23,700 tons (21,500 t). At around this time, marijuana seizures at the Mexican border increased, from 2.6 million pounds

**FIGURE 8.5**

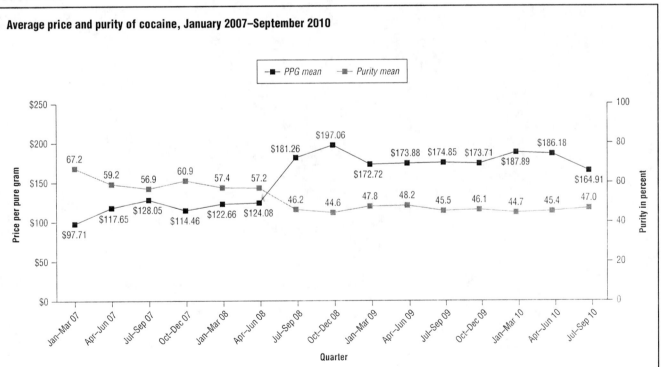

**Average price and purity of cocaine, January 2007–September 2010**

PPG = price per pure gram.
Note: From January 2007 through September 2010, the price per pure gram of cocaine increased 68.8%, from $97.71 to $164.91, while the purity decreased 30%, from 67% to 47%.

SOURCE: "Figure 7. Cocaine Price and Purity Data," in *National Drug Threat Assessment, 2011*, U.S. Department of Justice, National Drug Intelligence Center, August 2011, http://www.justice.gov/archive/ndic/pubs44/44849/44849p.pdf (accessed February 16, 2013)

(1.2 million kg) in 2008 to 3.7 million pounds (1.7 million kg) in 2009, before dropping again to 3.3 million pounds (1.5 million kg) in 2010.

Mexican drug traffickers and others also cultivate marijuana in the United States to avoid border seizure of the drug and transportation costs. One favored type of location for growing marijuana is public land that is out of the way. The NDIC reports that in 2010 over 4.5 million cannabis plants were eradicated from federal lands, 44% of all plants eradicated that year. Some growers cultivate the plant indoors to avoid detection and to benefit from year-round, easily controlled growing conditions. Growers may cultivate a dozen or so plants in a closet or operate elaborate, specially constructed (sometimes underground) greenhouses where thousands of plants grow under intense electric lighting or in sunlight. Indoor cultivators often use hydroponics, in which the plants are grown in nutrient solution rather than in soil.

Nondomestically grown marijuana arrives in the continental United States via the southwest border with Mexico and the northern border with Canada. (See Table 8.5.) The movement of marijuana across the United States between FYs 2008 and 2010 is charted in Figure 8.6. The NDIC states that in 2011 Mexican DTOs controlled most of the wholesale distribution of marijuana throughout the United States, and predicted they would continue to do so for many years. In addition, the NDIC reports that ethnically Asian Canadian-based criminal organizations were involved in smuggling marijuana into the United States across the northern border

**FIGURE 8.6**

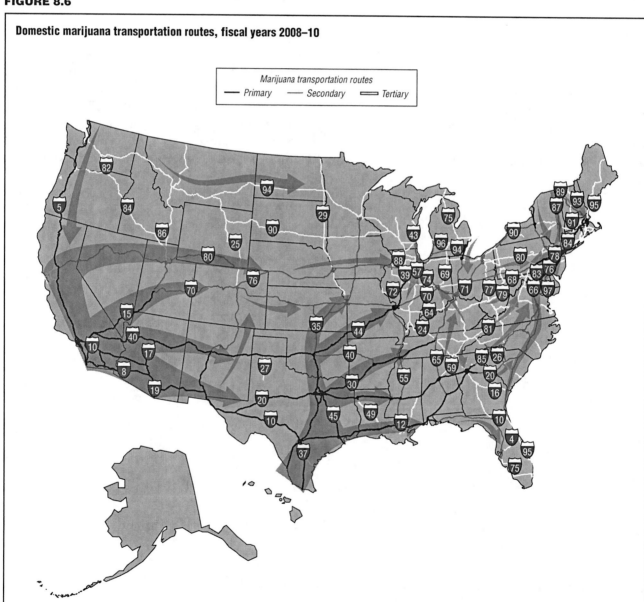

Domestic marijuana transportation routes, fiscal years 2008–10

SOURCE: "Figure 4. Internal Marijuana Movement, FY2008–FY2010," in *National Drug Threat Assessment, 2011*, U.S. Department of Justice, National Drug Intelligence Center, August 2011, http://www.justice.gov/archive/ndic/pubs44/44849/44849p.pdf (accessed February 16, 2013)

TABLE 8.8

## Marijuana potency, 1985–2010

[Percent Delta-9 THC concentrations and number of samples tested]

| | Non-domestic samples (federal seizures) | | | | | | Domestic samples (state and local eradication) | | | | | |
|---|---|---|---|---|---|---|---|---|---|---|---|---|
| | Type of cannabis | | | | | | Type of cannabis | | | | | |
| | Marijuana | | Sinsemilla | | All types[a] | | Marijuana | | Sinsemilla | | All types[a] | |
| Year | Potency[b] | Number[c] | Potency[b] | Number[c] | Potency[b] | Number[c] | Potency[b] | Number[c] | Potency[b] | Number[c] | Potency[b] | Number[c] |
| 1985 | 3.44% | 745 | 7.95% | 12 | 3.48% | 767 | 2.19% | 703 | 7.07% | 40 | 2.22% | 845 |
| 1986 | 2.75% | 711 | 8.78% | 14 | 2.80% | 753 | 1.95% | 661 | 8.16% | 18 | 1.84% | 803 |
| 1987 | 3.16% | 1,110 | 8.29% | 17 | 3.20% | 1,147 | 2.46% | 441 | 7.69% | 26 | 2.38% | 553 |
| 1988 | 3.62% | 1,127 | 8.30% | 29 | 3.70% | 1,171 | 2.20% | 513 | 7.33% | 69 | 2.56% | 651 |
| 1989 | 3.68% | 725 | 7.13% | 29 | 3.78% | 761 | 1.71% | 350 | 6.86% | 57 | 2.00% | 511 |
| 1990 | 3.78% | 756 | 9.59% | 16 | 3.82% | 788 | 2.09% | 352 | 10.29% | 45 | 2.58% | 475 |
| 1991 | 3.18% | 1,498 | 11.20% | 29 | 3.26% | 1,564 | 2.90% | 651 | 10.10% | 46 | 2.57% | 943 |
| 1992 | 3.09% | 2,461 | 9.67% | 33 | 3.16% | 2,515 | 3.05% | 875 | 7.72% | 43 | 2.96% | 1,025 |
| 1993 | 3.67% | 1,994 | 4.64% | 5 | 3.65% | 2,010 | 2.83% | 1,039 | 5.82% | 118 | 2.75% | 1,346 |
| 1994 | 3.76% | 2,052 | 6.92% | 10 | 3.75% | 2,074 | 2.95% | 980 | 7.55% | 94 | 3.02% | 1,210 |
| 1995 | 3.95% | 3,730 | 9.64% | 17 | 4.00% | 3,793 | 2.55% | 701 | 7.26% | 147 | 2.92% | 999 |
| 1996 | 4.41% | 1,377 | 11.30% | 22 | 4.54% | 1,422 | 2.90% | 767 | 8.94% | 146 | 3.48% | 1,029 |
| 1997 | 4.93% | 1,313 | 12.02% | 18 | 5.16% | 1,377 | 3.34% | 954 | 11.50% | 104 | 3.99% | 1,119 |
| 1998 | 4.73% | 1,298 | 11.88% | 37 | 4.96% | 1,361 | 3.36% | 778 | 12.58% | 64 | 3.75% | 922 |
| 1999 | 4.36% | 1,749 | 13.49% | 55 | 4.67% | 1,859 | 3.76% | 691 | 13.31% | 81 | 4.43% | 833 |
| 2000 | 5.10% | 1,861 | 12.87% | 62 | 5.40% | 1,963 | 3.96% | 1,057 | 12.72% | 51 | 4.10% | 1,185 |
| 2001 | 5.77% | 1,587 | 12.05% | 95 | 6.18% | 1,707 | 3.58% | 805 | 7.86% | 140 | 3.97% | 1,009 |
| 2002 | 5.66% | 1,380 | 14.41% | 302 | 7.26% | 1,710 | 3.27% | 409 | 7.29% | 226 | 4.29% | 703 |
| 2003 | 5.62% | 1,516 | 14.00% | 347 | 7.18% | 1,892 | 2.38% | 377 | 7.21% | 191 | 3.67% | 625 |
| 2004 | 6.17% | 1,418 | 14.06% | 485 | 8.33% | 1,943 | 2.55% | 395 | 7.67% | 246 | 4.20% | 694 |
| 2005 | 5.92% | 1,608 | 13.04% | 681 | 8.09% | 2,348 | 2.25% | 354 | 7.78% | 250 | 4.21% | 656 |
| 2006 | 6.49% | 1,409 | 13.59% | 668 | 9.08% | 2,116 | 1.99% | 362 | 6.81% | 364 | 4.15% | 775 |
| 2007 | 7.19% | 1,303 | 13.40% | 833 | 10.27% | 2,231 | 1.92% | 340 | 7.21% | 503 | 4.86% | 883 |
| 2008 | 7.16% | 1,054 | 13.08% | 942 | 10.25% | 2,074 | 1.82% | 302 | 7.53% | 370 | 4.84% | 701 |
| 2009 | 7.15% | 1,024 | 12.36% | 1,042 | 9.91% | 2,117 | 2.43% | 435 | 7.37% | 490 | 4.89% | 962 |
| 2010 | 6.71% | 885 | 12.92% | 1,337 | 10.98% | 2,315 | 2.79% | 290 | 11.84% | 97 | 4.89% | 405 |

THC = Tetrahydrocannabinol.

[a]The category "All types" of cannabis tested includes ditchweed and a small number of Thai sticks.

[b]These percentages, indicating potency, are based on simple arithmetic means calculated by dividing the sum of the delta-9THC concentrations of each sample by the number of seizures and are not normalized by weight of seizure.

[c]Number of tested samples that yield the potency in prior column.

SOURCE: "Table 66. Potency of Tested Cannabis from Federal Seizure and State and Local Eradication Samples, by Type, 1985–2010 (Percent Delta-9 THC Concentrations and Number of Samples Tested)," in *National Drug Control Strategy: Data Supplement 2012*, Executive Office of the President, Office of National Drug Policy, 2012, http://www.whitehouse.gov/sites/default/files/page/files/2012_data_supplement_final.pdf (accessed February 16, 2013). Data from University of Mississippi, National Center for Natural Products Research, Research Institute of Pharmaceutical Sciences, *Quarterly Report*, no. 116, March 26, 2012, and *Quarterly Report*, no. 107, January 12, 2010.

with Canada, and had been implicated in an increasing number of domestic marijuana production operations.

## THC Content and Price

The active ingredient in marijuana is THC (delta-9-tetrahydrocannabinol), which is mostly concentrated in the flowering tops (colas or buds) of the cannabis plant. The flowering tops of female plants that have not yet been pollinated and, therefore, have not yet produced seeds, have the highest THC content. This plant part is called sinsemilla (literally, "without seed"). In contrast, feral hemp, commonly called ditchweed, contains a low THC content and is generally not a product drug users want.

The ONDCP notes in *National Drug Control Strategy: Data Supplement 2012* (2012, http://www.whitehouse.gov/sites/default/files/page/files/2012_data_supplement_final.pdf) that between 1985 and 1995 the THC content of marijuana in federal seizure samples averaged less than

4% and that in state and local eradication samples THC was less than 3%. (See Table 8.8.) The potency found in federal seizure samples increased dramatically as the years went on; by 2007 the THC content in these samples reached a peak of 7.2%, before gradually dropping to 6.7% by 2010. The THC content in state and local eradication samples increased to just under 4% in 2000; it then began to decrease. In 2008 the THC content in these samples dropped to 1.8%, before rising again to reach 2.8% by 2010.

In 1996 the THC content for sinsemilla in federal seizure samples was 11.3%; by 2002 it peaked at 14.4%. (See Table 8.8.) By 2010 the THC content had dropped to 12.9%, but this level was still considered high. In 2010 the THC content of state and local eradication samples of sinsemilla was 11.8%.

The average price of marijuana at the retail level rose from $9.53 per gram in 1981 to $27.78 per gram in 1991.

## TABLE 8.9

**Average price of marijuana, 1981–2011**

[In 2011 dollars]

| Year | Purchases of 10 grams or less[a] Price per gram ($) | Purchases greater than 10 but less than 100 grams[b] Price per gram ($) |
|---|---|---|
| 1981 | 9.53 | 4.45 |
| 1982 | 10.19 | 5.72 |
| 1983 | 12.69 | 10.57 |
| 1984 | 12.98 | 5.49 |
| 1985 | 12.20 | 7.15 |
| 1986 | 26.31 | 12.02 |
| 1987 | 23.37 | 8.63 |
| 1988 | 22.83 | 9.48 |
| 1989 | 24.21 | 9.77 |
| 1990 | 24.65 | 11.98 |
| 1991 | 27.78 | 11.15 |
| 1992 | 25.26 | 9.17 |
| 1993 | 23.80 | 13.88 |
| 1994 | 19.99 | 12.84 |
| 1995 | 15.41 | 7.32 |
| 1996 | 14.10 | 7.96 |
| 1997 | 12.96 | 6.04 |
| 1998 | 12.35 | 7.54 |
| 1999 | 13.83 | 10.42 |
| 2000 | 12.95 | 6.62 |
| 2001 | 14.19 | 7.15 |
| 2002 | 16.84 | 12.17 |
| 2003 | 18.04 | 10.14 |
| 2004 | 16.29 | 7.84 |
| 2005 | 16.18 | 9.50 |
| 2006 | 16.19 | 10.80 |
| 2007 | 16.51 | 10.09 |
| 2008 | 16.71 | 6.79 |
| 2009 | 14.67 | 11.55 |
| 2010 | 16.95 | 9.77 |
| 2011 | 14.26 | 11.36 |

[a]Quantities purchased at the "retail" level.
[b]Quantities purchased at the "dealer" level.

SOURCE: "Table 65. Average Price of Marijuana in the United States, 1981–2011 (2011 Dollars)," in *National Drug Control Strategy: Data Supplement 2012*, Executive Office of the President, Office of National Drug Policy, 2012, http://www.whitehouse.gov/sites/default/files/page/files/2012_data_supplement_final.pdf (accessed February 16, 2013). Data from Institute for Defense Analyses, *The Price and Purity of Illicit Drugs: 1981–2007*, October 2008, and unpublished data, April 2012.

(See Table 8.9.) The price then fell to $12.35 per gram in 1998, rose to $18.04 per gram in 2003, and then stabilized at about $16.20 per gram for several years. The average price of marijuana at the retail level in 2011 was $14.26 per gram.

## HEROIN

Heroin users represent the smallest group using a major drug. According to SAMHSA, in *Results from the 2011 National Survey on Drug Use and Health: Summary of National Findings*, there were 300,000 current heroin users in the United States in 2011. (See Figure 4.2 in Chapter 4.)

### Heroin Production and Distribution

**PRODUCTION PROCESS.** The source of heroin is the opium poppy. After the leaves of the poppy fall off, only the round poppy pods remain. Heroin production begins by scoring the poppy pod with a knife. A gummy substance begins to ooze out. This opium gum is scraped off and collected. The rest of the process is explained by the Central Intelligence Agency (CIA) in "From Flowers to Heroin" (April 23, 2009, http://www.erowid.org/plants/poppy/poppy_article2.shtml):

> Once the opium gum is transported to a refinery, it is converted into morphine, an intermediate product. This conversion is achieved primarily by chemical processes and requires several basic elements and implements. Boiling water is used to dissolve opium gum; 55-gallon drums are used for boiling vessels; and burlap sacks are used to filter and strain liquids. When dried, the morphine resulting from this initial process is pressed into bricks. The conversion of morphine bricks into heroin is also primarily a chemical process. The main chemical used is acetic anhydride, along with sodium carbonate, activated charcoal, chloroform, ethyl alcohol, ether, and acetone. The two most commonly produced heroin varieties are No. 3 heroin, or smoking heroin, and No. 4 heroin, or injectable heroin.

The CIA explains that this generic process produces heroin that may be 90% pure. Variations in the process are introduced as the heroin is diluted to increase its bulk and profits. The pure heroin is mixed with various substances including caffeine, baking soda, powdered milk, and quinine.

**OVERVIEW OF THE TRADE.** Opium poppies are intensely cultivated in four regions of the world: Southeast Asia, Southwest Asia, Mexico, and South America. The INL reports in *International Narcotics Control Strategy Report: Volume I, Drug and Chemical Control* that in 2011 Afghanistan accounted for approximately 90% of the world's illicit opium, harvesting 324,000 acres (131,000 ha) of opium poppies to produce 6,400 tons (5,800 t) of raw opium.

Mexico produces a variety of heroin called black tar because it looks like roofing tar. It was once considered inferior to Colombian and Asian heroin, but it has reached a level of purity high enough that it can be snorted or smoked. Mexican heroin is targeted almost exclusively to the U.S. market. The long U.S.-Mexican land border provides many opportunities for drug smugglers to cross. Female couriers are used more frequently than male couriers. Mexican heroin is smuggled in cars, trucks, and buses and may also be hidden on or in the body of the smuggler. Many smugglers send their drugs by overnight-package express services.

The bulk of heroin from South America comes from Colombia. Many Colombian coca traffickers have been requiring their dealers to accept a small amount of heroin along with their normal deliveries of coca. This has allowed the Colombian producers to use an existing network to introduce a pure grade of heroin into the U.S. market. Much of Colombian heroin production is sent through Central America and Mexico by smugglers raveling on commercial airline flights into the United States. These smugglers hide the drugs in false-sided luggage, clothing, hollowed-out shoe soles, or inside their bodies. The Colombian-based heroin traffickers have established distribution outlets throughout the eastern half of the United States. However, according to the NDIC, in *National Drug Threat Assessment, 2011*, by 2009 the volume of South American heroin smuggled into the United States had begun to decline, due to decreased cultivation of opium poppies in Colombia. Between 2004 and 2009 the volume of heroin seized from commercial aircraft—the predominant means of smuggling heroin from South America into the United States—fell from 2,004 pounds (909 kg) to 707 pounds (321 kg).

## Purity and Price

According to the NDIC, in *National Drug Threat Assessment, 2010* (February 2010, http://www.justice.gov/archive/ndic/pubs38/38661/38661p.pdf), the DEA's Heroin Signature Program (HSP) measured South American heroin to be 57% pure in 2008. The HSP found that Mexican heroin was 40% pure that same year. In terms of weight, 58% of the heroin tested by the HSP in 2008 originated from South America, compared with 39% that came from Mexico. This was the highest percentage of Mexican heroin measured since 1987.

Purity is important to heroin addicts because low-purity heroin must be injected to get the most out of the drug. Many people feel uncomfortable using needles and fear contracting the human immunodeficiency virus (HIV), which can be spread by sharing a needle with an infected user. Higher purity heroin can be smoked or snorted, which makes heroin more attractive to potential users who do not want to use needles. Despite these so-called advantages of higher purity heroin, an estimated three out of five heroin users continue to inject the drug no matter what its purity.

## PHARMACEUTICALS

The NDIC notes in *National Drug Threat Assessment, 2011* that abuse of controlled prescription drugs (CPDs) poses a "problem second only to the abuse of marijuana in scope and pervasiveness in the United States; the problem is particularly acute among adolescents." Between 2008 and 2009 the number of individuals aged 12 years and older who used CPDs for nonmedical purposes rose from 6.2 million to 7 million, an increase of 12%. The NDIC also notes that opioid pain relievers were the most widely abused CPDs in 2009. Although there has traditionally been little trafficking in CPDs by DTOs, law enforcement officials have noted a steady increase in organized distribution of prescription drugs by street gangs. The NDIC states that in 2010 more than half (51.2%) of the nation's state and local law enforcement agencies reported involvement of street gangs in trafficking of CPDs, up from 48% in 2009.

## CHAPTER 9

# ANTIDRUG EFFORTS AND THEIR CRITICISMS

The Harrison Narcotic Act of 1914, which outlawed opiates and cocaine, was the first legislation aimed at prohibiting the possession and use of mood-altering drugs. Following that act, laws were passed or amended at intervals, but the war on drugs did not begin in earnest until the early 1970s with the Comprehensive Drug Abuse Prevention and Control Act of 1970. The phrase "War on Drugs" was coined in 1971 during the administration of Richard M. Nixon (1913–1994). A national effort was launched after that to bring illicit drug use under control, and it is still very much under way in the 21st century.

Not everyone agrees with governmental efforts to control or prohibit the use of mood-altering substances. Prohibition of alcohol came to an end in 1933 because of massive public disobedience. (See Chapter 1.) Data from the 2011 National Survey on Drug Use and Health (NSDUH), which are published in *Results from the 2011 National Survey on Drug Use and Health: Summary of National Findings* (September 2012, http://www.samhsa .gov/data/NSDUH/2k11Results/NSDUHresults2011.pdf) by the Substance Abuse and Mental Health Services Administration (SAMHSA), suggest a similar public response to laws that prohibit the use of drugs. For example, SAMHSA (September 2012, http://www.samhsa .gov/data/NSDUH/2011SummNatFindDetTables/NSDUH-DetTabsPDFWHTML2011/2k11DetailedTabs/Web/PDFW/ NSDUH-DetTabsCover2011.pdf) notes that in 2011, 47% of people aged 12 years and older (121.1 million people) had used an illicit drug at some point during their life. Just fewer than 15% (38.3 million) had done so in the past 12 months, and 8.7% (22.5 million) had used an illicit drug during the past 30 days. According to SAMHSA (February 5, 2009, http://www.oas.samhsa.gov/nhsda/PE1996/artab 007.htm#E8E11), the percentage of lifetime users increased during the preceding three decades; in 1979, 31.3% of people aged 12 years and older reported using an illicit drug at some point during their life.

One criticism leveled at governmental efforts to control or prohibit the use of mood-altering substances is that they appear to be inconsistent with the public health issues they raise. Tobacco and alcohol cause many deaths per year, yet both are legal substances. In the fact sheet "Health Effects of Cigarette Smoking" (January 10, 2012, http://www.cdc.gov/tobacco/data_statistics/fact _sheets/health_effects/effects_cig_smoking/), the Centers for Disease Control and Prevention (CDC) estimates that 443,000 premature deaths occur each year as a result of smoking and exposure to secondhand smoke. Donna L. Hoyert and Jiaquan Xu report in "Deaths: Preliminary Data for 2011" (*National Vital Statistics Reports*, vol. 61, no. 6, October 10, 2012) that 26,256 people died of alcohol-related causes in 2011. The National Highway Traffic Safety Administration reports in "Traffic Safety Facts, 2011 Data: Alcohol-Impaired Driving" (December 2012, http://www-nrd.nhtsa.dot.gov/Pubs/811700.pdf) that in 2011, 9,878 people died from car crashes that were alcohol related. In comparison, drug abuse produced 39,147 deaths in 2009, according to the Office of National Drug Control Policy in *National Drug Control Strategy: Data Supplement 2012* (2012, http://www.whitehouse .gov/sites/default/files/page/files/2012_data_supplement _final.pdf). SAMHSA shows in *Drug Abuse Warning Network, 2010: Area Profiles of Drug-Related Mortality* (May 2012, http://www.samhsa.gov/data/2k12/DAWN MEAnnualReport2010/DAWN-ME-AnnualReport-2010 .pdf) that marijuana, which is preponderantly the drug used by most of those classified as illicit drug users, causes few fatalities and virtually none by itself.

## NATIONAL DRUG CONTROL STRATEGY

The Anti-drug Abuse Act of 1988 established the creation of a drug-free nation as a U.S. policy goal. As part of this initiative, Congress created the Office of National Drug Control Policy (ONDCP; http://www.white house.gov/open/around/eop/ondcp) "to establish policies, priorities, and objectives for the Nation's drug control program. The goals of the program are to reduce illicit drug use, manufacturing, and trafficking, drug-related crime and violence, and drug-related health consequences." The ONDCP director develops the National Drug Control Strategy annually, which describes the nation's antidrug program and puts forth the proposed budget of the ONDCP.

The first National Drug Control Strategy was prepared by William J. Bennett (1943–), the first ONDCP director, and submitted to Congress by President George H. W. Bush (1924–) in 1989. Reduction of demand was a priority and has remained such over the years. The strategy also called for directing efforts at countries where cocaine originated, improving the targeting of interdiction (the interception of smuggled drugs), increasing the capacity of treatment providers, accelerating the efforts aimed at drug prevention, and focusing on the education of youth. In its details, the drug strategy laid emphasis on law enforcement activities and the expansion of the criminal justice system.

Since that time the basic building blocks of the National Drug Control Strategy have remained the same, but the specific emphases have changed. Some presidents lean more toward enforcement, others more toward fighting drug traffickers, and yet others more toward treatment and prevention. Whatever the model, all strategies to date have had the same components: prevention and treatment (together constituting demand reduction); and law enforcement, interdiction, and international efforts (together constituting supply disruption). The emphasis given to each of these components has been reflected in federal budgets.

In January 2009 President Barack Obama (1961–) appointed Edward H. Jurith (1955–), the former general counsel of the ONDCP, as the office's acting director. As early as the spring of 2009, only a few months into his presidency, President Obama had given indications of the direction his administration would take in the War on Drugs, including nominating a "drug czar" who favored treatment over incarceration and developing a major initiative to curtail violent drug trafficking on the U.S.–Mexican border. (See Chapter 1.) In May 2009 Gil Kerlikowske (1949–) was sworn in as director of the ONDCP and shortly thereafter the phrase "War on Drugs" was dropped.

As the ONDCP states in "Policy and Research" (2013, http://www.whitehouse.gov/ondcp/policy-and-research), the Obama administration's inaugural National Drug Control Strategy report, published in April 2010, was founded on a commitment "to using science and research to inform policy decisions." Central to this new policy was the recognition that drug addiction is a disease, one that demands an emphasis on prevention, treatment, and

recovery programs. In *Epidemic: Responding to America's Prescription Drug Abuse Crisis* (2011, http://www.whitehouse.gov/sites/default/files/ondcp/policy-and-research/rx_abuse_plan.pdf), the ONDCP outlines a four-point "Action Plan" aimed at stemming prescription drug abuse, which includes a strategy for monitoring the distribution of prescription drugs on the state level, as well as programs to promote the safe disposal of unused medication. The *National Southwest Border Counternarcotics Strategy* (2011, http://www.whitehouse.gov/sites/default/files/ondcp/policy-and-research/swb_counternarcotics_strategy11.pdf) provides a detailed overview of the ONDCP's strategy for combating illegal drug trafficking along the nation's border with Mexico, which includes an emphasis on both bolstering border security and interdiction efforts, and on promoting drug treatment and prevention programs within border communities.

## THE FEDERAL DRUG BUDGET

The national drug control budget is shown in Table 9.1. The data span fiscal year (FY) 2005 to the budget request for FY 2013. The federal fiscal year begins October 1 and ends September 30, so that FY 2013 dollars, for example, include funding for the last quarter of 2012 and the first three quarters of 2013. The total drug control budget has grown from $20.4 billion in FY 2005 to $25.6 billion in FY 2013, an increase of 25.6%. The budgets for FYs 2005 through 2009 were determined during the administration of President George W. Bush (1946–). The budgets for FYs 2010 through 2013 were determined during the Obama administration. The 25% increase in the budget took place primarily during the Bush years; the budgets during the Obama administration show a slight drop in FY 2011 and FY 2012, and then a slight rise in FY 2013.

The budget is divided into two broad components: reducing the demand for drugs and disrupting their supply. Reducing the demand for drugs supports research and programs that help communities work toward a drug-free environment and encourage young people to reject drug use. In Table 9.1 the funding categories related to reducing demand are "drug abuse treatment" and "drug abuse prevention." Funding to disrupt the supply of drugs supports efforts to keep individuals and organizations from profiting from trafficking in illicit drugs, both domestically and internationally. In Table 9.1 these funding categories are "domestic law enforcement," "interdiction," and "international." Significant portions of the international budget are spent on supporting international eradication efforts that, in turn, depend on the cooperation of other countries and on the U.S. drug certification program, which may temporarily deny funding to certain regimes.

Table 9.2 shows the overall supply and demand proportions from FY 2011 to FY 2013. A little more than 40% of drug control spending in 2013 was allocated to

TABLE 9.1

**Distribution of federal drug control spending, by function, fiscal years 2005–13**

[Budget authority in millions]

| Functions | Fiscal year 2005 Final | Fiscal year 2006 Final | Fiscal year 2007 Final | Fiscal year 2008 Final | Fiscal year 2009 Final | Fiscal year 2010 Final | Fiscal year 2011 Final | Fiscal year 2012 Enacted | Fiscal year 2013 Request |
|---|---|---|---|---|---|---|---|---|---|
| **Demand reduction** | | | | | | | | | |
| Drug abuse treatment | 6,761.8 | 6,811.0 | 7,135.0 | 7,422.9 | 8,426.9 | 8,937.2 | 8,953.90 | 8,747.5 | 9,150.5 |
| Drug abuse prevention | 2,040.0 | 1,964.5 | 1,934.2 | 1,841.0 | 1,954.0 | 1,566.4 | 1,478.10 | 1,400.5 | 1,387.6 |
| **Total demand reduction** | 8,801.9 | 8,775.5 | 9,069.2 | 9,263.9 | 10,380.9 | 10,503.6 | 10,431.98 | 10,148.0 | 10,538.2 |
| Percentage | 43.2% | 41.5% | 40.8% | 41.2% | 40.5% | 40.5% | 40.80% | 40.3% | 41.8% |
| **Supply reduction** | | | | | | | | | |
| Domestic law enforcement | 7,266.1 | 7,525.2 | 7,921.2 | 8,268.9 | 8,994.0 | 9,155.5 | 9,143.0 | 9,357.5 | 9,418.9 |
| Interdiction | 2,433.6 | 2,924.1 | 3,045.9 | 2,968.7 | 3,699.2 | 3,662.4 | 3,977.1 | 3,591.6 | 3,680.9 |
| International | 1,873.7 | 1,895.8 | 2,191.4 | 1,998.5 | 2,532.6 | 2,595.0 | 2,027.6 | 2,087.6 | 1,962.0 |
| **Total supply reduction** | 11,573.4 | 12,357.2 | 13,158.5 | 13,236.1 | 15,225.9 | 15,412.9 | 15,147.7 | 15,036.6 | 15,061.8 |
| Percentage | 56.8% | 58.5% | 59.2% | 58.8% | 59.5% | 59.5% | 59.2% | 59.7% | 58.8% |
| **Total** | 20,375.2 | 21,1207.7 | 22,227.7 | 22,500.0 | 25,606.8 | 25,916.5 | 25,579.7 | 25,184.6 | 25,599.9 |

SOURCE: "Table 3. Historical Drug Control Funding by Function, FY 2004–FY 2013," in *FY 2013 Budget and Performance Summary: Companion to the National Drug Control Strategy*, Executive Office of the President, Office of National Drug Control Policy, April 2012, http://www.whitehouse.gov/sites/default/files/ondcp/fy2013_drug_control_budget_and_performance_summary.pdf (accessed February 16, 2013)

TABLE 9.2

**Federal drug control spending, by function, fiscal years 2011–13**

[Budget authority in millions]

| Function | FY 2011 Final | FY 2012 Enacted | FY 2013 Request | FY12–FY13 change Dollars | FY12–FY13 change Percent |
|---|---|---|---|---|---|
| Treatment | 8,953.9 | 8,747.5 | 9,150.5 | +403.0 | +4.6% |
| Percent | 35.0% | 34.2% | 36.3% | | |
| Prevention | 1,478.1 | 1,400.5 | 1,387.6 | −12.9 | −0.9% |
| Percent | 5.8% | 5.5% | 5.5% | | |
| Domestic law enforcement | 9,143.0 | 9,357.5 | 9,418.9 | +61.4 | +0.7% |
| Percent | 35.7% | 36.6% | 37.4% | | |
| Interdiction | 3,977.1 | 3,591.6 | 3,680.9 | +89.3 | +2.5% |
| Percent | 15.5% | 14.0% | 14.6% | | |
| International | 2,027.6 | 2,087.6 | 1,962.0 | −125.6 | −6.0% |
| Percent | 7.9% | 8.2% | 7.8% | | |
| **Total** | $25,579.7 | $25,184.7 | $25,599.9 | +$415.3 | +1.6% |
| **Supply/demand split** | | | | | |
| Demand reduction | 10,431.9 | 10,148.0 | 10,538.2 | +390.2 | +3.8% |
| Percent | 40.8% | 40.3% | 41.2% | | |
| Supply reduction | 15,147.7 | 15,036.6 | 15,061.8 | +25.2 | +0.2% |
| Percent | 59.7% | 58.9% | 59.3% | | |
| **Total** | $25,579.7 | $25,184.7 | $25,599.9 | +$415.3 | +1.6% |

SOURCE: "Table 1. Federal Drug Control Spending by Function, FY 2011–FY 2013," in *FY 2013 Budget and Performance Summary: Companion to the National Drug Control Strategy*, Executive Office of the President, Office of National Drug Control Policy, April 2012, http://www.whitehouse.gov/sites/default/files/ondcp/fy2013_drug_control_budget_and_performance_summary.pdf (accessed February 16, 2013)

drug abuse treatment and prevention; a greater proportion (nearly 60%) was allocated to disrupting the drug supply.

Table 9.3 summarizes the drug control budget by agency. The agencies that work to reduce the demand for drugs include the ONDCP; the U.S. Departments of Education, Health and Human Services, Interior, Transportation, and Veterans Affairs; and the U.S. Small Business Administration. The agencies that work to disrupt the drug supply include the U.S. Departments of Defense, Homeland Security, Justice, State, and the Treasury.

Most domestic law enforcement funds are spent by the U.S. Department of Justice, or on its behalf, and underwrite the operations of the U.S. Drug Enforcement Administration (DEA), the chief domestic drug control agency. Interdiction funds are managed by the U.S. Department of Homeland Security, which oversees all

**TABLE 9.3**

## Distribution of federal drug control spending, by agency, fiscal years 2011–13

[Budget authority in millions]

| | Fiscal year 2011 Final | Fiscal year 2012 Enacted | Fiscal year 2013 Request |
|---|---|---|---|
| **Department of Agriculture** | | | |
| U.S. Forest Service | 15.3 | 15.3 | 14.7 |
| Court Services and Offender Supervision Agency for the District of Columbia | 52.8 | 53.1 | 52.4 |
| **Department of Defense** | | | |
| Drug Interdiction and Counterdrug Activities[a]/OPTEMPO[b] | 1,743.3 | 1,828.8 | 1,630.3 |
| Defense Health Program | 93.3 | 96.5 | 94.9 |
|     Total DoD | 1,836.5 | 1,925.3 | 1,725.2 |
| **Department of Education** | 123.9 | 64.9 | 108.3 |
| Federal Judiciary | 1,126.9 | 1,133.3 | 1,164.5 |
| **Department of Health and Human Services** | | | |
| Administration for Children and Families | 20.0 | 20.0 | 20.0 |
| Centers for Medicare & Medicaid Services[c] | 4,643.8 | 4,467.4 | 4,751.1 |
| Health Resources and Services Administration | 16.9 | 18.1 | 18.3 |
| Indian Health Service | 96.0 | 98.1 | 96.8 |
| National Institute on Alcohol Abuse and Alcoholism | 56.9 | 57.0 | 56.8 |
| National Institute on Drug Abuse | 1,048.8 | 1,052.1 | 1,054.0 |
| Substance Abuse and Mental Health Services Administration[d] | 2,576.8 | 2,565.8 | 2,470.9 |
|     Total HHS | 8,459.2 | 8,278.6 | 8,467.9 |
| **Department of Homeland Security** | | | |
| Customs and Border Protection | 2,238.3 | 2,280.3 | 2,276.4 |
| Federal Emergency Management Agency[e] | 8.3 | 7.5 | 0.0 |
| Federal Law Enforcement Training Center | 47.8 | 48.5 | 46.3 |
| Immigration and Customs Enforcement | 504.5 | 523.5 | 503.1 |
| United States Coast Guard[f] | 1,408.1 | 977.3 | 1,124.9 |
| Office of Counternarcotics Enforcement | 2.9 | 1.8 | 0.0 |
|     Total DHS | 4,209.9 | 3,838.9 | 3,950.7 |
| **Department of Housing and Urban Development** | | | |
| Community Planning and Development | 464.2 | 446.0 | 542.4 |
| **Department of the Interior** | | | |
| Bureau of Indian Affairs | 10.0 | 10.0 | 10.0 |
| Bureau of Land Management | 5.1 | 5.1 | 5.1 |
| National Park Service | 3.3 | 3.3 | 3.3 |
|     Total Interior | 18.4 | 18.4 | 18.4 |
| **Department of Justice** | | | |
| Assets Forfeiture Fund | 214.7 | 224.8 | 236.0 |
| Bureau of Prisons | 3,287.7 | 3,396.9 | 3,517.3 |
| Criminal Division | 12.3 | 12.3 | 12.6 |
| Drug Enforcement Administration | 2,305.9 | 2,347.0 | 2,387.9 |
| Organized Crime Drug Enforcement Task Force Program | 527.5 | 527.5 | 524.8 |
| Office of Justice Programs | 226.3 | 162.0 | 244.6 |
| National Drug Intelligence Center | 34.0 | 20.0 | 0.0 |
| U.S. Attorneys | 82.2 | 79.5 | 80.6 |
| U.S. Marshals Service | 237.7 | 248.9 | 250.8 |
| U.S. Marshals Service—Federal Prisoner Detention | 533.0 | 580.0 | 604.0 |
|     Total Justice | 7,461.3 | 7,598.9 | 7,858.5 |
| **Department of Labor** | | | |
| Employment and Training Administration | 6.6 | 6.6 | 6.5 |
| **Office of National Drug Control Policy** | | | |
| High Intensity Drug Trafficking Areas | 238.5 | 238.5 | 200.0 |
| Other Federal Drug Control Programs | 140.6 | 105.6 | 118.6 |
| Salaries and Expenses | 27.1 | 24.5 | 23.4 |
|     Total ONDCP | 406.2 | 368.6 | 342.0 |
| Small Business Administration | 1.0 | 0.0 | 0.0 |

border-control functions and the U.S. Coast Guard. International funds are divided roughly equally between the U.S. Departments of State and Defense. The Department of State's Bureau of International Narcotics and Law Enforcement Affairs (INL) is the lead agency that manages international programs. The Department of

TABLE 9.3

**Distribution of federal drug control spending, by agency, fiscal years 2011–13** [CONTINUED]

[Budget authority in millions]

| | Fiscal year 2011 Final | Fiscal year 2012 Enacted | Fiscal year 2013 Request |
|---|---|---|---|
| **Department of State** | | | |
| Bureau of International Narcotics and Law Enforcement Affairs[g] | 575.3 | 513.2 | 507.8 |
| United States Agency for International Development | 198.6 | 283.3 | 179.1 |
| **Total State** | **773.9** | **796.5** | **686.9** |
| **Department of Transportation** | | | |
| Federal Aviation Administration | 27.9 | 28.7 | 28.8 |
| National Highway Traffic Safety Administration | 2.7 | 2.7 | 4.0 |
| **Total Transportation** | **30.6** | **31.4** | **32.8** |
| **Department of the Treasury** | | | |
| Internal Revenue Service | 60.1 | 60.3 | 60.6 |
| **Department of Veterans Affairs** | | | |
| Veterans Health Administration[h] | 532.9 | 548.7 | 568.2 |
| | **$25,579.7** | **$25,184.7** | **$25,599.9** |

Note: Detail may not add due to rounding.

DOD = Department of Defense.
OPTEMPO = Operational tempo.
ONDCP = Office of National Drug Control Policy.
FEMA = Federal Emergency Management Agency.
USCG = United States Coast Guard.
VA = Veterans Administration.

DOD amounts include funding appropriated or requested for overseas contingency operations.

OPTEMPO funding (flight hours and steaming days) is reported by the military services and is not part of DOD's counter-drug activities budget request.

The Department of Health and Human Services' (HHS) Centers for Medicare and Medicaid Services (CMS) outlay estimates include substance abuse treatment expenditures for both Medicare and Medicaid. While CMS's Office of the Actuary (OACT) developed the Medicare estimates, Medicaid estimates were developed as a placeholder by ONDCP, based on data in the 2008 Report from HHS entitled 'SAMHSA spending estimates: MHSA spending projections for 2004–2014'. OACT did not develop or approve the Medicaid estimates. Medicaid estimates are not consistent with the fiscal year 2013 President's Budget Medicaid baseline projections, and do not incorporate the impact of recent legislation (including the Recovery Act and the Affordable Care Act), or recent economic and policy changes to the programs. These estimates are for use while HHS develops a more precise estimate consistent with current program spending.

Includes budget authority and funding through evaluation set-aside authorized by Section 241 of the Public Health Service (PHS) Act.

FEMA amount reflects Operation Stonegarden grant funding.

The USCG budgets by appropriation rather than individual missions. The USCG projects resource allocations by mission through use of an activity-based costing system. Actual allocations will vary depending upon operational environment and mission need. In fiscal year 2011, the USCG anticipated allocating $1,162.3 toward the drug interdiction mission. According to the USCG operations database, however, actual end-of-year allocation totaled $1,408.1 million.

State Department amounts include funding appropriated or requested for overseas contingency operations.

VA Medical Care receives advance appropriations; fiscal year 2013 funding was provided in the Consolidated Appropriations Act, 2012 (Public Law 112–74).

SOURCE: "Table 2. Federal Drug Control Spending by Agency," in *FY 2013 Budget and Performance Summary: Companion to the National Drug Control Strategy*, Executive Office of the President, Office of National Drug Control Policy, April 2012, http://www.whitehouse.gov/sites/default/files/ondcp/fy2013_drug_control_budget_and_performance_summary.pdf (accessed February 16, 2013)

Defense is involved in supporting anti-insurgency programs in the Andean region and elsewhere. (Insurgencies are organized, armed rebellions against governments.)

## INTERNATIONAL WAR ON DRUGS

The links among drugs, organized crime, and insurgencies outside the United States have long been known. A connection to terrorism is a contemporary emphasis that arose in the aftermath of the September 11, 2001 (9/11), terrorist attacks against the United States. In *Fiscal Year 2004 Budget: Congressional Justification* (May 20, 2003, http://www.state.gov/documents/organization/22061.pdf), the INL made a case for the convergence between the War on Drugs and the War on Terror:

The September 11 attacks and their aftermath highlight the close connections and overlap among terrorists, drug traffickers, and organized crime groups. The nexus is far-reaching. In many instances, such as Colombia, the groups are the same. Drug traffickers benefit from terrorists' military skills, weapons supply, and access to clandestine organizations. Terrorists gain a source of revenue and expertise in the illicit transfer and laundering of money for their operations. All three groups seek out weak states with feeble justice and regulatory sectors where they can corrupt and even dominate the government. September 11 demonstrated graphically the direct threat to the United States by a narcoterrorist state such as Afghanistan where such groups once operated with impunity. Although the political and security situation in Colombia is different from the Taliban period in Afghanistan—the central government is not allied with such groups but rather is engaged in a major effort to destroy them—the narco-terrorist linkage in Colombia poses perhaps the single greatest threat to the stability of Latin America and the Western Hemisphere. It also potentially threatens the security of the United States in the event of a victory by the insurgent groups. The bottom line is that such groups invariably jeopardize international peace and freedom, undermine the rule of law, menace local and regional stability, and threaten both the United States and our friends and allies.

The key to the international War on Drugs is disruption of the drug supply. The ONDCP states in *National Drug Control Strategy, 2006* (February 2006, http://www.usdoj.gov/olp/pdf/ndcs06.pdf) that market disruption "contributes to the Global War on Terrorism, severing the links between drug traffickers and terrorist organizations in countries such as Afghanistan and Colombia, among others. It renders support to allies such as the administration of President Alvaro Uribe [1952–] in Colombia. Market disruption initiatives remove some of the most violent criminals from society, from kingpins such as the remnants of the Cali Cartel to common thugs such as the vicious MS-13 street gang." As outlined in *National Drug Control Strategy, 2012* (April 2012, http://www.whitehouse.gov/sites/default/files/ondcp/2012_ndcs.pdf), the Obama administration emphasizes a balanced approach to drug control efforts but remains committed to policies that will "increase security along the Nation's borders and disrupt and dismantle the transnational criminal organizations that seek to traffic illicit drugs across them."

## DISRUPTING THE DRUG SUPPLY

Internationally, the federal effort is concentrated on what the INL calls the Andean ridge, the northwestern part of South America where Colombia, Ecuador, and Peru, running north to south, touch the Pacific and where landlocked Bolivia lies east of Peru. In *International Narcotics Control Strategy Report, Volume I: Drug and Chemical Control* (March 2012, http://www.state.gov/documents/organization/187109.pdf), the INL estimates that 95.5% of all cocaine entering the United States comes from Colombia. The remaining cocaine comes from Bolivia and Peru. Besides focusing on Colombia, the INL also concentrates on Mexico because the country is a major transmission route of drugs to the United States and because it is a significant source of heroin, marijuana, and methamphetamine.

The centerpiece of the disruption effort is the eradication of coca and poppy by providing airplanes and funds for spraying herbicides that kill the plants. Efforts also include assisting foreign law enforcement agencies and foreign governments with counternarcotics and anti-corruption activities, and providing financial support through the U.S. Agency for International Development (USAID) for the planting of legal crops and improving infrastructure (roads and bridges) so that farm goods can be delivered to market. The latter measures are necessary because many of the people who are involved in cultivating drug-producing plants live in remote and undeveloped regions, and this is the only source of income. The USAID programs are intended to give them alternatives.

Elsewhere, the INL is concentrating on Afghanistan and Pakistan. In all, INL programs extend to about 150 countries and involve assistance in law enforcement and in the fight against money laundering (making illegally acquired cash seem as though it was legally acquired). What follows is a brief encapsulation of the INL strategy in selected high-focus areas.

### Colombia

The primary effort to disrupt the drug supply in Colombia is coca eradication. The coca tree (*Erythroxylon coca*) is a densely leafed plant that is native to the eastern slopes of the Andes mountains and is heavily cultivated in Colombia.

Table 9.4 shows the amount of coca leaf that was cultivated between 1986 and 2009, and Table 9.5 shows the amount of coca leaf that was eradicated between 1987 and 2009. The area cultivated in Colombia increased from 1986 to 2001 about ninefold, from 46,200 acres (18,700 ha) to 419,600 acres (169,800 ha). The area of cultivation then declined through 2003, rose again through 2007 to near-2001 levels, and then dropped dramatically in 2008 to 294,100 acres (119,000 ha), falling further to 286,642 acres (116,000 ha) in 2009. U.S. aerial eradication efforts in Colombia increased dramatically from 104,484 acres (42,283 ha) in 2000, to a high of 424,065 acres (171,613 ha) in 2006. This was a fourfold increase in eradication. Eradication declined from 2006 to 2009, with 258,897 acres (104,772 ha) eradicated in 2009.

When the source of a drug such as cocaine is diminished, two things happen: the purity of the finished product (the drug) declines, and the price of it rises. A lag time occurs, however, between the eradication of source plants and the detection of the decline in purity and the rise in the price of the drug in the United States. Figure 8.5 in Chapter 8 shows the decline in purity and the rise in price of cocaine beginning in the first quarter of 2007, reflecting the results of coca eradication from years prior.

Poppy eradication takes place in Colombia as well because this country supplies a great deal of the heroin entering the United States. Table 9.6 shows Colombian opium poppy eradication between 1990 and 2010. In 2001 aerial eradication efforts removed 6,383 acres (2,583 ha) of the plants; in 2004 aerial and manual efforts together removed 11,261 acres (4,557 ha). Eradication then fell by about half in 2005 and 2006, as aerial eradication of poppies was discontinued in April 2006 to focus on the aerial eradication of coca. Additionally, Colombian cultivation of opium poppy declined from

## mount of coca leaf cultivated, 1986–2009

| ear | Net coca cultivation (hectares) | | | | Potential pure cocaine production (metric tons) | | | |
|---|---|---|---|---|---|---|---|---|
| | Total | Bolivia | Colombia | Peru | Total | Bolivia | Colombia | Peru |
| 86 | 162,500 | 37,800 | 18,700 | 106,000 | 710 | 220 | 30 | 460 |
| 87 | 175,700 | 41,300 | 25,600 | 108,800 | 740 | 220 | 40 | 480 |
| 88 | 193,300 | 48,900 | 34,000 | 110,400 | 750 | 225 | 55 | 470 |
| 89 | 215,700 | 52,900 | 42,400 | 120,400 | 755 | 220 | 70 | 465 |
| 90 | 211,700 | 50,300 | 40,100 | 121,300 | 775 | 220 | 65 | 490 |
| 91 | 206,200 | 47,900 | 37,500 | 120,800 | 805 | 220 | 60 | 525 |
| 92 | 211,700 | 45,500 | 37,100 | 129,100 | 835 | 225 | 60 | 550 |
| 93 | 195,700 | 47,200 | 39,700 | 108,800 | 720 | 240 | 65 | 415 |
| 94 | 201,700 | 48,100 | 45,000 | 108,600 | 745 | 255 | 70 | 420 |
| 95 | 203,900 | 48,600 | 50,900 | 104,400 | 900 | 240 | 210 | 450 |
| 96 | 201,700 | 48,100 | 67,200 | 86,400 | 770 | 215 | 255 | 300 |
| 97 | 187,100 | 45,800 | 79,500 | 61,800 | 680 | 200 | 265 | 215 |
| 98 | 185,500 | 38,000 | 101,800 | 45,700 | 690 | 150 | 380 | 160 |
| 99 | 179,900 | 21,800 | 122,500 | 34,700 | 650 | 70 | 460 | 120 |
| 00 | 187,500 | 19,600 | 136,200 | 31,700 | 770 | 80 | 530 | 160 |
| 01 | 221,800 | 19,900 | 169,800 | 32,100 | 1,055 | 100 | 700 | 255 |
| 02 | 200,750 | 21,600 | 144,450 | 34,700 | 975 | 110 | 585 | 280 |
| 03 | 166,300 | 23,200 | 113,850 | 29,250 | 790 | 100 | 445 | 245 |
| 04 | 166,200 | 24,600 | 114,100 | 27,500 | 755 | 115 | 410 | 230 |
| 05 | 204,500 | 26,500 | 144,000 | 34,000 | 875 | 115 | 500 | 260 |
| 06 | 224,800 | 25,800 | 157,000 | 42,000 | 890 | 115 | 510 | 265 |
| 07 | 232,500 | 29,500 | 167,000 | 36,000 | 815 | 130 | 475 | 210 |
| 08 | 192,000 | 32,000 | 119,000 | 41,000 | 695 | 195 | 285 | 215 |
| 09 | 191,000 | 35,000 | 116,000 | 40,000 | 700 | 195 | 280 | 225 |

ᴑURCE: "Table 118. Andean Net Coca Cultivation and Potential Cocaine Hydrochloride Production, 1986–2009," in *National Drug Control Strategy: Data Supplement 2012*, Executive Office of the President, Office of National Drug Policy, 2012, http://www.whitehouse.gov/sites/default/files/page/files/2012_data_supplement_final.pdf (accessed February 16, 2013)

## mount of coca leaf eradicated, 1987–2009

[n hectares]

| ear | Eradicated | | |
|---|---|---|---|
| | Bolivia[a] | Colombia | Peru |
| 987 | 1,040 | 460 | 355 |
| 988 | 1,475 | 230 | 5,130 |
| 989 | 2,500 | 640 | 1,285 |
| 990 | 8,100 | 900 | NA |
| 991 | 5,486 | 972 | NA |
| 992 | 3,152 | 959 | NA |
| 993 | 2,397 | 793 | 0 |
| 994 | 1,058 | 5,412 | 0 |
| 995 | 5,493 | 32,432 | 0 |
| 996 | 7,512 | 15,407[b] | 1,259 |
| 997 | 7,026 | 31,663[b] | 3,462 |
| 998 | 11,621 | 49,641[b] | 7,825 |
| 999 | 16,999 | 39,113[b] | 13,800 |
| 000 | 7,653 | 42,283[b] | 6,200 |
| 001 | NA | 77,165[b] | 3,900 |
| 002 | 11,839 | 102,225[b] | 7,000 |
| 003 | 10,000 | 132,817[b] | 7,022 |
| 004 | 8,437 | 136,555[b] | 7,605 |
| 005 | 6,073 | 138,775[b] | 8,966 |
| 006 | 5,070 | 171,613[b] | 10,137 |
| 007 | 6,269 | 153,133[b] | 11,057 |
| 008 | 5,484 | 133,496[b] | 10,143 |
| 009 | 6,314 | 104,772[b] | 10,025 |

A = Data not available.
ᴮeginning in 2001, United States Government (USG) surveys of Bolivian coca take place ᴠer the period June to June.
ᴄolombian figures pertain to aerial eradication from 1994 to 2009.

ᴑURCE: "Table 119. Amount of Coca Leaf Eradicated, 1987–2009 ᴴectares)," in *National Drug Control Strategy: Data Supplement 2012*, ᴇxecutive Office of the President, Office of National Drug Policy, 2012, ᴛtp://www.whitehouse.gov/sites/default/files/page/files/2012_data_ ᴜpplement_final.pdf (accessed February 16, 2013)

16,062 acres (6,500 ha) in 2001 to 2,718 acres (1,100 ha) in 2009.

Along with the eradication of coca and poppy in Colombia, USAID and other international organizations have conducted "alternative livelihoods" programs that provide farmers involved in cultivating coca and poppy with alternative crops. USAID began operating such programs in Colombia late in 2000 and in Afghanistan in 2004, although the idea had been implemented in other areas more than 30 years earlier.

Besides Colombia's aggressive seizure of drugs within its borders, the country is working with the United States in the resumption of the Air Bridge Denial (ABD) program. The ABD program works by forcing or shooting down aircraft that appear to be taking part in drug trafficking activities. The program was halted in 2001, when a civilian aircraft was downed in Peru and two U.S. citizens were killed. It was resumed in 2003. According to the INL in *International Narcotics Control Strategy Report*, as of 2012 the government of Colombia had assumed control over the ABD program, taking responsibility for maintaining the program's fleet of 72 aircraft.

Colombia, however, illustrates some of the fundamental dilemmas of interdiction. The drug trade there has been one symptom of a festering civil war. Through the 1990s and into the first decade of the 21st century antigovernment insurgent groups and illegal paramilitary groups were heavily funded by the drug trade. However, the Central Intelligence Agency notes in *World*

TABLE 9.6

**Amount of opium poppy cultivated and eradicated, 1990–2010**

[In hectares]

| Year | Afghanistan | Pakistan | Burma | Laos | Thailand | Colombia | Guatemala | Mexico |
|---|---|---|---|---|---|---|---|---|
| **Cultivated** | | | | | | | | |
| 1990 | 12,370 | 8,220 | 150,100 | 30,580 | 3,435 | NA | 845 | 5,450 |
| 1991 | 17,190 | 8,205 | 160,000 | 29,625 | 3,000 | 1,160 | 1,145 | 3,765 |
| 1992 | 19,470 | 8,170 | 153,700 | 25,610 | 2,050 | NA | NA | 730 |
| 1993 | 21,080 | 6,280 | 146,600 | 18,520 | 2,110 | NA | 440 | 438 |
| 1994 | 29,180 | 7,270 | 154,070 | 19,650 | 2,110 | NA | NA | 50 |
| 1995 | 38,740 | 6,950 | 154,070 | 19,650 | 1,750 | 6,540 | 150 | 5,050 |
| 1996 | 37,950 | 3,400 | 163,100 | 25,250 | 2,170 | 6,300 | 90 | 5,100 |
| 1997 | 39,150 | 4,100 | 155,150 | 28,150 | 1,650 | 6,600 | NA | 4,000 |
| 1998 | 41,720 | 3,030 | 130,300 | 26,100 | 1,350 | 6,100 | NA | 5,500 |
| 1999 | 51,500 | 1,570 | 89,500 | 21,800 | 835 | 7,500 | NA | 3,600 |
| 2000 | 64,510 | 515 | 108,700 | 23,150 | 890 | 7,500 | NA | 1,900 |
| 2001 | 1,685 | 213 | 105,000 | 22,000 | 820 | 6,500 | NA | 4,400 |
| 2002 | 30,750 | 213 | 77,700 | 23,200 | 750 | 4,900 | NA | 2,700 |
| 2003 | 61,000 | 1,714 | 47,130 | 18,900 | NA | 4,400 | NA | 4,800 |
| 2004 | 206,700 | NA | 36,000 | 10,000 | NA | 2,100 | 330 | 3,500 |
| 2005 | 107,400 | NA | 40,000 | 5,600 | NA | NA | 100 | 3,300 |
| 2006 | 172,600 | NA | 21,000 | 1,700 | NA | 2,300 | NA | 5,000 |
| 2007 | 202,000 | NA | 21,700 | 1,100 | NA | 1,000 | NA | 6,900 |
| 2008 | 157,000 | NA | 22,500 | 1,900 | NA | NA | NA | 15,000 |
| 2009 | 131,000 | NA | 17,000 | 1,000 | NA | 1,100 | NA | 19,500 |
| 2010 | 119,000 | 1,700 | NA | 3,500 | NA | NA | NA | NA |
| **Eradicated** | | | | | | | | |
| 1990 | NA | 185 | NA | 0 | 720 | NA | 1,085 | 4,650 |
| 1991 | NA | 440 | 1,012 | 0 | 1,200 | 1,156 | 576 | 6,545 |
| 1992 | NA | 977 | 1,215 | 0 | 1,580 | 12,858 | 470 | 11,583 |
| 1993 | NA | 856 | 604 | 0 | 0 | 9,821 | 426 | 13,015 |
| 1994 | NA | 463 | 3,345 | 0 | 0 | 3,906 | 150 | 11,036 |
| 1995 | NA | 0 | 0 | 0 | 580 | 3,760 | 86 | 15,389 |
| 1996 | NA | 867 | 0 | 0 | 880 | 6,028 | 12 | 14,671 |
| 1997 | NA | 654 | 10,501 | 0 | 1,050 | 6,972 | 3 | 17,732 |
| 1998 | NA | 2,194 | 16,194 | NA | 715 | NA | 5 | 17,449 |
| 1999 | NA | 1,197 | 9,800 | NA | 808 | NA | 1 | 15,469 |
| 2000 | NA | 1,704 | 0 | NA | 757 | 9,254[b] | 1 | 15,300 |
| 2001 | NA | 1,484 | 9,317 | NA | 832 | 2,583[b] | 1 | 19,115 |
| 2002 | NA | NA | 25,862 | NA | 507 | 3,371[b] | 1 | 19,157 |
| 2003 | NA | 3,641 | 683 | 18,900 | 767 | 2,994[b] | 1 | 20,034 |
| 2004 | NA | 4,426 | NA | NA | NA | 4,557[b] | NA | 15,925 |
| 2005 | NA | 707 | NA | NA | NA | 2,121[b] | NA | 21,609 |
| 2006 | NA | 363 | NA | NA | NA | 2,161[b] | NA | 16,889 |
| 2007 | NA | 614 | NA | NA | NA | 375[b] | NA | 11,046 |
| 2008 | NA | 0 | NA | NA | NA | 361[b] | NA | NA |
| 2009 | NA | NA | 4,087 | NA | NA | 148[b] | NA | NA |
| 2010 | NA | NA | NA | NA | NA | 545[b] | 918 | 14,842 |

NA = Data not available.

[a]The eradication figures shown for 1992–2001 are derived from data supplied by Mexican authorities to International Narcotics Control Strategy Report (INCSR). The effective eradication figure is an estimate of the actual amount of crop destroyed—factoring in replanting, repeated spraying of one area, and other factors.

[b]Eradication figures shown for Colombia represent aerial eradication from 2000 to 2003; combined aerial and manual from 2004 to 2006; and manual eradication since 2007 after aerial eradication was discontinued in April 2006 to put all aerial assets against coca cultivation.

SOURCE: "Table 114. Amount of Opium Poppy Cultivated and Eradicated, 1990–2010 (Hectares)," in *National Drug Control Strategy: Data Supplement 2012*, Executive Office of the President, Office of National Drug Policy, 2012, http://www.whitehouse.gov/sites/default/files/page/files/2012_data_supplement_final.pdf (accessed February 16, 2013)

*Factbook: Colombia* (March 26, 2013, https://www.cia.gov/library/publications/the-world-factbook/geos/co.html) that "more than 31,000 former paramilitaries had demobilized by the end of 2006 and the United Self Defense Forces of Colombia as a formal organization had ceased to function. In the wake of the paramilitary demobilization, emerging criminal groups arose, whose members include some former paramilitaries.... The Colombian Government has stepped up efforts to reassert government control throughout the country and now has a presence in every one of its administrative departments."

In "Colombian Paramilitaries' Successors Called a Threat" (NYTimes.com, February 3, 2010), Simon Romero reports that as of early 2010 the Colombian security policy was not working as well as expected to thwart the paramilitaries. Romero notes that the group Human Rights Watch issued a report explaining that these groups were massacring, raping, and displacing Colombians while continuing to be funded by the drug trade. The largest of the insurgent groups is the Fuerzas Armadas Revolucionarios de Colombia (FARC; Revolutionary Armed Forces of Colombia). However, Romero ndicates in "Rebels' Second in Command Has Been Killed, Colombia Says" (NYTimes.com, September 23, 2010) that in September 2010 government security forces killed Mono Jojoy (1953–2010), the FARC's second in command, and 20 other FARC members during a bombing raid. This attack on the FARC was a major setback to the insurgent group.

With an internal conflict that has lasted nearly 50 years, quite some time may pass before civil order is totally restored in Colombia and economic development has advanced enough to make coca and poppy cultivation unattractive.

## Bolivia and Peru

According to the INL in *International Narcotics Control Strategy Report*, Bolivia is the third-largest producer of cocaine and "is a significant transit zone for Peruvian-origin cocaine." Bolivia is poor and has had an unsettled history (nearly 200 coups since its independence in 1825). The country has been under democratic rule since the 1980s, but successive governments have been reluctant to support eradication programs energetically because coca cultivation (but not cocaine production) is legal in Bolivia. Coca is a traditional crop in this country, and the coca leaf is chewed by the inhabitants; eradication has resulted in a popular antiestablishment movement.

Table 9.6 shows the amount of coca leaf that has been eradicated in Bolivia, from 29,255 acres (11,839 ha) in 2002 to 15,602 acres (6,314 ha) in 2009. These eradication efforts are offset by replanting, and eradication is sometimes violently opposed by the population. As a result, the amount of coca leaf that was cultivated in Bolivia increased 51.3% during this period, from 53,375 acres (21,600 ha) in 2002 to 86,486 acres (35,000 ha) in 2009. (See Table 9.4.)

The INL explains that Peru is the second-largest producer of cocaine in the world and a major importer of cocaine precursor chemicals. However, unlike the Bolivian government, the Peruvian government is committed to counternarcotics activities. Regardless, the government's actions are hampered by organized bodies of *cocaleros* (coca growers), who enjoy sufficient popular support. Thus, in Peru as in Bolivia, replanting frequently follows eradication efforts. Nonetheless, Table 9.4 shows that the cultivation of coca leaf in Peru decreased dramatically from a peak of 319,013 acres (129,100 ha) in 1992 to a low of 67,954 acres (27,500 ha) in 2004. Data are unavailable for many years, but eradication increased sixfold between 1996 and 2004, from 3,110 acres (1,259 ha) to 18,792 acres (7,605 ha). Cultivation rose after 2004 to 98,842 acres (40,000 ha) in 2009, but eradication increased as well, to 24,772 acres (10,025 ha) in 2009.

## Mexico

Mexico is one of the principal producers of marijuana, methamphetamine, and heroin entering the United States. It also serves as a thoroughfare for cocaine, which is produced in South America and sent north to the United States.

From 2000 to 2006 the Mexican president Vicente Fox (1942–) and the Mexican government were energetic in the eradication of the cannabis and poppy crops. (Cannabis is the botanical name of the plant from which marijuana is derived.) Mexican officials were vigorous, as well, in the arrest and prosecution of members of drug cartels, even though these efforts were hampered by severe budget constraints, corruption, and inefficiencies within the law enforcement and criminal justice institutions. In 2006 Felipe Calderón (1962–) succeeded Fox as the president of Mexico. According to the INL in *International Narcotics Control Strategy Report*, during the first two years of the Calderón administration significant progress was made in attacking drug trafficking and consumption. In October 2008 Presidents Bush and Calderón announced the Mérida Initiative, a plan to achieve stronger law enforcement cooperation between the United States and Mexico. During the Bush administration, the initiative was primarily focused on strengthening law enforcement capabilities, largely through arming and training Mexican counterdrug agencies.

In March 2010 President Obama implemented an overhaul of the Mérida Initiative. As Clare Ribando Seelke and Kristin M. Finklea of the Congressional Research Service report in *U.S.–Mexican Security Cooperation: The Mérida Initiative and Beyond* (January 14, 2013, http://www.fas.org/sgp/crs/row/R41349.pdf), the shift in policy was aimed primarily at strengthening political institutions in Mexico, both as a means of eliminating corruption in the criminal justice system and as a way of restoring public faith in government. According to Seelke and Finklea, President Obama's new strategy was founded on "four pillars": "1) disrupting organized crime groups; 2) institutionalizing the rule of law; 3) building a 21st-century border; and 4) building strong and resilient communities." Highlights of the new strategy included a shift away from providing equipment to Mexican security personnel in favor of emphasizing training and technical assistance; helping install new "criminal procedure codes" in individual Mexican states; and developing "bilateral policies" as a means of strengthening border security and rooting out corruption among border officials. Community-building, with an emphasis on educational outreach and the development and strengthening of social institutions, was also a hallmark of Obama's revised initiative.

As Seelke and Finklea report, between FY 2008 and FY 2012 the U.S. Congress appropriated $1.9 billion in funding for the Mérida Initiative. In his FY 2013 budget request, President Obama included a request for an additional $234 million in Mérida Initiative funding. On two occasions Congress delayed payment on a portion of the initiative's funds, in order to ensure that the program was upholding its commitment to combating human rights abuses within the Mexican military and police force. According to Seelke and Finklea, the initiative began to show some signs of success between 2011 and 2012; drug-related violence fell during this span, and by December 2012, 22 of the 32 Mexican states had begun to overhaul their criminal codes. Shortly after his election in November 2012, the new president, Enrique Peña Nieto (1966–), reaffirmed Mexico's commitment to the initiative, while stressing that his administration's top priority in further cooperation with the United States would be on reducing drug-related violence.

Table 9.7 shows that cannabis cultivation in Mexico decreased ninefold from 86,610 acres (35,050 ha) in 1990 to 9,637 acres (3,900 ha) in 2000. After 2000 it began to increase, reaching 43,243 acres (17,500 ha) in 2009. The table also shows that eradication of marijuana crops in Mexico increased from 16,680 acres (6,750 ha) in 1990 to a high of 90,404 acres (36,585 ha) in 2003. Eradication leveled out at about 74,000 acres (30,000 ha) through 2006, but fell to 42,529 acres (17,211 ha) in 2010.

Table 9.6 shows the eradication of 39,352 acres (15,925 ha) of the Mexican opium poppy crop in 2004, 27,295 acres (11,046 ha) in 2007, and 36,675 acres (14,842 ha) in 2010. No data were available for 2008 and 2009. In spite of eradication efforts, poppy cultivation nearly quadrupled between 2006 and 2009, from 12,355 acres (5,000 ha) to 48,185 acres (19,500 ha).

Along with marijuana and heroin, one of the drugs imported to the United States over the U.S.-Mexican border is methamphetamine, a synthetic drug that is made in illegal laboratories. This drug has become an increasing problem in the United States. (See Chapter 4.) U.S. law enforcement agencies have done much to combat the spread of this drug domestically, but they are also active in stopping the flow of methamphetamine and its precursors (other substances that are used to make methamphetamine) into the country. In general, increased production of methamphetamine within Mexico is indicated by increased seizures at the U.S. southwest border. Table 8.5 in Chapter 8 shows that methamphetamine seizures along the Mexican border doubled between 2008 and 2010, from 4,896 pounds (2,221 kg) to 9,890 pounds (4,486 kg).

## Afghanistan

In *International Narcotics Control Strategy Report*, the INL indicates that Afghanistan produces roughly 90%

**TABLE 9.7**

**Amount of cannabis cultivated and eradicated by foreign countries, 1990–2010**

[In hectares]

| Year | Cultivated | | | Eradicated | | |
|------|---------|--------|----------|--------|--------|----------|
|      | Mexico* | Jamaica | Colombia | Mexico | Jamaica | Colombia |
| 1990 | 35,050 | 1,220 | 1,500 | 6,750 | 1,030 | 500 |
| 1991 | 17,915 | 950 | 2,000 | 10,795 | 833 | 0 |
| 1992 | 16,420 | 398 | 2,000 | 16,872 | 811 | 49 |
| 1993 | 21,190 | 1,200 | 5,050 | 16,645 | 456 | 50 |
| 1994 | 19,045 | 1,000 | 5,000 | 14,227 | 692 | 14 |
| 1995 | 18,650 | 1,000 | 5,000 | 21,573 | 695 | 20 |
| 1996 | 18,700 | 1,000 | 5,000 | 22,961 | 473 | NA |
| 1997 | 15,300 | 1,060 | 5,000 | 23,576 | 743 | NA |
| 1998 | 4,600 | NA | 5,000 | 23,928 | 705 | NA |
| 1999 | 3,700 | NA | 5,000 | 33,583 | 894 | NA |
| 2000 | 3,900 | NA | 5,000 | 33,000 | 517 | NA |
| 2001 | 4,100 | NA | 5,000 | 28,699 | 332 | NA |
| 2002 | 7,900 | NA | 5,000 | 30,775 | 80 | NA |
| 2003 | 7,500 | NA | 5,000 | 36,585 | 445 | NA |
| 2004 | 5,800 | NA | 5,000 | 30,851 | NA | NA |
| 2005 | 5,600 | NA | NA | 30,842 | NA | NA |
| 2006 | 8,600 | NA | NA | 30,162 | NA | NA |
| 2007 | NA | NA | NA | 22,348 | NA | NA |
| 2008 | 12,000 | NA | NA | 15,756 | NA | NA |
| 2009 | 17,500 | NA | NA | NA | 633 | NA |
| 2010 | NA | NA | NA | 17,211 | 447 | NA |

NA = Data not available.

*The eradication figures shown for 1992–2001 are derived from data supplied by Mexican authorities to the International Narcotics Control Strategy Report (INCSR). The effective eradication figure is an estimate of the actual amount of crop destroyed—factoring in replanting, repeated spraying of one area, and other factors. Reported cultivation is described as harvestable/net production.

SOURCE: "Table 122. Amount of Cannabis Cultivated and Eradicated by Foreign Countries, 1990–2010," in *National Drug Control Strategy: Data Supplement 2012*, Executive Office of the President, Office of National Drug Policy, 2012, http://www.whitehouse.gov/sites/default/files/page/files/2012_data_supplement_final.pdf (accessed February 16, 2013)

f the world's opium supply. When Afghanistan was under he control of the zealously religious and conservative Taliban regime, cultivated poppy acreage dropped precipitously, from 159,408 acres (64,510 ha) in 2000 to 4,164 acres (1,685 ha) in 2001. (See Table 9.6.) The United States invaded Afghanistan in 2001, in a response to the 9/11 terrorist attacks, and the Taliban was driven from power. An unintended consequence of these events was that poppy cultivation resumed, rising to 75,985 acres 30,750 ha) in 2002. By 2004 poppy cultivation reached a staggering 510,767 acres (206,700 ha) but then dropped by nearly half to 265,391 acres (107,400 ha) in 2005. The recultivation of poppy was in part a response to a continuing drought in the region: opium poppy is hardy and can grow under adverse conditions, supplying income to farmers. By 2007 poppy cultivation in Afghanistan had nearly reached 2004 levels at 499,153 acres (202,000 ha), but by 2010 it had dropped to 294,055 acres (119,000 ha).

Afghanistan's post-Taliban government officially banned opium poppy cultivation and has pressured its regional governors to suppress the drug trade. Despite these efforts, the situation in Afghanistan was, in the immediate post-Taliban era, similar to the situation in Colombia, with a weak central government unable to assert itself in areas where autonomous warlords hold de facto (virtual) power. Other countries and organizations have tried to help. For example, USAID has been active in establishing alternative development programs. According to the *FY 2013 Budget and Performance Summary: Companion to the National Drug Control Strategy* (April 2012, http://www.whitehouse.gov/sites/default/files/ondcp/fy2013_drug_control_budget_and_performance_summary.pdf), a portion of USAID's budget of $179.1 million in FY 2013 was dedicated to ongoing efforts to promote alternative agricultural development initiatives in Afghanistan, with the aim of reducing the nation's dependence on revenues generated by opium production. However, as Alissa J. Rubin reports in "In Afghanistan, Poppy Growing Proves Resilient" (NYTimes.com, January 1, 2012), efforts to reinvent the agricultural economy in Afghanistan had shown little progress by 2012, as annual poppy yields continued to climb.

The DEA developed the Foreign-Deployed Advisory Support Teams program in Afghanistan to identify, target, investigate, and disrupt or dismantle transnational drug trafficking operations in the region. A major goal of this program is to help develop Afghanistan's antidrug abilities. Training began in 2004, and operations began in 2005. Even though results were initially positive, the INL indicates in *International Narcotics Control Strategy Report* that "although opium poppy cultivation is largely confined to insecure provinces in the south, Afghanistan's narcotics industry continues to threaten efforts to establish security, governance, and a licit economy throughout the country."

## FOSTERING INTERNATIONAL COOPERATION: THE DRUG CERTIFICATION PROCESS

The United States uses a drug certification process to promote international cooperation in controlling drug production and trafficking. Section 490 of the Foreign Assistance Act of 1961 requires the president to annually submit to Congress a list of major drug-producing and drug-transiting countries. The president must also assess each country's performance in battling narcotics trade and trafficking based on the goals and objectives of the 1988 United Nations Convention against Illicit Traffic in Narcotic Drugs and Psychotropic Substances. Countries that have fully cooperated with the United States or that have taken adequate steps to reach the goals and objectives of the 1988 convention are "certified" by the president. U.S. aid is withheld from countries that are not certified. Many countries resent the process, but most work toward certification.

## TRANSIT-ZONE AGREEMENTS

Other countries not on the list are frequently reluctant to cooperate with the United States to stop drug traffickers. The Caribbean basin, for example, is a major transit zone for drug trafficking. The Caribbean basin countries are those that border, or lie in, the Gulf of Mexico and the Caribbean Sea, such as the island nations of the West Indies, Mexico, Central American nations, and northern South American nations. Bermuda is also included, even though it is in the Atlantic Ocean. Most of the islands have bilateral agreements with the United States, but these agreements are limited to maritime matters that permit U.S. ships to seize traffickers in the territorial waters of particular Caribbean islands. Few transit-zone countries permit U.S. planes to fly in their airspace to force suspected traffickers to land. Some transit-zone countries have no maritime agreements with the United States.

## DOMESTIC DRUG SEIZURES

The DEA is also at work within the United States to disrupt the drug supply. Table 8.5 in Chapter 8 shows drug seizures across the United States between 2006 and 2010. While seizures of cocaine dropped during that span, seizures of heroin, methamphetamine, marijuana, and MDMA (ecstasy) all increased. Of all of these illicit drugs, seizures of methamphetamine grew at the largest rate, increasing by nearly 56% between 2006 and 2010, from 12,297 pounds (5,578 kg) to 19,178 pounds (8,699 kg).

In 2006 the Combat Methamphetamine Epidemic Act was signed into law, establishing stricter national controls for the over-the-counter (nonprescription) sale of products containing the methamphetamine precursor drugs ephedrine and pseudoephedrine. Before this act, many states had imposed restrictions on the retail sale

**TABLE 9.8**

### Methamphetamine super lab seizures by state, 2000–10

| State | 2000 | 2001 | 2002 | 2003 | 2004 | 2005 | 2006 | 2007 | 2008 | 2009 | 2010 |
|---|---|---|---|---|---|---|---|---|---|---|---|
| Alabama | 0 | 0 | 1 | 0 | 0 | 0 | 0 | 0 | 0 | 0 | 0 |
| Arizona | 0 | 0 | 1 | 0 | 0 | 0 | 0 | 0 | 0 | 0 | 0 |
| Arkansas | 0 | 0 | 2 | 0 | 0 | 0 | 0 | 0 | 0 | 0 | 0 |
| California | 123 | 214 | 124 | 125 | 42 | 28 | 14 | 10 | 15 | 15 | 6 |
| Colorado | 0 | 0 | 2 | 0 | 0 | 0 | 0 | 0 | 0 | 0 | 1 |
| Georgia | 0 | 0 | 0 | 0 | 0 | 1 | 1 | 0 | 1 | 1 | 0 |
| Illinois | 0 | 0 | 0 | 2 | 0 | 0 | 0 | 0 | 0 | 0 | 0 |
| Indiana | 0 | 0 | 1 | 0 | 0 | 0 | 0 | 0 | 0 | 0 | 0 |
| Louisiana | 0 | 0 | 1 | 0 | 0 | 0 | 0 | 0 | 0 | 0 | 0 |
| Missouri | 0 | 0 | 0 | 1 | 1 | 1 | 1 | 1 | 0 | 0 | 0 |
| Montana | 0 | 0 | 0 | 0 | 0 | 0 | 0 | 0 | 1 | 0 | 0 |
| Nevada | 0 | 3 | 1 | 0 | 0 | 0 | 0 | 0 | 0 | 0 | 0 |
| North Dakota | 0 | 0 | 1 | 0 | 0 | 0 | 0 | 0 | 0 | 0 | 0 |
| Ohio | 0 | 0 | 0 | 0 | 1 | 0 | 2 | 0 | 0 | 0 | 0 |
| Oklahoma | 1 | 0 | 2 | 0 | 1 | 2 | 0 | 0 | 0 | 0 | 1 |
| Oregon | 3 | 5 | 2 | 1 | 4 | 1 | 0 | 0 | 0 | 0 | 1 |
| South Carolina | 0 | 0 | 0 | 0 | 1 | 0 | 0 | 0 | 0 | 0 | 0 |
| Tennessee | 0 | 0 | 0 | 1 | 0 | 0 | 0 | 0 | 0 | 0 | 0 |
| Texas | 3 | 9 | 2 | 0 | 2 | 0 | 0 | 0 | 0 | 0 | 0 |
| Utah | 0 | 0 | 0 | 0 | 0 | 1 | 0 | 0 | 0 | 0 | 0 |
| Washington | 1 | 5 | 2 | 0 | 1 | 0 | 0 | 0 | 0 | 0 | 0 |
| West Virginia | 0 | 0 | 1 | 0 | 0 | 0 | 0 | 0 | 0 | 0 | 0 |
| Wisconsin | 0 | 0 | 0 | 0 | 1 | 0 | 0 | 0 | 0 | 0 | 0 |
| **Total** | **131** | **236** | **143** | **130** | **54** | **34** | **18** | **11** | **17** | **16** | **9** |

Note: Super lab capacity is 10 pounds or more.

SOURCE: "Table 92. States with Methamphetamine Seizures of Super Labs by State, 2000–2010," in *National Drug Control Strategy: Data Supplement 2012*, Executive Office of the President, Office of National Drug Policy, 2012, http://www.whitehouse.gov/sites/default/files/page/files/2012_data_supplement_final.pdf (accessed February 16, 2013)

of pseudoephedrine. These state and national restrictions have resulted in a significant decline in methamphetamine laboratory seizures, because without these precursor drugs the laboratories cannot manufacture methamphetamine. Table 9.8 shows that the number of superlab seizures (laboratories that are capable of producing more than 10 pounds [4.5 kg] of methamphetamine per production run) has decreased as well. The table shows that 236 superlabs were seized in 2001, compared with nine in 2010.

## MARIJUANA LEGALIZATION MOVEMENT

In the United States the legalization of drugs almost invariably refers to the legalization of marijuana rather than, for example, heroin or cocaine. The use of "hard drugs" such as these is relatively limited, and most Americans consider them to be highly addictive and damaging to one's physical and mental health. Marijuana's situation is different. According to SAMHSA in *Results from the 2011 National Survey on Drug Use and Health*, more than 80% of all current drug users in 2011 were using marijuana, and 64.5% of all current drug users used only marijuana and no other drugs. Some studies suggest significant harm from marijuana use, including effects on the heart, lungs, brain, and social and learning capabilities. Other studies find little or no harm from moderate marijuana use. Regardless of what the research says, marijuana is generally thought of as a relatively mild drug, an opinion that is supported in

Canada by those who introduced repeated initiatives to decriminalize marijuana possession and in the Netherlands, where marijuana sales are tolerated in coffee shops.

### Public Opinion

The polling data that the Gallup Organization gathered for selected years between 1970 and 2012 show public opinion increasingly favoring the legalization of marijuana. (See Figure 9.1.) In 1973, 81% of the public opposed legalization, and 15% favored it. By 2012 those opposed had declined to 50% of the public, whereas 48% were in favor. As Table 9.9 shows, support for legalizing marijuana was highest among those aged 18 to 29.

With the support of this age group, a number of initiatives and referenda attempting to legalize marijuana for medical purposes or to decriminalize possession of modest quantities have appeared on state ballots. Many states and local jurisdictions have decriminalized certain uses of specific amounts of marijuana. Decriminalization means that the state or local jurisdiction no longer considers uses of marijuana in the amounts and manners it specifies as illegal, but the jurisdiction may still consider these uses as civil infractions and may impose civil fines, drug education, or drug treatment. Nevertheless, the possession and use of marijuana is still illegal under federal law, and this law supersedes state and local marijuana decriminalization laws. Therefore, a person residing in a

**FIGURE 9.1**

**Public opinion on legalizing marijuana use, selected years 1970–2012**

DO YOU THINK THE USE OF MARIJUANA SHOULD BE MADE LEGAL, OR NOT?

**TABLE 9.9**

**Public opinion on legalizing marijuana use, by age and political affiliation, 2012**

DO YOU THINK THE USE OF MARIJUANA SHOULD BE MADE LEGAL, OR NOT?

|  | % yes | % no |
|---|---|---|
| 18 to 29 | 60 | 39 |
| 30 to 64 | 48 | 51 |
| 65+ | 36 | 61 |
| Republicans | 33 | 66 |
| Independents | 50 | 47 |
| Democrats | 61 | 38 |

state that has decriminalized the possession and use of marijuana can still be arrested and prosecuted by federal officials under federal law.

In November 2012 this potential opposition between federal and state authority became an actuality, after voters in Colorado and Washington passed referenda legalizing possession of small quantities of marijuana for recreational purposes. As Tim Dickinson reports in "The Next Seven States to Legalize Pot" (RollingStone.com, December 18, 2012), the passage of these new laws "fundamentally changed the national conversation

about cannabis." In the wake of the marijuana legalization bills in Colorado and Washington, Dickinson writes, several other states were poised to pass similar laws in the near future, among them California, Maine, and Oregon. According to Dickinson, by December 2012 President Obama was beginning to hint that enforcement of marijuana laws was not a high priority for his administration, suggesting that federal interdiction efforts might prove more relaxed toward states where the drug was legal.

**Arguments for and against Legalization**

FOR LEGALIZATION. Most of those who favor legalization in some form (for medical use, decriminalization, or regulation) use two arguments in combination. The first argument is that an approach to drugs based on prohibition and criminalization does not work, produces excessive rates of incarceration, and costs a lot of money that could be more productively spent on treatment and prevention. The second argument is that drug use is an activity arbitrarily called a crime. It is imposed by law on some drugs and not on others, and can be seen as criminal at one time but perhaps not at another. Murder, rape, and robbery have always been considered inherently criminal acts, but drug use is just a consumption of substances; its control is arbitrary and follows fashions. For example, alcohol consumption was once prohibited but is now legal. Likewise, during the early 1900s opiates were sold in pharmacies, and the soft-drink Coca-Cola contained small quantities of cocaine.

Some who advocate the legalization of drugs believe the government has no right telling people what they may and may not ingest. However, most legalization proponents recognize that many drugs can be harmful (though many dispute the degree), but they do not see this as a reason to make their use illegal. They point out that tobacco use and alcohol abuse are harmful—possibly more harmful or addictive than some drugs that are illicit—but their use is legal. The policy these legalization advocates recommend is based on educational and public health approaches such as those that are used for tobacco and alcohol. They believe that a greater harm is imposed on society by prohibiting such substances, as evidenced by the consequences of the Prohibition period of the early 20th century, during which alcohol was banned and crime, racketeering, and homicide rates soared.

Many proponents argue that legalization will result in decreased harm and crime from trafficking, gang wars, and illegal activities committed to obtain drugs; lower incarceration rates and associated cost savings; and more funds available for treatment from savings and from taxes on legally distributed drugs. Legalization of drugs is also seen as making available marijuana in medical applications, such as relieving the suffering of cancer and acquired immunodeficiency syndrome (AIDS) patients.

AGAINST LEGALIZATION. The federal government's case against legalization is summarized by the DEA in the brochure *Speaking out against Drug Legalization* (2010, http://www.justice.gov/dea/pr/multimedia-library/publications/speaking_out.pdf). The 10 arguments presented by the DEA are shown in Table 9.10.

Like legalization proponents, the DEA's position is organized around the concept of harm. Certain drugs are illegal or controlled because they cause harm. In the DEA's view, the legalization of drugs—even if only marijuana—will increase the harm already suffered by the drug-using public by spreading use to ever larger numbers of people. The agency makes the point that drugs are much more addictive than alcohol and invites the public to contemplate a situation in which commercial interests might be enabled to promote the sale of currently illicit substances.

Would legalization reduce crime? The DEA does not believe it would. Under a regulated drug-use system, age restrictions would apply. A criminal enterprise would continue to supply those under age. If marijuana were legalized, trade in heroin and cocaine would continue. If all three of the major drugs were permitted to be sold legally, other substances, such as phencyclidine and methamphetamine, would still support a criminal trade. The DEA does not envision that a black market in drugs could be eliminated entirely because health authorities

TABLE 9.10

**Top ten facts on legalization of drugs cited by the Drug Enforcement Administration (DEA), 2010**

**Fact 1:** Significant progress has been made in fighting drug use and drug trafficking in America.

**Fact 2:** A balanced approach of prevention, enforcement, and treatment are the keys in the fight against drug abuse.

**Fact 3:** Drug use is regulated and access to drugs is controlled because drugs can be harmful.

**Fact 4:** Smoked marijuana has never been and will never be scientifically approved medicine.

**Fact 5:** Drug control spending is a minor portion of the U.S. budget. Compared to the social costs of drug abuse and addiction, government spending on drug control is minimal.

**Fact 6:** Legalization of drugs will lead to increased use and increased levels of addiction.

**Fact 7:** Crime, violence, and drug use go hand-in-hand.

**Fact 8:** Alcohol and tobacco have caused significant health, social, and crime problems, and legalized drugs would only make the situation worse.

**Fact 9:** Europe's more liberal drug policies are not the right model for America.

**Fact 10:** Most non-violent drug users get treatment, not jail time.

SOURCE: Adapted from "Summary of the Top Ten Facts on Legalization," in *Speaking out against Drug Legalization*, U.S. Department of Justice, Drug Enforcement Administration, 2010, http://www.justice.gov/dea/pr/multimedia-library/publications/speaking_out.pdf (accessed February 16, 2013)

would never permit potent drugs to be sold freely on the open market.

For all these reasons, the DEA advocates the continuation of a balanced approach to the control of drugs including prevention, enforcement, and treatment.

## MEDICAL MARIJUANA

The medicinal value of THC (delta-9-tetrahydrocannabinol), the active ingredient in marijuana, has long been known to the medical community. The drug has been shown to alleviate the nausea and vomiting caused by chemotherapy, which is used to treat many forms of cancer. Marijuana has also been found useful in alleviating pressure on the eye in glaucoma patients. Furthermore, the drug has been found effective in helping to fight the physical wasting that usually accompanies AIDS. AIDS patients lose their appetite and can slowly waste away because they do not eat. Complicating matters, many of the newer AIDS remedies must be taken on a full stomach. Marijuana has been found effective in restoring the appetite of some AIDS patients. This is not to say that all scientists agree that marijuana is healthy or useful. For example, some studies find that marijuana suppresses the immune system and contains a number of lung-damaging chemicals. Still, the potentially beneficial uses of marijuana as a medicine have led to an advocacy movement for it to be made legally available by prescription.

Opponents of the medical legalization of marijuana often point to Marinol (a laboratory-made form of THC) s a superior alternative. Marinol provides a standardized THC content and does not contain impurities, such as leaves, mold spores, and bacteria, which are generally found in marijuana. However, many patients do not respond to Marinol, and the determination of the right dosage is variable from patient to patient. Nonresponding patients claim that smoking marijuana or eating it incorporated into foods such as brownies allows them to control the dosage that they need.

Marijuana has been used illegally by an unknown number of cancer, glaucoma, and AIDS patients on the recommendation of their doctors. Nonetheless, the medical use of marijuana is not without risk. The primary negative effect is diminished control over movement. In some cases users may experience unpleasant emotional states or feelings. In addition, the usefulness of medicinal marijuana is limited by the harmful effects of smoking, which can increase a person's risk of cancer,

lung damage, and problems with pregnancies (such as low birth weight). However, these risks are usually not important for terminally ill patients or those with debilitating symptoms. Also, the drug can be eaten to be effective.

Some states and local jurisdictions have decriminalized the cultivation of marijuana for personal medical use. As mentioned previously, however, the cultivation of marijuana is still illegal under federal law, which supersedes state and local marijuana decriminalization laws. In addition, such state and local rulings do not necessarily establish that the use of marijuana is medically appropriate. That issue is hotly debated in the media and among Americans, but no nationally recognized medical organization—including the American Academy of Pediatrics, the American Cancer Society, or the American Medical Association—has endorsed the medical use of smoked marijuana.

# IMPORTANT NAMES AND ADDRESSES

**AAA Foundation for Traffic Safety**
607 14th St. NW, Ste. 201
Washington, DC 20005
(202) 638-5944
FAX: (202) 638-5943
E-mail: info@aaafoundation.org
URL: http://www.aaafoundation.org/

**Action on Smoking and Health**
701 Fourth St. NW
Washington, DC 20001
(202) 659-4310
FAX: (202) 289-7166
E-mail: info@ash.org
URL: http://www.ash.org/

**Adult Children of Alcoholics**
PO Box 3216
Torrance, CA 90510
(562) 595-7831
URL: http://www.adultchildren.org/

**Al-Anon Family Group Headquarters**
1600 Corporate Landing Pkwy.
Virginia Beach, VA 23454-5617
(757) 563-1600
FAX: (757) 563-1655
E-mail: wso@al-anon.org
URL: http://www.al-anon.alateen.org/

**Alcoholics Anonymous World Services**
PO Box 459, Grand Central Station
New York, NY 10163
(212) 870-3400
URL: http://www.aa.org/

**Beer Institute**
122 C St. NW, Ste. 350
Washington, DC 20001
(202) 737-2337
URL: http://www.beerinstitute.org/

**Bureau of International Narcotics and Law Enforcement Affairs**
**U.S. Department of State**
2201 C St. NW
Washington, DC 20520
URL: http://www.state.gov/j/inl/

**Campaign for Tobacco-Free Kids**
1400 Eye St. NW, Ste. 1200
Washington, DC 20005
(202) 296-5469
FAX: (202) 296-5427
URL: http://www.tobaccofreekids.org/
index.php

**Cocaine Anonymous World Services**
21720 S. Wilmington Ave., Ste. 304
Long Beach, CA 90810-1641
(310) 559-5833
FAX: (310) 559-2554
E-mail: cawso@ca.org
URL: http://www.ca.org/

**Distilled Spirits Council of the United States**
1250 Eye St. NW, Ste. 400
Washington, DC 20005
(202) 628-3544
URL: http://www.discus.org/

**Drug Policy Alliance**
131 West 33rd St., 15th Floor
New York, NY 10001
(212) 613-8020
FAX: (212) 613-8021
E-mail: nyc@drugpolicy.org
URL: http://www.drugpolicy.org/

**Nar-Anon Family Groups**
22527 Crenshaw Blvd., Ste. 200B
Torrance, CA 90505
(310) 534-8188
1-800-477-6291

FAX: (310) 534-8688
E-mail: wso@nar-anon.org
URL: http://nar-anon.org/Nar-Anon/Nar-
Anon_Home.html

**Narcotics Anonymous World Services**
PO Box 9999
Van Nuys, CA 91409
(818) 773-9999
FAX: (818) 700-0700
URL: http://www.na.org/

**National Council on Alcoholism and Drug Dependence**
217 Broadway, Ste. 712
New York, NY 10007
(212) 269-7797
FAX: (212) 269-7510
E-mail: national@ncadd.org
URL: http://www.ncadd.org/

**National Institute on Alcohol Abuse and Alcoholism**
9000 Rockville Pike
Bethesda, MD 20892
(301) 443-2857
E-mail: niaaaweb-r@exchange.nih.gov
URL: http://www.niaaa.nih.gov/

**National Institute on Drug Abuse**
6001 Executive Blvd., Rm. 5213,
MSC 9561
Bethesda, MD 20892-9561
(301) 443-1124
URL: http://www.nida.nih.gov/

**National Organization for the Reform of Marijuana Laws**
1600 K St. NW, Mezzanine Level
Washington, DC 20006-2832
(202) 483-5500
FAX: (202) 483-0057
E-mail: norml@norml.org
URL: http://www.norml.org/

**Office of National Drug Control Policy**
**Drug Policy Information Clearinghouse**
PO Box 6000
Rockville, MD 20849-6000
1-800-666-3332
FAX: (301) 519-5212
URL: http://www.whitehouse.gov/ondcp

**Office on Smoking and Health**
**Centers for Disease Control and Prevention**
4770 Buford Hwy., MS K-50
Atlanta, GA 30341-3717
1-800-232-4636
E-mail: tobaccoinfo@cdc.gov
URL: http://www.cdc.gov/tobacco/osh/

**SAMHSA's Health Information**
**Network**
PO Box 2345
Rockville, MD 20847-2345
1-877-726-4727
FAX: (240) 221-4292
URL: http://store.samhsa.gov/

**Substance Abuse and Mental Health**
**Services Administration**
One Choke Cherry Rd.
Rockville, MD 20857
1-877-726-4727
URL: http://www.samhsa.gov/

**U.S. Drug Enforcement Administration**
**Office of Diversion Control**
8701 Morrissette Dr.
Springfield, VA 22152
(202) 307-1000
URL: http://www.justice.gov/dea/index.shtml

**Wine Institute**
425 Market St., Ste. 1000
San Francisco, CA 94105
(415) 512-0151
FAX: (415) 356-7569
URL: http://www.wineinstitute.org/

# RESOURCES

The various agencies of the U.S. Department of Health and Human Services (HHS) produce important publications on the consumption of alcohol, tobacco, and illicit drugs in the United States and their health effects. Reports of the U.S. surgeon general and special reports to Congress are published through this office.

The Substance Abuse and Mental Health Services Administration (SAMHSA) produces the annual National Survey on Drug Use and Health. SAMHSA also tracks treatment services. The most recent report is *National Survey of Substance Abuse Treatment Services (N-SSATS): 2011, Data on Substance Abuse Treatment Facilities* (November 2012). SAMHSA also tracks reported episodes of drug abuse; the most recent published results are in *Treatment Episode Data Set (TEDS) 2000–2010: National Admissions to Substance Abuse Treatment Services* (June 2012). The agency also operates the Drug Abuse Warning Network, which collects data from emergency departments.

The HHS also publishes the bimonthly *Public Health Reports*, the official journal of the U.S. Public Health Service. This journal is a helpful resource on health problems, including those that are caused by alcohol and tobacco. The Association of Schools of Public Health has been a partner in the publication of *Public Health Reports* since 1999.

The National Institute on Alcohol Abuse and Alcoholism (NIAAA) publishes the journal *Alcohol Research and Health*. This journal contains current scholarly research on alcohol addiction issues. The NIAAA also publishes the quarterly bulletin *Alcohol Alert*, which disseminates research findings on alcohol abuse and alcoholism.

The National Center for Health Statistics, in its annual *Health, United States*, reports on all aspects of the nation's health, including tobacco- and alcohol-related illnesses and deaths. The *Morbidity and Mortality Weekly Report* is published by the Centers for Disease Control and Prevention (CDC), which also publishes many studies on the trends and health risks of smoking and drinking. Additionally, the American Cancer Society and the American Lung Association provide many facts on cancer and heart disease.

The U.S. Department of Agriculture (USDA) was responsible for several helpful reports concerning tobacco up until 2005. Its publications *Tobacco Outlook* and *Tobacco Briefing Room* monitored tobacco production, consumption, sales, exports, and imports. These publications were discontinued in 2005 after the government ended the decades-old tobacco quota system. (See Chapter 7.) The USDA still publishes the annual *Agricultural Statistics*, which provides valuable information about farming, and *Food Consumption, Prices, and Expenditures*, which compiles data on how the nation spends its consumer dollars. Other useful information is provided by the Economic Research Service of the USDA and the U.S. Department of Labor's Bureau of Labor Statistics, which examines how people spend their income, including spending on cigarettes and alcohol.

The National Highway Traffic Safety Administration of the U.S. Department of Transportation produces the annual *Traffic Safety Facts*, which includes data on alcohol-related accidents.

The Bureau of Justice Statistics monitors crime in the United States and focuses on criminal prosecutions, prisons, sentencing, and related subjects. Particularly helpful are *Drug Use and Dependence, State and Federal Prisoners, 2004* (Christopher J. Mumola and Jennifer C. Karberg, October 2006) and the annual publications *Compendium of Federal Justice Statistics* and *Sourcebook of Criminal Justice Statistics*. The Federal Bureau of Investigation's annual *Crime in the United States* provides arrest statistics for the United States. The U.S. Department of the

Treasury's Alcohol and Tobacco Tax and Trade Bureau provides alcohol and tobacco tax information.

Other important annual surveys of alcohol, tobacco, and illicit drug use in the United States are conducted by both public and private organizations. The CDC's Youth Risk Behavior Surveillance monitors not only alcohol, tobacco, and illicit drug use but also other risk behaviors, such as teenage sexual activity and weapons possession. The Monitoring the Future survey of substance abuse among students from middle school through college is conducted by the National Institute on Drug Abuse and the University of Michigan Institute for Social Research. The most recent reports are *Monitoring the Future National Survey Results on Drug Use, 1975–2011, Volume I: Secondary School Students* (Lloyd D. Johnston et al., June 2012) and *Monitoring the Future National Survey Results on Drug Use, 1975–2011, Volume II: College Students and Adults Ages 19–50* (Lloyd D. Johnston et al., July 2012). The *Pride Surveys Questionnaire Report for Grades 6 to 12, National Summary Statistics for 2009–10* (September 2010), which is based on a survey of youth and parents, is produced by the Pride Survey.

The Wine Institute, the Distilled Spirits Council of the United States, and the Beer Institute are private trade organizations that track alcoholic beverage sales and consumption, as well as political and regulatory issues. Action on Smoking and Health publishes reviews that are concerned with the problems of smoking and the rights of nonsmokers. The Campaign for Tobacco-Free Kids provides information on tobacco-related federal, state, and global initiatives; cigarette taxes; tobacco advertisements; tobacco and smoking statistics; and tobacco-related special reports.

The Gallup Organization provides important information about the attitudes and behaviors of the American public.

The national policy on combating drug abuse is centered in the Office of National Drug Control Policy (ONDCP). The ONDCP, which prepares a drug control policy each year for the president and coordinates efforts across the federal bureaucracy, is an excellent source for statistics that are collected from many other agencies. Publications consulted for this volume include *National Drug Control Strategy: Data Supplement 2012* (May 2012), *FY 2013 Budget and Performance Summary* (April 2012), and *National Drug Control Strategy, 2012* (2012) and earlier reports.

Domestic law enforcement and interdiction activities fall under the U.S. Department of Justice. The U.S. Drug Enforcement Administration (DEA) oversees all domestic drug control activities. The DEA publishes *Drugs of Abuse* (June 2011), a resource tool that educates the public about drug facts and the inherent dangers of illegal drugs.

The effort to control drugs beyond the nation's borders is largely under the supervision of the U.S. Department of State. The agency within the Department of State in charge of the drug control effort is the Bureau of International Narcotics and Law Enforcement Affairs. An excellent source of information is the bureau's annual *International Narcotics Control Strategy Report*.

Gale, Cengage Learning sincerely thanks all the organizations listed here for the valuable information they provide.

# INDEX

National Drug Intelligence Center, 131

National Highway Traffic Safety Administration, 10

National Institute on Alcohol Abuse and Alcoholism, 10, 21

National Institute on Drug Abuse, 93, 103, 106

National Survey of Substance Abuse Treatment Services, 94–95

National Survey on Drug Use and Health, 95

Native Americans, 10, 12

Nicotine, 3, 39–41, 50

Nicotine replacement therapy, 50

Nixon, Richard M., 14

# O

Obama, Barack
  drug control policies, 15, 16
  Family Smoking Prevention and Tobacco Control Act, 44, 80
  marijuana legalization, 157
  Mérida Initiative, 153–154
  National Drug Control Strategy, 146
  tobacco advertising, 2

Occupational Safety and Health Administration, U.S., 118

Office of National Drug Control Policy, 15, 16, 145–146

Opium
  Afghanistan, 154–155
  Colombia, 150–151
  cultivation, 15, 16, 131
  history of use, 12
  morphine, 57

Out-of-state alcohol sales, 116–118

Overdose
  heroin, 63
  stimulants, 58

Oxycodone, 56–57

# P

PACT Act, 118–119

Pain relievers, 56–57, 57t

Pakistan, 150

Paramilitary organizations, 152–153

Parental alcoholism, 24

Parental education levels, 75t, 78, 82

Passive smoke. See Secondhand smoke

PCP, 62

Pedestrian fatalities, 33, 33(t2.13)

Pemberton, John, 12

Peña Nieto, Enrique, 154

Peru, 153

Peyote, 12, 61

Pharmaceuticals, trafficking in, 143

Phencyclidine, 62

Philip Morris, 123

Physiology
  alcohol, effects of, 25–28, 25f
  anabolic steroids, 63–64
  antidrug vaccines, 106
  marijuana, effects of, 54–55
  MDMA, 61
  nicotine, effects of, 39–41
  substance use, factors in, 6–7
  tobacco use, 35
  underage drinking, 75

Pipe smoking, 10, 39

"Plan Colombia," 16

Poppies. See Opium

Population density
  adolescent alcohol use, 75t
  adolescent tobacco use, 82

Potency, marijuana, 54

Pregnancy
  alcohol consumption, 28–30, 28t, 29t
  drug use, 64, 65t
  smoking, 49–50, 49f

Premature aging, 42–43

Prescription drugs
  commonly abused drugs, 5t
  labeling, 13
  nonmedical use of pain relievers, 56–57, 57t
  smoking cessation, 50
  trafficking in, 143
  See also Medications

Preteen substance abuse, 71–72

Prevent All Cigarette Trafficking (PACT) Act, 118–119

Prevention
  adolescent smoking, 80, 81
  National Drug Control Strategy, 146
  smoking prevention and cessation programs, 123, 126t
  substance abuse, 106
  tobacco prevention spending vs. tobacco company marketing, by state, 127t

Prices
  cocaine, 139
  heroin, 143
  marijuana, 141–142, 142t
  methamphetamines, 136–137, 138f

Prisoners, 67t, 68t

Production
  cocaine, 138
  drugs, 131
  heroin, 63
  MDMA, 61, 88
  methamphetamines, 134–135
  PCP, 62
  See also Cultivation

Productivity loss, 119, 120, 120t

Professional sports, 64

Prohibition, 9–10, 116

Protective factors, 71, 106

Pryor, Richard, 60

Psilocybin mushrooms, 12

Psychic disorders, 62

Psychological issues
  children of alcoholics, 24
  MDMA, 61
  smoking, 41
  substance use, factors in, 6–7

Psychosocial factors, 22t, 23–24

Psychotherapeutics, 52–53, 56–59, 57t, 58f, 59f

Psychotropic substances Act, 62

Public health and smoking, 44–50

Public Health Cigarette Smoking Act, 11, 44

Public opinion
  drug problem priority, 15
  harmfulness of secondhand smoke, 47f
  marijuana legalization, 156–157, 157f, 157t
  smoking, harmfulness of, 35, 36f
  smoking bans, 47, 48f

Punishment. See Sentencing, drug offense

Pure Food and Drug Act, 13

Purity
  cocaine, 139, 139f
  heroin, 142, 143
  Marijuana potency, 141t
  methamphetamines, 135–137, 138f

# R

Race/ethnicity
  adolescent alcohol use, 72t, 74t, 75t, 78, 79t
  adolescent tobacco use, 80t, 81t, 82
  alcohol use, 19t
  alcohol use among females, by pregnancy status, 29(t2.9)
  alcohol use disorders, 21
  binge drinking, 20
  drug arrests, 65–66
  drug offense convictions, 66–67
  drug treatment admissions, 95
  drug use, 51, 52t
  early alcohol, tobacco, or marijuana use, 71–72
  pain relievers use, 57t
  smoking, 37, 37t, 39, 39(f3.6)
  state prisoner drug use, 68t
  substance abuse treatment admissions, 100t, 101, 102t

Raves, 61

Reagan, Nancy, 14

Reagan, Ronald, 14, 15

Reciprocity legislation, 116–117

Referrals, substance abuse treatment, 103, 105t

Regulations
  alcohol, 116–118
  drugs, 13–14
  tobacco, 44, 118–119

Rehabilitation, 98

tranquilizers, 57–58, 84–85, 87*f*

362.29 ALC
Alcohol, tobacco, and illicit drugs

EK

9 781569 957